CW01431415

Crisis Management and Recovery for Events:
Impacts and Strategies

Vassilios Ziakas, Vladimir Antchak and Donald Getz

 **Goodfellow Publishers Ltd**

0596226

(G) Published by Goodfellow Publishers Limited,
26 Home Close, Wolvercote, Oxford OX2 8PS
http://www.goodfellowpublishers.com

British Library Cataloguing in Publication Data: a catalogue
record for this title is available from the British Library.

Library of Congress Catalog Card Number: on file.

ISBN: 978-1-911635-91-8

DOI: 10.23912/9781911635901-4692

The Events Management Theory and Methods Series

Copyright © Vassilios Ziakas, Vladimir Antchak, Donald Getz, 2021

Design and typesetting by P.K. McBride, www.macbride.org.uk

Cover design by Cylinder

Printed by Printforce, Biggleswade

Distributed by UK Marston Book Services, www.marston.co.uk

Contents

Introduction to the Events Management Theory and Methods Series		v
Preface		vii
Contributors		xv

1 Theoretical Perspectives of Crisis Management & Recovery for Events — 1
Vassilios Ziakas, Vladimir Antchak and Donald Getz
Background: Understanding the concept of crisis for events — 2
Event crisis recovery and resilience planning — 15
Building resilience for events — 18

2 Crisis: The Juncture of Stability and Development — 30
William O'Toole
Crisis, back to normal — 30
Maturity model — 31
Standards level 4 — 33

Practice Insight 1: Interview with Steven Wood Schmader — 41

3 From Risk to Resilience: Contemporary Issues in Event Risk Management — 49
Peter Ashwin
The perception of risk: Making sense of the risk management construct — 50
Decision-making under uncertainty — 55
The emergence of domestic terrorism threats — 57
Cyber-criminal risks and digital age of events — 62

4 Stakeholder Management — 76
Donald Getz
Classifying stakeholders and formulating strategies in a time of crisis — 77
Strategy and action — 84
Resilience and the roles of stakeholders — 92

Practice Insight 2: Interview with Rebecca Cotter — 96

5 Events Employment: Crises' Impacts and Resolutions — 100
Richard N.S. Robinson and Yawei Jiang
Importance of event workforces — 101
Case Study #1 — 105
Case Study #2 — 107
Discussion and conclusions — 110

Practice Insight 3: Interview with Vern Biaett — 118

6 Redesigning Events in the Post COVID-19 Crisis: A Design Thinking Approach — 120
Kom Campiranon
Literature review — 122
Redesigning events with design thinking — 125
Implementation (Prototype and Test) — 129

Practice Insight 4: Interview with Neil Alderson   139

7   The Future of Events will be Hybrid   142
Tim Brown
Virtual events   143
Defining virtual and hybrid events   144
COVID-19 and the pivot to online   147
Benefits of virtual and hybrid events   149
Designing virtual and hybrid event experiences   151
Current trends of virtual and hybrid events   155
The future of events will be hybrid   158

Practice Insight 5: Interview with Dr. Amanda Cecil   165

8   Response and Recovery through Event Portfolio Management   167
Smita Singh and Eric D. Olson
Festivals and events in Des Moines   168
Impact of COVID-19 on the Des Moines event industry   169
The future of Des Moines events   175

Practice Insight 6: Case study of Transrockies Inc.   186

9   Swedish Sports Clubs and Events during the Covid-19 Pandemic   193
John Armbrecht, Erik Lundberg, Robert Pettersson and Malin Zillinger
Theoretical background: Crisis management and resilience   194
Methodology   196
Findings   198

Practice Insight 7: Case study of Musikfest   213

10   A Chronicle of Event Postponement and Reorganization:
     Coming Back Stronger   217
Danai Varveri and Vassilios Ziakas
Organizational context and case study approach   218
Making the decision and rescheduling   219

11 Agility in the Events Sector: A Case Study of a Business Event in Finland   233
Valentina Gorchakova and Ekaterina Berdysheva
2020: A crisis or a VUCA situation?   234
Agility   236
New technology and virtual events   238
Case study: Overview of SHIFT festival   239
Discussion and Conclusion   244

12   Crisis Management and Recovery for Events: Issues and Directions   248
Vassilios Ziakas, Vladimir Antchak and Donald Getz
Stages in crisis management   248
Issues and processes: A crisis management framework for events   250
Lessons from industry insights   254
Trends and transformations   255
Future research   257

Index   261

Introduction to the Events Management Theory and Methods Series

Event management as a field of study and professional practice has its text-books with plenty of models and advice, a body of knowledge (EMBOK), competency standards (MBECS) and professional associations with their codes of conduct. But to what extent is it truly an applied management field? In other words, where is the management theory in event management, how is it being used, and what are the practical applications?

Event tourism is a related field, one that is defined by the roles events play in tourism and economic development. The primary consideration has always been economic, although increasingly events and managed event portfolios meet more diverse goals for cities and countries. While the economic aspects have been well developed, especially economic impact assessment and fore-casting, the application of management theory to event tourism has not received adequate attention.

In this book series we launch a process of examining the extent to which mainstream theory is being employed to develop event-specific theory, and to influence the practice of event management and event tourism. This is a very big task, as there are numerous possible theories, models and concepts, and virtually unlimited advice available on the management of firms, small and family businesses, government agencies and not-for-profits. Inevitably, we will have to be selective.

The starting point is theory. Scientific theory must both explain a phenom-enon, and be able to predict what will happen. Experiments are the dominant form of classical theory development. But for management, predictive capa-bilities are usually lacking; it might be wiser to speak of theory in develop-ment, or theory fragments. It is often the process of theory development that marks research in management, including the testing of hypotheses and the formulation of propositions. Models, frameworks, concepts and sets of prop-ositions are all part of this development.

The following diagram illustrates this approach. All knowledge creation has potential application to management, as does theory from any discipline or field. The critical factor for this series is how the theory and related meth-ods can be applied. In the core of this diagram are management and busi-ness theories which are the most directly pertinent, and they are often derived from foundation disciplines.

Knowledge creation
concerning planned events

Theory of relevance to
Event Studies in general

Business
organizational &
management theory
to inform events
management & event
tourism

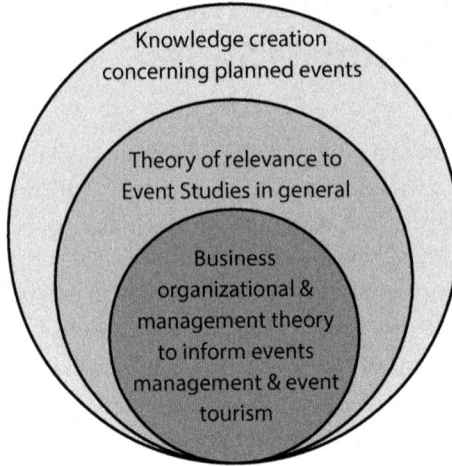

All the books in this series will be relatively short, and similarly structured. They are designed to be used by teachers who need theoretical foundations and case studies for their classes, by students in need of reference works, by professionals wanting increased understanding alongside practical methods, and by agencies or associations that want their members and stakeholders to have access to a library of valuable resources. The nature of the series is that as it grows, components can be assembled by request. That is, users can order a book or collection of chapters to exactly suit their needs.

All the books will introduce the theory, show how it is being used in the events sector through a literature review, incorporate examples and case studies written by researchers and/or practitioners, and contain methods that can be used effectively in the real world.

Preface

The growth of planned events has been exponential in the last decades. A growth that was, however, disrupted suddenly by the COVID-19 pandemic crisis in 2020. Doubts and fears about the present and future of events surfaced across the globe. Events inevitably face the consequences of the systemic changes the pandemic accelerated, triggering a restructuring of the world economy and broader socio-cultural transformation. In this rapidly changing context that the event sector operates, the academic community seems to have been caught by surprise. Little advice and strategic foresight has been offered as to how events can be effectively managed in times of a major crisis and fully recover. The rarity and magnitude of the pandemic crisis can be a reason explaining this lack of timely academic response. But as with any crisis, this is a good time to reflect on the key assumptions and modalities that have shaped the event sector and how, in turn, events are being treated and studied. Even a cursory glance at the event-related scholarship reveals the dearth of specialized know-how on crisis management grounded in the distinctive nature of planned events and their resultant phenomena. Instead, current practice is, as in most event-related scholarship, to rely on established knowledge from general disciplines (especially tourism and business) by borrowing their principles and models and applying them to the context of events. Is this enough to engender or advance learning and strategic intelligence for event crisis management?

This book takes the stance that it is now time to start building specific theory on crisis management for planned events. Still, of course, cross-disciplinary investigations and borrowing from general disciplines are important, but such efforts should be placed in a specialized context with the focus on producing distinctive theory and acumen about events. This is the way to move forward and advance the discourse. While the contribution of this book to such theory-building is rather modest and with limitations, it aspires to set up a robust stage for future inquiries. A major limitation of the book concerns the swift and pressured timeline that was completed in the midst of the pandemic. But this timeline was important in itself. Because the book is a first-hand response and reflection to the issues and changes brought about by the pandemic crisis, which at first stage need to be reported, debated and examined, so that future research can generate more broadly knowledge about all types of crises and inform more wisely evidence-based practice. Capturing timely the essence of the multifaceted pandemic effects on the event sector helped also to realize that effective crisis management for events should be structurally adaptive to wider systemic transformations (e.g., politics, society, environment, culture, etc.). For this reason, the volume is not focused on operational risk management processes per se or communication strategies for handling reputation or image recovery, but instead, by taking a more comprehensive perspective, is centered on structural change at meso and micro levels (i.e., community, market, institutional, organizational and operational); change both exogenous and of events themselves as triggered by macro-level transformations, in managing crisis and achieving recovery of events. Understanding the nature and impacts of change serves to explain its causes and the reasons behind the way individual events (and the whole sector at large) are reconfigured, adapted and function in the new conditions. This approach can establish solid grounds for effective event crisis management embedded within host community structures and processes.

Overview

Events are from their nature temporal and short-lived, and so susceptible to environmental change, volatility and impeding crises. The advent of the COVID-19 pandemic crisis has exposed the innate fragility of events and calls for rethinking long-established supply models in events, better understanding the changing consumer behavior, and overall questioning the sustainability of the whole sector. The landscape of the event sector has dramatically changed, putting more pressure and demands for event organizations to adapt in the new conditions, as well as identify and appropriately leverage new opportunities. This means that for any crisis, events should develop capacity for readiness, adaptability and resilience to achieve first their own recovery, survival and prosperity, as well as, in turn, to nurture versatility in terms of how they can be employed to serve their host communities' needs in post-crisis recovery. However, as noted above, there is limited scholarship and comprehensive evidence regarding crisis management for events. Therefore, this volume seeks to build knowledge on the particular aspects of crisis management that events are facing.

Given the huge impact of the COVID-19 crisis on the event sector, the volume uses it as a case to explore how event organizations can cope with sudden and unexpected crises, including natural disasters and economic crises. There is a two-fold purpose that grounds the underlying logics of this volume: (1) managing effectively events in times of crisis; as well as (2) redesigning and leveraging events for achieving post-disaster recovery and resilience. The book is intended to bring together theoretical and practical insights in order to set up a robust ground for effective crisis management and recovery strategies of events. For this reason, particularly, it incorporates insights of practitioners between chapters presenting interviews and case studies. We would like to thank for their generous time and invaluable contributions to this book: Steven Wood Schmader (CFEE President & CEO International Festivals & Events Association), Rebecca Cotter (Manager, Communications Operations & Events, Corporate Communications & Community Engagement, City of Markham, Ontario, Canada), Vern Biaett (Consultant, expert witness, retired

Event Management Professor, and long-time event manager and volunteer), Neil Alderson (Events Nova Scotia and Sport Tourism Canada), Dr. Amanda Cecil (2012 PCMA Foundation's Educator Honoree, 2012 MPI "Member of the Year" RISE Award, Professor IUPUI), Aaron McConnell (CEO TransRockies), and finally from Musikfest, Gabriela Laracca (PR Coodinator) and Curt Mosel (COO) of the event's organizer, ArtsQuest.

Book outline

Rationale and aims

Taking the pandemic crisis as a case in point, our basic argument is that the events sector has not been sustainable in any triple-bottom-line sense, as under the dominant neo-liberal, capitalist regime there has been more or less a free market in creating events, huge competition bidding on events, investment in the biggest and best venues resulting in over-supply, and an emphasis on event tourism and place marketing that has resulted in over-tourism in many cities. The pandemic crisis exacerbated the unsustainable state of the event sector. Existing intense competition for resources has been combined with diminishing demand and financial support, resulting in structural change. This is not a globally uniform process – some cities and countries have been hit harder than others.

The event sector is now more vulnerable than ever, but the need for social, cultural, and healthier events is likely to increase. In corporations, cities and destinations around the world a serious re-think of goals, policies and strategies is already occurring, if only due to a reduced capacity to offer financial support and to produce events. To assist in this process, this edited volume offers a number of insights and principles to foster change and in particular to increase resilience of the event sector. In doing so, the volume sets out to:

- Explore models and practices of crisis management for events;
- Establish a framework for event crisis management and recovery;
- Assess the impacts of the pandemic crisis on events;
- Determine how events have responded to, and can recover from, the pandemic crisis;
- Provide a roadmap to build resilience in the event sector.

Structure and contents

The chapters are briefly introduced and described in this section following the running order and conceptual coherence of the book. Between chapters a number of vignettes in the form of verbatim interviews and case studies are included, titled as 'practice insights' in order to throw light on the perceptions and voices of professionals dealing with crisis in the industry.

1. Theoretical perspectives of crisis management and recovery for events

The first chapter is written by the editors and provides a comprehensive introduction to the theoretical perspectives and intricacies of crisis management and recovery for events. It contextualizes the distinctive parameters and exigencies of crisis management for events and thereby sets up the ground for generating specific theory and evidence-based practice on this highly complex and emergent organizational landscape. It is emphasized that the event sector has to move now to integrated models of event management and develop event-focused frameworks for crisis management. This calls for a change in mind-set both in theory and praxis. The chapter outlines fundamental principles of a holistic mind-set and directions for determining requirements of effective crisis management and recovery, building resilience of event ecosystems and fostering their sustainable growth and prosperity. Overall, the chapter establishes firm foundations for reshaping the event sector utilizing complex-systems theory, resilience principles and the event portfolio perspective as a way to nurture a holistic mind-set on crisis management for events.

2. Crisis: The juncture of stability and development

The second chapter, by O'Toole, takes an evolutionary view on the development of the event sector identifying its dynamic and self-organizing characteristics that create five phases in the sector maturity. This is described by the Events Sector Maturity Model, which considers development as an emergent result of the complexity of events and event management. Within his context, a crisis is one of the factors and stimuli that have helped create a development model for events. The logics underpinning this chapter are that 'normal' in a complex system, such as the event sector, over time is dynamic and, moves through phases determined by self-organization and survival combined with the globalization of the sector. Instead of using business crisis management tools, the chapter examines the phenomenon of crisis as a disruption that opens up many opportunities for events. It is argued that a major crisis such as the pandemic may allow the more agile and creative events and event teams an inflexion point to move the sector into an innovative phase with wide diversity of unique events. This realist and optimistic perspective suggests that a crisis for events stands at the juncture of their stability and flexibility/adaptation and standard risk management can be applied as the management of opportunities. Therefore, more broadly crisis management can be viewed as the treatment of emerging opportunities and the analogous adaptation of events.

3. From risk to resilience: Contemporary issues in event risk management

The chapter by Ashwin provides an analysis of contemporary insights into how event organizers and industry professionals approach risk management, decision-making, resilience, event team preparedness and readiness.

First, it discusses the interdependent constructs pertaining to socio-cultural theoretical perspectives of risk and how event organizers' perception of risk influences their approach to risk management and decision-making to prepare for and respond to adverse events. Following on, the second part of the chapter addresses two contemporary risks, both of which present potential for catastrophic impacts to the sustainability and viability of an event: (1) cyber-criminals who are increasingly focusing their cyber-attacks on vulnerable, event digital ecosystems given the upsurge of virtual delivery formats, and (2) domestic terrorism and the threat to events from homegrown violent extremists, domestic violent extremists and unaffiliated lone offenders.

4. Stakeholder management

This chapter, by Getz, presents concepts and principles for stakeholder management of events in a time of crisis, and how stakeholder management is an essential part of events recovery and resilience. It highlights that the very definition of stakeholders and the mapping of stakeholder relationships must evolve during a crisis. This is because stakeholders may be the cause of a crisis or differentially impacted through the phases of crisis response and recovery. Drawing from stakeholder salience and the parameters of legitimacy, power and urgency, the chapter contextualizes and delineates stakeholder mapping and subsequent strategies in event crisis management and recovery. It views mapping and strategies as situation-dependent and dynamic, requiring a flexible approach to stakeholder management during and after a crisis. Especially, it is emphasized that collaborative action becomes even more important in order to implement effectively response plans and maintain stakeholder relations when events are cancelled and re-scheduled.

5. Events employment: Crises' impacts and resolutions

Robinson and Jiang in their chapter look at how organizations and employees in the event industry respond to crisis. Particularly, they focus on organizational responses to crises that have deleterious impacts on their operations and revenue. The chapter first reviews pertinent literature about workforce impacts of crises and strategies to mitigate risks and build resilience. It summarizes this body of work and references emergent work treating the COVID-19 pandemic impacts before presenting case studies from two very dissimilar Australasian event organizations. Despite their differences, these businesses used remarkably similar strategies to respond and recover from the crisis. These are critically reviewed in conclusion before pondering future research opportunities.

6. Redesigning events in the post-COVID-19 crisis: A design thinking approach

The chapter by Campiranon focuses on design thinking as one of problem-solving methods which can be used to cope with crisis. It underscores the need to generate de-thinking, re-thinking and un-thinking of pre-assumptions and mindsets. Specifically, the chapter discusses the role of design thinking during the COVID-19 pandemic to generate innovative solutions to address unique challenges in the events sector. It identifies a three-stage design thinking process that comprises inspiration (empathize and define), ideation and implementation (prototype and test). As indicated, event organizers need to have an action plan and an appropriate event method for each crisis management stage. It is also postulated that although virtual events have mostly been adopted during the crisis, they can be more effective in the post-crisis stage in order to achieve a higher level of engagement among participants. Design thinking is an important area for crisis management research in events. The chapter suggests that future studies can examine how organizers can redesign events by employing the latest technologies such as extended reality, which covers new and emerging technologies, including virtual, augmented, and mixed reality, to create immersive digital event experiences.

7. The future of events will be hybrid

The chapter by Brown explores the context of business events in relation to the evolution, development and benefits of virtual and hybrid events. It particularly examines the impact of COVID-19 on the event industry and the responding pivot to online events with designing virtual and hybrid experiences. It posits that hybrid events will be a cornerstone of this new event landscape. Given the sudden pivot to virtual events and expected growth in hybrid events, the chapter notes the lack of research on this area and the opportunity for academia and industry to collaborate to examine best practice for this new event context. Current trends and future directions of virtual and hybrid events are discussed as emerging from the COVID-19 pandemic crisis. The chapter highlights the considerable potential for developing this literature further and exploring hybrid events. Therefore event scholarship needs to keep an eye on how the event industry has been experimenting with hybrid events and provide best practice guidance and advice.

8. Response and recovery through event portfolio management: A case study from Des Moines, Iowa

This chapter by Singh and Olson takes the festival and event sector in Des Moines, Iowa as a case study to highlight the challenges of recovery and response to the COVID-19 pandemic. In particular, it examines how Des Moines's event portfolio management can position the city for effective recovery in the sector. It discusses how event organizers in Des Moines have been responding to the impact of COVD-19. The case study indicates that Des Moines should use effective event portfolio management strategies through the collaboration of its key stakeholders (attendees, local businesses, and event organizers) as a method for recovery and adaptation to the challenges presented by COVID-19. It is shown how Des Moines events have adapted within a portfolio context by implementing creative strategies to boost the art, culture, and heritage of the region. The chapter provides suggestions to overcome the COVID-19 crisis by recommending forming an umbrella organization to brainstorm, share best practices, and build partnerships across the portfolio. This case demonstrates the potential of portfolio management as a crisis management tool for the event sector.

9. Sport clubs and event recovery in Sweden

The chapter by Armbrecht, Lundberg, Pettersson, and Zillinger is a national case study of the pandemic effects on sport clubs and events in Sweden. It provides a snapshot of the heavily affected event industry in Sweden during the pandemic. In this context, the study analyzes the consequences of cancelled events staged by sports clubs. It also describes important strategic reactions of sports clubs in response to the crisis alongside their adaptive capacities and vulnerabilities. It is shown that many sport clubs in Sweden have suffered in economically and non-economic terms during the COVID-19 pandemic. Sports clubs took different strategies, adapting and innovating events. Cancelled events have been identified as the main driver of lost revenues. The case reveals the strong relationship between clubs and events as clubs primarily rely on events for generating revenue. It is suggested that a common portfolio approach among different clubs can help in recovery and resilience of events through diversification and risk reduction during a crisis and development of collaborative strategies supporting the economic resilience among clubs. The study points that the pandemic might, in turn, lead to new travel patterns and changed environmental impacts with the need to create new sport events.

10. A chronicle of event postponement and reorganization: Coming back stronger

The chapter by Varveri and Ziakas describes the case of a national ballet competition in Greece that was postponed and re-organized as a virtual event during the pandemic. The case study throws light on how event organizers are responding to the crisis and adapting to the new conditions. It focuses on the empirical decision-making of event organizers to deal with the consequences of the crisis. It is shown that event organizers have to rely on their own abilities, resourcefulness and adaptability in order to stay in business. This case provides an example of organizers' adaptive thinking and methodical decision-making to re-organize the competition as a virtual event, as well as manage the human bond between the dancers and the audience within a virtual reality environment. Similar characteristics and requirements span across artistic, sporting, cultural and entertainment events with which such organizers can relate.

11. Agility in the events sector: A case study of a business event in Finland

This chapter by Gorchakova and Berdysheva presents a case study of a business festival organized in Turku, Finland, discussing analytically the decision-making process, stakeholder involvement and feedback, establishment of a new modus operandi and a new event format. Underpinned by agile planning principles, it applies this approach to the context of the case study, drawing important implications for agile event management. This can serve as foundation for implementing innovative agile strategies in event crisis management and recovery.

12. Crisis management and recovery for events: Issues and directions

The last chapter, written by the editors, provides a concise conclusion to the book. It portrays the changing structural landscape of the event sector as a result of the pandemic crisis. It highlights that events have to learn to run under conditions of constant or episodic crisis and turbulence. A holistic mindset in crisis management needs to be developed to create tools and strategies for enabling the effective adaptability, recovery, and resilience of events. To this end, the chapter outlines the pillars of a holistic crisis management perspective that makes use of complex adaptive systems, event portfolio and resilience theories. It also sums up major issues in the crisis management of events and puts forward an integrative framework that brings together crucial elements and processes. Finally, the chapter discusses key trends and transformations of the event sector, and within this context, it suggests directions for future research.

Sum and substance: Breaking the void

In breaking the silence of event scholarship regarding crisis management and recovery, this book identifies and assesses the impacts of crises on events and explores strategies for effective response, recovery and resilience-building. In sum, this collection of papers, interviews and case studies fills a broad gap in the event management literature. It assembles contributions and insights from both academics and practitioners, thereby bridging theory and praxis. It combines cross-disciplinary approaches applied to different contexts and regions of the world. It thus sheds light on the complex subject matter of crisis management and recovery for events providing evidence that can inform event policy and practice. Ultimately, the book opens up avenues for future inquiries to build specific theory and intelligence on this complex subject. As the pandemic crisis made imperative to create knowledge on how to make events resilient, the book sets the ground towards reimagining and reconfiguring apposite perspectives, models and practices for the event sector.

Editors

Vassilios Ziakas, PhD, studies sport and leisure policy through an interdisciplinary lens that explores strategic linkages among sport, recreation, leisure, tourism and events. His primary emphasis is on strategic planning for obtaining a range of sustainable community benefits. Dr. Ziakas is the author of the monograph *Event Portfolio Planning and Management* (Routledge, 2014), co-author of *Event Portfolio Management* (Goodfellow, 2019), and co-editor of the *Routledge Handbook of Popular Culture and Tourism* (2018) as well as *Creating and Managing a Sustainable Sporting Future* (Routledge, 2019).

Vladimir Antchak, PhD, is Senior Lecturer in Applied Management at the University of Derby, UK. His research interests focus on event portfolio design and management, event experience, placemaking and strategic storytelling. He has over ten years of experience in events management, including organisation of business forums and conferences, cultural exhibitions, international business visits and presentations.

Professor Getz is editor in chief of the book series *Events Management Theory and Methods* by Goodfellow Publishers. Dr. Getz is Professor Emeritus, the University of Calgary, where he worked in the Haskayne School of Business from 1991 through 2009. Following his retirement he held part-time research positions at the University of Queensland (Australia), University of Stavanger (Norway), and the University of Gothenburg (Sweden). He has authored and co-authored numerous papers related to events and tourism and a number of relevant books including *Event Studies, Event Tourism, Event Evaluation,* and *Event Impact Assessment.*

Contributors

John Armbrecht, PhD is affiliated to the Centre for Tourism and researcher at the School of Business, Economics and Law at Gothenburg University. He received his PhD in marketing and has published research on experiential and non-use values within empirical fields such as cultural tourism, cultural economics and event and festival management and economics.

Peter Ashwin is one of industry's leading authorities on risk management and security to enable event organizers to meet the challenges of today's complex and uncertain world. He has led multi-national teams in seven countries over six Olympic Games (2000 – 2012), 2015 Baku European Games (Azerbaijan), 2015 ICC Cricket World Cup, 2010 G8/G20 Summit (Toronto) and a number of iconic festival and events across North America. He is a former Australian Army special forces officer who now calls Montreal, home.

Ekaterina Berdysheva is an MSc in Economics and Business Administration from the Turku School of Economics and a finance and project management professional with experience from international organizations like the Finnish Consulting Group and IF P&C. She is currently a board member of Boost Turku Entrepreneurship society, which is the founder of SHIFT Business Festival. Ekaterina was in charge of international development at SHIFT Business Festival in 2020 and was involved in developing marketing campaigns, international sales strategy and productization. Ms. Berdysheva is a guest lecturer at Business School of Åbo Akademi in Turku, Finland, and the University of Derby, UK.

Tim Brown, PhD, is Programme Leader of Events Management and Senior University Teaching Fellow at the University of Chester, UK. Tim's research interests include charity fundraising and charitable events, events management operations, experiential learning, event marketing and promotion, event technology, and the economic and socio-cultural impacts of events.

Kom Campiranon, PhD, is an Assistant Professor in the Service Innovation Program of the College of Innovation at Thammasat University, Thailand. He has extensive experience and is widely published in events, service innovation and design, design thinking, smart tourism, and tourism crisis management.

Valentina Gorchakova, PhD, is an experienced academic and marketing professional. She obtained a MA in International Relations from St. Petersburg State University and worked in business, not-for-profit organisations and the UN Development Programme before returning to academia several years later. Valentina is currently a Senior Lecturer and Programme leader of an online Business and Management BSc programme at the University of Derby, UK. Her major research interests lie in the areas of destination management, visitor experience and behaviour, cultural and urban tourism, and leadership.

Yawei Jiang is a PhD candidate in the Business School of The University of Queensland. Her research focuses on small business resilience in the face of extreme weather events. She has published several academic articles in peer-reviewed journals as well as book chapters in the relevant field. Her research interests include strategic management in tourism crisis and disasters, organizational recovery, and resilience in managing environmental uncertainties, and risk communication strategies for tourism destinations.

Erik Lundberg, PhD, is a researcher and lecturer in Marketing and at the Centre for tourism, University of Gothenburg, Sweden. He received his PhD in 2014 where he describes and analyses tourism and event impacts from a sustainable development perspective. He has published in journals such as

Tourism Management, Journal of Sustainable Tourism, Scandinavian Journal of Hospitality and Tourism Management, and *Event Management.*

Eric D. Olson, PhD, is an Associate Professor, Program Director for the Event Management Program, and Event Management Director of Graduate Education in the Department of Apparel, Events, and Hospitality Management at Iowa State University. His research focuses on LGBT+ tourism and events and customer evaluation of service encounters and service recovery.

William O'Toole is an events development specialist. He has worked in over 20 countries developing their events strategies, specific event development advice and event/festival audits, curriculum development and professional training of event teams in risk and project management. His latest textbooks are *Risk Management for Events* (2021) and *Crowd Management: Risk, Security, Health* (2020). He developed the courses and teaches Masters (Event Management) in France, USA and Australia. Bill began his career creating and managing concerts, festivals and special events around the world.

Robert Pettersson holds a PhD in Human Geography and is an Associate Professor in Tourism Studies. He works as director at the ETOUR Research Centre at Mid-Sweden University. His research focuses on event and destination development, tourism trends and tourism as a catalyst for regional development. Dr. Pettersson has a close relation to actors outside academia after several years as the head of the external relations office at the university. He also has many assignments in external boards and groupings.

Richard N.S. Robinson joined the University of Queensland in 2005. He has taught undergraduate and postgraduate courses in hospitality, tourism and event management, and professional development. His research projects, many nationally and internationally funded, explore tourism, hospitality and event workforce policy and planning, skills development, foodies' travel and event behaviours, and designing and evaluating education programs. He currently holds an Advance Queensland Industry Research Fellowship, to develop a tourism workforce crisis resilience and recovery strategy.

Smita Singh is currently a Ph.D. candidate in the Department of Apparel, Events, and Hospitality Management at Iowa State University. Her research focuses on event technology and destination marketing.

Danai Varveri, PhD, is a researcher of sport policy and Managing Director of the National Classical and Contemporary Dance Competition held annually in Greece. Her work is dedicated to enable the sport sector to increase its potential as a social, health and economic driver and her expertise lies on promoting sport-for-development programs for active living and well-being.

Malin Zillinger is a human geographer, affiliated to Lund University and the tourism research institute Etour at Mid Sweden University. Her work is devoted to digitalization within the tourism system, events, innovation, and tourist information search. She has been dedicated to themes related to risk and risk management and in 2020, this interest was related to the pandemic that strongly hit all sectors of the tourism industry. Zillinger is enthusiastic in knowledge sharing with actors outside academia.

1 Theoretical Perspectives of Crisis Management and Recovery for Events

Vassilios Ziakas, Vladimir Antchak and Donald Getz

Introduction

The world is always subject to crises and many times significant developments or changes occur in the aftermath of a crisis. In this regard, any crisis can be viewed as a turning point or critical juncture, though typically characterized by ambiguity, volatility and grave worries about the future. A crisis can cause continuing existential and socio-economic impacts; however, it also provides opportunities for creativity and innovation by re-imagining and reconfiguring the strategic purpose of organizations. Crises are apposite circumstances for reflection on management approaches, decision-making and the overall stability and sustainability of any system within which individual organizations operate. Arguably, any crisis prompts change to systems and organizations analogous to its scale and extent of multifaceted impacts.

The recent COVID-19 pandemic is a case in point of a multifaceted crisis as it is not only a health emergency. It entirely disrupted the social world and its commerce bringing about serious repercussions to the everyday life of people. The event sector, being a mirror of society, has been affected dramatically. Compulsory closures and regulations regarding social distancing led to innumerable postponements or cancellations of planned events, from the Summer Olympic Games in Tokyo to the smallest of community celebrations. Professional and amateur sports alike postponed or cancelled their seasons. Businesses of all scales all along the supply chain, including the venues, entertainers, and suppliers of goods and services, suffered enormous economic losses.

It appears that the full recovery of the interdependent event, hospitality and tourism industries inevitably requires a thorough re-thinking of the current approaches to city event planning and to event tourism. The pandemic crisis showed vividly that the development of the event sector worldwide has neither been salubrious nor sustainable. This is mainly because it has been expanding too rapidly, without regard for the health of whole event populations or the feasibility of managing event portfolios for long-lasting resilience. In other words, growth has been unregulated and inconsiderate of its lifelong systemic consequences to the range of preexisting events. As a result, competition has been intense, to acquire the most prestigious events, to build the most attractive 'eventful cities', or to produce the most benefits from event tourism. Exorbitant costs and detrimental impacts are widely evident for mega and major events, while in many cities over-tourism and the pandemic generated debate about whether there have been too many events staged with ever-increasing investment of public money. The pandemic crisis has exacerbated this erratic state of the event sector, clearly illustrating its unsustainable growth and the need to consider events operating within broader service ecosystems.

Nevertheless, the literature lacks specific frameworks and models focused on events, determining requirements for effective crisis management and recovery, building resilience of event ecosystems and fostering their sustainable growth and prosperity. The purpose of this chapter is to contextualize the distinctive parameters and exigencies of crisis management for events and thereby set the ground for generating specific theory and evidence-based practice on this highly complex organizational landscape.

Background: Understanding the concept of crisis for events

What is a crisis? What does it entail when it comes to events? To answer these questions, first we must clarify the difference between crises and disasters. In general, crises involve a disruption that physically affects a system as a whole and threatens its basic functions and existence (Pauchant & Mitroff, 1992). Disasters are circumstances that trigger a sudden unpredictable catastrophic change over which stakeholders have little control (Scott & Laws, 2005). In the literature, the distinction is clear, relating a crisis to an internal organizational failure to act, while attributing a disaster due to an external event over which the organization has no control (Ritchie & Jiang, 2019). In addition, disasters are distinguished into natural (e.g., earthquakes, flooding, etc.) and human-made disasters (e.g., terrorist attacks, political or financial crises). However, these distinctions in the practical context of events are blurred as a crisis and a disaster may overlap; event organizers often fail to act appropriately in ominous situations of the external environment who they have no control over. For example, the COVID-19 pandemic is both a natural (virus) and human-made (socio-economic) external disaster that caused event failures and terminations. Therefore, a crisis and a disaster should be defined in particular contexts and issue areas considering their causes.

It is heuristically useful to contrast and compare the types of crisis causes for planned events. A crisis in general has either an external cause or exists in the response to an incident or general societal/economic crisis such as the pandemic. As well, smoldering or invisible crises can occur within organizations due to culture and leadership weaknesses, malfeasance or incompetence. How people and organizations respond to an incident, such as an attack or injury, or respond to a general crisis like a pandemic, is as important as the cause. For instance, witness the poor response of some governments and some events to the COVID-19 pandemic that resulted in avoidable 'super spreaders' and deaths. Table 1.1 provides a comprehensive list of possible external and internal causes of crises, followed by a list of response crises. External causes include natural, human error, human malfeasance, economic and socio-cultural conditions. Internal causes comprise organizational culture conflict, weak or incompetent management, failure to act in time or appropriately, and system-wide chaos. The causes are often interrelated, affecting one another and thus increasing the complexity of crises and the severity of impacts.

Integral to the concept of crisis is the extent of risk faced by people and organizations. O'Toole, Luke, Semmons, Brown, and Tatrai (2020) have examined the full range of risks facing events noting that catastrophes or worst-case scenarios are not part of normal risk assessment and require a different level of contingency planning. This brings to the fore another important distinction between the terms 'incident' and 'crisis'. Literature on crisis communication and risk management operates within these two interrelated terms. An incident is an unintended occurrence that disrupts normal operations, and generally incidents at events and surrounding events are minor and predictable within normal risk management.

An incident is one-off and relatively manageable, whereas a crisis can best be defined as "*a specific, unexpected, and non-routine event or series of events that create high levels of uncertainty and threaten or are perceived to threaten an organization's high-priority goals*" (Seeger, Sellnow, & Ulmur, 1998, p. 233). It is marked by a "*sense of urgency, close observation by the media and interrupts normal business operations with a potential loss of revenues and credibility*" (Williams & Treadaway, 1992, p. 57). Parsons (1996) classifies three types of crises. These are: a) an immediate crisis with little or no warning, and the organization is unable to prepare; b) a slower-in-developing, emerging crisis in which the negative impacts can possibly be stopped or minimized by organizational actions; and c) a sustained crisis with a long-term time frame.

Table 1.1: The causes of crises and disasters

EXTERNAL CAUSES

Natural (e.g., wind, hail, snow, flood, earthquake, extreme temperatures, tsunami, lightning, wildfires, infectious diseases and pandemic)

- disease and pandemic may have natural origins but their transmission is subject to human intervention;
- fire is often human caused, or attributable to malfunctions and accidents, but wildfires may be caused by lightning;
- extreme temperatures, snow, excessive rain, wind and lightning (i.e., dangerous storms) can often be predicted by monitoring weather and weather radar;
- flooding and tsunamis are sometimes predicted, but earthquakes are often not;
- any natural cause can lead to secondary and even cascading negative impacts on the ecosystem, geology, structures, events, and whole communities, generating long-term crises such as financial losses, negative publicity, loss of goodwill and complete organizational failure;
- natural disasters may have a direct, on-site impact on events, or events might experience indirect effects such as loss of access, community disengagement or shifting priorities by governments.

Human error (e.g., injury caused by vehicular accidents and work practices; fires started by improper installation or maintenance; collapse of structures like stages; human crushes or trampling; panic without a clear cause)

- the question of legal liability may arise when human error is the cause of injury or damage to life and property, but error is also found in the responses or lack of adequate response; a basic principle of risk management is to impose waivers on attendees and participants in events, but these do not fully exempt organizations and individuals from lawsuits where negligence can be proved;
- an on-site crisis exists until immediate threats are removed and/or injuries and damages have been effectively dealt with according to emergency response procedures; however, the aftermath, including the possibility of legal action as well as damage to reputation can be prolonged.

Human malfeasance (terrorism, cybercrime, robbery, fraud, riots, fights, use of weapons, sexual assault, impaired operation of vehicles and equipment, slander)

- some types of malfeasance might remain invisible for a period of time, resulting in a delayed crisis – for example cybercrime, fraud and robbery;
- substance abuse is a special case, as it might not result in any visible or immediate problems; there is always the potential for accidents and injuries or damage to reputation to result from alcohol or drug abuse;
- on-site security is mostly taken for granted, but organizations also need a permanent system of internal crime prevention;

- slander, or rumor mongering, can harm an organization; a permanent and live system of monitoring and response for social media is necessary;
- a cover-up will only delay the inevitable fallout from human-caused problems; that the cause might be fixed but the crisis for the organization emerges later.

Economic conditions (recession, unemployment, loss of credit, major economic policy shifts, changes in corporate strategy; competition)

- trends have to be monitored, but not all of these potential sources of financial problems are predictable;
- competition is a fact of life and it applies to resources, demand, and attention; events that fail to maintain a competitive advantage are at risk;
- the financial health and potential resilience of venues and events is always a major concern for owners and managers;
- few organizations ever prepare for worst-case scenarios like the pandemic-imposed cancellations and (for many) complete loss of revenue – the result is numerous bankruptcies and permanent closures.

Social and cultural conditions (de-population, demographic shifts,e.g., ageing, immigration, value shifts,e.g., towards greater sustainability or away from certain activities, cause-related protests and boycotts)

- careful attention to trends and issues can alleviate some of these potential problems, but essentially organizations have to adapt to changing conditions;
- inclusiveness, both internally and regarding the customer bases, is one way to guard against the potential negative impacts of social and cultural shifts.

INTERNAL CAUSES

Organizational culture conflict

- the role of founders and charismatic leaders in shaping organizational culture is potentially a source of problems; strategic planning should take into account the fact that organizations must adapt to both internal and external change;s
- a crisis will occur when internal divisions threaten stability and unity of purpose;
- a crisis might arise if there is uncertainty about how to respond, or a political/ values-based impasse over the necessary/best response to incidents and problems;
- a crisis can arise from organizational misdeeds , such as ignoring pollution, cover-ups of mistakes, not adequately protecting the health and safety of customers or stakeholders, a lack of care for the resources of others (i.e., fiduciary responsibility), or false advertising; presumably there will be internal conflict over the values that encourage or permit such misdeeds, and inevitably they will result in public exposure and demands for accountability or legal action.

Weak or incompetent management

- bad decisions and inadequate management systems can lead to emergencies; financial weaknesses can make an effective response to a crisis impossible; human-resource weaknesses such as a lack of training or inadequate numbers can make it more likely that a financial problem or on-site incident will occur; technological problems can arise from both external hacking and internal mistakes;
- these are problems that should not occur in a well-managed organization, and they can be anticipated; mistakes have to be followed by corrective action;
- root-cause analysis should be completed by experts for all management failures;
- the crises attributable to bad management might be long-term and hidden from public view until they result in a major incident or complete organizational/financial failure;
- management systems can fail if they have never been tested.

Failure to act in time or appropriately:

(a) scenario 1 – there is a lack of relevant or sufficient information upon which to base decisions; scenario 2 – information is available and a correct response is known but no or inadequate action is taken (this could be a political issue such as a lack of leadership, or related to inadequate management systems)

- constant monitoring and feedback systems both internally and from external stakeholders are essential for timely responses;
- contingency plans must be in place and staff/volunteers empowered to act in a timely manner;
- even in well-managed and adequately resourced organizations, there will be a natural hesitation to cancel or postpone scheduled events; during the 2020 pandemic many events failed to prevent 'super-spreader' conditions.

System-wide chaos:

- in a worst-case scenario all or many social, economic, political and technological systems fail, resulting in general chaos; no organization can be expected to cope with such a large-scale disaster unless and until order and essential systems are restored;
- following the 2020 pandemic it is clear that resilience planning for tourism, hospitality, leisure, entertainment, venues and events must include the probability of many failures and specific incentives and assistance will be needed for a 'new normal'.

As noted above, it is common that a crisis can be caused by a disaster. A commonly accepted definition in the literature portrays the concept of disaster as *"unpredictable catastrophic change that can normally only be responded to after the event, either by deploying contingency plans already in place or through reactive response"* (Laws & Prideaux, 2005, p. 6). Such disasters are often generated by technological or natural forces and can include explosions, political upheaval, riots, crime, terrorism, war (Pforr & Hosie, 2008), hurricanes, earthquakes, floods (Quarantelli, 1988) or the COVID-19 pandemic.

Hermann (1963) argues that crises present a restricted amount of time to make an appropriate and sufficient response in order to minimize the risks threatening the values, functionality and overall sustainability of an organization. The responses are critical in reducing, offsetting and containing negative impacts of a crisis occurred (Seeger et al., 1998). There are at least three general types of crisis responses, including inaction, routine responses, and novel, original responses (Billings, Milburn, & Schaalman, 1980). Inaction or routine responses are appropriate when an organization is dealing with a low-level crisis with the expectation that the problem will be solved on its own. In a time of a high-level crisis, new approaches are required to operate in unfamiliar and risky circumstances.

Turner (1976) put forward an analytical framework of crisis or disaster development. According to this framework, a collapse takes place when inaccuracy or inadequacy in the accepted norms happens. A chain of discrepant events develops and accumulates, generally unnoticed during the incubation period, and results in a precipitating event which arouses close attention and leads to the revision of the general perception. The immediate consequences of the collapse become evident, and this is followed by a rescue-and-salvage stage when those impacted recognize the critical features of the failure and develop strategies for overcoming the negative consequences. Finally, full readjustment occurs with new norms and regulations adjusted to fit new realities. It is evident that the event industry should acknowledge many unavoidable risks and consequences of crises and therefore must develop more effective coping strategies.

Health-related disasters such as the 2003 Severe Acute Respiratory Syndrome (SARS) that affected 26 countries and resulted in more than 8,000 cases, or Avian (bird) flu influenza in South East Asia in 2003-2004 severely affected tourist mobility within and to various regions. SARS resulted in a number of countries issuing warnings or restricting travel to some destinations in East Asia, while taking health safety precautions at their own borders (Hall, Timothy, & Duval, 2004). In the case of Toronto, SARS so seriously disrupted tourism, sports and events that government agencies invested heavily in a recovery event featuring the Rolling Stones (Strange, 2006). Yet, as McKercher and Hui (2004) claim, most tourists have relatively short memories and usually resume travelling when they feel the immediate threat to their health and wellbeing has passed. Several scholars such as Pforr and Hosie (2008) as well as McKercher and Hui (2004) determine that such outbreaks do not tend to have lasting impact on travel and visitor flows in the long term, and that tourism consumer confidence restores promptly.

Overall, the thesis we take in this chapter views a crisis in the context of events as an exogenous or endogenous incident unfolding in various ways by a combination of causal patterns that create complex dimensions and effects. Along these lines, we highlight that a crisis for events is:

♦ unexpected (unplanned) by the people and organizations affected;

♦ out of the immediate control of those people;

♦ expected to grow rapidly if not solved soon;

♦ increases the uncertainty of planned actions.

Crisis management through a systems perspective: Chaos and complexity theories

A complex systems perspective is useful to capture the unfolding of crises, their effects and responses of event organizers within their complex environments (Faulkner, 2001; Paraskevas, 2006; Speakman & Sharpley, 2012). Contrary to traditional linear-reductionist models of crisis management, chaos and complexity theories assume the nonlinear nature of the world, environment and observed phenomena. They provide important lines of inquiry for crisis management by viewing events as complex adaptive systems of interactions and relationships. In particular, chaos theory investigates the behavior of non-linear systems and illuminates their state (Boukas & Ziakas, 2014), as shown by its basic principles in Table 1.2. It is associated with complexity theory but these perspectives are not identical. The focus of chaos theory is how simple systems give rise to complicated unpredictable behaviors, while complexity theory focuses on how systems consisting of many interdependent elements can lead to well-organized and nearly predictable behaviors (Olmedo & Mateos, 2015). The interconnection between chaos and complexity is known to make up a *chaordic* system: that is a complex adaptive system of dynamic connections between elements that form a unified whole, whose behavior is simultaneously unpredictable (*chaotic*) and *orderly* (Olmedo & Mateos, 2015). Events operate within chaordic systems characterized by dynamic structures, complex and nonlinear relationships between organizations, which evolve through time creating new emergent properties, and although their evolution is hardly predictable, it shows patterns of order. Any crisis causes turbulence to the already volatile environment within which events are embedded until 'self-organization' takes place as the consequence of bifurcation where order re-emerges out of a random and chaotic phase (Boukas & Ziakas, 2014).

Events themselves can be seen as complex adaptive systems. Such systems have the ability to alter and learn from past experiences. From a crisis management standpoint, we need to know how events and their stakeholders adapt to their environments and how they cope with conditions of high uncertainty.

Table 1.2: Basic principles of chaos theory

Explanation	Implications for events
Butterfly effect	
Insignificant changes in early stages of development may lead to a chain reaction which climaxes to the production of larger outcomes; these can dramatically shift the structure of the system.	The sensitive dependence of events on initial conditions and small changes which may suddenly occur influencing them catastrophically at national/international levels.
Lock-in-effect	
Inherited innovations in the past may have a lasting effect, even though changes in the conditions may have made the initial response redundant.	Mistakes of the past continue to happen by event organizers.
Edge of chaos	
A condition of extreme readiness for radical change as equilibrium is fragile and may be unexpectedly disrupted.	Events must be ready to cope with changes; extinction of unsustainable or 'unfit' events, while creating new opportunities for events capable of adapting.
Bifurcation	
The system overwhelms a critical point of the space phase and moves into a new phase.	Events enter in a new situation characterized by chaos and disequilibrium, a state where overwhelming changes exceed all current knowledge and response capabilities. It may lead to an event's break-down, resulting in its end, or break-through to one of various new states of order.
Self-organization	
New levels of form, organization and complexity often arising from interchanges between organisms and their context. A consequence of bifurcation where order re-emerges out of a random and chaotic phase.	An event becomes more suitable to deal with external or internal obstacles because of more optimized available resources. The crisis enters a resolution stage and the event enters a new normality.
Strange attractor	
The new behavior that is a departure from the previous norms that would be difficult to duplicate.	The values, codes, contradicting pressures and needs or oppositional paradoxes to which events logically and repetitively return.

Source: Boukas & Ziakas (2014).

This will inform the formulation of recovery strategies to changing conditions and contexts. By viewing events as adaptive systems, we can comprehensively examine and better understand how the individual and collective behavior of stakeholders adapts and self-organizes recovery strategies. Crisis management, thus, is an elusive balancing between chaos and order (stasis). Notions of emergence and self-organization can shed light on how social contexts become collective realities, where the 'whole' is more than the cumulative sum of its elements. Walby (2009) suggests that we need to understand the intersectionality of interacting systems upon one another making the environment in which a system operates as populated by competing, overlapping systems. Events are innately intersectional as their operations and delivery usually span across different system sectors. Viewing events as chaordic systems can reveal the emergent properties and interacting elements of events with the environment in order to make short-term decisions. This is essential for events since there can be several types of crises that make them highly susceptible to environmental changes and exogenous shocks. Therefore, we need to examine the complex adaptive interactions among event stakeholders in order to understand the complexity of environmental conditions and the contribution of each stakeholder to the recovery process of events. Quite surprisingly, however, chaos and complexity theories have not yet been applied to events to study operational and policy issues and so our event-specific chaordic knowledge is very limited about crisis management.

Nonetheless, in the academic literature and in praxis a 'systemic' turn has been made in how events are viewed and treated. This marks a progression from exclusively thinking about single events to event portfolio management in many cities and destinations (Antchak, Ziakas, & Getz, 2019). Still, there has been little if any discourse on the paradigm shift required to ensure resilience in the event sector. We can place this evolution of theory and praxis within two contexts of discourse, including neo-liberal capitalism being the source of intense competition and growth- oriented policies, and sustainability – with a considerable doubt about continued growth of the sector, a doubt now punctuated by the near collapse of international travel and tourism.

Evidently, sustainability in the event sector is much more than the greening of events and venues, and more than using a triple-bottom-line or balanced scorecard approach when evaluating outcomes. It is important to recognize that sustainability is not an end state, but a process of continuous improvement with sights set on the long-term. The continued existence and prosperity of individual events, and of managed event portfolios, especially in times of crisis, is a pertinent question. Within an organizational-ecology perspective, births and deaths are not the key point when considering population health or resilience (Andersson, Getz, & Mykletun, 2013). Instead, the core question is: how can we achieve a healthy and sustainable population or managed portfolio of events within each city and destination?

The COVID-19 pandemic crisis and the event sector

The COVID-19 pandemic crisis, with its high unpredictability and world-wide coverage, intensified uncertainty and distress about the future. For a long time, no one was able to give any reassurance of a quick and full bounce-back. The catastrophe of the COVID-19 pandemic caused a socio-political, existential and operational crisis threatening lives and businesses around the world. Responses in many places exacerbated the negative impacts because it appeared that no government or business was adequately prepared. Figure 1.1 provides a timeline outlining three stages in the pandemic and subsequent responses that pertain to the event sector.

Undoubtedly, the 2020 pandemic is proving to be much worse than SARS in 2003 or any other health-related disasters in contemporary history. It is prominent in the following ways:

♦ COVID-19 is the most severe pandemic since 1918; it is global and universal in extent; hardly anyone or any country was prepared for the scale of the disaster and grave impacts on health and the world economy;

♦ most health-related threats in the past were ephemeral (although with often lasting consequences); the 2020 pandemic took place over more than a year, including a second wave with re-infections;

♦ broader structural economic and social/political changes resulted, especially in the realms of leisure, tourism, events and hospitality;

♦ although by January 2020 most countries knew a novel coronavirus was spreading, they were not adequately prepared to prevent it, taking into account advice given over past decades about how to prepare for the next pandemic (Friedman, 2020), and deal effectively with the consequences.

The lack of timely response by the event sector to the pandemic indicates signs of organizational procrastination and structural inertia. Specifically, it is evident that there was a large and damaging gap between the time when global knowledge of the spreading pandemic was available and when national, regional and local officials took action. In most places, events were postponed or cancelled following announcement of a health emergency, while many events were held during the gap, when the public and those in charge of staging events all knew it was coming but either did not want to face the consequences with crucial decisions or lacked appropriate guidance and advice from authorities. For example, Mardi Gras in New Orleans was allowed to take place in late February 2020 without adequate warning about the risk from the federal officials. As some analysts argue, the event became a major transmission source in the area (Perlstein, 2020). In Italy, a home Champions League game between Atalanta and Valencia had been named 'Game Zero' by local media as it was held two days before the first confirmed case of locally transmitted COVID-19 (Sky News, 2020).

2020 PANDEMIC: indeterminate duration

-Origin: Wuhan China, Dec. 2019 or earlier

-Covid 19 was known to be spreading globally by January 2020

-WHO declares it a pandemic on March 11

-European countries' infections peak before June, while growth in infections and deaths continued to increase elsewhere

-By June, The Americas witnessed the largest number of new cases and resultant deaths while China declared few new cases

-"Second wave" of infections was expected in Autumn or late 2020

-The capability for mass vaccinations was not expected until 2021, but fast-tracking of research and development was being mandated by governments

Immediate impacts & responses

-From as early as February in Italy and through the summer of 2020 there were global travel restrictions imposed, social distancing required or recommended, events cancelled or postponed

-most sport leagues were postponed indefinitely; the summer Olympics were postponed until 2021 (if feasible then)

-In February many events were held in North America even as the pandemic spread, such as Mardi Gras New Orleans

-increasing efforts were being made to track the disease, test the population and develop vaccines through the remainder of 2020

-some countries and cities began a return to the "new normal", even when the infections continued to spread, placing many people at risk

Long-term impacts & responses

-Structural changes are expected in response to economic recession or depression; reduced globalization is expected

-new health regulations might become permanent

-it is predicted that there will be a very slow recovery of demand for leisure and travel, and altered patterns of leisure are expected

-permanent changes in employment expected, with marginalized people facing higher levels of structural un- or under-employment

-many planned events might be discontinued and event organizations fail, in line with other small businesses in tourism, retail, hospitality

-more digital events and digital augmentation is expected; will there be permanent restrictions on size and interactions?

-planning for and managing resilience in the tourism, hospitality and events sectors becomes essential; cities and destinations are expected to view proactive event portfolio management as a necessary function

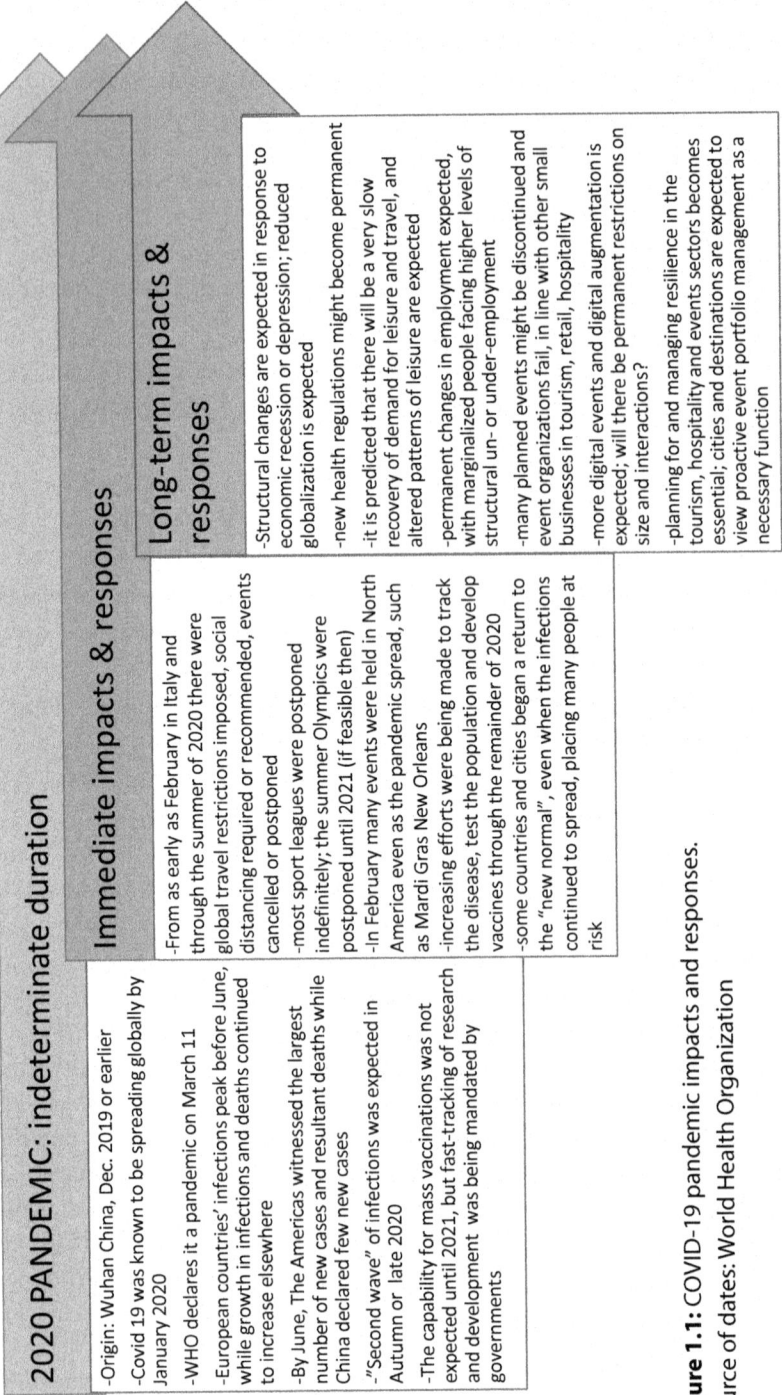

Figure 1.1: COVID-19 pandemic impacts and responses. Source of dates: World Health Organization

Exploring trajectories of the event life cycle, Holmes and Ali-Knight (2017) identify a so-called strategy of 'hiatus', a temporary lapse with the intention to return. Usually, relevant decisions are accompanied by an announced reconvening, but that was made difficult by the uncertainties surrounding the pandemic crisis. Event cancellations and postponements require specialized management wisdom, methodical decision-making, operational adaptation and tailored strategies.

In fact, very few events have the luxury of announcing an indefinite postponement because they are restricted by the availability of venues, potential clashes with other events (some keeping to their scheduled dates, others searching for new time slots), other logistical challenges such as re-booking suppliers and entertainers, and a lack of financial resources. In 2020, many postponements of events were made with the intent or promise of holding the event at its usual time next year, but for some that proved to be unfeasible. Cancellation for one-time events means the potential experience (and its potential benefits, but not all costs) is gone forever. Planned termination of events occurs when producers and supporters believe there is no viable future after the crisis.

While postponement is apparently the most common reaction, the resulting financial and image effects are still largely unknown. The British independent festival sector, for example, has been at risk of collapsing with many events cancelled and insufficient government support measures for event companies. The UK live music event sector expected a £900m loss in 2020 (The Guardian, 2020a). Some events are venue-dependent, such as theatre. The famous Globe Theatre in London was facing bankruptcy as of May 19, 2020 (Jeffery, 2020) owing to its complete closure during the months of lockdown; a similar prospect faced the Shakespearean Theatre in Stratford, Canada, as it was forced to suspend its entire season and instead offered digital recordings of past plays, a substitute that offered no prospect of earning income (Maga, 2020).

Evidently, as of the time writing this chapter (January 2021), it is striking that no sufficient levels of contingency planning and professional expertise have yet been made available to prepare appropriately event and venue managers for the severe consequences of the 2020 pandemic. The role of industry associations becomes critical in a situation when the industry requires consolidation and clear guidance. For example, as a response to COVID-19 crisis, the UK's Association of Event Organizers (AEO) has prepared a set of key measures for small scale and more complex events to be applied in conjunction with the risk assessment. A 5P framework (Protect all, Protect contractors, Protect visitors/exhibitors/speakers, Protect event teams and Protect events) entails the key areas of event planning and staging with an emphasis on:

- Density calculation (visitor flow, crowd management, entry/exit arrangement);
- Hygiene measures and touch-free arrangements;
- Medical plans for identifying and managing people who may be infected/ symptomatic;
- Controlling numbers of workers on-site throughout the build and break phases;
- Limiting equipment usage by multiple people where possible;
- Clear communication pre-show and on-site;
- Reviewing the profile visitor and exhibitor attendance for vulnerable groups – over 70s, asthma, etc.;
- Minimization of numbers of people in organizer's offices, and introduction of one-way system in and out of offices if possible;
- Strong knowledge transfer plans;
- Training for key personnel in managing COVID risk.

(AEO, 2021)

This framework could become a starting point in developing more effective and sustainable solutions for the event industry in the post-COVID era; it includes critical elements of risk management that were usually neglected by the practitioners in the past.

The special case of mega and hallmark events

Mega-events like the Olympics are planned years in advance, following more years of consideration and bidding, and are difficult to postpone or cancel, given the enormous investment of resources and prestige. According to a number of commentators, the Olympics and other mega-events such as the World Cup generally do not deliver on promised economic or tourism benefits (e.g., McGillivray & Turner, 2017; Zimbalist, 2015), yet are still highly valued by some cities and countries. Hence it was controversial when Tokyo, after considerable international pressure, reluctantly agreed to move its 2020 Summer Olympic Games to 2021 (The Guardian, 2020b). This announcement came without changing the nominal date of the event, presumably in order to protect the value of its large stock of merchandise dated 2020.

A challenge also exists for those periodic events that have achieved hallmark status. These are typically festivals and sporting events (often packaged together) that have become co-branded with the city; they are valued traditions and popular tourist attractions (Getz, 2013). These events are so important in terms of tourism, economic impacts, prestige and place identity that postponing or cancelling them requires decisions at a very high level. For example, when Hurricane Katrina devastated New Orleans in 2005 there was great controversy about whether or not to hold the next Mardi Gras (Root, 2006) and the city mayor proclaimed that the event was the 'heart of the city' and would be held as usual, although it had a reduced program. Similarly, when Calgary's Stampede, an annual rodeo, exhibition, and festival held in summer, was threatened by flood waters in 2013, the decision was made to fast-track a clean-up and repair of the site so that it could go ahead as scheduled; but in 2020 it was reluctantly cancelled for the first time in over 100 years for health reasons (Gilligan & Pearson, 2020).

As a whole, three major conclusions can be drawn from the pandemic impacts on the event sector. First, no amount of risk planning and preparation was adequate (even where it was in place) to prevent worst-case impacts that comprised the postponement and/or cancellation of numerous events, and closure of many venues around the world; this brought about deleterious effects on the entire supply chain serving tourism, hospitality, cultural and entertainment sectors. Second, there is unlikely to be a swift, complete recovery, and indeed there might be a global depression to inflict further damage. Clearly, the event sector, alongside the allied tourism and hospitality industry, has suffered considerably, and it seems that lasting damage has been done to their economic viability, resulting in a reduction of the number and diversity of events and venues. Third, a new paradigm is required to guide cities and destinations in order to overcome any type of crisis, become more resilient in adverse conditions and adapt to a new environment. To this end, attention is needed to be drawn on recovery and resilience planning of events.

Event crisis recovery and resilience planning

As with any crisis, it is not expected that all event organizations can survive the negative impacts and unfavorable new conditions. Individual events, event-producing companies, venues and suppliers need to make a range of basic strategic decisions as illustrated in Figure 1.2, applied to the context of the pandemic crisis. This straightforward decision-tree identifies first the option of not responding to a crisis with postponement or cancellation; however this carries certain risks and the impacts of the decision should be wisely assessed. Events that decided to ignore a crisis like the pandemic (or for inescapable reasons fail to act in a timely manner) might suffer from negative publicity and their future might be in doubt. If they are able to continue in the future, they will have to reconsider the options facing events that have been cancelled or postponed.

The schematic illustration provides a set of cascading decisions about events that are cancelled or postponed because of a crisis. Eventually, they might fail and have to terminate because of debt, declining corporate and public-sector support, faltering consumer demand, or logistical reasons such as an inability to find a venue or time slot. If they choose to come back, along the way there is a need to sustain engagement with key stakeholders and this can be accomplished through social-media platforms and digital scheduled events. The last three options facing all events that try to recover are re-scheduling, reconfiguration through some form of change (redesign, reposition, rebrand), and restructuring within a network such as a managed event portfolio. This latter option relocates individual events into the core of strategic partnerships, generates new mutually beneficial synergies among stakeholders that add value to events, and ultimately reshapes the way cities and destinations plan for event resilience.

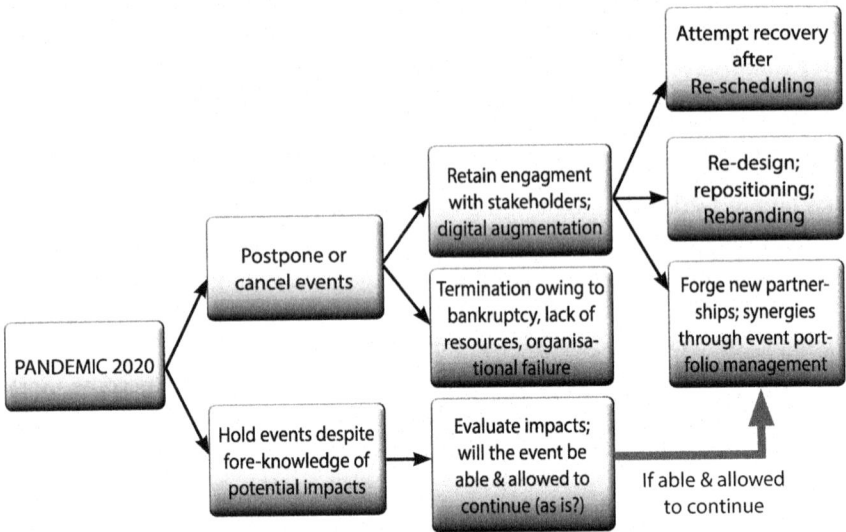

Figure 1.2: Decision-making in times of crisis

Several deviations in the decision-making of event organizers might take place necessitating a different suite of strategies. Hallmark events are a special case and their absence might lead to even greater levels of support and demand. For instance, publics who have missed the event might be asking to bring it back so that they can enjoy its qualities, and so local authorities, in turn, might quickly call for additional funding to re-instate their leading hallmark events. One-time peripatetic mega-events like the Olympics confront the following challenge, as the Tokyo 2020 shows: how can the organizers (both the governing and local organizing bodies) of a world-class event with a regular schedule adapt to postponement or outright cancellation? The investment both in hallmark and mega events is so immense, with expectations of financial returns and image enhancements, that some form of compromise is likely to happen. The same applies to popular sports that have lost part of their season or their championships.

Flexibility and adaptability are both requisite processes in the recovery phase. To adapt means to respond creatively to changes with new strategies and actions, while flexibility is required for organizations that cope with uncertainty. Several options will have to be taken into account such as deciding across a variety of venues, sponsors, dates and programming. The adaptable event organization must embrace and encourage innovation, while simultaneously be flexible in responding to both constraints and opportunities. In this context, every event, event organization as well as supporting agencies and corporations should be engaged in recovery planning. Figure 1.3 portrays the principal elements of planned event recovery that relate to any type of crisis.

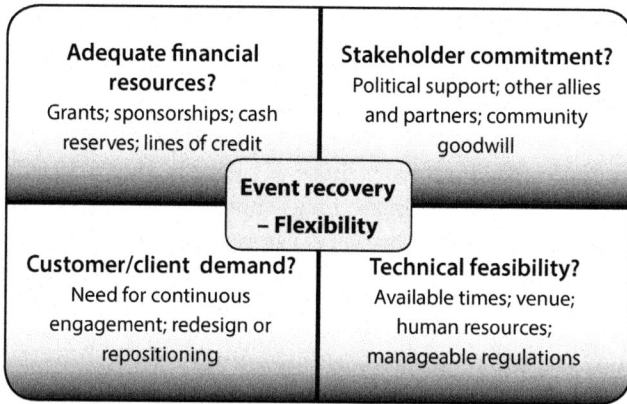

Figure 1.3: The basic elements of event recovery planning

First of all are financial resources, as lost revenues from postponed and cancelled events can lead directly to bankruptcy. Organizations with cash reserves and lines of credit have a better chance of weathering a crisis. Inability to renew or find alternative grants and corporate sponsorships are another path to failure. Much of the financial burden confronted by recovering events pertains to stakeholder commitment. As noted earlier, permanent, hallmark events are much more likely to receive commitments from local government and other supporters. Events working within inter-organizational networks and managed portfolios should be able to support each other, but that does not mean failures cannot be tolerated. Although seemingly insensitive, there is an argument to be examined and tested concerning whether the weak events should be allowed to perish and investments made only according to a new strategy.

Community goodwill must be sustained or established, as this can translate into customer demand, volunteers, and a more favorable political position. Future demand for events is never certain, as even those with loyal audiences that return year after year can be impacted by normal audience aging (raising the necessity to attract new segments) and be hit by adverse environmental conditions such as health and safety concerns or increased competition. Accordingly, a recovery plan requires unceasing engagement with all stakeholders and especially past customers or participants. A full redesign or repositioning option is possible, but risky in terms of being able to predict latent demand or the ability to capture market share.

The last fundamental element for recovery is technical feasibility or operational know-how. Rescheduling requires the ability to book a venue (e.g., even public streets and parks will have restrictions), find the same or at least a suitable time slot, recover all suppliers or get new ones, bring back volunteers and staff or recruit and train new ones, and be able to manage any new regulations, especially rules and guidelines pertaining to health and safety.

Building resilience for events

All venues and events practice risk management. The most common threats being taken into consideration are those of safety related to accidents, security related to crime and terrorism, image linked to perceived failures, and financial losses resulting from the very common inability to secure revenues to cover all costs. Health has typically been seen as a matter of meeting regulations, such as those pertaining to food, alcohol, energy, water, sanitation, evacuation and building standards – certainly not of responding to a pandemic. However, the pandemic crisis raised new health concerns and threats for public safety. Most event-producing organizations and venue managers had little or no experience with the new health demands and standards brought by the pandemic. That lack of preparedness, given the rarity of pandemics, is in itself a cause of organizational and system-wide crisis. To build resilience in the event sector, three levels of resilience planning have to be put into play: the event and its organization; the community; and the entire event population and managed event portfolio in a given area.

The event and its organization

The concept of resilience generally means the capacity to recover swiftly from difficulties or adverse conditions. There is a great amount of literature available on building a resilient organization. Such an organization is able to withstand changes in its environment and still function either without having to adjust or adapting to new conditions in a manner that better suits the new environmental conditions (McCarthy, Collard, & Johnson, 2017). Organizational resilience has been defined as:

> "The ability of an organization to anticipate, prepare for, respond and adapt to incremental change and sudden disruptions in order to survive and prosper. Organizational resilience encourages businesses to look beyond risk management towards a more holistic view of business health and success. A resilient

organization should not only survive over the long term but should also flourish – passing the test of time."

(BSI group, 2021)

Being prepared is a key requirement of proactive risk management and resilience planning. O'Toole et al. (2020, p. 157) suggest a PPRR emergency and risk management framework, including the phases of Prevention, Preparedness, Response and Recovery. *"While much of the focus will often be on the response phase, investing in prevention builds resilience, preparedness ensures scalability and capacity to manage surge and recovery operations are restorative and focus on lessons learnt to be carried forward."* O'Toole et al. (2020, p. 26) also emphasize the notion of antifragility, citing Taleb's (2012) definition as the ability to strengthen as a result of stress or crisis. It includes learning from mistakes, which is part of being a learning organization (Senge, 1990).

Nohria (2006) highlights the necessity for organizational adaptability as a strategic reaction on global crises. Contingency plans are necessary but not always sufficient. The most robust organizations have developed continuous sensing and response capabilities. When comparing adaptable organizations with the less robust, the following characteristics are evident:

♦ networked, with distributed leadership (as opposed to hierarchical and centralized);

♦ loosely coupled with a dispersed workforce (rather than greater interdependence among parts and a concentrated workforce);

♦ a cross-trained, generalist workforce guided by simple yet flexible rules, and not a bunch of specialists who are policy and procedure driven.

The matter is that a planned event might not be adaptive by its very nature: over-dependence on funding from one or a few sources; focusing on a niche market that is vulnerable to competitive pressures or economic conditions; an organizational culture that resists change, or leadership that lacks adaptive skills. All of these weaknesses can be reduced within a managed and balanced event portfolio, a strategic grouping of multiple events. It must be noted, however, that this will not prevent bankruptcies and other failures of portfolio assets.

Community resilience

Resilient communities are those that have the capacity to use available resources to respond to, withstand, and recover from adverse situations allowing for their adaptation and growth after a crisis or disaster strikes (Bosher & Chmutina, 2017; Norris et al., 2008). This level of resilience planning is critical, given the close relationships between many events, venues and residents and the direct involvement of numerous local governments and other public agencies in the event sector. Community resilience has been defined as:

"[…] the ability of a system (like a community) to absorb disturbance and still retain basic function and structure. Building resilience means intentionally guiding the system's process of adaptation in an attempt to preserve some qualities and allow others to fade away, all while retaining the essence—or "identity"—of the system. In a human community, identity is essentially determined by what people value about where they live."

(Resilience, 2021)

This definition places emphasis on preserving identity and values. Derrett (2008, p. 107) suggests a model to show how festivals and other events can help develop community resistance, which she defined as the *"future capacity of that community to meet challenges that might beset them"*. Collaboration, stakeholder engagement, participation by residents and effective governance are key elements. Events are catalysts, and therefore the management and governance of the event sector is important to the community's well-being.

As shown by the pandemic crisis, individual events alone are more vulnerable to negative impacts. We contend, however, that if they are part of a portfolio, then they can benefit from a series of collaborative, synergistic and complementary effects. These portfolio effects can support individual events, which are expected, in turn, to create aggregate value for the portfolio. Certainly, given the perennial problem of scarce resources, tough decisions will have to be made for concerted portfolio provision. Attention should be given to both selecting those events to receive support, and to the ones allowed to cease. That is the beginnings of thorough efforts to build portfolio resilience.

Event portfolio and event population resilience

In the context of cities and destinations, the practice of portfolio management can help achieve long-term sustainability when the aim is to have a salubrious and diverse population of events. Although it is not possible to make all events resilient in any jurisdiction, the resilience of managed portfolios can ensure that the most valued events as well as a selected array of events are always present. This warrants the permanency of events in the host community as part of a systemic configuration. From a financial standpoint, portfolio resilience brings together the notions of diversification to minimize risk, which can be seen as a defensive strategy, and proactive investments to secure advantages from disruptions in the market or from a crisis. In the event sector these concepts can be applied as follows:

♦ **Defensive**: A diversified event portfolio will protect from any loss of target market segments by sustaining an array of event types, through the entire calendar year, in different locations and venues;

♦ **Proactive**: Event bids are often structured as unique opportunities for bringing a range of benefits to a city or country; direct creation of new events or supporting innovation and entrepreneurship in the event sector is also proactive.

Nevertheless, it should be emphasized that normal portfolio resilience strategies will not necessarily be sufficient when a major crisis shuts down entire economic sectors, including travel, hospitality and events. Godschalk (2003) proposed critical elements in building resilient systems, which can be viewed as goals in resilience planning for event portfolios or the event sector overall. Accordingly, we contextualize these elements in the events realm below:

1   **Redundancy**: Failure of one or more events cannot be allowed to disintegrate the entire portfolio or population. Thus, it is important to ascertain from the outset which events must carry on, foster multiple nodes in the network for obtaining and sharing resources, ensure multiple venues are available for key events, and work along with other agencies, the private sector and other layers of government to manage portfolios. A minimum strategy is, at least, to coordinate overlapping event portfolios with each of them performing important functions for different strategic and policy purposes.

2   **Diversity**: The values and goals should be explicit in creating a balanced portfolio, encompassing all types of events, with an annual program; further goals should be to attract multiple target markets, cater to diverse social and cultural interest groups, and provide services and experiences to all segments of society.

3   **Efficiency**: Here policies and procedures should be introduced and established to ensure the efficient allocation of resources. For example, should financially vulnerable events that fail in a crisis be saved? Portfolio managers have to know where and how scarce resources get allocated, and in doing so, it is pivotal to decide if priority should be given to sustain permanent hallmark events or to create new ones and perhaps bid for one-off events.

4   **Autonomy**: Portfolio management does not suggest a lack of autonomy to facilitate independent action by events and other organizations to respond to a crisis by following their own recovery plans. What is highly problematic for individual events is that they tend to develop resource dependencies on key stakeholders and there are also controls imposed by regulators that can limit an event's capacity to take protective and recovery action. On the other hand, portfolios can manage this structural weakness of individual events. A crucial matter is how to coordinate a portfolio of events that sustains both synergies and autonomy.

5   **Strength**: Robust events, venues and suppliers should be able to withstand threats or absorb shocks. Strength can be amplified and optimized at the portfolio level, not the level of individual events or whole populations. Social systems are inherently strong as evidenced by community-

based initiatives to help people cope with the crisis and support events. Here it is essential to preserve previous market demand and/or attract new segments to events. Also, effort is required to secure the return of volunteers and staff or foresee the need to recruit new ones.

6   **Interdependence**: Events are interconnected elements in a portfolio as a systemic configuration. This is a fundamental principle of portfolio management, realized through fostering strong networks, versatile synergies and common goals.

7   **Governance**: Typically one focal organization leads in portfolio development and management. Nevertheless, in many cities and destinations there are multiple portfolios to take into account, generating additional governance challenges. Effective portfolio governance requires collaboration and networking within a distinct policy structure as well as dedicated action planning specific to events.

8   **Adaptability**: To optimize adaptability it is essential to facilitate learning in events by applying evidence-based decision-making at the organizational and portfolio levels; this requires a comprehensive system of controls, evaluation and impact assessment. Also, it is important to provide guidance and support on organizational change, to share experiences from a crisis and to constantly modify the portfolio by reflecting on environmental conditions and trends.

9   **Collaboration**: Event portfolios are contingent upon collaboration among different stakeholders. As such, portfolio managers should aim to strengthen existing collaborative networks and forge new cross-industry partnerships or community alliances. Residents, representing the local population and not just a customer base or target segments, are always a key stakeholder group requiring regular communication, consultation and research on values, attitudes and perceived impacts. How residents react to the crisis and its effects determine future possibilities for the event sector.

On the whole, the above elements are useful for elaborating on the properties and attributes of event portfolios, which contribute to resilience. Based on this analysis, we distinguish a set of key processes that make up portfolio resilience. These processes can produce significant added value to the event sector in times of crisis. As noted earlier, the portfolio processes are inherently integrative and systemic concerning how different events as interconnected elements are reconfigured to form a new whole program that adapts to environmental changes (Antchak et al., 2019; Ziakas, 2019, 2020; Ziakas & Costa, 2010). In particular, we discern five processes: network synergies, operational efficiencies, multipronged leverage, market supplementarities, and ecosystem continuity. Each process is explained below as follows.

Network synergies

Bringing together a range of stakeholders in a portfolio may develop relationships and foster collaboration. Stakeholder exchanges and interactions create a network that is instrumental for portfolio planning and delivery. Coordination of the event portfolio network is crucial in order to nurture and utilize synergies among the different events and supporting organizations. Synergies can be categorized as thematic or inter-organizational. Thematic synergies strengthen the meanings of events, thereby amplifying their impact on attendees. Inter-organizational synergies facilitate the forging of alliances, the garnering of community support and the establishment of local supply chains, which are required for the effective implementation of individual events and the whole portfolio. A well-coordinated event portfolio network can cultivate and sustain collective action, which is vital for enabling collaboration across the array of events. This calls for the formation or appointment of a local agency with the responsibility to coordinate the portfolio network, relationship-building and stakeholder management. Garnering wide-ranging community support for the portfolio may also engender opportunities for attracting alternative sources of funding from corporate and civic groups.

Operational efficiencies

Portfolio implementation is reliant on an integrated set of resources that are used interchangeably across events. Deploying shared resources can reduce operational costs as there will not be a need to find required resources from other sources. For instance, the same venues and facilities can be used, and volunteers can be chosen from a common volunteer pool. The goal is to attain the optimal use of resources avoiding their under-utilization or depletion. If demand for events exceeds resource capacity, then this is a sign that no further event development should be taken in the portfolio. If, on the other hand, several resources are not used, further investment is needed to build demand for events and develop new ones in the portfolio. Likewise, the portfolio context enables resource development to take place through knowledge exchange and investing in common assets.

Portfolio efficiency is also apparent in the execution of leveraging strategies and tactics aimed to obtain, amplify, and sustain event benefits. Leveraging requires that joint strategies be crafted to achieve multiple outcomes. Simply put, one action should seek out to obtain several benefits. For instance, if we lengthen the duration of an event, then visitor stays and expenditures will be increased, exposure of event messages boosted, destination experience enhanced, and the festival atmosphere elevated with augmentations to the program. These benefits can then be magnified providing that the same strategy is employed for selected events in the portfolio. To achieve this, portfolio efficiency stipulates another critical function: the synchronization of events and activities, which prevent overflows or time conflicts. For example, events can be scheduled in the off-peak period to overcome seasonality or sequenced across specific periods to build momentum and attract tourist flows. Synchronizing a portfolio, therefore, dictates the optimal sequencing of events, comprehensive programming and timely scheduling.

Multipronged leverage

Event portfolio management is based on a multipronged strategic approach that indicates the value of a balanced composition synergizing different event types in a portfolio. Balance further relates to the economic and social benefits being sought. To reach balance, multipronged portfolio leverage takes into account multiple perspectives and views, which are represented by the different events, and creates participatory mechanisms for stakeholder dialogue, deliberation and consensus-building. The array of events is viewed as a coherent group of assets that provide opportunities for community interventions. Based upon local consultation, interventions can be undertaken in the form of programs, campaigns or other actions to amplify the portfolio benefits. This requires a comprehensive view of events and their elements, community assets and intended outcomes. The underlying purpose is to identify ways to integrate events and the portfolio into the local mix of products and services that can enable cross-leverage between community assets and events. Comprehensiveness of portfolio leverage develops strategic acumen and ability to adapt events and strategies according to environmental changes and new conditions.

Market supplementarities

A portfolio can augment a community's market reach through the array of events that target supplementary audiences with different motivations and interests. For example, core markets can be served alongside accompanying and incidental markets by building up events and activities in the portfolio that appeal to each of them. As a result, there is a need for comprehensive design of the marketing mix of a portfolio, rather than of each single event as current praxis tends to do. A change of mind-set is thus imperative. This considers each event (and its elements) as part of the portfolio marketing mix and the challenge is to interrelate and synergize the different events based on the overall marketing strategy. From this perspective, market supplementarities can be leveraged. Supplementarity concerns three domains: (1) expanding audience reach through the number of events offered and their scope, (2) replacing missed audiences with further events that attract new markets, and (3) developing niche markets through specialized events.

Ecosystem continuity

Portfolio thinking principally entails the strategic patterning of events into a system. Unavoidably, through time some events will fail while others will carry on. The portfolio, however, will remain as a structure keeping consistency and integrity of event-related offerings at the host community. Subsequently, a comprehensive stance on portfolios serves the overarching purpose to maintain their continuity as service ecosystems. From this perspective, the matter is how each event contributes to the ecosystem; on this ground, decisions can be made as to which events should be terminated and which ones to be kept and assisted. In a similar vein, the turn to digital events needs to be assessed in terms of how it affects the portfolio and what should be the balance between digital and live events. Learning can be generated in this manner to improve portfolio implementation and adaptability to changing conditions. The primary aim is to guard the event portfolio ecosystem continuity. Concerted action that builds the strength of a portfolio and ensures its continuity can have positive effects on the reputation and image of the host community as an event provider.

The aforementioned processes, when acting in tandem, contribute cumulatively to building portfolio resilience. As depicted in Figure 1.4, portfolio resilience comprises the following interdependent domains: balance, synergies, community support, learning and adaptability/flexibility. In all, these elements generate opportunities for creativity, joint marketing, resource-sharing and synergistic strategy-making to deal with volatility and turbulent change. We contend that this is a practical, realistic, comprehensive and systematic means to enhance the resilience of the event sector, especially in times of crisis.

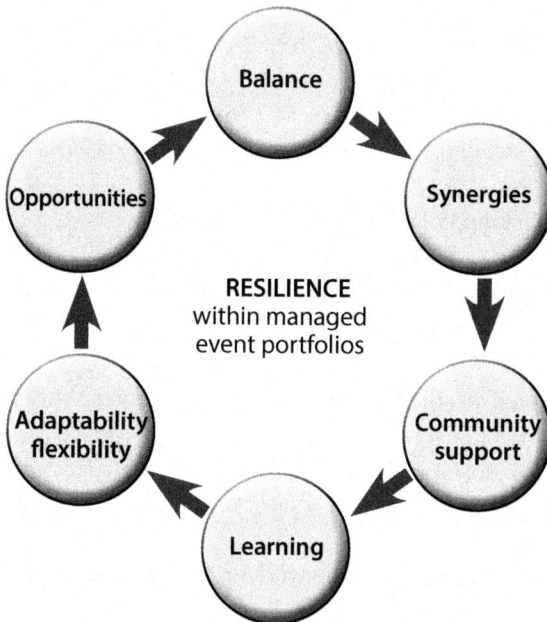

Figure 1.4: Building resilience in the event sector

Conclusion

The arrival of COVID-19 crisis exposed the fragility of the event sector with often erratic, unplanned foundations in many cities and destinations. It also accelerated structural change, reconfiguring key assumptions, practices and processes. The new landscape of the event sector has to move now, more than ever, from its innate fragmentation to integrated models of event management and develop event-focused frameworks for crisis management if it is to build resilience in the sector. This calls for a change in mind-set both in theory and praxis. In this chapter, we outlined fundamental principles of a holistic mind-set and directions towards generating specific theory in the complex area of crisis management and recovery for events. This makes up an important area for future research and thus requires considerable scholarly attention. The chapter establishes firm foundations for reshaping the event sector utilizing complex systems theory, resilience principles and the event portfolio perspective as a way to nurture a holistic mind-set on crisis management for events.

References

AEO (2021) https://www.aeo.org.uk/covid-19

Andersson, T., Getz, D., & Mykletun, R. (2013). Sustainable festival populations: An application of organizational ecology. *Tourism Analysis, 18*(6), 621-634.

Antchak, V., Ziakas, V., & Getz, D. (2019). *Event Portfolio Management: Theory and practice for event management and tourism*. Oxford: Goodfellow.

Billings, R., Milburn T., & Schaalman, M. (1980). A model of crisis perception: A theoretical and empirical analysis. *Administrative Science Quarterly, 25*, 300-316.

Bosher, L., & Chmutina, K. (2017). *Disaster Risk Reduction for the Built Environment*. Hoboken, NJ: John Wiley & Sons.

Boukas, N., & Ziakas, V. (2014). A chaos theory perspective of destination crisis and sustainable tourism development in islands: The case of Cyprus. *Tourism Planning and Development, 11*(2), 191-209.

BSI group (2021) https://www.bsigroup.com/en-GB/blog/ Organizational-Resilience-Blog/6-steps-to-Organizational-Resilience/

Derrett, R. (2008). How festivals nurture resilience in regional communities. In, J. Ali-Knight, M. Robertson, A. Fyall & A. Ladkin (Eds.), *International Perspectives of Festivals and Events: Paradigms of analysis* (pp. 107-124). Oxford: Butterworth Heinemann.

Faulkner, B. (2001). Towards a framework for tourism disaster management. *Tourism Management, 22*(2), 135–47.

Friedman, U. (2020). We Were Warned! *The Atlantic*, March 18, https://www. theatlantic.com/politics/archive/2020/03/pandemic-coronavirus-united-statestrump-cdc/608215/; accessed June 23, 2020.

Getz, D. (2013). *Event Tourism: Concepts, international case studies and research*. New York: Cognizant.

Gilligan, M. & Pearson, H. (2020). 2020 Calgary Stampede cancelled for first time in over 100 years amid COVID-19. Global News, April 24. https://globalnews.ca/news/6815098/covid-19-2020-calgary-stampede-update/; accessed June 23, 2020.

Godschalk, D. (2003). Urban hazard mitigation: Creating resilient cities. *Natural Hazards Review, 4*(3), 136-143.

Guardian, The (2020a). UK live music festivals sector at risk coronavirus, May 13. https://www.theguardian.com/music/2020/may/13/uk-live-music-festivals-sector-at-risk748coronavirus; accessed June 1, 2020.

Guardian, The (2020b). Tokyo Olympics 2021 last chance agrees IOC chief, May 21. https://www.theguardian.com/sport/2020/may/21/tokyo-olympics-2021-last-chanceagrees-ioc-chief; accessed June 1, 2020.

Hall, C.M., Timothy, D., & Duval, D. (2004). Security and tourism: Towards a new understanding? *Journal of Travel and Tourism Marketing,15,*(2-3), 1-18.

Hermann, C. (1963). Some consequences of crisis which limit the viability of organizations. *Administrative Science Quarterly, 8*(1), 61-82.

Holmes, K., & Ali-Knight, J. (2017). The event and festival lifecycle: Developing a new model for a new context. *International Journal of Contemporary Hospitality Management, 29*(3), 986-1004.

Jeffery, L. (2020). Shakespeare's Globe May Not Survive Pandemic, U.K. Lawmakers Warn. London: NPR. https://www.npr.org/sections/coronavirus-liveupdates/2020/05/19/858754044/shakespeares-globe-may-not-survive-pandemic-u-klawmakers-warn; accessed June 1, 2020.

Laws, E., & Prideaux, B. (2005). Crisis management: A suggested typology. *Journal of Travel and Tourism Marketing,19*(2-3), 1-8.

Maga, C. (2020). Stratford Festival suspends 2020 season indefinitely due to COVID-19. *The Star*, April 27. https://www.thestar.com/entertainment/stage/2020/04/27/stratford-festival-suspends-2020-season-indefinitely-due-to-covid-19.html; accessed June 1, 2020.

McCarthy, I., Collard, M., & Johnson, M. (2017). Adaptive organizational resilience: An evolutionary perspective. *Current Opinion in Environmental Sustainability, 28*, 33-40.

McGillivray, D., & Turner, D. (2017). *Event Bidding: Politics, persuasion and resistance*. Abingdon: Routledge.

McKercher, B., & Hui, E. (2004). Terrorism, economic uncertainty and outbound travel from Hong Kong. *Journal of Travel and Tourism Marketing, 15*(2-3), 99-115.

Nohria, N. (2006). Collaboration: Survival of the Adaptive. *The Harvard Business Review* (May). https://hbr.org/2006/05/preparing-for-a-pandemic#post3; accessed June 23, 2020.

Norris, F.H., Stevens, S.P., Pfefferbaum, B., Wyche, K.F., & Pfefferbaum, R.L. (2008). Community resilience as a metaphor, theory, set of capacities, and strategy for disaster readiness. *American Journal of Community Psychology, 41*(1-2), 127-50.

Olmedo, E., & Mateos, R. (2015). Quantitative characterization of chaordic tourist destination. *Tourism Management, 47*, 115-126.

O'Toole, W., Luke, S., Semmons, T., Brown, J., & Tatrai, A. (2020). *Crowd Management: Risk, security and health.* Oxford: Goodfellow.

Parsons W. (1996). Crisis management. *Career Development International, 1*(5), 26-8.

Paraskevas, A. (2006). Crisis management or crisis response system? A complexity science approach to organizational crises. *Management Decision, 44*(7), 892–906.

Pauchant, T.C., & Mitroff, I.I. (1992). *Transforming the Crisis-prone Organization: Preventing individual, organizational, and environmental tragedies.* San Fransisco: Jossey-Bass Inc.

Pforr, C., & Hosie, P. (2008). Crisis management in tourism. *Journal of Travel and Tourism Marketing, 23*(2-4), 249-264.

Perlstein, M. (2020). Mardi-gras may have been the perfect petri dish for coronavirus experts say. New Orleans: WWWLTV, March 17. https://www.wwltv.com/article/news/health/coronavirus/mardi-gras-may-have-been-theperfect-petri-dish-for-coronavirus-experts-say/289-d6f081f4-82f1-4847-9685-8a645f1406b1; accessed June 1, 2020.

Quarantelli, E.I. (1988). Disaster crisis management: A summary of research findings. *Journal of Management Studies, 25*, 273-385.

Resilience (2021) Six Foundations for Community Resilience. https://www.resilience.org/six-foundations-for-community-resilience

Ritchie, B.W., & Jiang, Y. (2019). A review of research on tourism risk, crisis and disaster management: Launching the annals of tourism research curated collection on tourism risk, crisis and disaster management. *Annals of Tourism Research, 79*, 102812.

Root, J. (2006). Mardi Gras will party on despite Hurricane Katrina's destruction. LJWorld.com. https://www2.ljworld.com/news/2006/feb/18/mardi_gras_will_party_despite_hurricane_katrinas_d/; accessed June 1, 2020.

Scott, N., & Laws, E. (2005). Tourism crises and disasters: Enhancing understanding of system effects. *Journal of Travel and Tourism Marketing, 19*(2/3), 151-160.

Seeger, M., Sellnow, T., & Ulmer, R. (1998). Communication, organization, and crisis. *Annals of the International Communication Association, 21*(1), 231-276.

Senge, P. (1990). *The Fifth Discipline: The art and practice of the learning organisation.* New York: Doubleday.

Sky News (2020). Coronavirus: Champions League match a 'biological bomb'. https://news.sky.com/story/coronavirus-champions-league-match-a823biological-bomb-that-infected-bergamo-experts-say-11963905; accessed June 1, 2020.

Speakman, M., & Sharpley, R. (2012). A chaos theory perspective on destination crisis management: Evidence from Mexico. *Journal of Destination Marketing and Management, 1*(1–2), 67-77.

Strange, C. (2006). Postcard from plaguetown: SARS and the exoticization of Toronto. In: A. Bashford (Ed.), *Medicine at the Border: Disease, globalization and security, to the present* (pp. 219–240). New York: Palgrave Macmillan.

Taleb, N. (2012). *Antifragile: Things that gain from disorder.* New York: Random House.

Turner, B. (1976). The organizational and interorganizational development of disasters. *Administrative Science Quarterly, 21,* 378-397.

Walby, S. (2009). *Globalization and Inequalities: Complexity and contested modernities.* London: Sage.

Williams, D.E., & Treadaway, G. (1992). Exxon and the Valdez accident: A failure in crisis communication. *Communication Studies, 43,* 56-64.

Ziakas, V. (2019). Issues, patterns and strategies in the development of event portfolios: Configuring models, design and policy. *Journal of Policy Research in Tourism, Leisure and Events, 11*(1), 121–158.

Ziakas, V. (2020). Leveraging sport events for tourism development: The event portfolio perspective. *Journal of Global Sport Management,* In Press, DOI:10.1080/24704067.2020.1731700.

Ziakas, V., & Costa, C.A. (2010b). Explicating inter-organizational linkages of a host community's events network. *International Journal of Event and Festival Management, 1*(2), 132–147.

Zimbalist, A. (2015). *Circus Maximus: The economic gamble behind hosting the Olympics and the World Cup.* Washington D.C.: Brookings Institution Press.

2 Crisis: The Juncture of Stability and Development

William O'Toole

Introduction

The development of the events sector over the last 40 years has shown a remarkable consistency. Not necessarily on the ground with specific events, but certainly looking at the management processes at a meta-level, there is a longitudinal pattern that has emerged. It seems the startling diversity of events, their independent development, the variety of personalities and work practices in every country and city of the world has produced a model of development. I have been fortunate to observe and, to a small degree, influence this development. I have experienced and worked in its various phases. From working in events in over 40 countries ranging from the Liberia to the USA, the pattern is unmistakable. This pattern is dynamic and self organizing. The development pattern creates five phases I have described here. The maturity levels become phases when we introduce the dimension of time. But what has this to do with 'crisis'. In an innovative and disruptive industry such as events, crisis is one of the factors that powers the pattern in development. From the Global Financial Crisis (GFC), to terrorism, to the COVID crisis, these are stimuli that have help create a development model.

Crisis, back to normal

A large part of the literature on crisis, disasters and crisis response concerns the management of the recovery. These stress the ability to 'return to normal' and resilience. Resilience is measured by the length of time required to return to normal (US Department of Homeland Security, 2010). The British Standards Institution, for example, focuses on business continuity management. In this chapter I will examine crisis as a mechanism for change. Instead of returning to the previous state of normal, it is a tool of development along a maturity path.

PAS 200:2011 defines a crisis as an *"inherently abnormal, unstable and complex situation that represents a threat to the strategic objectives, reputation or existence of an organization."* (British Standards Institution, 2011). As with all statements that include the concept of 'strategic objectives', this assumes that the objectives are never in opposition. For example, an objective of an event may be to adapt to new evolving condition to expand their audience. This can come under the general title of 'audience development'. This may clash with the objective to provide a stable platform for sponsors. Developing new sponsors can almost certainly clash with retaining current sponsors. It is this juncture of development and stability that is exposed in a crisis.

According to Regester Larkin's Assessment of PAS 200, quoted by Hamidovic (2012):

"[Crises] develop in unpredictable ways, and the response usually requires genuinely creative, as opposed to preprepared solutions. Indeed, it is argued that preprepared solutions (of the sort designed to deal with more predictable and structured incidents) are unlikely to work in complex and ill-structured crises. They may, in fact, be counterproductive."

This last statement is the core of the movement along the maturity path. The plans, standards, rules and regulations become inertia. Mathematically it can be demonstrated that hazards and risks are a result of frequency analysis of past incidents and therefore are inherently conservative. In a stable environment the past is indeed a measure of the future. However events are by their very nature 'new'. When combined with the diversity, independent development and complexity of the events sector, perhaps it takes a crisis to overcome this stultification.

Maturity model

The basis of this chapter is the assumption that the events sector follows the other sectors in society, such as engineering, accountancy, medicine and moves through the phases outlined in Figures 2.1 and 2.2. This concept originates from the Capability Maturity Model (CMM) of the Software Engineering Institute of Carnegie Mellon University (1994). The CMM is set out as a prescriptive model to ensure optimization of software development.

In the Events Sector Maturity Model, the development is an emergent result of the complexity of events and event management. Each city, town and country has over the last 30 years independently developed their part of the events sector. It has organically grown through localized demand, failure and success. Events compete for resources and an audience and therefore it can be regarded as an evolutionary model. Most festival and other community level events were globally isolated and the event teams focused on delivering their specific event. They were not concerned with global standards.

The maturity model for event management was introduced in *Events Feasibility and Development* (2011). The suggested levels and their characteristics are described in Figure 2.1.

Informal	Formal	Accountable	Adaptable
The event is organized on an ad hoc basis, little is written down. Depends on personality of the event manager. Highly adaptive and flexible. Management system is not accountable.	The event has structured management with delegation. Project planning tools are used.	Includes the competencies of the Formal level and the management can account for their management and decisions. Documented and integrated management system.	Includes the Accountable competencies. The event management can respond positively to change and improve for each event.

Figure 2.1: Adapted from Maturity Table for Event Management, (O'Toole, 2011, p. 162) and Competencies and Maturity Models (O'Toole, 2002).

Carrying this event management model further to describe the formation and progress of the events sector, the author has created and tested the table shown in Figure 2.2.

	Maturity path				
	1	2	3	4	5
Maturity Level	Ad hoc	Isolated planning	Integrated Planning	Standards	Stable with flexibility and adaptation
Characteristics	No formal plans; quick to set up and flexible. Often driven by one personality.	Single areas such as Marketing and Schedule use plans. Delegation is formalized.	Repeatable events. Solid organization structure. Management seen as an asset. Each event improves the planning. Codes and guidelines are introduced.	Input from best practice and International standards and mandatory standards. Event specific laws. Decision hierarchy with complete accountability.	Plans are one input to decisions. Decision making is distributed and networked. Best practice is studied at all levels. Competency is measure of staff. Risk is also opportunity.
Limits	Cannot be repeated or sold. Unaccountable decisions.	Not fully accountable.	Good plans become the objective.	Bureaucratization. "Box ticking". Inflexible. Fragile, open to disasters.	Not understood by Levels 3 and 4.

Figure 2.2: Events Sector Maturity Model (O'Toole, 2021)

The Festival of the Winds is a good example of an event growing organically and responding to opportunities. It was not part of any policy or worldwide trend and it was initially driven by a local personality. Also as the numbers of participants and spectators grew, the event became more economically important to the local businesses such as the restaurants and shops. At a time when the beach would not attract large numbers, i.e. windy September, the festival dramatically increased the number of people coming to the area. As one local put it *"Years ago the shops cursed the wind, now they pray for it"*. The local businesses are now financially dependent on the event going ahead and hence the local Council invests more resources into it and ensures it is a safe event. At the same time the events sector in the state of New South Wales (NSW) was growing, festivals were starting to be linked and Occupational Health and Safety (OHS) and other workplace standards became a mandatory part of the festival. It then moved into Level 4. Almost all the public festivals and events in the area, such as Sculpture by the Sea, Garage Sale Trail, Bondi to Bronte Ocean Swim and City to Surf have followed this path.

This model of self organization and adaptation[1] is replicated around the world to the millions of public events, celebration events and festivals. For many years they were independently developing, but still following a certain path. It seemed to be the logic of growth and development.

Standards level 4

At the local level, the yearly events progressed by responding to opportunities as well as complying with the new rules and regulations and the requirement of the stakeholders. Arising from this natural growth all these events are moving through the phases in Figure 2.2.

There are a number of factors that drive this along. These include:

1. Globalism

The interconnected world means the Festival of the Winds, for example, can now connect with other kite festivals around the world. In the 1990s, for example, they were sponsored by Malaysia Airlines. Their logo is a kite. The airline's sponsorship included transporting to Bondi a number of fighting kites and flyers from Malaysia to the event. This was then used to publicize the event. The Taif Rose festival began in Saudi Arabia in 1996 as a response to the needs of the local farmers. It has now connected with the Portland Rose festival in the USA. The cross communication and training has moved the festival along the maturity path. It was in 2019 a major part of the 11 festivals around Saudi Arabia promoted worldwide.

---

1   Surprisingly similar to the models in evolutionary biology such as found in Stuart Kaufman's *The Origin of Order*, 1993.

Globalism includes international logistics, just-in-time management and, as a result, the standardization of many aspects of the event including its management system. Live Nation Entertainment, for example, own and operate venues around the world. Their contracts, methods of working and professionalism have an effect on events that hire Live Nation as a supplier of performers and ticketing.

2. Risk

The nature of public events means that any disaster will be well publicized. According to Kahneman and Tversky (1979), people will over-estimate the probability of disasters. The risk management solution to this situation is more planning. This leads to more standards, codes and regulations. Initially the event had to submit their plans for the event to be approved. Hence the event management team needs to implement formal planning. With the introduction of risk management standards, the plans must be integrated. The perception of risk and risk aversion has been a strong impetus to the movement along maturity path for events.

3. Economic impact

Small events, such as weddings, small concerts and special events are distributed and therefore their combined economic impact may be great but not noticed by a central government. As events grew larger the economic impact became more pronounced and this became a driving factor in the move along the maturity path.

4. Tourism

Tourism is related to economic impact and also concerned with risk. An event that included tourists is exposed to the world in term of risk. The 2006 Dhow disaster in Bahrain, for example, took the event from a local celebration to an issue in the International Court. The implication is that the internationalization of certain events by attracting tourists leads to an expectation of professionalism. The professionalism is measure by the standard in the international industry. Hence it is a factor in the movement towards the fourth column in Figure 2.2.

Figure 2.3 shows a simple causal diagram of the drivers along the maturity path.

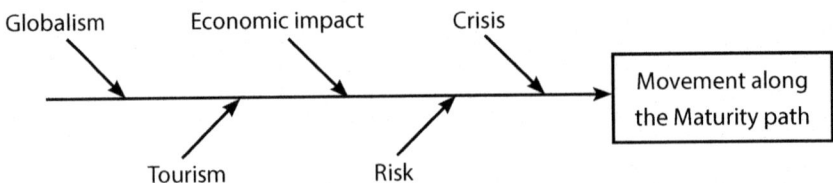

Figure 2.3: Factors in the development of the events sector

Health crisis

The COVID crisis, like the GFC, the SARS crisis and the terrorism crisis can be seen as accelerating the movement of events and therefore, ultimately, the event sector along the maturity path.

In events sector, a crisis may be described as an unexpected change that is outside the abilities of current resources to solve and is time dependent when inaction can make the risk far worse.

On a micro level, for the event management, the health crisis is straight forward as it entails how an event will comply with the directives of the government. The problem is that the directives of the government are often contradictory; may not take into account the special circumstances of events; and may change before there is time to implement them. However, on the macro level the crisis will push the lagging regions along the maturity model.

To be compliant the event team needs risk management plans to submit to the authorities. This drives the events in the Ad Hoc and Isolated Planning phase forward to the Integrated Planning phase. Risk management is a method of integrating all the planning functions. Cities, regions and events that are already in Level 3, Integrated planning, will move more towards the Standards level as government requirements for events will become more pervasive and stringent. This is not just in the area of health, but also includes compliance in risk, OHS and all operational areas of events including security, drones and temporary structures. The City of Greater Geelong (2011) *Event Planning Guide*, for example, with a population of 200,000, comprises 152 pages of standards and codes of practice that must be understood and planned before applying for permission to hold a public event.

In the same way that Government woke up to the power of events to attract tourists and therefore bring in new money, events are now seen to affect society as spreaders of diseases.

On that point it is interesting to consider the literature on public health and events. Most of the early event management textbooks rarely mention it. As stated by Dr Stephen Luke in *Crowd Management: Risk, Security, Health*:

> "Mass casualty incidents at public events are front page news, especially if terrorism is suspected. Pandemic influenza and Ebola Viral Disease are high profile global health issues. The lethality of heat wave is becoming increasingly understood. Mass drug overdoses at music festivals may result in catastrophic loss of life and inevitably evoke passionate community debate. Why then is health so often an after-thought in event planning?"

O'Toole et al. (2020, p. 147)

With the growth of mega events, the World Health Organization (2015) produced the detailed and wide-ranging publication *Public Health for Mass Gatherings*. The Hajj in Saudi Arabia, for example, has been concerned with public health for many years due to its global nature, drawing people from around the world to stay in close proximity. As a result of medical crises, such as meningitis, hepatitis B and polio, the Government has enacted various laws and regulations to minimize the risks (Allen, et al. 2011; Almutairi, et al., 2018; Memish, et al. 2019). The many articles in the *Lancet* and similar publications indicate that the public health issue is often driven by incidents and presentations at large events. As explained earlier, standards and codes are set up to control the risk at mega events. As they are mandatory, they are enforced for smaller events. This moves the events sector into the fourth phase. Smaller festivals and public events do not have the resources to follow these mandatory standards. An example of this is the other crisis which now has been going for so long that it is no longer referred to as a crisis: terrorism and events. The introduction of new security standards has forced smaller events and festivals to pay for extra security, or to close if they could not afford to fulfil the new security requirements. Note that, initially, this was regardless of whether the event was possibly a terrorist target or not. Examples of this are worldwide, such as 2019 St Patrick's Day parade in Washington DC. Perhaps this is a further example of Kahneman and Tversky's (1979) prospect theory of risk perception. Following that logic, is obvious that mandatory standards will be introduced to events with regard to public health. The COVID crisis will then move the event sector in many regions along the maturity path.

This concept of crisis as a reset or readjustment of a complex system is not new. Ecological crisis as part of the biological evolution is well known. Disasters, crises that quickly become completely out of control for a period, are a part of history and the readjustment can be seen as contributing towards progress. The bushfire crisis in Australia in 2018, for example, reintroduced control management of the bushlands and prepared Australia for the COVID crisis.

Stable/Flexible phase

The next level along the maturity path is the Stable/Flexible phase. This phase is in response to the growth of rules, regulations, permits, licenses and codes that can easily stifle the creativity of events. The Byzantine growth of detailed form filling and permissions, as well as the long time to obtain licenses and permits and the tendency for bureaucracies to be risk averse, leads to the 'box ticking' that has become part of event management. For example, erecting a temporary tent or marquee at an event for only one day involves at least 11 detailed standards as well as the Work Health and Safety Regulation of 2011. These standards range from AS/NZS 1680.0 – Interior lighting – Safe movement, to AS1170 – Structural design actions. These standards, codes and regulations must be followed regardless of the time the tent is in use. Whereas with very large events, the costs associated with these standards can be amortized over the time period of the asset, a small community event does not have that possibility. As well, it is an upfront cost. As described, the new security costs are not an issue with the mega events when compared with the many smaller public festivals and events. To take one example, the Fêtes de Bayonne in north France estimated their new security cost to be one third of the overall cost of the event. There are many examples of smaller events being cancelled due to the extra mandatory security costs such as The Rice Street Festival in Minneapolis and the Tweed Valley Banana Festival. The relatively small community festivals are subject to the same hazard analysis as mega events when it comes to hostile attacks. One can see expression of this issue in the illegal raves and dance parties such as the Quarantine Raves that were springing up around the world. These types of events circumvent all permits, rules and regulations by using the social networks to promote the event just before it occurs.

As ever, Edinburgh is far ahead of this and their strategy includes this very non-bureaucratic statement:

"Occasionally, an event opportunity will arise which is so exceptional that it will be grasped even if it doesn't quite meet the key criteria. A flexible approach will ensure that not only can we act quickly, but also that we can balance such opportunities with our ongoing commitments."

(City of Edinburgh Council, 2007, p. 10)

They are constantly seeing opportunity in risk. A major issue they faced was that the accommodation providers (hotels) dramatically increased their prices during the festival. This is quite common for successful events and is a result of the stability of the festival and its worldwide reputation. It was very expensive for the aspiring artists, particularly the new performers, who, after all, provide the new ideas and keep the Fringe Festival fresh and attractive. The Fringe Festival's solution was to launch a 'put-up-a-performer' campaign to the people of Edinburg and surrounding areas. They suggested here was an opportunity for the local people to share their home with an artist. Being open to innovation and able to manage a risk and create an opportunity is the key characteristic of the column five in the Events Sector Maturity Model (Figure 2.2).

A further example of the Stable/Flexible phase is the response by Dubai Tourism Commerce and Marketing (DTCM) to the COVID crisis. They focused on their 'Dubai Fitness Challenge 2020'. One result was an astounding 20,000 cyclist taking part in December 2020 at the inaugural event. An interesting use of the crisis to create social capital.

The COVID crisis may be a wake-up call for mega events. The large events and international event companies have grown rapidly with the stability of the world economy. Due to their political and economic impact mega events such as the Olympics, huge concerts and festivals, are now defining the industry. They are reliant on stable economies, international logistics and the free flow of people around the world. They can be highly geared. They can borrow large amounts of money, make a surplus and pay it back easily with interest, as the interest paid back is far less than the profit. But they are fragile. They are highly exposed to what Nassim Taleb called fat tail risks (Taleb, 2012). These are unexpected catastrophic risks. The cost of mandatory standards has comparatively little impact on the economy of these mega events. In some cases they can create their own mandatory standards through legislation in the host country. They live and thrive in the Standards column of the Maturity Model. The standards, rules and regulations become a wall or entry cost that stops any upcoming competition.

The international events and event supplier companies are in the same column. Live Nation was reportedly on their way to bankruptcy in April of 2020. Their business included over 4000 performers, numerous venues around the world and planned festival and concerts. The Government of Saudi Arabia saved them by buying half a billion dollars in shares of the company. This can be compared to the small agencies, festivals and venues who have survived by scaling back the size of their events, using the time to be innovative and training their staff. In Australia, the NSW State Government decided to support 1000 small concerts distributed around the country. Called Great Southern Nights, it was a COVID compliant alternative to the mega concerts.

All these may be indicative of a reset. The mega events may not come back in the same way. It may be an opportunity for small events and smaller event companies to replace the mega events and international companies. This may introduce a new flexibility in the event sector and allow the agile companies to find a new place.

Conclusion

At the beginning of the COVID crisis many event professionals and experts feared the worst. As expected by Kahneman and Tversky's (1979) prospect theory, and shifting the risk needed by bureaucratic decision making, it was seen as a major disruption and the question was how to get back to normal once it was over. The concept underpinning this chapter is that 'normal' in a complex system over time is not a static state. It is dynamic and, in the case of the event sector, moves through phases determined by self organization and survival combined with the globalization of the sector. Instead of using such tools as business continuity management, this chapter examines the crisis as a disruption that opens many opportunities. It breaks the dominance the past mega events have in the sector. They are slow moving, exposed to crisis and hence, fragile. The crisis may allow the more agile and creative events and event teams an inflexion point to move the sector into an innovative phase with wide diversity of unique events. In this phase risk management is also used as the management of opportunities.

References

Allen, J., O'Toole, W., Harris, R., & McDonnell, I. (2011). *Festival and Special Events Management*. Hoboken: John Wiley & Sons.

Almutairi, M., Alsalem, W., Hassanain, M., & Hotez, P. (2018). Hajj, Umrah, and the neglected tropical diseases, *PLoS Neglected Tropical Diseases. 12*(8), e0006539. doi: 10.1371/journal.pntd.0006539.

British Standards Institution. (2011). *PAS 200:2011 Crisis Management. Guidance and good practice*.

Carnegie Mellon University, Software Engineering Institute. (1994). *The Capability Maturity Model*. Addison Wesley Longman, Inc.

City of Edinburgh Council. (2007). *Inspiring Events Strategy 2007,* www.edinburgh. gov.uk, p10.

City of Greater Geelong (2011). *Event Planning Guide*. www.geelongaustralia.com. au.

Hamidovic, H. (2012). *An Introduction to Crisis Management*. ISACA, 5.

Kahneman, D., & Tversky, A. (1979). Prospect Theory: An Analysis of Decision under Risk. *Econometrica, 47*(2), 263-291.

Kauffman, S. (1993).*The Origin of Order; Self Organisation and Selection in Evolution*. OUP.

Memish, Z. Steffen, R., White, P., Dar, O., Azhar, E., Sharma, A., & Zumla, A. (2019). Mass gatherings medicine: public health issues arising from mass gathering religious and sporting events. *Lancet, 393*(10185), 2073–2084. doi: 10.1016/S0140-6736(19)30501-X

O'Toole, W. (2002). Competencies and Maturity Models. [Paper presentation] International Special Event Society Conference , Sydney, Australia. http://epms. net/information/.

O'Toole, W. (2011). *Events Feasibility and Development: From Strategy to Operations*. Butterworth-Heinemann.

O'Toole, W. (2021). *Events Feasibility and Development: From Strategy to Operations*. (2nd ed.). Taylor & Francis.

O'Toole, W., Luke, S., Semmens, T., Brown, J. & Tatrai, A. (2020). *Crowd Management: Risk, Security, Health*. Goodfellow.

Taleb, N. (2012). *Antifragile, Things That Gain from Disorder*. Random House.

US Department of Homeland Security. (2010). *DHS Risk Lexicon*. https://www.dhs.gov/xlibrary/assets/dhs-risk-lexicon-2010.pdf.

World Health Organization. (2015) *Public Health for Mass Gatherings: Key considerations*. WHO Press, Switzerland.

Event websites and online media reports

Dubai Fitness Challenge 2020, https://www.dubaifitnesschallenge.com/

Dubai Fitness Challenge 2020, Report: https://www.ritzmagazine.in/hamdan-bin-mohammed-joins-more-than-20000-cyclists-in-first-dubai-ride/

Festival of the Winds, https://www.festivalofthewinds.com.au/

Sculpture by the Sea, https://sculpturebythesea.com/

Garage Sale Trail, https://www.garagesaletrail.com.au/

City to Surf, https://city2surf.com.au/

Bondi to Bronte Ocean Swim, http://www.bonditobronte.com.au/

Great Southern Nights, https://www.greatsouthernnights.com.au/

Practice Insight 1:

Interview with Steven Wood Schmader, CFEE President & CEO International Festivals & Events Association (IFEA World)

Steve Schmader, with 40+ years' experience in the festivals & events industry, including 20 years as the President & CEO of the IFEA, was asked several questions about the impacts of the COVID-19 pandemic on the global festivals and events sector, as he is in a unique position of being able to relate to events and their many stakeholders all over the world.

Q: Can you tell us a little about the IFEA, as a professional organization?

A: The best way to do that is to provide a brief organizational overview:

Founded in 1956 as the Festival Manager's Association, the International Festivals & Events Association (IFEA World) today is 'The Premier Association Supporting and Enabling Festival & Event Professionals Worldwide.' In partnership with global affiliates under the umbrellas of IFEA Africa, IFEA Asia, IFEA Australia / New Zealand, IFEA Europe, IFEA Latin America, IFEA Middle East, and IFEA North America, the organization's common vision is for "A Globally United Industry that Touches Lives in a Positive Way through Celebration." Toward that end, we now also count "IFEA Academia," providing a common home for students, faculty and institutions around the world who share a festival and event management focus and a common goal of preparing future industry leaders; a forum for important industry-related research and discussions; and an effective junction of the academic and professional pathways of our industry.

With a target audience that includes all those who produce and support quality celebrations for the benefit of their respective "communities", the IFEA's primary focus is identifying and providing access to the professional resources and networks that will, as stated in our mission, inspire and enable those in our industry to realize their dreams, build community and sustain success through celebration.

The IFEA exists to serve the needs of our entire industry, all those who share our core values of excellence & quality; the sharing of experience, knowledge, creativity and best practices; and the importance of "community" building both locally and globally. Our success lies in the success of those we serve through professional education, programming, products and resources, networking and representation.

The IFEA enjoys the active support of over 3000 Premier Members, a self-selected group of industry leading professionals and organizations who continue to set and raise the bar for themselves and everyone in our industry with regard to creativity, quality, professionalism, experience, and success. These members (including all event categories, budget and attendance levels), while representing only a part of the festivals and events industry as a whole, have learned the value of active and continued involvement with their professional peers at the highest levels and have set themselves apart from the pack. They represent the very best of our industry brand and through their involvement the IFEA is able to build a stronger foundation for our common industry.

Q: From your unique vantage point, what have been the primary impacts of the 2020 COVID-19 pandemic on the global festivals and events sector?

A: The COVID-19 pandemic is unlike anything we have ever faced before – as an industry and as the world. As a result, that has also changed the resulting impact and our approaches to managing and responding to it. The pandemic is unlike past challenges, such as the attacks of 9/11, where events were used as part of the broader national response in the United States – bringing communities and the country together to show that life would go on, paying tribute to lives lost, and bonding people together, as no other industry can; or following a mass shooting/vehicular attack on an event, anywhere in the world, where the response is a more natural progression of shock and empathy, followed by a focused effort and determination to learn from what happened, being thankful it wasn't our own event(s), learning from what occurred, and then creating a new set of 'best practices' as a professional industry, to ensure that we reduce the likelihood of the same thing being allowed to happen at any other event(s) moving forward.

The Coronavirus pandemic hit fast – closing down our entire industry of 'mass gatherings' in a matter of weeks following our first knowledge of the virus; it affected everyone, everywhere – including all of our stakeholder groups; and presented us with the worst set of considerations possible. The global festivals and events industry is made up, primarily, of driven, optimistic, creative leaders, who specialize in coming up with creative, lemonade-from-lemons, solutions to any problem, when given the parameters they must work within; but the global COVID-19 pandemic gave us no parameters, no end-date, no past examples to compare to, and no 'best practices' to follow. With our well-planned processes and well-oiled event machines looking forward to our annual preparations for a normal year as we celebrated the start of the 2020 New Year, little did we recognize that we were all about to be enrolled in a Masters Degree program that none of us asked for.

While it could rightfully be presented as a 'shock and awe' impact on us all, I think it can more accurately be compared to an impact more like the five stages of grief:

- ☐ *Denial* – We (the global industry 'we') began by slowly denying the impact that we were seeing/hearing/reading about, or seeing/hearing/reading as projected by the health and medical experts, and could not imagine that it would go on very long, and that it certainly would not affect 'our' events. Possibly 'others,' but not 'us.' Nothing had ever stopped our events from occurring… not wars, or economic downturns, or terrorism, or weather. We had always persevered, and would again. We would all be the first event on the other side of the problem, with the public masses clamoring to regather and celebrate pre-pandemic 'normalcy' again with us.

- ☐ *Anger* – When we started to be told by our cities and health experts that mass gatherings (our events) could no longer take place safely, we became angry. 'They' had no right to tell us what we could do or not do. Our stakeholders expected us to go on; our boards expected us to go on; our volunteers and attendees expected us to go on. And when we, as industry leaders, started to more fairly and logically explore the 'what if's' of this new equation, others got angry at us.

- ☐ *Bargaining* – This phase took many angles for our industry. We began bargaining with our host communities to believe in us and our ability to produce a safe event, even while others had resulted in a 'super-spreader' result. We bargained with our attendees to please follow all of the new safe-distancing, masking and sanitation rules, but quickly learned – as did many other industries – that most of our global societies and citizenry do not want to be told what they can and cannot do. We bargained with our sponsors to continue supporting us, as we shifted to new virtual renditions of our events; promised to be back 'bigger and better' than ever in a few months, or next year; and started realizing the massive impact on our budgets and reserves if we could not produce our primary annual revenue source.

- ☐ *Depression* – As it became more and more apparent that we had no control over this pandemic, nor its impact on our events, organizations, travel, stakeholders, etc., we all went through an individual and mass depression stage. Fortunately we were all there for each other to empathize and help us all to better get through this stage, although there is likely to be more of this ahead, as we watch the unfortunate closure of some events and organizations forever, as a result.

- ☐ *Acceptance* – And, now, while we are still, as an industry, going through several of the above stages of grief simultaneously (depending upon global regions, control measures and success, and government leadership), most have come to some level of acceptance of the realities that we are facing; the extended time frame that we are likely needing to prepare for and be sustainable through, looking forward to the promise of a widely-used and effective vaccine; and to coming back, full-circle, using our global network and creative brain-trust to come out not only whole, but better, than our pre-pandemic days.

Other key impacts of the pandemic on the global festivals and events industry, as well as so many others, include:

☐ *Financial* - The loss of our primary annual revenue sources; the loss of (through necessary usage) cash reserves, for those lucky enough to have had them; and unimaginable (under any normal scenario) expense cuts, including staff layoffs and furloughs, office space, asset reduction, etc. The battle for government funding support, across-the-board for all businesses, organizations and industries, has identified and put the spotlight on many fault-lines in countries around the world, shutting down and/or damaging many smaller businesses and even some iconic ones (at this writing, Disney has announced planned furloughs and layoffs of 32,000+ global employees) in the wake, while putting many individual segments of every industry in competition with their normally allied partners and counterparts. And the financial impact on sponsors, suppliers, entertainers, host communities and countless others has created/will continue to create a new need for everyone to work together with an 'all in this together' attitude and a determination to get everyone through the pandemic whole and sustainably on the other side. This will not be a short process and may take many years.

Other financial considerations will be the addition of many new – and not yet clearly defined – expenses, created as the result of new regulations, health and safety standards, changes in staffing and volunteer needs and skill sets, and more. How those will be covered (hand-sanitizer and liability insurance are not great sponsorable assets) are still to be determined, but most event budgets were already stretched pretty thin to begin with.

☐ *Risk management* – Concern for the safety (literally life and death) of our attendees, staffs and volunteers will be at a new level – arguably beyond protection measures/levels that were necessarily put into place as a result of increased terrorism attacks and concerns over recent decades – including new insurance considerations for if those efforts and precautions are not effective.

☐ *Understanding that all of our 'Best Practices' no longer count.* While many are focusing on becoming a quick-study, using past skill sets and experience as a starting point, there are not yet any experts on what we are dealing with, since no one has been through this before. Every event, no matter their longevity, from this point forward, will be a 'first-time' event and we will all be learning together.

☐ *Back to the future* – To ensure our survival, I think that we will see a return to events of the past, as we move forward, and a much greater connectivity to relationships (new and old); in-kind sponsorship support; and a re-focusing on securing, involving, driving and participating in local support efforts and communications for our events moving forward.

☐ *New creativity* – While we are not there yet, you can see the gears starting to turn and I believe that one of the most positive impacts of the pandemic will be new levels of creativity and plans for protecting against similar surprises moving forward.

☐ *Realization & appreciation for the value of events* – Because of the cancellation of so many festivals and events around the world, and our societal inability to gather for such an extended period of time, I believe that there has been, and will continue to be, a renewed appreciation for the essential role that events play in holding the fabric of our communities and world together.

Q: What is being done and planned for recovery of the industry?

A: Because, as noted in my previous comments, no one has ever been through the challenges that we are currently going through, there is no pre-defined approach as to how to plan and prepare for the recovery of our industry. In fact, we are still defining the full impact, the new expectations that lay ahead, and what future we may be planning for. While there are glimmers of hope in the production of new vaccines, there is still no pre-determined end date, and the return to pre-pandemic 'normalcy' will likely be a gradual one and not an immediate flip of a switch.

All that accepted, the global festivals and events industry has taken a number of proactive steps toward understanding the progression of the pandemic and ensuring our readiness along each step of the journey:

☐ *Communication, networking, education and awareness* – Through professional associations like the IFEA, representing every unique niche of our industry, communication and networking have never been at such an active and supportive level, around the world. While distanced in-person, we have mastered technology to connect us at every level… one-on-one, across borders and cultural barriers, and across industry differences. We have opened up communications and education lines with allied associations; health and risk management organizations such as the CDC, WHO, DHS, and CISA; those we knew before and those we have met through our common need to learn and support. And we have opened up new channels of media communications that have expanded a greater global awareness for our industry, our impact on and our reliance on so many others.

Additionally, most professional associations have quickly created and presented valuable new educational webinar series, expanded networking opportunities, as well as publications focused on global media coverage and case studies of how our global peers are being impacted by and responding to the pandemic. While almost all professional associations, like those they serve, have had to cancel their annual educational conventions and gatherings in-person, experiencing the same financial sustainability challenges as their members, the global networks of those they serve have helped to ensure their health and continuation.

The IFEA Task Force

The IFEA created a focused IFEA Task Force to utilize the creative brain-trust that makes up our industry, in an effort to begin and continue our conversations regarding our pandemic response at every phase. The Task Force included the following committees:

☐ *RE-PRESENT: The when, why and how considerations behind re-presenting a postponed or cancelled event.*

As events of all sizes, budgets and histories are placed in the previously unimagined position of having to postpone and/or cancel those events, due to local, state, regional or national COVID-19 safety restrictions, how do we effectively Re-Present those same events to protect our brands, help drive revenues, protect sponsorship values, support our communities, and/or meet other stakeholder obligations. And, acknowledging likely finite staff and fiscal resources, should we? This committee addressed the important considerations involved in assessing next best steps and selected examples of what seems to be working for others reinventing their own wheel.

☐ *RE-CONNECT: Partnering with our communities & stakeholders to ensure long-term success for everyone*

Perhaps one of the most positive outcomes of this global pandemic, has been the (re)opening of doors/conversations with many community stakeholders that we may have lost touch with, or never thought to work in partnership with before. We know what our events contribute to our respective communities and that is usually one of the primary personal drivers/rewards for those in our industry. This committee addressed how our events/organizations might lead the efforts to keep our communities bonded during these difficult times, to ensure the long-term health of all events, and how we might work more closely with our cities, other events and organizations, volunteers, artists and vendors, sponsors, etc. to help all of our communities come through this storm stronger and keep all of our events financially secure and healthy.

☐ *RE-STRUCTURE: Protecting the financial sustainability of our events with an eye on the future*

☐ The future success of our events will be more important than ever to our communities and world, and to all of our many stakeholders and audiences who value them so much, but first, we must take steps to ensure the short- and long-term financial sustainability of those events and organizations. This committee researched and debated the steps necessary to get us all back to our comfort zones, with an eye on a bright, secure and important future.

☐ *RE-OPEN: What re-opening our events may look like and how to prepare now for maximum success*

☐ In the midst of many challenges that we do not yet control, it is important that we do everything possible to proactively lead, drive and map where we are headed. Understanding that the future will include many new expectations, it is important that we start preparing now for when we may be able to reopen our festivals and events. This committee began to define the new expectations that all events can use to overlay with their formally 'normal' events, with the goal of reimagining how you might put those expectations into place and prepare for the effects they may have on operational plans, as well as financial and human resources.

☐ *RE-IMAGINE: The future of events in an extended and/or post-pandemic world*

Nothing usually excites event professionals like a blank canvas of change and new possibilities... that we control! If we find that it may realistically be 1 to 3 years before a large, mass-gathering event can safely reopen, this committee explored and researched how we can successfully manage the likely new regulations and hurdles that we will all face as an industry (e.g., safe-distancing, mask requirements, sanitation and other services, temperature checks, limited capacities, et al.) and how we can/might still create/present a new event model(s) that are able to provide the energy, creativity, community participation, sponsor support and activation, etc., that we all desire, while also maintaining financial sustainability.

This Task Force process will continue throughout the pandemic and our recovery process, however long that may prove to be, changing along the way to address new and recurring challenges, questions, needs, and updating current committee findings to the next level, along the way. Our greatest strength as an industry, globally, has always been our willingness to share with our peers – our successes and failures; our challenges; our creativity; our best ideas – and it will be that willingness to share that will get us all through this time in history that is unlike any other that we, or our world, has experienced.

Messaging & Operational Support

As new vaccines are approved and distributed around the world, it is clear that our best hope of returning to a pre-pandemic normalcy will depend upon a high percentage of the population getting vaccinated as soon as allowed, suggested and available. At that time it is the plan of the IFEA, and hopefully all of our allied event industry associations, to use the messaging and outreach capabilities of our industry to encourage everyone, in communities around the globe, to get vaccinated and help us bring back events and the world we serve. Additionally, some event producers around the world, are/ have been offering their organizational and operational expertise, as well as some of their venues, to serve in support of the care of those with COVID-19 and the processing of those who wish to be inoculated.

Q: Who are the key stakeholders in the survival and recovery of the festivals and events industry?

A: There are many key stakeholder groups (listed below) touched by and impacted by the festivals and events industry, just as we are touched by and impacted by each of them, respectively. In one or more of the many ways described in my previous answers, all of them will play a critical role in the survival and recovery of our industry. The future may find that we reimagine our relationships with each one, but hopefully we will only be drawn closer together, becoming more creative and resilient as a result, as we continue to provide the unique gift that events bring to the world.

- ☐ Individual festivals & events
- ☐ Staffs, boards, and volunteers
- ☐ Host communities
- ☐ Sponsors
- ☐ Suppliers to the industry
- ☐ Venues
- ☐ Attendees, families and friends
- ☐ Professional industry associations
- ☐ All those individuals who make up, serve and support the success of all those listed above.

3 From Risk to Resilience: Contemporary Issues in Event Risk Management

Peter Ashwin

Our brains tend to go for superficial clues when it comes to risk and probability, these clues being largely determined by what emotions they elicit or the ease with which they come to mind

Nassim Nicholas Taleb

Introduction

In today's volatile, uncertain, complex and ambiguous global risk society, national boundaries are blurred, inter-connected markets are exposed to delocalized risks with consequences that may stretch over extended or indefinite periods of time. Under these uncertain conditions, event organizers find themselves planning and delivering events in an environment characterized by disruptive effects of the Covid-19 pandemic and extant risks from homegrown violent extremism, cyber-criminal threats, supply chain disruptions and event cancellations (Beck, 2006; Hall, et al., 2019; Piekarz et al., 2015; Reid & Ritchie,2011; Rutherford Silvers, 2008; Tarlow, 2002).

It is widely acknowledged that risk management should be viewed by event organizers and event professionals as a fundamental responsibility for planning and delivering a world class guest experience in a safe and secure environment (Berlonghi, 1990; Piekarz et al., 2015; Rutherford Silvers, 2008; Tarlow 2002;). However, in stark contrast, many event organizers concede that they do not have an event risk management plan (Ashwin & Wilson, 2020; Sturken, 2005 cited in Robson, 2009; Robson, 2009). In light of the recent proliferation of violent attacks on festivals and events, from the 2013 Boston Marathon bombing to the recent 2019 Gilroy Garlic Festival (California) shooting, there has been an increasing public discourse and emerging legislative requirements for event organizers to demonstrate an evidence-based approach to risk management decisions with the ability to explain the rationale behind those decisions in clear, objective and transparent terms (US Department of Homeland

Security, 2020; UK Center for the Protection of National Infrastructure, 2020).

Drawing upon the existing body of literature for event risk management, from Berlonghi (1990) to the recent 2019 event industry survey investigating event organizers approaches to risk management and resilience (Ashwin & Wilson, 2020), this chapter will explore contemporary risk issues in today's volatile, ambiguous, complex and uncertain world. First, it will discuss the inter-related risk constructs pertaining to socio-cultural theoretical perspectives of risk and how an event organizer's perception of risk influences their approach to risk management and decision-making. Then the chapter will address two contemporary risks, both of which present the potential for catastrophic consequences: cyber-criminals who are increasingly focusing their cyber-attacks on vulnerable, event digital eco-systems; and domestic terrorism and the threat from homegrown violent extremists, domestic violent extremists and unaffiliated lone offenders ('lone wolves'). Finally, pragmatic, risk-based approaches to mitigating these risks will be discussed, specifically, preventative risk control measures and opportunities for enhancing organizational resilience to cyber-crime and terrorism.

The perception of risk: Making sense of the risk management construct

…risk cannot be eliminated: there will be incidents, so we must focus on resiliency under all conditions…
Caitlin Durkovic[1]

In order to understand the approach an organizer adopts for managing risks to their event or organization, one must first explore the phenomenon of the perception of risk. This has been theorized in social scientific literature through three major theoretical perspectives: (1) the naïve realist or techno-scientific, (2) cognitive psychology and (3) sociocultural (Lupton, 2013). The techno-scientific perspective contends that risk is a product of a hazard or threat (risk source or trigger), measured through the calculations of likelihood and the consequences, an underlying premise, which is consistent with the International Standards Organization *ISO 31000 (20018) Risk Management – Guidelines*. Techno-scientific theorists also argue that the layperson's, reliance on intuition and their perceived lack of risk knowledge and subjective approach, results in inferior decisions and responses as compared to a techno-scientific perspective (Lupton, 2013). Beck (1999), however, contends that one should not have to choose between a natural-scientific objectivism (naïve realist) or a cultural relativism (subjective) approach for risk management, but rather use each when it is appropriate to understand the complex

---

1   Assistant Secretary, Infrastructure Protection, US Department of Homeland Security, 2016

and ambivalent nature of the risk environment. This position is supported by the social-constructionist argument that risk judgements are in part based on prior knowledge, personal embodied experiences, discussions with others and access to expert knowledge about how relevant industries and regulatory bodies have tended to deal with risk in the past (Lupton, 2013; Slovic, 2000).

Within the events context, risk perception has been described *"the concerns of the various entities involved in the event"* (Berlonghi, 1990, p. 19) and that the risks identified by the event organizers may not be accurate nor verifiable, particularly in the absence of an event risk assessment. An event organizer's perception of risk is not only based on perceptive or objective fact, but also by their background, experience, the organizational culture and the influence of the senior management team attitude to risk (Robson, 2009). Event organizers often rely on intuitive risk judgments based on a foundation of experience, which seldom incudes direct experience with the risk event but this in itself should not be considered erroneous or biased, if event organizers' opinions differ from that of expert risk assessments (Lupton, 2013; Rogers, 1997).

In summary, given the inherent limitations of risk-based decision-making within uncertain environments and the fundamental processes of human risk perception, it is clear that the subjective decision-making will always be part of the event risk assessment process (Talbot, 2011).

Risk management: Current approaches and practices

While there is a relatively large body of literature asserting that risk management is fundamental to planning and delivery of safe and secure events, there still remain gaps in research and literature specific to event organizers' approaches to risk management (Khir, 2014; Robson, 2009). Furthermore, the existing body of literature on risk management within the events industry focuses, in the most part, on insurance and legal obligations, vendor agreements, indemnifications, waivers and insurance policies, but not on the role of event managers and their responsibilities as operational risk 'owners' (Rutherford Silvers, 2008).

Berlonghi (1990) was amongst the first academic practitioners to highlight risk management as an integral part of the event management process: the process by which an event is planned, prepared and produced (Goldblatt, 2011; Rutherford Silvers, 2008). Within the events context, risk management can be described as the process of making and carrying out decisions that minimize the adverse effects of the potential losses of an event or simply stated as *"making events as safe and secure as possible"* (Berlonghi, 1990, p.3), or alternatively:

"a comprehensive approach to risk management that engages organizational systems and processes together to improve the quality of decision making for

managing risks that may hinder an organization from achieving its objectives" (US Department of Homeland Security, 2011, p. 13)

Effective risk management requires the assessment of inherently uncertain events through two dimensions: (1) how likely is the risk event, and (2) what are the potential consequences (impacts) to the successful achievement of the organization's mission and objectives? The probabilistic risk assessment (PRA) is one of the most commonly used tools to quantify risk through an assessment of the aforementioned factors of likelihood (probability) and consequence to provide a risk estimate or rating, commonly referred to as the level of risk (Ostrom & Wilhelmsen, 2012). If sufficient rigor has been put into defining the context of the risk statement, the likelihood and the consequence metrics, then a meaningful risk estimate (risk rating) can be quickly and consistently obtained from a risk matrix (Talbot, 2011).

PROBABLILITY	RISK LEVEL				
ALMOST CERTAIN (5)	LOW (5)	MEDIUM (10)	HIGH (15)	VERY HIGH (20)	VERY HIGH (25)
LIKELY (4)	LOW (4)	MEDIUM (8)	HIGH (12)	HIGH (16)	VERY HIGH (20)
POSSIBLE (3)	LOW (3)	MEDIUM (6)	MEDIUM (9)	HIGH (12)	HIGH (15)
UNLIKELY (2)	LOW (2)	LOW (4)	MEDIUM (6)	MEDIUM (8)	HIGH (10)
RARE (1)	LOW (1)	LOW (2)	LOW (3)	MEDIUM (4)	MEDIUM (5)
CONSEQUENCE	INSIGNIFICANT (1)	MINOR (2)	MODERATE (3)	SIGNIFICANT (4)	SEVERE (5)

Figure 3.1: Probabilistic risk assessment matrix (heat map)

Figure 3.1 provides an example of a risk matrix (heat map), typically referred to as a '5 x 5' risk matrix, where both probability (likelihood) and consequence are qualitatively described and quantitatively scored, for example the probability of occurrence 'almost certain' is rated as five, as opposed to 'rare' which is rated as one. The risk score or estimate is calculated by multiplying the assessed probability rating by the consequence rating.

Although semi-quantitative in nature, risk matrices provide a visual presentation of ranked risks which then allows event decision-makers to make value judgements to prioritize resource allocation to mitigate the risks to a level as low as reasonably possible (ALARP principle) or to fall within the designated risk appetite of the event senior management team (International Standards Organization, 2018; Hopkin, 2010).

Probability risk assessments are often viewed by event organizers as being an overly complex and challenging endeavor, given the requirement to construct likelihood and consequence metrics and risk level statements, and compounded by the fact that event organizers typically have limited risk management knowledge or experience. An alternative approach to event risk assessments, is 'risk ranking', a comparative, subjective risk assessment exercise to rank and prioritize management of risks within an organization (Hancock, 2019; Florig et al., 2001). Another advantage of the risk ranking exercise is that it provides team-based opportunities for all levels of event management to engage in risk discourse, fostering a heightened level of risk awareness and the opportunity for horizontal integration across typically, siloed event functional areas.

A risk ranking exercise for event organizing committee involves the following steps, the indicative outcome of which is summarized in Table 3.1.

1   Event senior management and the operational management team come together for a risk ranking workshop;

2   As a group, identify and collectively agree on a list of risks (risk register) which collectively 'keep them up at night'; for the purpose of this example, the risk register is assumed to contain five risks;

3   Then each individual is asked to assign a numerical ranking value, one being for the lowest risk and five for the highest risk;

4   The scores per risk are added to provide an aggregated risk score;

5   Finally, the risk register is resorted/prioritized based on the final risk scores.

Table 3.1: Risk ranking exercise

Risk Statement	#1	#2	#3	#4	#5	Total Score	Risk Ranking
(1) Inability to attract, recruit and retain high caliber staff due to the disruption of Covid-19 pandemic	5	4	3	4	3	19	1
(2) Severe weather event triggers evacuation of event site and event cancellation	2	2	1	3	2	10	5
(3) Active assailant firearms attack inside the event site	3	4	2	3	4	16	3
(4) Disruption to IT network and data access due to cyber-criminal ransomware attack	2	1	3	3	2	11	4
(5) Ticket sales do not meet forecasted targets resulting in significant budget shortfalls	3	5	4	2	3	17	2

One key point to note, is that agreement among participants is not, in itself, an objective of the risk ranking exercise because individual participants should be encouraged to disagree about the relative levels of risk based on their perception of risk.

Risk ranking offers event organizers an opportunity to add process to their subjective risk assessments to better inform future decision-making and communication of risk information within the organization. However, event organizers should remain cognizant of the fact that subjective risk assessments are prone to bias, error, the potential for over-estimation or under-estimation of risk, which may result in ill-informed decisions (Hillson, 2016; Lupton, 2013; Piekarz et al., 2015; Slovic & Peters, 2006).

If event organizers collected and analyzed statistical data from after-action reports, near misses and incident reports, this dataset provides opportunities to gain valuable risk insights to support objective and informed judgments for risk mitigation (Reason, 1990, 1997; Robson, 2009). This argument is supported by the findings from Ashwin and Wilson's (2020) survey into the event industry's risk management practices, eliciting 160 responses from festival and event leaders across 11 countries. Only 18% of the respondents indicated that they had a current risk management plan and 35% indicated they did not have a risk management plan and or, did not know if they had a plan. In the absence of personal or organizational experience with risk events, organizers and event professionals will look externally for opportunities to leverage accumulated risk management experience and knowledge from other event organizers and industry trade associations like the International Festival and Events Association (IFEA) to assess risk trends and frequency within the industry, gain insights into the severity of past risk events and to identify industry best practices for risk mitigation. Industry research also provides opportunities for event organizers to leverage information across the industry, for example, Figure 3.2 provides a summary of perceived risks versus actual risk events from Ashwin and Wilson's (2020) industry survey.

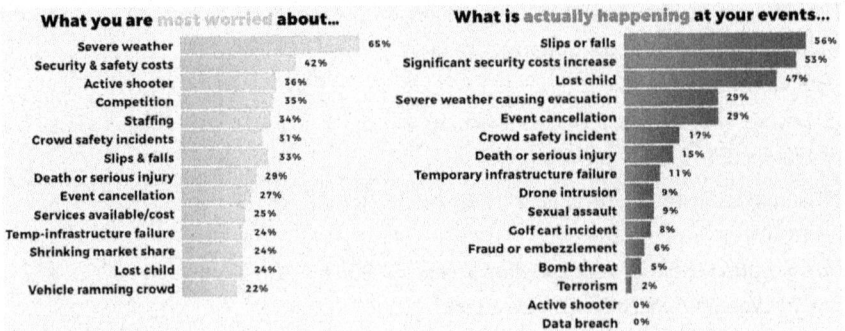

What you are most worried about…		What is actually happening at your events…	
Severe weather	65%	Slips or falls	56%
Security & safety costs	42%	Significant security costs increase	53%
Active shooter	36%	Lost child	47%
Competition	35%	Severe weather causing evacuation	29%
Staffing	34%	Event cancellation	29%
Crowd safety incidents	31%	Crowd safety incident	17%
Slips & falls	33%	Death or serious injury	15%
Death or serious injury	29%	Temporary infrastructure failure	11%
Event cancellation	27%	Drone intrusion	9%
Services available/cost	25%	Sexual assault	9%
Temp-infrastructure failure	24%	Golf cart incident	8%
Shrinking market share	24%	Fraud or embezzlement	6%
Lost child	24%	Bomb threat	5%
Vehicle ramming crowd	22%	Terrorism	2%
		Active shooter	0%
		Data breach	0%

Figure 3.2: 2019 Event industry survey results: Perceived risk ranking versus actual risk events

The awareness and maturity of risk management within the events industry is undeniably growing as event managers migrate from an insurance-led approach to an event management led approach. However, it remains evident that the events industry faces ongoing challenges developing a mature level of capability to proactively manage event risks; be it subjective, value-based judgments through risk ranking or quantitatively through probability risk assessments. As an industry, we must continue to pursue further academic research into event risk management and to provide opportunities for professional development of our next generation of events leaders in risk management.

Decision-making under uncertainty

Are event management decisions primarily driven by a deliberate and rational analysis or a more intuitive, heuristic-based approach? This section of the chapter will review theoretical approaches to decision-making under uncertainty and how the perception of risk may also influence event organizers' decision-making.

Klein's (1993, 1998) research on recognition prime decision (RPD) model concludes that decision-making is a perpetual process, situationally based to facilitate fast effective decision-making, based on previous experience and intuitive knowledge that enables the decision-maker to generate fast and effective courses of action. The recognition primed decision model reasons that fast, effective decision-making is possible within time critical situations when the decision-maker has the expertise and situational awareness, combined with a battery of experience-based, intuitive knowledge (Klein, 1993, 2008).

Event organizers often rely on intuitive risk judgments, known as heuristics (mental shortcuts) to make inferences and decisions based on what they individually and collectively remember observing or experiencing during previous risk events (Laybourn, 2003; Slovic, 2000). In contrast, rational theories of decision-making assume that decision-makers follow a rational procedure for making decisions, selecting the option that will produce the best outcome (Laybourne, 2003). Research into naturalistic decision-making (NDM) focused on how first responders utilized their expertise and experience to make effective decisions through utilizing systems of work known to have been successful in previous uncertain and high stress situations (Ash & Smallman, 2010). Slovic (2000) argues that people like event organizers may judge risks and hazards more efficiently, and make better decisions under pressure using heuristics rather than an analytical or systematic approach.

Event organizers will rarely have the necessary information and time for an analytical based decision-making process but under these conditions, naturalistic decision-making allows event organizers to leverage their expertise, experience and intuition to reach timely 'satisficing' decisions within dynamic and complex multi-agency environments (Klein, 1993, 2008; Tarlow, 2002). Yet conversely, 83 per cent of the 160 respondents from Ashwin's and Wilson's (2020) industry survey indicated that they had limited confidence in their event team 'mission readiness' and capability to respond and manage adverse events within volatile, ambiguous, complex and uncertain event environments.

Decision support models: The OODA loop

Event organizers, like other professionals, have great difficulty making decisions and judgements under uncertainty and operating environments characterized by multiple situational inputs (Plous, 1993). An event organizer's decision-making can be improved through adopting a repeatable and systematic decision-making model; one such model which is applicable to the events environment, is the 'observe, orient, decide and act' decision-making model, otherwise known as the OODA loop (Boyd, 1979). Developed in 1979 by United States Air Force Colonel John Boyd, the OODA Loop comprises four interrelated, multi-dimensional elements: observation, orientation, decision and action, which encompass both time and space (Rule, 2013).

Adopted from Boyd's OODA loop, Figure 3.3 provides a simplified but structured checklist approach to support decision-making under uncertainty by event organizers and their operational management team. This model has improved effective decision-making by event professionals from team supervisors to senior management.

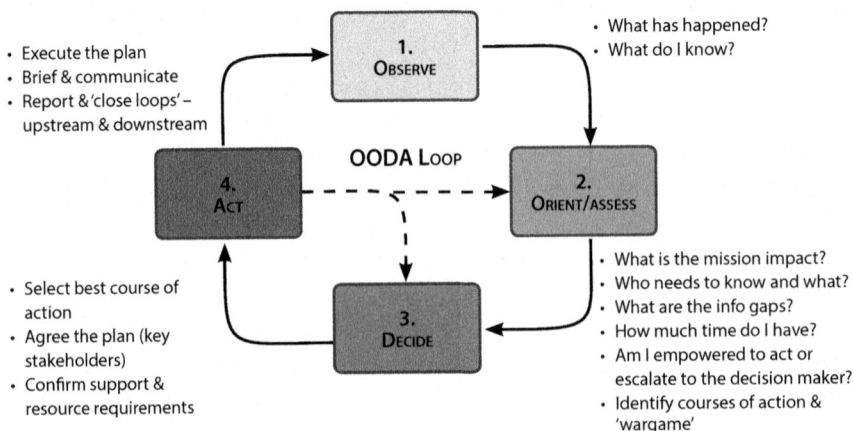

Figure 3.3: Decision support methodology for event organizers – the OODA Loop

The emergence of domestic terrorism threats

An evolving threat landscape

Since 9/11, the threat of terrorism and targeted violence against vulnerable soft targets and mass gatherings (festivals and events) remains one of the most serious risks to the United States homeland security (Department of Homeland Security [DHS], 2020). The current threat landscape highlights the proliferation of home-grown violent extremism and domestic violent extremism, giving rise to new configurations of low capability, high impact, asymmetric attacks utilizing firearms, edged weapons, vehicles as weapons, and improvised explosive devices to violently attack soft targets as evidenced by the attacks on the Boston Marathon, 2013; the Pulse nightclub, 2016 (Orlando); Route 91 Harvest Country Music Festival, 2017 (Las Vegas), Ariana Grande Concert, 2017 (Manchester, UK) and the Gilroy Garlic Festival, 2019 (California). Accessible, crowded, mass gatherings like festivals and events will continue to remain attractive targets for various threat actors into the foreseeable future (DHS, 2020; Hesterman, 2015).

Terrorism in today's global risk society is a complex problem. It is widely recognized that the underlying causes of terrorism and other forms of violent extremism are manifested through many sources of conflict, including ethnic, religious, political, economic and ideological influences which may accelerate an individual's pathway to radicalization or extremism (Clarke & Newman, 2006). Post-modern domestic terrorism is often characterized as a leaderless resistance, where individuals and groups connect through a shared ideology enabled through the internet without any defined leadership (Hesterman, 2015). Understanding the pre-conditions and precipitants that trigger a terrorist or violent lone offender to embark on a pathway to violence, provides an opportunity for event organizers, the private security sector and law enforcement to apply a targeted, risk-based security counter measures (risk controls) to reduce terrorism related risks. A risk-based approach identifies security countermeasures to reduce the likelihood of a terrorist attack occurring (deter and detect) and in the event of a terrorist attack, identifying response and recovery measures to reduce the severity of the consequences to people, property and reputation (Bjorso & Silke, 2019).

The 2020 US Department of Homeland Security threat assessment for mass gatherings assesses the three primary threats to events: (1) lone offenders who lack a clearly discernible political, ideological or religious motive; (2) small cells of individuals categorized as domestic violent extremists, motivated by racial or anti-authoritarian factors to commit unlawful acts of violence; and (3) homegrown violent extremists inspired by, or directed by foreign terrorist organizations to engage in ideologically motivated, terrorist activities (DHS, 2020).

The evolving sophistication and adaptive capability of terrorists, criminals and other malicious threat actors is routinely underestimated (Hesterman, 2015; Mcllhatton, et al., 2019). Threat actors adapt their tactics based on the lessons learnt from the successes and failures of other terrorist attacks, both domestically and internationally (Haberfeld & von Hassell, 2011). Furthermore, the internet enables exchange of secure web-based global conversations over the 'dark web' and social media channels between disconnected, like-minded individuals and other virtual communities, to share and acquire the know-how to execute highly lethal attacks on soft targets (Bouhana et al., 2018; Mcllhatton et al., 2019). Terrorist attacks are rarely sudden and impulsive; a terrorist's or other threat actor's ability to modify and adapt their tactics to the target environment should not be underestimated, nor should there be an over reliance on past events to predict the probability of future attacks (Clarke & Newman, 2006; Hesterman, 2015).

A successful terrorist attack is catastrophic – substantial loss of life, property damage, severe financial loss and irreparable reputational harm to the organization and its executive leadership (Mcllhatton et al., 2019). Recent low sophistication attacks in the US are frequently characterized by the use of firearms as opposed to other methods, where little or no training expertise (capability) is required and can be easily and inexpensively acquired (Bouhana et al., 2018). This is evidenced by two recent lethal attacks within the events industry: the 2016 Pulse nightclub terrorist attack in Orlando resulting in 49 fatalities and 53 wounded patrons (Ellis et al., 2016) and the 2017 Harvest 91 Country Music Festival resulting in 58 fatalities and a 2020 settlement of $800 million for the victims of the shooting by MGM Resorts (Ferrara, 2020). Event organizers have a legal responsibility and duty of care obligation to provide a safe environment and reduce the potential of harm from foreseeable risks for their guests, workforce and other client groups/stakeholders who attend their events (Clark & Saviour, 2018).

Reducing terrorism risks through situational crime prevention

Terrorism risks to events and mass gatherings cannot be eliminated, however, a risk-based approach provides opportunities to enhance an event's security posture, preparedness and resilience to known terrorist threats. Terrorism risk can be defined as a function of threat, vulnerability, and consequence; where the existent threat and the inherent vulnerabilities of the organization represent the 'likelihood' that an attack will be successful (Willis, 2007). By identifying potential threats and assessing potential vulnerabilities when exposed to known threats, appropriate risk controls (security counter measures) can be identified and aligned to available resources within predetermined budgets (Ezell et al., 2010).

Given the inherent uncertainty of terrorism risks and the difficulty to assess the level of terrorism risk with a high level of confidence (Aven & Renn, 2009), an alternate approach to mitigating terrorism risk was postulated by Clarke and Newman (2006) to utilize situational crime prevention (SCP) principles to reduce the risk of a terrorist attack. Underpinned by two criminological theoretical perspectives, rational activity theory and rational choice theory, Clarke and Newman's (2006) seminal SCP publication, *Outsmarting the Terrorists*, provides a pragmatic and effective approach for counterterrorism through five SCP strategies: (1) increasing the effort, (2) increasing the risks, (3) reducing the reward, (4) reducing provocation and (5) removing excuses. Table 3.2 provides examples for SCP that can be applied by event organizers and their security partners to enhance the event security and resilience.

Table 3.2: The counter terrorism application of SCP for events

SCP Principle	Event based examples
(1) Increase the effort	Increasing the difficulty for a threat actor during pre-attack surveillance or final dry rehearsals, provides opportunity to disrupts their attack vector pathway.
(2) Increase the risk	Increase the risk of detection and detainment through highly visible police presence, security patrols and an event workforce who have enhanced security and situational awareness for reporting suspicious activity (training).
(3) Reduce the reward	Reducing the reward involves implementing strategies that make the target less attractive or reducing the gain or pleasure from executing the attack. For events, this attribute is closely aligned to increasing the risks and increasing the effort.
(4) Reduce provocation	While not directly applicable to counter terrorism for event per se, reduced provocation strategies provide opportunities to de-escalate situations before they trigger public safety or criminal situations, for example, 'verbal judo' techniques to de-escalate situations with non-compliant guests.
(5) Remove excuses	Removal of excuses through the use of signage, terms and conditions of entry, prohibited and restricted items policies, makes it difficult for offenders or threat actors to use excuses for their behavior, for example unauthorized access into controlled or restricted areas.

In summary, SCP attempts to shape, influence, or intervene in the terrorists or criminal offenders decision-making process by influencing environmental opportunities that reduce the attractiveness of the target and increase the perceived risk of being caught.

EVIL DONE: Reducing terrorism risk through 'thinking like a terrorist'

Terrorist decision-making and target selection is largely governed by environmental opportunities and constraints in relation to planning, capabilities and resources (Freilich et al., 2019). Through understanding a terrorist's decision-making criteria for target selection, the attractiveness of an event as a potential terrorist target can be evaluated, inherent vulnerabilities identified and reduced, and opportunities identified to enhance the resilience and preparedness of the event team's capability to respond and recover from a terrorist incident.

To identify effective counter terrorism measures, event organizers must think like a terrorist. Adopting a threat actor's targeting mindset, allows event organizers to subjectively assess their event's attractiveness and vulnerability to a terrorist attack, where vulnerability refers to the *"inherent features of the target that are more susceptible or attractive to attack by terrorists"* (Clarke & Newman, 2006, p. 90). Clarke and Newman (2006) theorized that the terrorist target selection was based on a combination of eight attractiveness criteria, according to whether the potential target was: exposed, vital, iconic, legitimate, destructible, occupied, near, and easy; summarized by the acronym 'EVIL DONE'. Terrorist target pre-selection is conditioned by a combination of these factors; more vulnerable targets possess a greater number of these attributes (Boba, 2009). Table 3.3 provides a practical approach for event organizers to subjectively assess the attractiveness and vulnerability of their event to a terrorist threat through EVIL DONE.

Risk-based counter terrorism strategies for events

Terrorists and other threat actors plan attacks in observable stages which include the conduct of initial target surveillance, pre-attack surveillance (hostile reconnaissance) and final dry rehearsal before initiation of the attack. Through understanding the planning stages of a hostile event or terrorist attack, event organizers have the opportunities to deter and detect potential terrorist attacks and other criminal activities through risk-based counter measures to increase the threat actors' efforts required and their likelihood of detection or discovery during the attack planning cycle (Anarumo, 2011; Clarke & Newman, 2006; DHS, 2019; US National Counterterrorism Center, 2020).

Table 3.4 provides examples of applied counter terrorism, event security measures based on risk-based principles: (1) preventative risk control measures (deter, detect and delay) which reduce the likelihood of a terrorist attack through increasing the effort and risk; and (2) responsive risk control measures (respond and recover) designed to enhance the preparedness and resilience of event workforce to respond confidently and effectively in a post terrorist incident environment.

Table 3.3: EVIL DONE: Event attractiveness and vulnerability target attributes

EVIL DONE	Event attractiveness and vulnerability target attributes
Exposed	Visible, exposed target (event site or venue), easily accessible for pre-attack surveillance and dry rehearsals by the threat actor.
Vital	Police and security patrols, enhance workforce security awareness and suspicious activity reporting (training).
Iconic	The iconic attribute considers the target's symbolic value to the terrorist or threat actor. Other iconic characteristics include whether the event highly recognizable – locally, regionally, or nationally through mainstream media and social media platforms.
Legitimate	Target is perceived as appropriate to attack, demographics and attendance by a specific individual /s may influence the selection of the target by the threat actor.
Destructible	Requires the least amount of effort, security is perceived to be ineffective, weapon choice and tactics offer opportunities for mission 'success'.
Occupied	Terrorists are attracted to events with large, high density crowds within confined spaces to provide opportunities for enhanced lethality.
Near	Terrorism is a local event; proximity and familiarity with the intended target and terrain requires less pre-attack preparatory efforts by the threat actor. Criminological research demonstrates that most terrorists and criminal offenders select targets close to home (within 50 miles) or where their routine activities take them (Freilich et al., 2019).
Easy	An event site or venue location characterized by requiring minimum effort and logistical support, easy accessible approaches to the target and a range of options for escape and evasion.

While events and other gatherings will continue to remain attractive targets for various threat actors into the foreseeable future, it is possible for event organizers to reduce the risk of a terrorist attacks through counter terrorism solutions that are cost-effective, feasible and offer opportunities for enhancing an event team's resilience and capability to respond and recover from a critical incident through training and pre-event operational readiness and preparedness exercises.

Table 3.4: Counter terrorism risk reduction strategies for events

Preventative Risk Control Measures
Event Security and Safety management Plan (ES2MP) – a comprehensive and tested, security and safety management plan is a matter of good business and corporate responsibility (DHS, 2019).
Electronic surveillance systems e.g., CCTV cameras, where budget allows - technology should complement other human-based security measures as opposed to be the focus of the counterterrorism effort (Hesterman, 2015).
Deployment of highly visible police and private security patrols, pre-event and during the event.
Implement a security awareness training plan to enhance individual and collective capabilities to identify pre-attack surveillance indicators and reporting suspicious behaviors and activities.
Background checks as an employment / volunteer pre-condition to reduce the risk of insider threats.
Responsive Risk Control Measures
Conduct pre-event tabletop exercises to exercise and validate emergency response plans with security and safety stakeholders and active shooter training drills with local law enforcement.
Provide traumatic first aid training 'stop the bleed' for frontline staff and budget for, and purchase an appropriate number of 'bleed control kits' for the event staff as part of the medical plan.
Conduct pre-event emergency response drills with front line staff including risk-based scenarios for active assailant, multiple casualty incident and evacuation.
Pre-event testing of unified command, control and communications (C3) arrangements between the event operations team, law enforcement and event security.
Critical Incident Medical Plan.

Cyber-criminal risks and digital age of events

The transformative effect from the advent of computers in the 1980s and the subsequent launch of the world wide web in the 1990s, has led to the evolution of today's digital society and the unprecedented reach of digital technology and computer networks within the events industry (Stratton et al., 2016). Furthermore, the rapid onset of the digital age also created unprecedented opportunities for increasingly, sophisticated, and capable cyber-criminals and cyber-deviant entrepreneurs to engage in low risk, high return, cyber-crimes (Levi et al., 2017). The relative ungovernability of cyberspace and the revolutionary developments in technology, present a multi-dimensional challenge for information security professionals and law enforcement agencies pursuing the prosecution of cyber-criminals across a globally inter-connected network, where national borders and jurisdictions are no longer distinct or defined (Cavelty, 2018; Chang & Grabosky, 2014; Stratton et al., 2016).

CYBER SECURITY:
Stay lost in the music,
not in the cloud

Cyber resilience for festivals & events in today's uncertain world

Cybersecurity risks are a persistent and serious threat to the events industry digital ecosystems (Figure 3.4). Event organizers are highly dependent on secure and uninterrupted access to information and communication technology (ICT) networks to service their e-commerce operations, social media marketing, and data management tools from their 'business as usual' workplaces as well as temporary event sites, where thousands of attendees will expect uninterrupted, high quality access to event ICT networks for e-commerce, social media and other event related digital information (Hindduja & Kooi, 2013; Lakhani, 2017; Levi et al., 2017). Cybercriminals are agile, adapt and continuously evolve their tactics, techniques, and technologies to target and exploit the events industry ICT systems whose cyber-defenses are known to be far more vulnerable and less sophisticated than those of larger organizations.

KNOW THE BEAT: Cyber Criminal Risks and Threats

Cyber attacks are a persistent threat to the global festival and events industry. IT systems, networks and data are vulnerable to a wide range of risks both physical and cyber from sophisticated cyber-criminals and other malicious actors with intent to exploit vulnerabilities and seek opportunities to steal data, commit fraud or disrupt IT networks and systems.

RANSOMWARE	INSIDER THREATS	SOCIAL ENGINEERING
Malicious software (through phishing emails) designed to encrypt or deny access to computer systems or data; payment of a ransom is required to regain access	Insiders abuse your trust to maliciously disrupt operations, corrupt data, steal sensitive information for profit or compromise IT systems, causing loss or damage.	Cyber-criminals employ social engineering techniques: gaining trust through deception to access to sensitive data, exploit and compromise business email accounts or seek fraudulent payments

Figure 3.4: Cyber criminal threats to events

Cybercrime and its impact on the events industry

The concepts of cybercrime and cybersecurity have been in common usage throughout the public and academic domains since the 1990s; however, there still remains a limited consensus among criminologists on how cybercrime should be defined and how it can classified and aligned to criminal behavior within cyberspace (Gordon & Ford, 2006; Levi et al., 2017; McGuire & Dowling, 2013; Wall, 2001). Despite this lack of consensus, cybercrime has been described as any criminal offence that is specifically facilitated or committed using a computer, network, or hardware device or which has occurred in cyberspace (Chang & Graborsky, 2014; Gordon & Ford 2006). The question of how cybercrime could be classified and aligned to criminal behaviors and offences was largely unanswered by criminologists until Wall's (2001) seminal research into cybercrime. Wall's (2001) cybercrime typology consists of four categories aligned to harmful behavior rather than specific offenses:

◆ cyber-trespass (unauthorized access to data through hacking and malware);

◆ cyber-deception (the use of social engineering, malware, identify fraud and fraudulent scams);

◆ cyber-porn and obscenity; and

◆ cyber-violence (the ways and means through which individuals can bring interpersonal harm to others through the web).

Measuring the impacts and cost of cybercrime within the events industry is problematic for the followings reasons: first, there is a limited body of evidence from official crime surveys and statistics; second, under-reporting of offenses by victims and an inherent lack of understanding that cybercrime is an offense; third, inconsistencies in terminology, reporting and victim survey methodologies; fourth, cybercrime has been commonly used to describe a general range of criminal offences; and fifth, the lack of harmonized statutes and legislation between national and international jurisdictions, particularly given the trans-jurisdictional nature of cybercrime, whereby the victim, the offender and the impact of the offense may reside in different jurisdictions (Chang & Grabosky, 2014; Furnell et al., 2015; Levi et al., 2017; McGuire & Dowling, 2013; Stratton et al., 2017; Wall, 2001).

The events industry sector encompasses a diverse range of activities that includes festivals, parades, meetings, conventions, expositions, sport and other special events, planned, coordinated and executed by the event organizing committee; typically categorized as a not-for-profit small business with fewer than twenty paid staff (Goldblatt, 2011; Getz, 1997). Cybersecurity risks are uniquely challenging for the event industry sector, for not only do event organizers have to protect their 'business as usual' workplaces from cybercrime threats, but they must also protect ICT systems at temporary event sites, where thousands of attendees will access event ICT networks for e-commerce, social media and to access other event related digital information (Lakhani, 2017).

While there is a limited body of literature pertaining to cybercrime and its impact on the events industry sector, complementary evidence can be derived from 'like industry' sector cybercrime surveys and reports, including the Verizon (2020) Data Breach Information Report; the UK Federation of Small Business report (2016) Cyber Resilience: How to Protect Small Firms in the Digital Economy; UK Government Department for Digital, Culture, Media and Sport (2019) Cyber Security Breaches Survey; and the Australian Cyber Security Center (2020) Cyber Security and Australian Small Business report. However, it should be noted that while surveys do not measure criminal activities or police reported crimes, they do provide indicators and insights into cyber-enabled and cyber-dependent crime datasets (McGuire & Dowling, 2013).

Recent research into the cybercrime impacts by Verizon (2020) and the UK Department for Digital, Culture, Media and Sport (2019) on small businesses (comparable to event organizing committees) indicates 32 per cent have experienced cyber security breaches or attacks. The research indicates that the most common types of attacks were phishing and others impersonating an organization in emails for fraudulent, financial gain and malware including ransomware. The infographic depicted in Figure 3.5, provides a summary of key facts and figures from the research.

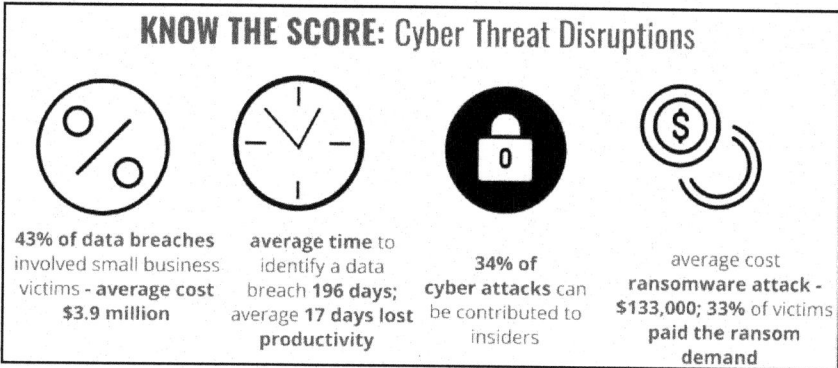

KNOW THE SCORE: Cyber Threat Disruptions

43% of data breaches involved small business victims - **average cost $3.9 million**	**average time** to identify a data breach **196 days;** average **17 days lost productivity**	**34% of** cyber attacks can be contributed to insiders	average cost **ransomware attack - $133,000; 33%** of victims **paid the ransom demand**

Figure 3.5: A summary of cyber threat disruptions

Data theft and malware – is your event at risk?

Data theft, a cyber-enabled crime, and malware, a cyber-dependent crime, are recognized as two of the most prevalent forms of cyber-attack vectors (Levi, et al., 2017; UK Dept. for Digital, Culture, Media and Sport, 2019). Data theft is an exploitation attempt by cybercriminals to obtain and exploit personal identifiable information (PII) for personal profit or financial gain through the use of technology, detailed online searches for personal information or social engineering techniques (Furnell et al., 2015; McGuire & Dowling, 2013). Within the UK arts, entertainment and recreation sector, 11 per cent of businesses reported being a victim of data theft. A recent high-profile event industry cyber-incident was the 2017 Coachella Valley Music and Arts Festival (Indio, California) reported a data breach involving 950,000 attendee PII records (Mercury News, 2017). It was subsequently reported that the Coachella attend PII accounts were being sold on the Dark Web for $300, presumably for targeted phishing campaigns (Hackread, 2017). While the financial and reputational cost from this data breach is unknown, it can be assumed to be significant; based on the average cost of USD $150 per record to compensate for consulting and legal services, restitution to victims, regulatory fines and recovery technologies (IBM Security 2020; Verizon, 2020).

The second prevalent cyber-dependent crime, malware, is software specifically designed to disrupt, damage or gain unauthorized access to computer systems. Its use by cybercriminals is primarily motivated by personal profit or financial gain (US Cybersecurity and Infrastructure Security Agency, 2020). Destructive malware attacks have become increasingly more common in the workplace, a recent 2020 survey indicated that more than 35 percent of small business respondents reported daily phishing, spoofing, malware, ransomware 'exploitation attacks' or other daily email threats (IMB Security, 2020). Malware as a cyberattack vector provides cybercriminals and other malicious actors with a low risk, high reward opportunity as evidenced through 21 per cent of UK small businesses reporting being a victim of malware (UK Federation of Small Business, 2016).

Cybercrime risk mitigation: A pragmatic approach for event organizers

The viability and success of events is predicated on secure ICT systems and maintaining the confidentiality, integrity and availability of proprietary information and customer data records, accomplished through an overarching information security framework (Andress, 2011; Hinduja & Kooi, 2013; Whitman & Mattford, 2005). Despite this, event organizers do not perceive their events to be an 'attractive and lucrative target' for cyber-criminals. However, contrary to this perception, recent cybercrime research indicates an increasing threat to the events industry from cyber-criminals and other malicious actors (Millaire et al., 2017; UK Federation of Small Business, 2016).

Recent arts and entertainment industry cybersecurity surveys indicated that 80 per cent of the sector (including event organizers) assessed their level of cybersecurity understanding as 'average' and their cybersecurity practices as 'below average' with an average cybersecurity investment of USD$2,600 per year (Australian Cyber Security Center, 2020; UK Department for Digital, Culture, Media and Sport, 2019). These findings provide valuable context, both financially and organizationally when considering the identification and selection of 'fit for purpose' cybercrime prevention and risk mitigation strategies for the events industry.

When considering the selection of cybercrime prevention strategies and other cybersecurity risk controls, foremost is the requirement to enhance the organizations IT security through a layered 'defense-in-depth' strategy and reduce technological organizational vulnerabilities, both internal and external (Cavelty, 2014; Whitman & Mattford, 2005). Furthermore, it should be recognized that event organizing committees like other small businesses, tend to be more vulnerable to technological and organizational weaknesses due to limited resources and capital, limited or no dedicated IT security staff, a lack of technical expertise and knowledge and conflicting business priorities (UK Federation of Small Businesses, 2016).

Considering the inherent cybersecurity vulnerabilities and the current levels of cyber-risk maturity of event organizers, the following cyber-security resilience measures provide a baseline for implementing a layered technical and organizational approach to information security, that is cost effective and sustainable. First, technological risk controls, including computer security software, data backed-up offsite or cloud based, regular updates of software and patches on all systems, secured wireless networks, encrypted data and communications capability, virtual private network. Second, organizational risk controls including strict password policy, security risk assessments at regular intervals, regular ICT system penetration tests, identify assurance/ background checks on all employees, cyber insurance policy and cyber-incident business continuity plans.

Identifying cybersecurity best practices is only helpful if they are implemented by event organizers. So how do theoretical perspectives influence the likelihood of successful implementation of cybercrime prevention strategies? The application of criminological theories and other research perspectives provide an evidence-based methodology to inform the development of polices, practices, protocols and the overall approach to information security and crime prevention (Hinduja & Kooi, 2013). Insider threats account for 33 per cent of 'cyberattacks' and data breaches. Understanding this threat profile, the general deterrence theory (GDT) can be utilized to identify risk controls for the mitigating insider threats, for example, cybersecurity and password protection policies, access control and cybersecurity awareness training for staff (Lee et al., 2004). It has been contended that situational crime prevention (SCP) provides a better theoretical perspective than traditional theories for cybercrime prevention (Hinduja & Kooi, 2013). Applying SCP to the context of cybercrime prevention, seeks to reduce vulnerabilities through ICT system design, increase the risk/decrease the reward through criminal legislation and internal InfoSec policies, increase the effort by 'hardening' the digital ecosystem through ICT security protocols and encryption, and reduce the use of excuses (workforce and staff) through ICT cybersecurity policies and training.

The successful implementation of cybercrime prevention strategies within the events industry is likely, if cybersecurity measures are cost effective and can be easily implemented without unduly impacting on workplace productivity (Kirlappos et al., 2014). The Figure 3.6 infographic provides a visual example of best practices for cyber resilience of any event, regardless of size or whether, volunteer or staff led.

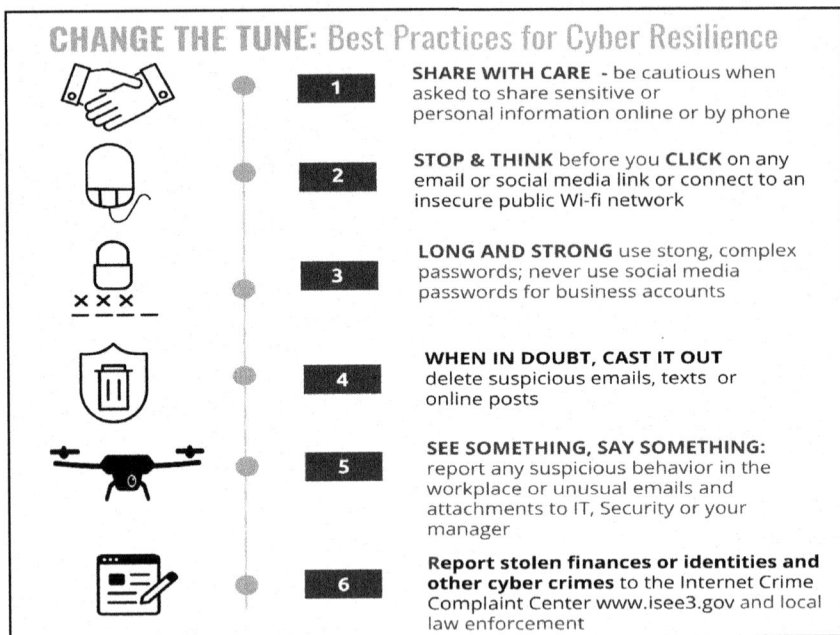

CHANGE THE TUNE: Best Practices for Cyber Resilience

1. **SHARE WITH CARE** - be cautious when asked to share sensitive or personal information online or by phone

2. **STOP & THINK** before you **CLICK** on any email or social media link or connect to an insecure public Wi-fi network

3. **LONG AND STRONG** use stong, complex passwords; never use social media passwords for business accounts

4. **WHEN IN DOUBT, CAST IT OUT** delete suspicious emails, texts or online posts

5. **SEE SOMETHING, SAY SOMETHING:** report any suspicious behavior in the workplace or unusual emails and attachments to IT, Security or your manager

6. **Report stolen finances or identities and other cyber crimes** to the Internet Crime Complaint Center www.isee3.gov and local law enforcement

Figure 3.6: Cyber security practices for event organizers

The convergence of cybersecurity within the event industry's digital ecosystem

Securing event ICT ecosystems in the future, where thousands of mobile devices connect to onsite wireless access points and dedicated Wi-Fi networks for cashless point of sales transactions, ticketing, social media and event information, remains a daunting task for event IT security teams (Lakhani, 2019). Moreover, this challenge will be further exacerbated through the COVID-19 global risk shock and the pivot from traditional office workplaces to the 'new normal' of tele-working from home-based workplaces and the emerging fourth industrial revolution, Industry 4.0; characterized by the integration of physical and computational elements and the emergence of cyber-physical technologies, such as the internet of things (IoT) and radio-frequency identification (Lal, 2020; US Cybersecurity and Infrastructure Security Agency, 2020; Xu et al., 2018).

Shaping the response to future cyber threats

What is the role of the public and private security sectors for shaping and influencing best responses to future cyber threats to the events industry sector? First, IT security professionals should seek to better understand the challenges confronting event organizers for the implementation of industry cyber security best practices, for example: resourcing and budget constraints; the lack of dedicated staff with an IT security focus; lack of cyber risk awareness and the severity of consequences from a cyber incident; lack of business continuity preparedness and organizational resilience to cyber-incidents and ICT system failures; appreciate that implementing complex cybersecurity policies practices and protocols are likely to have negatively impact on workplace productivity and less likely to be implemented (Cavelly, 2014; Kirlappos et al., 2014; Payne et al., 2019). Second, taking steps to improve the cybercrime evidence base through consistent use of language and methodologies for the collection and measurement of cybercrime data, encourage reporting of cybercrime in the workplace through cybersecurity awareness and training. Third, seek opportunities to strengthen domestic legislative frameworks and the harmonization of cybercrime legislation *between* transnational jurisdictions to increase the risk of prosecution for would-be cybercriminals and raise the cost of 'doing business' for cybercriminals (Stratton et al., 2017). Fourth, actively promote a culture of collaboration and digital trust within the events industry ecosystem through the public and private security sector industry to enhance access to timely cybersecurity and threat information.

Cybercrimes are a complex problem, global in nature and remain a persistent and serious threat to the organizers and their events. As the physical world and virtual space becomes increasingly integrated, ICT systems, networks and data will continue to remain vulnerable to existential cyber threats from sophisticated cyber-criminals and other malicious actors who possess the intent and capability to exploit vulnerabilities to steal data, commit fraud and disrupt access to data within the events digital ecosystems. To meet this challenge, event organizers supported by the public and private security sector partners must continue to converge and adapt their cyber-security defenses to meet these future cyber-threats. The ongoing convergence of the public and private security sectors, collective security initiatives for the provision of industry leading advice on cost effective, 'best of breed' cybersecurity tools and the availability of government sponsored cybersecurity training will significantly enhance the events industry resilience to cyber-incidents, malicious or accidental.

Cybercriminals are agile, adapt and continuously evolve their tactics, techniques, and technologies to target and exploit the events industry ICT systems whose cyber-defenses are known to be far more vulnerable and less sophisticated than larger organizations. While it has been noted that the events industry sector workplace is constrained by limited resources, workplace cyber-security training and cybercrime situational awareness remain fundamental building blocks for effective information security and the prevention of cyber-crime within the industry.

Conclusion

This chapter explored contemporary insights into event risk management and how event organizers approach risk-based decision-making in today's volatile, ambiguous, complex and uncertain world. The inter-related risk constructs pertaining to socio-cultural theoretical perspectives of risk were explored to provide insights into how event organizers perception of risk influences their approach to risk management, be it subjective or objective. It was concluded, that while event organizers rely on intuitive risk judgments based on a foundation of experience which seldom incudes direct experience with the risk event, this should not be considered erroneous or overly biased, as compared to probabilistic risk assessments. Following on, it was surmised that event organizers rarely have the necessary information and time to apply analytical based, decision-making processes but rather they relied on naturalistic decision-making (heuristics); leveraging their expertise, experience and intuition to reach timely and 'satisficing' decisions. Notwithstanding, it was noted that an event organizer's decision-making could be improved through adopting repeatable and systematic, decision-making models, such as the OODA loop.

The second part of the chapter considered two low probability, severe impact risks, domestic terrorism and cyber-criminals attacks. While events will continue to remain attractive targets for various terrorism threat actors into the foreseeable future, it is possible for event organizers to reduce the risk of a terrorist attacks through applying SCP counter terrorism solutions that are cost-effective, feasible and offer opportunities for enhancing an event team's resilience and capability to respond and recover from critical incidents. The rapid onset of the digital age has created unprecedented opportunities for increasingly, sophisticated, and capable cyber-criminals and cyber-deviant entrepreneurs to target event organizers whose vulnerable cyber-defenses are known to offer low risk, high return criminal opportunities. Cybercrimes will continue to remain a persistent and serious threat. Event organizers in collaboration with their public and private security sector partners must continue to converge and adapt their cyber-security defenses to meet these future cyber-threats.

The awareness and maturity of risk management within the events industry is undeniably growing as event managers migrate from an insurance-led approach to an event management led approach. However, it remains evident that the events industry faces ongoing challenges in developing a mature level of capability to proactively manage event risks; be it a subjective, risk ranking approach or more quantitatively, through probability risk assessments. As an industry, it is essential to pursue further academic research into event risk management and to provide opportunities for professional development of the next generation of events leaders in risk management.

References

Anarumo, M. (2011) The practitioner's view of the terrorist threat, in Kennedy, L., & McGarrell, E. (eds) *Crime and Terrorism Risk: Studies in Criminology and Criminal Justice.* pp. 56-89.

Andress, J. (Ed.) (2011). *The Basics of Information Security: Understanding the Fundamentals of InfoSec in Theory and Practice.* London: Elsevier.

Ash, J., & Smallman, C. (2010). A case study of decision making in emergencies. *Risk Management, 12*(3), 185-207.

Ashwin, P., & Wilson, M. (2020) *Event Industry Preparedness and Resilience Survey.* https://www.blerter.com/lp/event-preparedness-resilience-survey-report.

Australian Cyber Security Centre. (2020) *Cyber Security and Australian Small Businesses Survey Results.* https://www.cyber.gov.au/sites/default/files/2020-07/ACSC%20Small%20Business%20Survey%20Report.pdf (Accessed: 22 August 2020).

Aven, T., & Renn, O. (2009) The role of quantitative risk assessments of characterizing risk and uncertainty and delineating appropriate risk management options with special emphasis on terrorism risk, *Risk Analysis, 29* (4), pp. 587- 600.

Beck, U. (1999) *World Risk Society.* Cambridge: Polity Press.

Beck, U. (2006). Living in the world risk society. *Economy and Society, 35*(3), 329-345.

Berlonghi, A. (1990) *The Special Event Risk Management Manual.* Dayton, CA: Bookmasters Inc.

Bjorgo, T., & Silke, A. (2019). Root causes of terrorism. In A. Silke (Ed.) *Routledge Handbook of Terrorism and Counterterrorism* (pp.57-65). New York: Routledge.

Boba, R. (2009) 'EVIL DONE', in Freilich, J. and Newman, G. (eds). *Reducing Terrorism through Situational Crime Prevention.* pp.71-91, Monsey, NY: Criminal Justice Press.

Bouhana, N., Malthaner, S., Schuurman., Lindekilde, L., Thornton, A., & Gill, P. (2019) Lone actor terrorism: Radicalization, attack planning and execution, in Silke, A. (ed.) *Routledge Handbook of Terrorism and Counterterrorism.* New York: Routledge, pp.112-121.

Boyd, J. (1979). New Conception for Air-to-Air Combat. (Unpublished paper). Available at: http://dnipogo.org/john-r-boyd/.

Cavelty, M. (2014) Breaking the cyber-security dilemma: Aligning security needs and removing vulnerabilities, *Science, & Engineering Ethics, 20*(3), 701–715.

Chang, L., & Graboksy, P. (2014) Cybercrime and establishing a secure cyber world, in Gill, M. (ed) *The Handbook of Security.* 2nd edn. Basingstoke: Palgrave MacMillian, pp.331-339.

Clark, J., & Saviour, S. (2018) *Negligence: What is Reasonably Foreseeable.* https://stewartmckelvey.com/thought-leadership/client-update-negligence-what-is-reasonably-foreseeable, (Accessed:15 December 2020).

Clarke, R., & Newman, G. (2006) *Outsmarting the Terrorists.* Westport, Connecticut: Praeger Security International.

Department for Digital, Culture, Media and Sport. (2019) *Cyber Security Breaches Survey 2019.* https://assets.publishing.service.gov.uk/government/uploads/system/uploads/attachment_data/file/813599/ (Accessed: 12 August 2020).

Ellis, R., Fabtz, A., Karimi,F., & McLaughlin, E. (2016) *Orlando Shooting: 49 Killed, Shooter Pledged ISIS Allegiance.* Orlando shooting: 49 killed, shooter pledged ISIS allegiance (cnn.com) (Accessed: 1 December 2020).

Ezell, B., Bennett, S., Von Winterfelt, D., Sokolowki, J., & Collins, A. (2010) Probabilistic risk analysis and terrorism risk, *Risk Analysis, 30* (4), 575-589.

Ferrara, D. (2020) *Judge Approves $800 million Settlement for Route 91 Victims.* https://www.reviewjournal.com/crime/courts/judge-approves-800m-settlement-for-route-91-victims-2133490/ (Accessed:15 December 2020).

Freilich, J., Chermak, S., & Hsu, H. (2019) Deterring and preventing terrorism, in Silke, A. (ed.) *Routledge Handbook of Terrorism and Counterterrorism.* New York: Routledge, pp. 434-443.

Furnell, S., Emm, D., & Papadaki, M. (2015) The challenge of measuring cyber-dependent crimes, *Computer Fraud, & Security, 10,* 5-12.

Getz, D. (1997) *Event Management and Event Tourism.* New York: Cognizant.

Goldblatt, J, Dr. (2011). *Special Events: A New Generation and the Next Frontier.* 6th edn. New Jersey: John Wiley, & Sons Inc.

Gordon, S., & Ford, R. (2006) On the definition and classification of cybercrime, *Journal of Computer Virology, 2,* 13-20.

Haberfeld, M., & von Hassell, A. (2011). Proper proactive training to terrorist presence and operations in friendly urban environment. In M. Haberfeld, & A. von Hassell (Eds.), *A New Understanding of Terrorism: Case Studies, Trajectories and Lessons Learned* (pp. 9-22). New York: Springer.

Hackread. (2017) *Coachella Festival Website Hacked; User Data at Risk.* https://www.hackread.com/coachella-festival-website-hacked-user-data-at-risk/ (Accessed: 15 August 2020).

Hall, S., Manning, D., Keiper, M., Jenny, S., & Allen, B. (2019). Stakeholders perception of critical risks and challenges hosting marathon events: An exploratory study. *Journal of Contemporary Athletics, 13*(1), 11-22.

Hesterman, J. (2015) *Soft Target Hardening: Protecting People from Attack*. Boca Raton, FL: CRC Press.

Hillson, D. (2016) *The Risk Management Handbook: A Practical Guide to Managing the Multiple Dimensions of Risk*. London: Kogan Page Ltd.

Hinduja, S., & Kooi, B. (2013) Curtailing cyber and information security vulnerabilities through situation crime prevention', *Security Journal*, 26(4), 383-402.

Hopkin, P. (2010). *Fundamentals of Risk Management: Understanding, evaluating and implementing effective risk management* (2nd edn). London: Kogan Page.

IBM Security and Ponemon Institute (2020). *Cost of a Data Breach Report 2020*. New York: IBM Security.

International Organization for Standards. (2018). *ISO 31000: Risk Management – Guidelines*. 2nd ed. Zurich: International Organisation for Standards (ISO).

Khir, M.M. (2014). *Developing an Event Safety Typology: A Qualitative Study of Risk Perception amongst Event Planners and Venue Managers in Malaysia*. PHD Thesis. Liverpool John Moores University. Available at: http://researchonline.ljmu.ac.uk/id/eprint/4441/1/157529_2014masrurphd.pdf.

Kirlappos,I., Parkin, S., & Sasse, A. (2014). Learning from Shadow Security: Why understanding non-compliant behaviors provides the basis for effective security. Available at: https://discovery.ucl.ac.uk/id/eprint/1424472/1/Kirlappos%20et%20al.%20-%202014%20-%20Learning%20from%20%E2%80%9CShadow%20Security%E2%80%9D%20Why%20understanding.pdf.

Klein, G. (1993). A Recognition-Primed Decision (RPD) Model of Rapid Decision Making. In G. Klein, J. Ornaanu, R. Calderwood, & C. Zsambok (Eds.), *Decision Making in Action: Models and Methods* (pp. 138-147). Norwood, NJ: Ablex Publishing Corp.

Klein, G. (2008). Naturalistic decision making. *Human Factors: The Journal of Human Factors and Ergonomic Society*, 50(3), 456-460. Available from: https://journals-sagepub-com.ezproxy4.lib.le.ac.uk/doi/pdf/10.1518/001872008X288385.

Lakhani, A. (2019) *Ensuring Cybersecurity at Big Events this Summer*. https://www.fortinet.com/blog/business-and-technology/cybersecurity-big-summer-events (Accessed at: 26 August 2020).

Lal, A. (2020) *Building Cyber Resilience Post COVID-19 19*. https://www.cpomagazine.com/cyber-security/building-cyber-resilience-post-covid-19/ (Accessed: 28 August 2020).

Laybourn, P. (2003) Risk and decision making in events management, in Yeoman, I. (ed). *Festival and Events Management: An International Arts and Culture Perspective*. New York: Routledge.

Levi, M., Doig, A., & Gundur, R. (2017) Cyberfraud and the implications for effective risk-based responses: Themes from UK research, *Crime Law Society Change*, 67, 77–96.

Lupton, D. (2013). *Risk*. 2nd edn. New York: Routledge.

McGuire, M., & Dowling, S. (2013) Cybercrime: A review of the evidence, *Home Office Research Report 75*. London: Home Office Science.

Mcllhatton, D., Allen, A., Chapman, D., Monaghan, R., Ouillon, S., & Bergonzoli,,K. (2019). Current considerations of counter terrorism in the risk management profession. *Journal of Applied Security Research, 14*(3), 350-368.

Mercury News (2020). *Coachella Festival Website Hacked, Users Personal Data Stolen.* https://www.mercurynews.com/2017/03/01/coachella-festival-website-hacked-users-personal-data-stolen/ (Accessed: 20 August 2020).

Millaire, P. Sathe, A., & Thielen, P. (2017) *What all Cyber Criminal Know: Small and Midsize Businesses with Little or No Cybersecurity are Ideal Targets.* https://www.chubb.com/us-en/_assets/doc/17010201-cyber-for-small_midsize-businesses-10.17.pdf (Accessed: 21 August 2020).

Ostrom, L., & Wilhelmsen, C. (2012). *Risk Assessment: Tools, Techniques and their Application.* New York: John Wiley, & Sons Inc.

Payne, B., David C. May, D., & Hadzhidimova, L. (2019) America's most wanted criminals: Comparing cybercriminals and traditional criminals, *Criminal Justice Studies, 32*(1), 1-15.

Piekarz, M., Jenkins, I., & Mills, P. (2015) *Risk and Safety Management in the Leisure, Events, Tourism and Sports Industries.* Oxfordshire: CAB International Inc.

Plous, S. (1993). *The Psychology of Judgment and Decision Making.* NY: Mcgraw-Hill Book Company.

Reason, J. (1990). The contribution of latent human failures to the breakdown of complex systems. *Philosophical Transactions of the Royal Society of London. Series B, Biological Sciences, 327*(1241), 475–484. doi:10.1098/rstb.1990.0090.

Reason, J. (1997). *Managing the Risk of Organizational Accidents.* Surrey, UK: Ashgate Publishing Ltd.

Reid, S., & Ritchie, B. (2011) Risk management: Event managers' attitudes, beliefs and perceived constraints, *Event Management,15*, 329-341.

Robson, L. (2009) *Perceptions of Risk at Meetings and Conferences: An Event Planners Perspective.* PHD Thesis. University of Waterloo. https://uwspace.uwaterloo.ca/bitstream/handle/10012/4509/Robson_Linda.pdf.

Rogers, G. (1997) The dynamics of risk perception: How does perceived risk respond to risk events? *Risk Analysis,17*(6), 745 – 757.

Rule, J. (2013) *A Symbiotic Relationship: The OODA Loop, Intuition, and Strategic Thought.* Master of Strategic Studies, Dissertation. United States War College. https://www.scrummaster.dk/lib/AgileLeanLibrary/Topics/OODALoop/OODAASymbioticRelationship.pdf.

Rutherford Silvers, J. (2008) *Risk Management for Meetings and Events.* Oxford: Butterworth- Heinemann.

Slovic, P. (2000) *The Perception of Risk.* London: Earthscan Publications Ltd.

Slovic, P., & Peters, E. (2006). Risk perception and affect. *Current Directions in Psychological Science, 15*(6), 322-325.

Stratton, G., Powell, A., & Cameron, R. (2017). Crime and justice in digital society: Towards a 'Digital Criminology'?. *International Journal for Crime, Justice and Social Democracy, 6*(2), 17-33.

Talbot, J. (2011) .What Right with Risk Matrices? Available at: https://31000risk. wordpress.com/article/what-s-right-with-risk-matrices-3dksezemjiq54-4/

Tarlow, P. (2002) *Event Risk Management and Safety*. New York: John Wiley, & Sons Inc.

UK Centre for the Protection of National Infrastructure. (2020) *Recognizing Terrorist Threats Guide*. https://www.cpni.gov.uk/recognising-terrorist-threats-guide-0 (Accessed: 10 December 2020).

UK Federation of Small Businesses (2016). *Cyber Resilience: How to Protect Small Firms in the Digital Economy*. Available at: https://www.fsb.org.uk/resources-page/small-businesses-bearing-the-brunt-of-cyber-crime.html.

US Department of Homeland Security, Cybersecurity and Infrastructure Security Agency. (2011). *Risk Management Fundamentals*. Available at: https://www.dhs. gov/xlibrary/assets/rma-risk-management-fundamentals.pdf.

US Department of Homeland Security, Cybersecurity and Infrastructure Security Agency. (2019) *CISA Cyber Essentials*. https://www.cisa.gov/publication/cisa-cyber-essentials (Accessed: 22 July 2020).

US Department of Homeland Security, Cybersecurity and Infrastructure Security Agency. (2020) *COVID-19 Exploited by Malicious Cyber Actors*. https://us-cert. cisa.gov/ncas/alerts/aa20-099a (Accessed: 22 August 2020)

US Department of Homeland Security. (2020) *Homeland Threat Assessment*. https:// www.dhs.gov/sites/default/files/publications/2020_10_06_homeland-threat-assessment.pdf (Accessed: 30 November 2020).

US National Counterterrorism Center. (2020) *Counter Terrorism Guide for Public Safety Personnel*. https://www.dni.gov/nctc/jcat/index.html (Accessed: 20 November 2020).

Verizon. (2020) *2020 Data Breach Investigations Report*. https://enterprise.verizon. com/resources/reports/2020-data-breach-investigations-report.pdf (Accessed: 13 August 2020).

Wall, D. (2001) Cybercrimes and the Internet, in Wall, D (ed) *Crime and the Internet*. New York: Springer.

Whitman, M., & Mattord, H. (2005) *Principles of Information Security*, 2nd edn. Boston: Thompson Course Technology.

Willis, H. (2007). Guiding resource allocations based on terrorism risk. *Risk Analysis, 27*(3), 597-606.

Xu, L., Xu, E., & Li, L. (2018) Industry 4.0: State of the art and future trends, *International Journal of Production Research*, 56(8), 2941-2962.

4 Stakeholder Management

Donald Getz

Introduction

This chapter presents concepts and principles for stakeholder management in a time of crisis, and how stakeholder management is an essential part of recovery and resilience. Definitions, stakeholder theory, case studies and practical advice for event stakeholder management has been provided in the book *Event Stakeholders* by Mathilda van Niekerk and Donald Getz (2019). However, it was written before the 2020 pandemic and did not specifically address crisis management.

A number of interviews and case studies have been incorporated in this book, reflecting the views of experts in a wide range of event settings and types. The interviewees were asked to comment on the impacts of the Covid-19 pandemic on the events sector, from their perspectives, on actions taken and plans for recovery, and on the key stakeholders for recovery and building resilience. A summary of the interviews and case studies is contained in the final chapter. While not all crises are as serious as the pandemic, 2020 generally being seen as a worst-case scenario, this material is valuable in shedding light on any form of crisis facing events, and in particular on the vital roles played by internal and external stakeholders.

Who or what is a stakeholder? For a privately owned event, owners and direct investors are the *shareholders*, while *stakeholders* can broadly be defined as persons or organizations that have something to gain or lose by the actions of the event. They might have an investment in an event, or a perceived interest. An investment can be tangible or intangible. For example, tangible investments can be in the form of being a marketing or logistical partner, supplier, volunteer, paid employee, sponsor or other type of participant. Communities, cities and destinations invest in events and consider themselves to be important stakeholders, their investments being both tangible (e.g., money, venues, marketing, other services) or intangible (e.g., moral and political support, attendance, or – at a minimum – tolerance).

Just about everyone else who wants to have an influence, or feels impacted by the event (and this can include *potential* involvement and *possible* impacts) can be considered a stakeholder. When multiple events are considered, such as a managed portfolio or the entire population of events in a city, the number and interests of potential stakeholders becomes very large. This complexity is why many organizations classify stakeholders into *primary and secondary* types, or use even more sophisticated methods such as those described in this chapter to classify them on the basis of power, urgency and legitimacy, then develop appropriate strategies.

Drawing from the generic stakeholder literature, (Freeman, 1984, p. 46) defined stakeholder as "*Any individual or group who can affect the firm's performance or who is affected by the achievement of the organization's objectives*". Carroll (1993, p. 60) broadened the definition this way: "*those groups or individuals with whom the organization interacts or has interdependencies*", while Savage et al. (1991, p. 61) described stakeholders as "*groups or individuals who have an interest in the actions of an organization and [...] the ability to influence it.*" If a normative, or value-based approach to stakeholder management is taken, as advocated by Clarkson (1995) and in line with principles of corporate social responsibility, then all real and potential stakeholders should be acknowledged, given a voice, and their interests considered when making decisions.

In summary, an organization can define its stakeholders in narrow or broad terms, related to a number of criteria, and then apply management principles as necessary. In a time of crisis, however, adaptation will be required.

Classifying stakeholders and formulating appropriate strategies in a time of crisis

The nature of the crisis will influence stakeholder relationships and how they are managed. We first have to consider *incidents*, being one-off, sudden and unwanted threats or damages. Accidents with injury, crowd violence, terrorist attacks, damage during bad weather, or other incidents dictate that responses are immediate and hopefully pre-planned and rehearsed, so the number and types of stakeholders involved is set in policy. Staff and volunteers must have assigned duties through contingency planning and emergency-response drills, and liaison with professional first responders should ideally be automatic. These types of incidents can be resolved satisfactorily for all concerned if there is no lasting negative impact such as death or serious injury, lawsuits or other legal proceedings, or financial losses that threaten viability. Whether or not an incident becomes a crisis is therefore a matter of context and perspective.

Given that a crisis can be defined as either the cause or trigger of a problem, such as an incident described above, or the challenges imposed by organizational response (including uncertainty, chaos or do-nothing), we have to consider how stakeholders are related to both short-term and long-term crises. A smoldering or enduring crisis might also be evident in mismanaged organizations or where organizational culture has led to internal conflicts, but these are of quite a different nature than those caused by external stimuli because they might remain invisible or deliberately hidden for some time.

During long-term crises, with the focus on how the organization responds (assuming it has survived the initial shock), the participation of many more stakeholders will be necessary. The 2020 pandemic illustrates this point, as not only were events seriously impacted but also their venues, sponsors, performers, suppliers, audiences and communities all suffered. Events were forced to consider priorities and conduct risk-reward assessments when deciding if they should go on as usual (a few did, even after it was clear that a pandemic was spreading globally), postpone or cancel. In this context, outright cancellation was the extreme option, meaning there was no prospect of holding the event again (for one-time events) or the future was completely uncertain. Most periodic events elected to announce they would postpone and picked a later date or committed to returning next year, same time, if feasible. Some sports eventually created 'bubbles' to continue competition in tightly controlled venues with no live audiences. Many virtual events were created online, while the term 'hybrid event' took on new meanings. What the world witnessed in 2020 was an externally imposed crisis with immediate and severely negative impacts, followed by a prolonged period of uncertainty and planned recovery. The stakeholders for any given event or organization were radically redefined in terms of power, legitimacy and urgency.

Salience: Power, legitimacy and urgency

The famous 'salience' model of Mitchell et al. (1997) provides a useful starting point for thinking about stakeholder management during a time of crisis and for the purposes of planned recovery. It consists of three overlapping circles representing the attributes of *power, legitimacy and urgency* which together define salience and delimit seven categories of stakeholder. Outside the circles is an eighth category labelled 'non stakeholder', but it has to be asked if there is such a thing – in theory, anyone or any organization could potentially become important. High stakeholder salience means that organizations should give priority to managing these relationships. The categories are:

♦ *definitive stakeholders* possess all three attributes;

♦ *dependent stakeholders* have two attributes, but no power;

♦ *dangerous stakeholders* have power and urgency but no legitimacy; they pose a threat;

♦ *dominant stakeholders* have power and legitimacy;

♦ *dormant stakeholders* have only power;

♦ *discretionary stakeholders* possess only legitimacy;

♦ *demanding stakeholders* show urgency but without power or legitimacy.

Power

There are various sources of power, and it is used in different ways, but the exercise of regulatory power over events and venues by a few key stakeholders is most likely to be the biggest challenge during a crisis. Regulators (including police, health authorities, and law makers) can shut down events or severely influence their operations. This kind of power is often absolute, meaning it cannot be ignored or resisted. It might be in the form of restricting hours or denying access to venues, requiring substantial safety audits, making infrastructure changes or equipment repairs, re-designing the program (including performance cancellations), or imposing limits on attendance and hours of operations. Parades can face mandatory changes to routes taken and to permissible contents (such as the height of inflatables), sports might have to shift venues or change their alcohol and dining policies, and so on.

Financial institutions can also exert absolute or severe power over events. Banks and other lenders might terminate lines of credit or force repayment of debt. Suppliers can suddenly withdraw credit and demand cash. Events and venues that rely on ticket sales or pre-event registration fees are the most vulnerable when audiences are prevented from attending mass gatherings, thereby generating immediate and possibly fatal financial weakness.

Agencies and corporations with this kind of power over venues and events can never be ignored, and must always be fully engaged. In general, public health agencies have this power (they can be local, regional or national), as do local governments through various regulatory and enforcement departments. It is also important to recognize that local authorities are often both the regulator and the funding agency for many festivals and events; their support can also include coordination, provision of venues and services, marketing and lobbying, especially those with event departments and those practicing some degree of event portfolio management. These powerful stakeholders in times of crisis become possible lifelines, ideally providing additional funding or other forms of tangible support that enable events and venues to survive. On the other hand, they might run out of money and move priorities away from the events sector.

The increased need on the part of venues and events can result in amplified power for politicians and public agencies. The lengthy pandemic crisis also permits, and might require, a re-thinking of event and tourism-related strategy and priorities that might result in funding changes (will it result in more or less support?); regulations (health and safety requirements in particular will be stepped up); degree of engagement (will direct portfolio management become more popular?); and marketing (perhaps a new emphasis on hallmark and iconic events with potential to stimulate travel as opposed to local or resident-oriented events?).

In many countries governments provided financial support to workers, venues and companies, but what about not-for-profit events? What support is available for festivals and events that cannot be held but nevertheless have debts and financial obligations to suppliers? Without a financial safety net, failures are to be expected.

Who else has power that is amplified in times of crisis and for planned recovery? Certain key sponsors will have augmented power to either continue or suspend financial and other support for venues and events. In the case of corporate events outright cancellation is one decision managers and owners might take, while withdrawing support from independently-owned events is another. Suppliers and vendors often have little or no power, and so suffer when venues and events close down. Entertainers are in this category, and the pandemic resulted in many performers and artists losing their livelihood, while material and service suppliers had to struggle to find alternative sources of revenue – sometimes without viable options.

Legitimacy

The definition of legitimacy might have to change during a crisis because normal operations and relationships are of necessity altered. Three change scenarios might play out – and these hold implications for power and urgency as well as legitimacy. In the first, all current stakeholders remain legitimate and require normal attention, but new ones have to be urgently added. These will include health agencies that suddenly take on new powers, making them 'definitive' stakeholders at least for a period of time, and any others with the power to regulate and withhold financial support. All others have to be maintained, but the newly powerful stakeholders must be satisfied completely.

In the second scenario, some important stakeholders are lost. These could include segments of the population or existing audience that will not return, possibly for financial reasons or because of crisis-related changes in the event or venue's reputation, brand, positioning or program. Vendors and suppliers might be lost because of bankruptcy or a shift to other business models. Political and corporate support might disappear.

The third scenario is defined by uncertainty, and this might generate apprehension and poor decision making. In some crises the matter will be resolved quickly and recovery is certain, but the pandemic has imposed a great deal of uncertainty about the future. In a lengthy, complex crisis there might be disruption of important relationships, addition of new ones, and questions about who has to be involved in recovery. In the worst of crises there can be stakeholder chaos giving rise to questions like these: who is to be trusted to help us? where will support come from? will there be new agencies regulating us? what is happening in the marketplace?

Urgency

Not all events and venues will consider the customer, or the public in general, to have urgent needs in a time of prolonged crisis such as the 2020 pandemic. This is mainly because they are going to be preoccupied with health concerns, staying at home (lockdowns have been a common response) and worrying about financial solvency (can they get their jobs back? what will be the impact on employment prospects in general?). Many events have nevertheless gone to great lengths to maintain some level of engagement with known, loyal audiences such as subscribers, repeat visitors and particular communities or groups. Recovery – whether defined by bringing the same event back, modifying it, or holding a new one – will impose increasing urgency on communications, engagement, marketing and selling, so urgency is a dynamic consideration.

Dangerous stakeholders in a time of crisis

Some stakeholders like health authorities can gain power, presenting new threats, but others might decide to act more dangerously! Why? Because a crisis, and in particular chaotic situations, present opportunities for enemies and for entrepreneurs. Enemies can be described as 'the competition', those who oppose what you are doing on moral or ideological grounds (and perhaps want to shut down an event or part of its program), politicians who prefer to see support and funding go in other directions, and other stakeholders who see the potential for gain at someone else's expense. Many venues and events probably do not think in these terms, believing they have no enemies, but during a crisis and in chaotic environments do not be surprised if old tensions resurface, new ones appear, and enemies act against your interests while you are vulnerable.

Entrepreneurs on the other hand are looking for positive outcomes that might emerge during the crisis. This refers to not only starting something new or innovating within established parameters (such as starting a new festival because others have disappeared) but also to revolutionary changes that disrupt the established order. Entrepreneurs starting new venues create opportunities for events, but new event start-ups can represent increased competition for resources. The real danger to the established order within the events world comes from structural changes in the economy, in consumer behavior, and in the regulatory world. The 'market' for events might never be the same following the Covid-19 pandemic.

What are the possible structural changes that threaten existing venues and events while create entrepreneurial opportunities? Consider changes in the work environment (who wins and loses economically?); leisure and travel (have preferences and habits changed permanently?); values and social order (have health considerations become a new priority?); and technology (what is the new role of digital events?).

Discussing dangerous stakeholders raises the issue of impediments to crisis management and recovery, as outlined in the ensuing Table 4.1. This is an important exercise for event organizers to undertake in any crisis, incorporating risk-reward factors. Each event and organization will have a different list of stakeholders to consider, so this table is simply illustrating the approach.

Table 4.1: Potential impediments to crisis response and recovery from various stakeholders

Stakeholder	Potential actions to impede crisis response and recovery
Owners	Entrepreneurs and business owners might go bankrupt or face legal problems and therefore not pursue recovery; the ROI on events might appear to be unattractive during and following a crisis, compared to alternative investments.
Directors	In the not-for-profit sector, boards of directors might be pro-recovery, divided on the issue, or opposed; the composition of a board might be critical – are they all committed volunteers or are they appointees/ are some experts in professional fields or do they all lack experience and expertise? What is their risk-taking orientation? In the public sector it is both politicians and civil servants that might be pro or anti recovery.
Staff	Have they lost their jobs and can they be recalled or replaced?
Volunteers	Will they return or do new ones have to be recruited?
Funders	If there is no money to spend in advance of a scheduled event, recovery is impossible; lost sponsors and grant-givers are a risk.
Mass media	Media support, apathy or antagonism could result from a crisis, especially if the event is blamed for injuries or deaths or is perceived to be undesirable for other reasons – the absence of a positive presence by events could translate into general consumer apathy; negative messaging can harm recovery potential.
Social media	Does goodwill translate into tangible support such as grants and the easing of regulations to get an event into recovery mode? What priorities will be assigned to events and particular events by politicians? There is some reason to fear that the 2020 pandemic will lead to new and onerous health regulations for events and venues. Other disasters have resulted in event terminations when regulators react to (for example) injuries and deaths at event venues by imposing new controls.

The 'industry'	Lack of umbrella leadership and co-ordination results in a weak voice and poor results from lobbying (owing to inadequate or non-existent collaboration among professional associations, suppliers, academics, types of events, and the public, private and not-for-profit sectors.
Politicians; govern-ment	Whether due to apathy, new competition, lack of information or a general decline in the population's demand for entertainment, travel and tourism, certain segments and even whole audiences can be lost – the cost of winning new audiences might be high.
Lost audiences	Demands for the refund of deposits for cancelled or postponed events can result in bankruptcy; moneys paid in advance to suppliers, venues, performers and the owners of rights can be a substantial burden.
Demanding customers	They want their deposits back, imposing financial hardship on venues, suppliers and events; they demand constant event updates and infor-mation that is not available.

Vulnerable stakeholders in a time of crisis

Just as power shifts, so does dependency in a time of crisis. Suppliers and vendors have taken a hard and often fatal blow in the pandemic, so too have numerous venues, service providers and small business across the entire tourism, hospitality and leisure sectors. If some events and organizations survive, or perhaps even gain in support and resilience, will it be at the expense of dependent companies and individuals? What will happen to displaced volunteers and staff in the events sector?

The directly vulnerable include staff who might lose their jobs and income, suppliers that lose their revenue source, and the event organization that suffers a financial loss and possibly faces bankruptcy. Volunteers are not directly impacted financially but do lose valued engagement and might not want to return. Entertainers or performers might have their contracts cancelled and they will then lose money and access to live audiences, threatening their livelihoods. Sponsors who withdraw, or have no event to engage with, will lose valuable sales and marketing potential; small, local business sponsors might fare worse than major corporations. Students seeking internships and employment will have to wait – but for how long before they give up and move to other opportunities. Who of these stakeholders needs assistance the most, and where will it come from? Is mutual support feasible, either at the event level or through networks?

A considerable portion of any event's vulnerability relates to finances, and this is a function of the organization's business model. The business model is not always made explicit, especially in governmental and not-for-profit organizations, but it is crucial to consider the most fundamental questions: how do we create value for others while securing sufficient resources for our own continuation and health?

Events dependent on ticket sales or registration fees are probably the most at risk when a crisis arises; with cancellations and postponements, sales and pre-registration are suspended and there might arise claims for re-imbursement. Venues dependent upon events for their revenue face a similar financial crisis. Throughout the business world the effects of a loss of customer demand can be immediately disastrous. Reputation damage might be less immediate in its impacts, especially if it results in a slowing of demand and support as opposed to a sudden withdrawal, but in the long run a strong, positive reputation is vital to survival.

For many organizations there will be a moral imperative to assist those who are negatively impacted by a crisis, including financial losses incurred when events are cancelled or postponed. But how? If there are no cash reserves, committed external supporters, or lines of credit, it might be impossible to assist those who need it most.

It is for this reason that supportive networks have become imperative, either in the form of tightly-defined associations, such as city-sponsored event and venue networks and managed event portfolios, or through more broadly-defined tourism, culture, hospitality or other industry-based associations.

Strategy and action

In this section strategies and actions are discussed for stakeholder management during a crisis, and for recovery. Generic stakeholder management strategies have been presented in the van Niekerk and Getz book (2019), including the works of Savage, Nix, Whitehead and Blair (1991), Mitchell et al. (1997), Winch (2004), Lim, Ahn and Lee (2005), Boonstra (2006), and Freeman (2010). A *"blended strategy matrix for stakeholder management"* was developed by van Niekerk and Getz (2019, p. 74), modifying some of the more generic strategies to fit the situations faced by events, but further adaptation is required for crisis and recovery management, as provided in Figure 4.1.

The 'blended strategy matrix' combines a typology of stakeholders with appropriate strategies suggested by various authors. The matrix of four cells is defined by 'increasing potential for collaboration' on the vertical axis, which has been be expanded to cover increasing potential to provide immediate and lasting assistance, and 'increasing power and influence' on the horizontal axis, now expanded to include the potential for increasing interest and capability to do harm, in the context of a time of crisis and recovery. The top-right cell in this matrix thereby comes to represent the most important stakeholders on the basis of their ability to assist, but alternatively (bottom-right cell) those most likely to do harm. In a given situation the organization might be more focused on obtaining assistance and commitments or on defending against attacks.

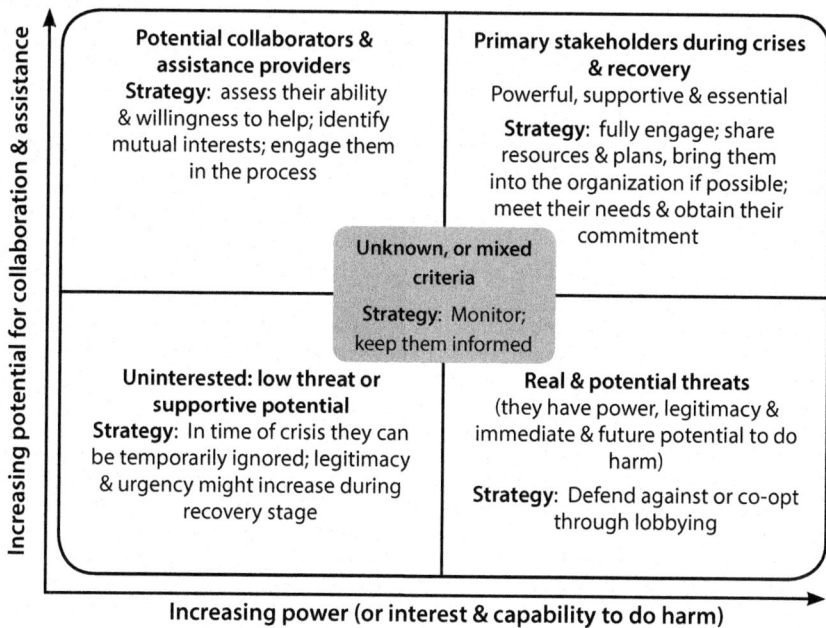

Figure 4.1: Event stakeholder management strategies in a time of crisis and for recovery (Adapted from van Niekerk, M. & Getz, D. (2019, p. 74)

As illustrated, the various strategies include a number of actions, or tactics, that are discussed below, including monitoring and assessment, engagement and communications, appeasement and obtaining commitment, and defense.

Monitoring and assessment: Stakeholder mapping

Stakeholder mapping is a standard tool, and it becomes critical in a time of crisis – or to avoid one. Stakeholder relationships are dynamic, so there is a need for organizations to incorporate monitoring and analysis into ongoing planning and evaluation, not leaving it only for occasional strategic planning projects.

Table 4.2 combines several dimensions of stakeholder mapping and management specifically for a time of crisis and recovery. Power, legitimacy and urgency are always considerations, but the dynamics of stakeholder relationships can require swift reactions so there is a need for anticipating changes. Power in particular is a crucial consideration within a crisis, so it is suggested that power to help or to harm (or hinder recovery) be explicitly included.

This kind of mapping exercise can begin with a list of internal and external stakeholders, suited to the context, and evaluation of their power, legitimacy and urgency as well as how that might change – or hopefully will change – during the crisis and recovery stages. That dynamic element requires some written indication of either foreseen or desired changes in status. Each cell in the matrix can contain a variety of relevant information. In some instances it might be useful to employ symbols.

Table 4.2: Stakeholder mapping in a time of crisis and recovery, emphasizing power, legitimacy and urgency

Power to help	Power to harm or hinder	Legitimacy	Urgency
Owners/investors			
Require accountability and a plan to recover; will they provide emergency funding?	Support could be withdrawn or a business sold; bankruptcy is possible.	To a large extent they determine who has a legitimate stake in the organization, event, and recovery.	Must consult and inform them throughout the crisis & recovery process.
Board directors			
Ask if they can assist through their networks, e.g., lobbying and finances.	Are they fully supportive of recovery plans? Do they challenge the CEO?	Constant (i.e., their legitimacy does not vary; might insist on a wider range of stakeholder engagement).	Same as above.
External funders (grants, sponsorship, donations)			
High: Will they provide emergency funding and will funding return to normal?	**High:** They have the power to provide or withdraw funding.	Constantly legitimate; they might make funding conditional on engagement with their own stakeholders.	Determine when they are to be approached for funding and what they need.
Legal/police			
Variable: They provide a necessary and immediate response to many incidents.	Legal requirements can prevent or restrict event size, access, activities.	Constant; cannot be ignored.	Urgency is related to whether or not police are needed and to legal proceedings such as lawsuits or trials.
Regulators			
To the extent that regulators and funders/supporters are the same (e.g., local government) there is the need to find a common ground.	Each crisis might result in new and restrictive standards or requirements.	Constant.	
Allies & supporters			
It is essential to find allies who will commit to recovery and help lobby for support (e.g., through formal event networks and managed event portfolios).	Weak links can be fatal during a crisis or lesson the potential for recovery; always build support networks.	Constant.	Will increase as a crisis lengthens or becomes more severe; crises that affect networks or portfolios will result in collective urgency.

Power to help	Power to harm or hinder	Legitimacy	Urgency
Audiences			
Audience or general market research can help by determining future demand; pre-paid registration or ticket sales can make future recovery feasible.	The power is related to demand – will they pay /attend / complain /endorse or recommend? Will customers demand refunds for postponed events?	Constant (for many events there will be no greater stakeholder legitimacy than loyal audiences).	Urgency to engage is greatest when events are postponed or cancelled, when rescheduling is announced, and when ticket sales or registration fees are to be collected.
Residents/the public			
Residents can indicate support and assist recovery through their elected officials and through media reports.	Negative attitudes towards events, reflected in politics and the media, can harm recovery potential.	Constant for community-based and all public events' others might have narrower constituencies.	Urgency can arise from negative media reports or political debates.
Paid staff			
Employees will be critical in planning and implementing recovery.	Staff might resign or be unwilling to support major changes.	Constant.	Commitment and action is urgent during incident response and recovery implementation.
Volunteers			
Volunteers should be kept engaged and asked to lobby for recovery.	Their loss can be an impediment to recovery.	Constant when there is a core of committed volunteers.	Urgent when bringing back volunteers for recovery.
Venues			
It is vital to ensure that venues will be available; conversely, venues need events and should be supportive.	Event venues might be seriously impacted, even closed, by incidents and lengthy crises.	Variable if venues can be substituted.	Urgent when venues have to be booked for scheduled events.
Suppliers			
Key supplies, including performers, should ideally be permanently engaged by events; they can lobby for recovery.	Cancelled /postponed events negatively impact on suppliers – they might fail or develop different supply chains to survive.	Variable if suppliers can be substituted; some might always be critical such as performers.	Urgent when supplies have to be committed and again when performers and supplies have to be delivered or on-site.
Mass media			
Have power over news and can shape pubic and political opinion - ideally in support of events & event tourism.	Bad publicity can be the cause of a crisis or impede recovery.	Constant where media are normally covering events.	Variable; it depends on what media coverage events get or can arrange.

Power to help	Power to harm or hinder	Legitimacy	Urgency
Social media			
Desirable to maintain a permanent presence in various social media and use these to inform, spread recovery stories and build support.	Complaints, negative reviews and stories, and hostile attitudes can spread quickly – needs to be monitored and countered.	Variable: in some settings social media will have much greater significance.	Urgent when there is a need to counter rumors, negative publicity, false news.
Sport governing bodies			
For certain sport events the governing bodies will take the lead in crisis response.	They have the power to withdraw support and insist upon changes to events and venues; terms for recovery have to be negotiated.	Constant, for governed sports.	Variable urgency depending on the nature of the crisis; rescheduling might be problematic.
Other			
Other powerful stakeholders will be context specific.			

A long list of potential stakeholders has been included in this table, drawing in part from the interviews and case studies presented in the chapter and elsewhere in this book.

The first stakeholder category shown is that of external owners or investors, as some event organizations will be accountable to government agencies, or to tourism and destination marketing organizations, corporate headquarters, shareholders, or perhaps sport governing bodies. This is followed by a list of possible stakeholders, all of them generic to planned events and venues.

In the example of owners/investors the diagram indicates they have a permanent and 'high' level of power, and that requires constant engagement and imposes the need for full accountability. Their legitimacy is obvious and constant, but engaging and reporting to them is likely to be intermittent and at scheduled, formal meetings. They want a plan and appropriate, approved action to solve the crisis and recover – or they will impose a plan based on their own, higher-level strategy. This option, imposed from above, is more likely to arise in a crisis where the event or portfolio of events is only one factor for an organization to consider. The notion of this vital stakeholder group being ally or enemy is not relevant, as they hold ultimate authority over the event or venue and its future.

External funders, on the other hand, could become neutral or uncaring during a crisis of their own, but are never enemies. If funding is withdrawn, allies should be mobilized to lobby for recovery of support. Strategies will be different for corporate sponsors as opposed to government grants and donations.

Audiences, particularly known loyal customers or constituencies (i.e., repeat visitors, subscribers, participants) might suddenly lose urgency (but never become irrelevant) in a crisis, as occurs when events are cancelled or subject to lengthy and uncertain postponement and all that can be done is keep them informed – that goes for residents in general. But at some point re-engagement is necessary and so urgency is variable. The power of audiences is in their ability to cancel subscriptions or tickets, demand refunds, or spend their time and money elsewhere. This power might be expressed immediately upon event cancellation through demands for refunds, or it might be a factor in slowing or preventing full recovery because interest has been lost or the marketplace structurally changed. This latter possibility is a real threat to events and venues following the 2020 pandemic as structural economic and social shifts are occurring and their effects on difference sectors is uncertain.

Appeasement and obtaining commitment

Whatever needs to be done to appease stakeholders and retain support is a good strategy. Ethics and organizational charters or mandates might limit the options, but in a truly desperate state the organization might not have any choice but to 'beg, borrow or steal' for essential support – and get confirmation that support is committed. Freeman (2010) advocated taking the offensive when a stakeholder is potentially supportive. This can include tactics such as trying to change their objectives or perceptions, adopting their position on important issues, or linking the event's program, brand or goodwill to the stakeholder for mutual benefit. Winch (2004) recommended meeting the needs and demands of powerful stakeholders to secure their support, and fully engaging them through a variety of tactics. For events, full engagement can mean bringing politicians and sponsors onto the board of directors so that their needs are translated into decisions and actions.

Established festivals, events and venues have the advantage of goodwill – and it can be leveraged during a crisis. Goodwill in the business world is an intangible asset related to its reputation and brand that gets valued in the process of purchases or takeovers, but in the world of not-for-profit organizations it is more a type of social capital that can be leveraged. Here is an example. A festival needs cash to survive and has debts that cannot be paid, so it faces bankruptcy. But because of its reputation and status (as a tradition, or a hallmark event, or an important asset within a managed event portfolio) creditors are willing to provide deferrals, banks or public agencies are willing to provide loans or grants, politicians support the event's recovery, and the public shows its love. So goodwill in this context is a matter of stakeholder relationships, and it might just carry the event through the crisis.

Defense

There might be stakeholders who attack when an organization is in crisis, for one of several reasons. Competition among events and venues for customers and supporters can be intense, resulting in dirty tactics to eliminate the perceived threat. During the 2020 pandemic bankruptcies were accelerating as cash flow dried up and costs, such as rent and debt repayments, were unsupportable. Small businesses were hard hit, while many major corporations sought bail-outs. This crisis extended across tourism, hospitality, entertainment and other economic sectors. Those who survive might not be in a mood for sharing, being charitable, or leaving room for competitors.

Many events have alienated segments of the population for reasons ranging from exclusion (e.g., they cannot afford to attend) to perceived or real negative impacts at the individual, neighborhood or community (e.g., noise, crime, traffic). Community anger or alienation might force politicians to act against the interest of events in crisis or to simply ignore appeals for assistance. But politicians might also harbor ideological-based antagonism to certain events or venues based on any of the widely-implemented justifications for public-sector intervention – they all cost money or consumer other precious resources. Lastly, in this category of potential enemies, are the media. Social media platforms are rife with conspiracy theories, negative reviews and open hospitality to just about everything, and this could include an event or venue caught up in a crisis. Mass media, largely the local televisions stations and newspapers, can elect to focus on problems or potentials, bad or good news stories. Are they partners or uninvolved observers?

Lim et al.'s (2005) 'defensive' strategy was to work with hostile stakeholders only to the extent necessary, but that approach to appeasement might not be enough. Freeman's (2010) defensive strategy included taking action to prevent competitive threats and the rather extreme option of launching a propaganda attack against them. Disinformation campaigns are unethical, but commonplace. Just how nasty is the hostile stakeholder and how serious is the threat they pose? Many in sports would say that the best defense is a strong offence, and who can argue with that wisdom in a time of crisis? Launch the offence before enemies can attack, meaning line up your powerful friends and allies to ensure that no vulnerability is evident.

Staying engaged, communications

Events can lose their audience because of cancellation or postponement, but the audience – or certain segments of it – might become disengaged for other reasons. It is of fundamental importance to maintain as much engagement as possible, hence the widespread use of various tactics during the 2020 pandemic, including augmentation or creation of the event's online and social-media presence, launching virtual events, proactive information campaigns, holding live shows and competitions without audiences or as drive-in/drive-by entertainment or spectacle, and running full championships in isolated 'bubbles' with only media audiences. Sports work without live audiences if there is TV coverage, but not all forms of live experiences can be substituted in this way.

Stakeholders acting together are stronger than individual events and organizations working alone. In particular, communications from event networks and event portfolio managers can be more effective when the audience is the public at large and mass media are employed. Individual events might be better at reaching their particular audiences through social media and their own customer databases.

Is the focus of the crisis on your event or organization, or are you incidental – one of the impacted? It makes a big difference. In the pandemic, events were casualties and each had to struggle with its own set of implications. In other crises, such as an attack or serious injuries to attendees, the event itself will be under intense scrutiny, leading to key people in the organization who will likely have to answer tough questions.

General principles for communications with stakeholders in a time of crisis include the following:

♦ Keep key stakeholders informed regularly, and get real news to them before it hits the media;

♦ Combat fake news and reputation-damaging stories;

♦ Be consistent in messaging, and keep channels open for stakeholder questions and input;

♦ Lay out the impacts and planned response to the crisis as quickly as possible, then regularly demonstrate progress;

♦ What is expected and asked from each stakeholder will have to be a matter of one-to-one engagement, not press releases;

♦ Engagement should include direct participation in response planning and recovery implementation, although only committed and crucial stakeholders are likely to accept such a challenge;

♦ Working through event networks and with portfolio managers will more likely ensure that key stakeholders are part of the process.

Audience development

To the greatest extent possible, events and venues should always try to engage with their audiences so that they remain loyal and return as the event is (re)scheduled. Money-raising campaigns, or lotteries, are another option, but these actions might not be realistic. The logical option is to cultivate new audiences, although it is not the easiest of choices. To bring audiences back and develop new ones requires resources, and how is that going to be feasible when cash-flow has dried up? Turning to powerful stakeholders for assistance might be the only real option.

Resilience and the roles of stakeholders

Resilience, or the ability to survive and adapt, requires both internal strengths and supportive external links. The internal strength will come first and foremost from financial resilience, the ability to ride out revenue losses or debt loads, then from people and their willingness and ability to persevere. Unfortunately, many venues, events and organizations are inherently vulnerable financially as their business model requires a continuous (or pulsating) intake through registration fees, ticket sales and merchandising, or through grants and sponsorship revenue that is tied to actual production of the event. How can this vulnerability be overcome?

The editors of this book have argued that networking and portfolio management are crucial for the events sector in cities and destinations, with details and examples provided in the book *Event Portfolio Management* (Antchak, Ziakas, & Getz, 2019). There is strength in numbers, that is a truism, but additional resilience can emerge from collaboration in marketing, coordination of scheduling and programming, target marketing, joint communications and lobbying within formally managed portfolios in which each event and venue is a valued asset.

As to people resilience, that relates to education, training, professionalism and organizational culture – including the vital role of leadership that prepares for crises, implements appropriate systems in a timely manner, and inspires all staff, volunteers and other stakeholders to stay the course leading to full recovery – even if recovery is within a 'new normal'.

Leadership

A resilient system, by definition, has the capacity to recover. The absence of strong, wise or legitimate leadership can be the cause of a crisis, and during an imposed crisis leadership might be weak, or fail altogether, for several reasons. Leaders are not always experienced in managing a crisis, and there are worst-case scenarios that cannot be anticipated and might not be survivable no matter what is done. No-one provided a recovery plan for the 2020 pandemic, so leaders and organizations in general had to learn on the go, or fail.

Incompetence is another factor to consider, as some leaders are good at motivating but not at strategy. Others are inflexible in their values and methods. In short, not all leaders are going to pull an event or venue through a major crisis. In such hard times leadership might have to be provided in the form of ground-up and collective action (i.e., by staff, volunteers and other key stakeholders), as well as being flexible (can decisions be made at a moment's notice to respond to opportunities and pressures?) and adaptable (e.g., can a longer-term vision be pursued even while remaining flexible?).

Ground-up, collective leadership is something that event organizations should be good at – and should put into practice at some level when times are good in order to help to prepare for the next crisis. Mark Lukens claims that both top-down and bottom-up leadership can be necessary and co-exist. He defines the bottom-up style this way:

"As an idea, bottom-up leadership emerged from the egalitarian ideals that swept the Western world in the 20th century. It emphasizes participation as a way of drawing on all the skills and knowledge an organization's employees have to offer. … To be sure, bottom-up leadership has its advantages. By getting many people's input, it crowdsources wisdom and information, allowing you to draw on the best ideas that are out there, rather than just dictating a certain task for someone to perform. It also gives people a sense of ownership over their work and workplace, which boosts engagement and motivation."

(Lukens, M., 2016)

Many organizations and events have already instituted bottom-up leadership and stakeholder collaboration, but if not, a crisis will likely force their hand. It is difficult to image a crisis scenario in which an event owner or its CEO makes all the decisions without at least wide and deep consultation among internal and external stakeholders. In particular this is likely to be required to overcome financial problems that could lead to bankruptcy.

Leadership is expected from government, elected officials, professionals with experience, and professional or industry associations. The accompanying profile of IFEA committee work during the pandemic demonstrates that kind of leadership (*Practice insight 1*, p. 45), and there are many other examples around the world of very active recovery planning for the events sector. What should not be lost during recovery planning is the need for building resilience at the micro and macro levels (i.e., both individual events and their organizations, and for networks and portfolios of events), and to make that work will require concerted efforts on the part of all stakeholders.

Conclusion

Maintaining close, supportive stakeholder relationships is a critical element in risk management, crisis recovery and long-term resilience for events and event portfolios. Entire populations of events in cities and destinations are structured by inter-stakeholder relationships and go a long way to sustaining a healthy event ecosystem.

This chapter commenced with a number of theoretical concepts related to the nature of stakeholders and their management. A key point is that the very definition of stakeholders and the mapping of stakeholder relationships must evolve during a crisis. Stakeholders, whether internal or external, may be the cause of a crisis or differentially impacted by it. The crisis may be imposed on an event or organization, or generated by it, affecting different stakeholders through the stages of crisis response and recovery.

Various theoretical models of stakeholder classification and strategies relate to the three key elements of stakeholder *salience:* legitimacy, power and urgency. These are often situation dependent and dynamic, requiring a flexible approach to stakeholder management during and after a crisis. Key questions arise from salience: who has the power and means to assist in crisis management and recovery, or to threaten us more? Where will support or resistance come from, and how can we manage those stakeholders? In a time of crisis some stakeholders can be become dangerous, better allies, or less relevant. Appropriate stakeholder management strategies may include being defensive, going on the attack, or implementing heightened monitoring and communications. Collaborative action becomes more important.

From an ethical perspective, it has to be recognized that crises are likely to make certain groups more vulnerable than others, and leaders have to determine how to help them. Many jobs were lost during the pandemic, and not all of them could be protected or will be reinstated in the future. Numerous businesses have failed. Who gains and who loses in a crisis might require urgent attention.

References

Antchak, V., Ziakas, V., & Getz, D. (2019). *Event Portfolio Management.* Oxford: Goodfellow.

Boonstra, A. (2006). Interpreting an ERP-implementation project from a stakeholder perspective. *International Journal of Project Management,* 24 (1), 38-52.

Carroll, A. (1993). *Business and Society: Ethics and Stakeholder Management,* 2nd. Edn. Cincinatti: Southwesterm.

Clarkson, M. (1995). A stakeholder framework for analyzing and evaluating corporations. *Academy of Management Review,* 20 (1), 92-118.

Freeman, R. (1984 [2010]). *Strategic Management: A Stakeholder Approach.* Cambridge University Press.

Getz, D. (2013). *Event Tourism.* N.Y.: Cognizant.

Lim, G., Ahn, H., & Lee, H. (2005). Formulating strategies for stakeholder management: A case-based reasoning approach. *Expert Systems With Applications,* 28, 831-849.

Lukens, M. (2016) The false choice between top-down and bottom-up leadership. www.fastcompany.com/3056551/the-false-choice-between-top-down-and-bottom-up-leadership. (accessed Nov. 25, 2020).

Mitchell, R., Agle, B., & Wood, D. (1997). Toward a theory of stakeholder identification and salience: Defining the principle of who and what really counts. *Academy of Management Review,* 22 (4), 853-886.

Savage, G., Nix, T., Whitehead, C., & Blair, J. (1991). Strategies for assessment and managing organizational stakeholders. *Academy of Management Executive,* 5 (2), 61-75.

Van Niekerk, M., & Getz, D. (2019). *Event Stakeholders.* Oxford: Goodfellow.

Winch, G. (2004). *Managing Construction Projects - An Information Processing Approach.* Blackwell Science.

Practice Insight 2:

Interview with Rebecca Cotter, M.A., CSEP, Manager, Communications Operations & Events, Corporate Communications & Community Engagement, City of Markham, Ontario, Canada

Q1: What have been the biggest impacts of the pandemic on municipal events?

A: Certainly the greatest impact of the pandemic has been the cancellation (or postponement) of hundreds of municipal events. The sheer absence of community festivals, concerts, fundraising events, etc., has had a significant economic and social impact on the well-being of communities and their residents, businesses and stakeholders. Some events have modified to virtual or alternative formats, to varying degrees of success. However, the underlying sentiment from communities and elected officials is that nothing replaces the spirit, connectivity and social benefits of in-person community events. The prospect that these events may not return for an extended period of time is starting to weigh heavily on both event organizers and local residents.

A municipal event organizer survey conducted by the Network of Municipal Event Planners (NMEP) in Ontario, Canada, in early-April 2020 revealed the following impacts:

☐ High level of event cancellation and postponements

☐ Limited number of events modifying to virtual format

☐ Reductions in grant dollars

☐ Reductions in sponsorships

☐ Reductions in cash revenue

☐ Reductions in economic impact

☐ Reductions in staff and volunteers

☐ Reductions in community partners, suppliers, vendors

Q2: What is being done for recovery and for greater resilience?

Municipalities for the most part are still focused on establishing their new operating model with regard to the ways and means through which events are planned and delivered. Meaning, some municipalities have cancelled all events indefinitely, laid off staff to improve the bottom line of the organization, and are not making any efforts at recovery or building resilience. The current focus seems to still be on operations, not long term strategy.

For those that have embarked on recovery efforts, these efforts largely involve implementing new public health and safety regulations, and creating or revising systems and structures for receiving, reviewing and approving event applications under federal, provincial and municipal restrictions.

Some larger municipalities have implemented event and festival support programs or financial aid funds in the early days of COVID to offset expenses already incurred for events that had to be cancelled. The City of Toronto brought in programs for embracing and supporting alternative format events. Webinars and re-opening guidance education programs are being developed to help event organizers understand and comply with COVID-related restrictions.

At this time [mid 2020] I am not aware of any broader, longer-term efforts to build greater resilience among individual festivals and events, or communities of event organizers.

Q3: Who are the main stakeholders in the recovery process, and what are their roles?

Stakeholders in the municipal event recovery process include:

Emergency Operating Committee (EOC)/Reopening Team

In response to the COVID-19 emergency orders, many Ontario municipalities activated established EOCs and/or pandemic response/reopening teams. These teams often consist of key staff within each organization that are responsible for guiding the municipality's business decisions and pandemic recovery.

EOCs are often responsible for guiding or approving the corporation's event recovery efforts and could be consulted for policies and frameworks to assist in their development.

Municipal Leadership Team

A municipality's executive leadership team may be comprised of individuals in various senior leadership positions within the organization, including Commissioners, Directors, and Managers. This team is typically responsible for guiding the strategic and operational deliverables of the organization.

In response to COVID-19, a municipality's executive leadership team is likely to be heavily involved in directing staff's recovery planning efforts. Maintaining appropriate communication with the organization's senior leadership may benefit event recovery by:

☐   Advocating for the development of common best-practices

☐   Developing and implementing effective hazard and risk management and safety measures

☐   Developing and implementing unified policies and procedures across the corporation

☐ Aligning staff efforts, tools and resources with EOC and/or pandemic response/reopening team standards

Special Event (Advisory) Team (SEAT/SET)

The planning and/or permitting of events in many municipalities follows a process that involves a team of event-affiliated subject matter experts (SMEs), referred to commonly as the municipality's Special Event (Advisory) Team, or SEAT/SET team. While the composition and function of municipal SEAT/SET teams vary by municipality, most often this group is comprised of municipal, regional and service agency members responsible for reviewing and/or approving outdoor event applications, in whole or in part.

Municipal event professionals with previously established SEAT/SET teams are encouraged to engage these SMEs in the development of local event recovery strategies. Municipal event professionals operating in jurisdictions without an established SEAT/SET team may wish to establish such a team as an outcome of the pandemic, in order to ensure all necessary SMEs are involved in the municipality's event recovery efforts.

The SEAT/SET team is responsible for reviewing and incorporating any new measures or requirements into the event application process, manuals or toolkits, as deemed appropriate by the municipality.

SEAT/SET teams typically include representatives from:

☐ Event services
☐ Building services
☐ By-law enforcement
☐ Communication services
☐ Cultural services
☐ Economic development
☐ Emergency medical services
☐ Fire and emergency services
☐ Health and safety
☐ Legal services
☐ Paramedic / first aid services
☐ Parks / facility operations
☐ Police services
☐ Public health
☐ Recreation services
☐ Risk management

- ☐ Road operations
- ☐ Transit services

Community event organizers

Municipal special events follow two delivery models:

1 'Direct Delivery' – whereby the community event is planned by a municipality's event office and/or municipal staff

2 'Third-party Delivery' – whereby the community event is planned by a third party event organizer who applies, obtains compliance and receives a permit for executing a community event on municipal property.

Third-party event organizers range from average residents and citizens who may or may not have any formal event planning training or experience, to professional event organizers working with organizations, agencies or production companies.

The number of direct-delivered and third-party events offered varies greatly across municipalities, however generally, a community is likely to have more third-party produced events than direct delivered events occur. As such, the role of third-party event organizers is very significant to the recovery of community events. The collaboration and commitment of these organizers will be critical to re-growing communities' vibrancy and animation through events, once it is safe and possible for large gatherings to resume.

However, building a recovery strategy that accommodates this stakeholder group is anticipated to be very challenging as the skills, abilities, capacity and experience of third-party event organizers varies greatly even under ideal circumstances. The added complexities of the pandemic's impact on event regulations and requirements will be very challenging for even the most skilled organizers with the greatest capacity for recovery and resilience, and may overwhelm those with less skill and capacity for compliance and change.

5 Events Employment: Crises' Impacts and Resolutions

Richard N.S. Robinson and Yawei Jiang

Introduction

The aim of this chapter is to consider employment in relation to the broader events industry and crisis. In doing so this contribution homes in on two substantial research gaps in the literature. The first, related to the intrinsic interdependency between the events industry and the tourism and hospitality industries (Getz & Page, 2016), is that there is a well-documented academic and policy-maker ambivalence towards workforce issues in the broader tourism, hospitality, and event industries relative to other topics in these domains (Baum et al., 2016; Liu, 2018; Muskat & Mair, 2020). The second gap is that although there is a rich literature related to tourism and events recovery from, and resilience to, crisis and disasters, their impacts on workforce, and the role they play in recovery is ill-understood (Ritchie & Jiang, 2019).

There is, however, also an interdependency between many of the entertainment, cultural and sporting industries and events (Getz, 1997). Almost without exception the global tourism (hospitality and events) and entertainment (cultural and arts) have been the hardest hit economically by the COVID-19 pandemic (Sigala, 2020). A focal point of this chapter, therefore, will be the consideration of not only direct event employment effects vis-a-vis crises but also the ripple effects on other workforces dependent on the 'soft infrastructure' that the event industry generates. In particular this chapter will:

♦ Demonstrate that workforce is a neglected area in events research relative to its importance;

♦ Outline what we know about event workforces and job creation (including multiplier effects);

♦ Reveal the impacts of crises on event workforces;

♦ Detail how organizational recovery strategies impact workforces when dealing with crises;

♦ Consider events employment-related recovery and resilience strategies.

Crises refer to institutional (organizational) responses or failures vis-à-vis disasters (Ritchie & Jiang, 2019). Disasters can be natural (e.g., flood, earthquake bushfire), human-induced (e.g., economic, terrorism or conflict) and epidemic events. Disasters can also be unfolding scenarios, for instance climate change, escalating nuclear armament tensions or rising inequality. In practice many of these are not discrete but interconnected – for example epidemic and economic disasters. As a case in point, the context for this chapter will be the impact of the COVID-19 pandemic on events, with a focus on Australasia, although in the first case study a crisis in late 2019 compounded the proceeding COVID-19 impacts. Nascent research suggests the impacts on tourism, hospitality and events workforces has been crippling – more than this, Baum, Mooney, Robinson and Solnet (2020) suggest COVID-19 (and by implication other crises) amplify existing workforce vulnerabilities and precarities (cf. Robinson et al., 2019). As such there are several imperatives for the consideration of the workforce impacts of crises on events, extending from the economic, social, political, and humanistic. These imperatives will unfold in this chapter thus. First the literature and background will be critically treated to generate a platform for the presentation of two Australasian case studies that bring the various surfaced perspectives to life. The chapter will conclude with the consideration of employment-related recovery and resilience strategies in both practical but also more abstracted dimensions.

Importance of event workforces

Events are operated on a temporary and project-based structure and are characterized by a high fluctuation of paid employees and volunteers (Muskat & Mair, 2020; Michopoulou, Azara, & Russell, 2020). Event workforces have their unique profiles (Abson, 2017; Kim & Cuskelly, 2017) which reflects in a highly heterogeneous workforce from a diverse nature of contract forms (e.g., long-term permanent employees, casual employees, volunteers, and external contractors) (Mair, 2009). The temporary and project-based structure also indicates a high speed/clear goal performance of event organizations, which rely on constant flu ctuations of employees during an event's operations period. This creates a series of workforce management problems to ensure business continuity (Clark et al., 2017; Van der Wagen & White, 2015), especially for small- to medium-size event organizations (SME) with a large number of part-time temporary workers (Michopoulou et al., 2020). For example, the difficulty around ongoing recruitment, employee retention (Muskat & Mair, 2020), storage of knowledge (Stadler, Fullagar, & Reid, 2014) and logistics of employee planning (Van der Wagen, 2007).

In the current uncertain global environment affected by natural disasters and health crises (e.g., COVID-19), event organizations are facing more challenging issues to adapt their strategic planning to achieve resilience. Crises and disasters can disrupt workforce availability and mobility and can create negative psychological effects to vulnerable populations (Santos et al., 2020). Therefore, workforce training is emphasized as one of the key dimensions in determining the ability of organizations to absorb or mitigate negative impacts (Nyaupane et al., 2020) or to reduce business interruption losses by maintaining functionality and productivity (Santos et al., 2014). However, despite the clear recognition of the heterogenous nature of event teams, existing literature largely focuses on volunteer understanding (e.g., Blackman, Benson, & Dickson, 2017; Kim, Fredline, & Cuskelly, 2018) with a neglect of paid part-time workers (Muskat & Mair, 2020). Event workforce strategies are under-researched in the context of events, specifically on increasing employee retention, improving upskilling, creating long-term positions (Baum et al., 2009; Michopoulou & Melpignano, 2019), and mitigating disruptions to achieve crisis/disaster-related resilience (Nyaupane et al., 2020).

Furthermore, event employment or workforce issues reside in what Muskat and Mair (2021) ascribe as 'inward' perspectives on events research, which include the machinations of organizational, managerial, and human resource matters. Among these 'inward' attributes, industry leaders need more creative strategies to attract and sustain quality workforces. However, the ability of event organizations to recognize the needs of its labor shortage and provide sufficient career development and training opportunities is relatively limited (McCabe, 2012). No specific research is available in discussing quality workforce in the event context. Although Getz and Robinson (2014; Robinson & Getz, 2016; Robinson, Getz, & Dolnicar, 2018) have argued that in some niche event areas there is preponderance of demand-side research in comparison to supply-side, employment issues in the event industry remain neglected.

Event workforce effects and management

Events provide substantial opportunities to create employment, develop new skills, accelerate short-term economic needs, and alleviate long term poverty (Maguire & Hanrahan, 2017). Many countries have leveraged events as an opportunity to build skill legacy and to enhance long-term employment for local people (Jago et al., 2010), and develop event education programs to provide a pipeline of skilled workers (cf. Robinson, Barron, & Solnet, 2008). Moreover, events can generate a large need for labor during events planning and preparation phases, such as construction of event-related infrastructure, maintenance of grounds and facilities, and security planning (Mills & Rosentraub, 2013). Furthermore, events can bring short-term employment effects in other sectors such as retail trade, accommodation and food services, arts, and entertainment (Feddersen & Maennig, 2013). The investment of public projects (e.g., transportation system upgrade, travel infrastructure renewal) can create other economic development opportunities and generate more new jobs (Mills & Rosentraub, 2013). In the longer term, skills from recruited external experts can be transferred to the local laboring market by skills training or apprenticeship type programs. This is an important positive effect the events industry brings to other economics, especially for poor countries where capacity building or skills development are lacking in the service delivery area (Jago et al., 2010).

Event workforce management is a wide-ranging activity that reflects the long-term strategic development of the event organization (Van der Wagen, 2007). A successful workforce management should help organizations to attain positive culture of commitment and cooperation development as the key outcomes. Key strategic approaches for workforce planning include the analysis of labor markets, analysis of skills requirements, and employee monitoring at multiple event phases (e.g., planning before the event and operation/deliver during the event) (Hanlon & Cuskelly, 2002). However, there is a lack of discussion of event workforce management in a crisis and disaster environment. For example, the current COVID-19 pandemic has created great financial stress on event operations. Choi (2020) reports that until the relaxation on social gathering rules, 87% of events have been cancelled or postpone, according to a survey of events' professionals in the US. Concomitantly, 90%of event businesses have reduced salaries and 58% have been forced into making redundancies (Choi, 2020). Company team culture has been negatively impacted due to mental health and communication issues (Levinson, 2020). A deeper investigation is needed to understand the impacts of these crises on event workforce management and how event workforce can implement successful and effective responses.

Impacts of crises on event workforce

The event industry is one of the most risky and uncertain industries as it comprises a complexity of activities, arrangements, and operational processes (Boyle & Haggerty, 2012). While events' economic and socio-cultural impacts have been widely studied in the literature, there has been limited research discussing the crisis impacts on the event industry, especially the event workforce. A growing number of studies have explored the COVID-19 impacts on hospitality and tourism workforce (e.g., Baum et al., 2020; Sönmez et al., 2020); while limited attention has been given to event workforce that is based on a temporary and project-based structure (Muskat & Mair, 2020). The tourism and hospitality industry has experienced workforce shocks during the pandemic, which not only trigger financial pressure to many individuals (Sönmez et al., 2020), but also exert significant stress on people's mental health and safety (Hsieh et al., 2013).

Lee and Goldblatt (2001) first investigated the impacts of the 2001 economic recession on the event industry, which included the decrease of event numbers, increased competition for small companies, and job losses. These have necessitated the event industry to identify niche markets and provide more personalized services to increase their competitive advantages. They also studied the global financial crisis's (2007-2009) impact on events and found a significant profit margin decrease, reduced sponsorship funding, and other revenue sources losses (Lee & Goldblatt, 2012). The COVID-19 pandemic has increased events' uncertainty levels due to social gathering restrictions (Parnell et al., 2020). Financial uncertainty is the single greatest challenge for event operators without a clear date to reschedule and resume operations (Ludvigsen & Hayton, 2020). This could trigger a series of subsequent effects on ceasing current labor contracts, venue cancellation, and activity rearrangement, talent and show procurement, event promotion etc.

Event workforce response to crises

Event organizers need to identify suitable strategies to respond to crises and prepare for the future. Lee and Goldblatt (2012) found four strategies post-crisis to maintain events operation. First, increased marketing efforts could help reduce financial exposure following a recession. Event operators should consider the 'new' needs and wants of customers and customize their business practices in the future. Second, the increased use of technology (e.g., social media, AI) in event marketing would be a new trend. Consistent and reliable information sharing is important to protect workforce and maintain customer relationships (Anderson, 2006) by adopting post-crisis stress reduction strategies such as peer interaction (Heath, 1998). Importantly, the use of technology can be further expanded to event operations (i.e., virtual events and festivals) in the COVID-19 environment to ensure the safety of employees and customers (Sigala, 2020). Third, securing sponsorship relationships and diversifying new revenue sources are important to mitigate financial pressure following a recession or other types of crises. Fourth, seeking out strong political support for events and festivals can be also critical for event organizers to remain sustainable.

In responding to the COVID-19 pandemic impacts, volunteer and security management are essential considerations for events and festivals stakeholders (Ludvigsen & Hayton, 2020). Event organizers rely on large numbers of volunteers to deliver service at all levels (Hoye et al., 2020), and thus can take on security-related tasks and duties in crowd control (Giulianotti & Klauser, 2010) to assist the social distancing rules. This requires a new training process to enable their acquisition of desirable skills. To cope with variations in demand in a crisis environment, event organizations could also use more casualized workforce to increase workforce flexibility (Anderson, 2006). Furthermore, the event industry needs to implement effective safety protocols, including measures to disinfect venue seats and public spaces after each use to prevent potential risk of virus transmission (Sönmez et al., 2020). More importantly in the long-term, event organizers need to re-design outdoor/indoor experiences to cater for smaller groups of customers (Sigala, 2020). It should comply with social distancing and gathering restrictions but without comprising the quality of experience for customers. They need to also integrate new technologies into their experience design, such as the robotic automation and AI to enable no-touch service delivery (Agrawal et al., 2020). Workforce reskilling and upskilling would become important in a post-pandemic era for new business models.

Case Study #1

Tough times call for empathic communication and community goodwill

Ramping up to becoming a NZ$1 billion/year operation, two crises befell Auckland's multi-purpose precinct, SkyCity Entertainment Group, in the space of a few months. Incorporating an international convention center drawing on the facilities of a casino, two hotels totaling 635 rooms (with another property nearing completion), multiple food and beverage outlets, a theater, and other public spaces, SkyCity is a jewel in Auckland's and New Zealand's, event and tourism landscape. Crowning the complex, Sky Tower alone attracts half a million visitors annually. In October 2019, a fire tore through the roof of the 'under construction' convention center. Due to the extensive structural and smoke damage and a black sooty pall that hung above Auckland's CBD, the executive took the tough decision to close for two days (three nights) rather than place the public, and just as importantly their employees, at any risk. Over the following three weeks SkyCity resumed trading but at a reduced scale, meaning many of their 3,500 strong full-time equivalent workforce was temporarily stood down. As labor costs represented nearly 40% of revenues for SkyCity, affirmative action was required.

In what became a dress rehearsal for responding to the imminent COVID-19 pandemic impacts, senior management worked diligently to minimize the crisis' impacts on their valued employees. Furloughed staff eligible for annual leave and other entitlements had this buffer enacted. *"Our primary concern was for the wellbeing of our staff and the community"*, related Colin McClean, General Manager of Hotel Operations. Communication became the fulcrum of their response. It was clear there would be job losses – the key was to reduce the impacts on individuals and the community. Over several weeks, communications, via email, text, and one-on-one and group Skype calls, occurred as often as every six hours each day. The messaging was empathetic, but a deliberate attempt was made not to sugar-coat the situation. Messaging was honest, and ultimately this built trust and loyalty. As a result, job losses were low, mainly through vacancy non-replacement, and business returned strongly through November and December of 2019. Many contingent staff returned to work, with any potential disaffection assuaged by the regular but frank communications. Gaming, then as into 2021, was the mainstay of Sky-City's recovery, accounting for over 50% of the venue's revenue.

Figure 5.1: SkyCity Convention Center Roof Fire and Sky Tower.
Source: https://pxhere.com/en/photo/1599680; Permissions: CC0/PD

Ironically, it was a slow decline in casino revenues, amongst a predominantly Asian-heritage patronage, that signaled an even greater disruption than the fire was afoot. Event and accommodation cancelations increased apace until March 2020 when the pandemic had reached New Zealand's shores and the government enforced lockdowns. All events were cancelled, and facilities closed. By April 2020, SkyCity was reporting monthly receipt losses of NZ$90 million. The New Zealand government wage subsidy enabled SkyCity to keep on many permanent staff, covering 80% of salaries, which the business was able to top-up. As elsewhere, contingently employed workers were not eligible. Mediation processes involved unions. Unite Union, representing most of the convention, casino and hospitality staff, was key to working collaboratively with SkyCity to enact objective measures in the 'right-sizing' process, including the 'last in first out' redundancy policy. So the communications, fine-tuned during the fire crisis, kicked in again, as the marketing personnel pivoted from an outward commercial to internal and community engagement strategy. Positive language framed decision making – for example, the staff-shedding process normally labelled 'down-sizing' was referred to as 'right-sizing'. Executives involved in the inevitable and difficult process of 'right-sizing' were not unaffected. They experienced grief at the plight of their former worker colleagues and were hurt by the inevitable media coverage that provided platforms for disaffected retrenched staff. *"It was like survivor syndrome"*, recalled Mr McClean. On the other hand, many employees were gracious in departure, appreciating SkyCity's incapacity to keep going but also their empathetic approach – and took to social media to express these sentiments.

Recovery has been slow but steady, driven by pent-up domestic demand particularly in the gaming portfolio. The events and hospitality side of the business, however, remains slow, and in those services resides most of the demand for labor. The theater remains closed. Nonetheless, rehiring commenced as lockdowns eased in mid-2020, prioritizing those staff who were retrenched. *"It's a win-win"*, said McClean, *"we are repaying their loyalty and atoning for the difficulties they and the community faced – but our former staff are already skilled up, know our business and are job-ready"*. In the meantime, reconstruction of the convention center recommenced in mid-2020 – creating jobs in construction, a sector often targeted by policymakers to reinvigorate economies. Alike events and tourism operators globally, SkyCity is waiting for international borders to reopen in a post-COVID-19 world, so they can welcome visitors and their employees back in equal measure.

With appreciation to Mr Colin McClean, General Manager of Hotel Operations, for his valued time and candid insights https://skycityauckland.co.nz/

Case Study #2

Performing arts organization creates employment amid COVID-19 disruption

Approaching five years of managing and representing performing artists, Cluster Arts was set to have its breakthrough year in 2020. Founded by experienced arts sector professional, Deb Wilks, Cluster Arts, based in Brisbane, Queensland, Australia, is a genuine SME, and provides 'backend' services to performing artists and specializes in representing bespoke circus troupes. Artist services include procurement of performances, or gigs (usually extended season tours), and managing their contractual, administrative, operational, compliance and developing business strategies. Additionally, Cluster Arts project manages events and festivals, or parts thereof. Increasingly, their footprint extended internationally as they managed or auspiced

Australian artists on the signature and 'fringe' festival circuit in the US and Canada, UK, mainland Europe, South Korea, and China.

Pre-COVID-19, Cluster Arts employed three people, Deb Wilks and her Executive Producer, Kate Malone, full-time, and a part-time Operations Manager – or 2.5 full-time equivalent (FTE) staff. Indirectly, via the circus troupes they represented, Cluster Arts created and sustained employment for nearly 40 performing artists. Their forecasts for 2020 projected (AUS)$500,000 in revenue. Grant acquisition was a significant but diminishing part of their portfolio, as the business sought greater independence.

Cluster Arts staff were with performers touring in China as COVID-19 broke. Over the coming months the international circuit collapsed and in February 2020 the Australian Government announced domestic lockdowns. The immediate impact of the pandemic was swift and devastating. Future business dried up and Cluster Arts was saddled with legacies – financial and administrative. For example, performers they represented were stranded overseas. Their revised budget reforecast earnings downwards by two-thirds – much of this income was derived in the early months of 2020.

In late March, the Australian Government announced the JobKeeper scheme, designed to enable employers to retain staff on reduced, but government subsidized income. While other players in the performing arts sector claimed JobKeeper for their staff but adopted a passive market positioning, Cluster Arts adopted a proactive strategy. In fact, by the close of 2020 Cluster Arts had doubled its staffing and nearly doubled the number of circus troupes they represented. How did they achieve these employment outcomes at a time when the arts and entertainment industry had been savaged globally by the impacts of the COVID-19 pandemic?

An immediate response was for Cluster Arts to reach out to all its constituents, in particular the performing artists they represented. As Deb Wilks stated, *"without the artists we would not have a job"*. Cluster Arts considered the artists as their clients and attended to their wellbeing; physical, emotional, and financial. Cluster Arts open plan office became a drop-in center for artists to meet and even train. JobKeeper applications were prepared on behalf of eligible artists, and ultimately 50% of their artists secured the safety net – and Cluster Arts even offered cash to artists who were in dire straits. Ensuring Cluster Arts had healthy relationships, trust and goodwill with their representative performers and advocating for them was key to retaining them as clients for when opportunities emerged.

Figure 5.2: Cluster Arts' Online International Circus Pitching program. Source: Cluster Arts; Permissions: Ms Deb Wilks, Executive Director.

Like many performing artists Cluster Arts experimented with virtual performances but quickly abandoned this strategy as the value proposition for all stakeholders, including audiences, was poor. Instead, Cluster Arts embarked on an engagement and outreach program. A positive affordance of the lockdown was extra time! As Deb Wilks quipped, *"the pandemic allowed us to work on our business rather than in our business"*. Cluster Arts used this time to network at the highest levels, government and corporate, to seek out opportunities – after all festival directors would be looking closer to home for performers as international travel became an impossibility. The hibernation of Circus Oz proved a boom. As the regional festival circuit picked up Cluster Arts became a go-to agency, especially as Queensland remained relatively unscathed but closed its borders to the southern states who were experiencing higher rates of community infection. Cluster Arts launched an online pitching program for international producers. They received 30 applications from Australian companies for six places and worked with successful candidates to prepare their international 'pitches' for strategically selected international presenters. Subsequently, several performers have signed up with Cluster Arts as their management company!

Cluster Arts 'front-foot' response to the impacts of the COVID-19 pandemic have reaped real and potential business and employment growth. Cluster Arts created several positions, supported by JobKeeper, to bring in-house services they previously contracted out. These include a producer, a marketer, and a bookkeeper, bringing the organizational FTE staff to nearly five. With opportunities created in the domestic market via networking and competitors falling by the wayside, Cluster Arts have provided gigs and tours for several of the troupes. And via its innovative outreach Cluster Arts have also grown the number of performer groups they represent from 9 to 15 – creating competitive advantage and further employment when international travel and the festival circuit relaunches.

With thanks to owner, Deb Wilks, for reflectively and openly sharing proprietary information https://www.clusterarts.com/

Discussion and conclusions

In the consideration of crises and their employment-related impacts in this chapter, it is apparent there is an urgent need for more and new knowledge. COVID-19 has been unprecedented in its impacts on the events and allied industries in the modern age, given that the affordances of the airline travel boom since the mid-twentieth century have transformed these sectors into multi-billion concerns employing millions of people (WTTC, 2020) even if many contingently. With travel curtailed, both international and domestically, event demand diminished. Social distancing regimes, implemented by most jurisdictions, deemed even the smallest events impossible. While technology has facilitated virtual events for some sectors (Sigala, 2020), in our case studies, virtual space was either inappropriate or uncommercial. As gatherings became periodically permitted, a focus on creating events for local markets became the focus. Even at this limited scale events organizations had to have recovery and resilience strategies in place to ensure they were 'geared to go' including being staffed with the requisite workforce.

The case studies both highlight government proactivity to massive workforce disruptions, albeit typically less dramatically disruptive than COVID-19. In Australia and New Zealand, as in many developing nations, active labor market policies (cf. Solnet et al., 2014) are a common cyclical intervention for attraction, retention, and regional workforce responses. This allowed businesses to retain a standing workforce for recovery, even if revenues almost entirely dried up. In parallel, although the events and allied tourism and hospitality industries are notoriously unrepresented in advocacy bodies for employees and stakeholders (cf. Robinson & Brenner, 2020), unions and peak industry bodies became key to negotiating for labor rights and lobbying governments to ease community and travel restrictions when appropriate. Bucking a trend in developed nations for organizations to resist collectivism, the SkyCity case demonstrated the benefits of embracing Union-facilitated negotiations to achieve transparent and fair processes – even if that meant redundancies in worst case scenarios.

As the literature alludes to, indirectly the event industry can have positive impacts on other sectors and the broader economy. Venues that support auxiliary tourism products and hospitality services (Feddersen & Maennig, 2013), like SkyCity, generate large-scale employment – and even though event recovery was slow these augmented services allowed for the retention or deployment of some staff. In terms of infrastructure and capacity building, so long as finance is available, capital can be invested into overdue renovations or new-builds (Mills & Rosentraub, 2013), creating extra-demand – and so invigorated employment opportunities – as markets normalize.

Drilling down to the firm and individual level, some themes from the literature resonate. Training and development are strategies to engage and motivate employees during downturns in business (Nyaupane et al., 2020). Micro-credentialling has become a go-to product to keep staff engaged while concomitantly up-skilling especially in the occupational and guest health, hygiene and safety regimes that will likely interface with normal services in the job descriptions of events employees (Sigala, 2020; Sönmez et al., 2020). Beyond this, investment in training, whether by employer or employee, constitutes professional development and can free up 'headspace' and stimulate creativity and innovation, as evident in the Cluster Arts case study.

In both case studies communication with employees/contractors was a key strategy in responding to the crises' impacts, particularly recognizing that individual and community wellbeing (Levinson, 2020) were key sensibilities. This is important because, as the literature confirms, event workforces, whether renumerated or volunteers, are often contingently engaged (Muskat & Mair, 2020; Michopoulou et al., 2020). Rather than treating them as disposable, the cases speak to communications strategies that acknowledged, dignified, and respected their workforces – not a universal tourism, hospitality, and event industry affordance (Higgins-Desbiolles, 2020b). Multiple media were harnessed in communications strategies to ensure cut-through, consistency and 'care' (cf. Anderson, 2006). It was clear that resilience, harnessing from the learnings of prior crises, was mobilized to more effectively navigate the challenges that the COVID-19 pandemic impacts conjured up. Our cases hint at the impact of crises on management left with tough decisions, who often become the targets of criticism. Their burden can be heavy and bring guilt – and responsibility to try to turn things around and bring back their employees more quickly. Employees who 'survive the cut' equally might feel uncomfortable, especially if they live and socialize in the same communities.

A paucity of literature prevents a comprehensive discussion of employment strategies related to crises. Nonetheless, the case studies highlight a number of practical strategies related to past learnings; clear consistent, regular and honest yet empathetic communications; harnessing technology and the reach of social media, a concern for individual and community wellbeing, collaboration with representative bodies to mitigate risks, negotiate fair settlements and normalize business, and accepting and leveraging from active labor market policies like wage subsidies (Solnet et al., 2014). Critically, event recovery, at least apparent from these case studies, is contingent on organizations being hopeful and proactive. Both the cases presented in this chapter demonstrated capacity building through investment in infrastructure, human capital, and organizational capabilities such that their organizations are well-positioned to be competitive and resilient for the inevitable turnarounds. After all, events and allied industries have historically demonstrated remarkable resilience and recovery from crises (Ritchie & Jiang, 2019).

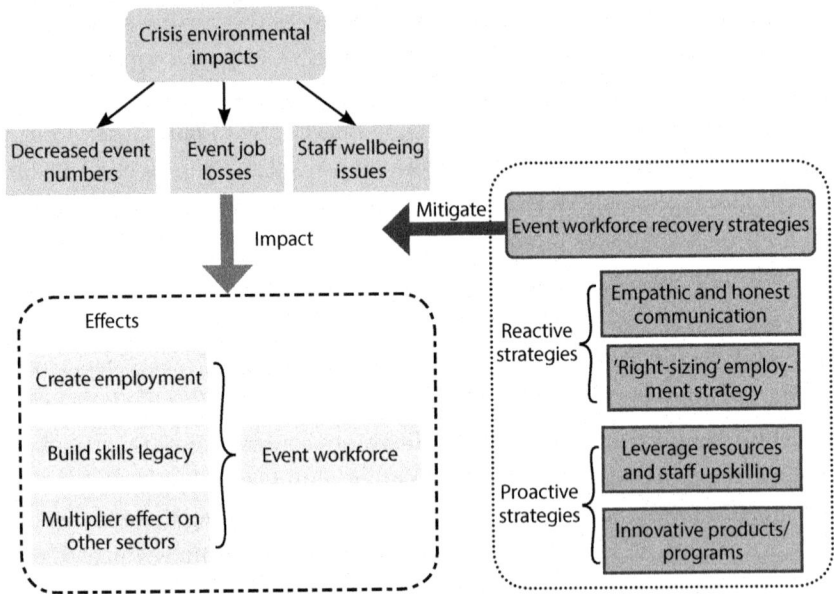

Figure 5.3: Event workforce crisis impact and resolution framework

In summary, this chapter has achieved its objectives in several ways. First, despite the fact that event workforces are unique and vulnerable in facing turbulent environments (e.g., crises and disaster), relevant research is still neglected in discussing how event workforces can be impacted by a disruptive crisis and what recovery and resilience strategies events organizations can generate to deal with employment-related issues. Following on, this chapter outlined several events workforce effects in creating employment, building skill legacies, and accelerating short-term economic needs, i.e., multiplier effects on other sectors such as retail, accommodation and food services, arts and entertainment. By using two case studies, on SkyCity and Cluster Arts, in a COVID-19 environment, this chapter has revealed key impacts of crises on event workforces including the decrease of event numbers, job losses, staff wellbeing issues, and financial challenges. Key crisis response strategies (e.g., regular communication using empathetic and honest messages) have been adopted to assuage negative emotions and ensure a smooth post-crisis staff return. For smaller event organizations, more proactive recovery and resilience strategies have been used to leverage the resource opportunities from external agencies to foster business model restructuring and innovative products. These have helped to expand their business operations and even employment growth. Figure 5.3 captures these key learnings from this chapter.

Future research

As others have noted, events employment is a relatively neglected field (Muskat & Mair, 2020). Equally, the employment-related impacts of crises are poorly understood (Ritchie & Jiang, 2019). Rich opportunities for research beckon. Given that event workforces are highly contingent, transient, and often-times low-skilled can create precarities. From an employer's perspective crises can impart sudden and dramatic impacts on operations – sometimes, as in the case of the case studies – complete shutdowns. Whole communities share the impacts. The state is not always able to step into the breach, although during COVID-19 governments did provide welfare safety nets in many developed countries. Given the complexities involved networked and system approaches to understanding events, employment and crises are likely to result in more holistic understandings. The search for 'solutions' is likely a futile exercise – conceptually or practically. More likely is a resolutions approach – whereby affected stakeholders negotiate crisis risk and resilience strategies that collectively mitigate impacts and mutually position each in good stead for recovery. Moreover, the two case studies presented in this chapter mostly consider employees as victims of crises befalling events organizations. Clearly, employees can also be agents of emergency responses to crisis on behalf of organizations, in the ways in which hotel staff might shield guests from harm (cf. Deshpandé & Raina, 2011).

Specifically, in a crisis/disaster environment where individual well-being faces tremendous challenges, more attention is needed for the psychological capital of events companies. How business owners, managers, and front-line employees can effectively cope with disturbances through their psychological capital are becoming critical to address sustainability issues for the events industry. Typical psychological capital – self-efficacy, hope, optimism, and resilience – have been found to impact organizational resilience through problem-based and emotion-based coping strategies post-disaster (Fang, Prayag, Ozanne, & de Vries, 2020). Future research should further navigate employees' emotional changes and different individual coping strategies during the recovery process following major crises and disasters. Unique event workforce attributes (e.g., part-time temporary or voluntary arrangements) can be compared to provide different insights.

To return to employees themselves, greater consideration is required of their plight as crises on the one hand demand more from them but also leave them so vulnerable to unemployment. Unlike other industries, their normal levels of compensation are not such that they can voluntarily 'rest-up' between gigs. Furthermore, volunteers represent a key events workforce (Baum & Lockstone, 2007) not explored in this chapter. A key limitation of this chapter is that sustainability issues as arising from the COVID-19 crisis have not been considered (Higgins-Desbiolles, 2020a) – key in relation to the social dimension which includes employment. Critical approaches will be required to work towards equitable strategies, especially for marginalized cohorts that disproportionately bear the brunt of crises (cf. Baum et al., 2020). Events, it is said, is a people industry – reflections going forward should ensure that definition is as inclusive of employees as of visitors and attendees.

References

Abson, E. (2017). How event managers lead: Applying competency school theory to event management. *Event Management, 21*(4), 403–419.

Agrawal, S., De Smet, A., Lacroix, S., & Reich, A. (2020). To emerge stronger from the COVID-19 crisis, companies should start reskilling their workforces now. McKinsey & Company.

Anderson, B. A. (2006). Crisis management in the Australian tourism industry: Preparedness, personnel and postscript. *Tourism Management, 27*(6), 1290-1297.

Baum, T., & Lockstone, L. (2007). Volunteers and mega sporting events: developing a research framework. *International Journal of Event Management Research, 3*(1), 29-41.

Baum, T., Deery, M., & Hanlon, C. (Eds.). (2009). *People and Work in Events and Conventions: A research perspective.* CABI.

Baum, T., Kralj, A., Robinson, R. N. S., & Solnet, D. J. (2016). Tourism workforce research: A review, taxonomy and agenda. *Annals of Tourism Research, 60,* 1-22.

Baum, T., Mooney, S. K. K., Robinson, R. N. S., & Solnet, D. (2020). COVID-19's impact on the hospitality workforce – new crisis or amplification of the norm? *International Journal of Contemporary Ho spitality Management, 32*(9), 2813-2829.

Blackman, D., Benson, A. M., & Dickson, T. J. (2017). Enabling event volunteer legacies: A knowledge management perspective. *Event Management, 21*(3), 233-250.

Boyle, P., & Haggerty, K. D. (2012). Planning for the worst: Risk, uncertainty and the Olympic Games. *British Journal of Sociology, 63*(2), 241–259.

Choi, K. (2020). *What will happen to the events industry after coronavirus?* https://www.plugandplaytechcenter.com/resources/what-will-happen-events-industry-after-coronavirus/ (Accessed 5 Nov 2020).

Clark, H., Dimanche, F., Cotter, R., & Lee-Rosen, D. (2017). Human capital challenges in the events industry of Canada: finding innovative solutions. *Worldwide Hospitality and Tourism Themes, 9*(4), 424–432.

Deshpandé, R., & Raina, A. (2011). The ordinary heroes of the Taj. *Harvard Business Review, 89*(12), 119-123.

Fang, S., Prayag, G., Ozanne, L.K., & de Vries, H. (2020). Psychological capital, coping mechanisms and organizational resilience: Insights from the 2016 Kaikoura earthquake, New Zealand. *Tourism Management Perspectives, 34*, 100637.

Feddersen, A., & Maennig, W. (2013). Mega-events and sectoral employment: The case of the 1996 Olympic Games. *Contemporary Economic Policy, 31*(3), 580-603.

Getz, D. (1997). *Event Management & Event Tourism*. Cognizant Communication Corp.

Getz, D., & Page, S. J. (2016). *Event Studies: Theory, research, and policy for planned events*. Routledge.

Getz, D., & Robinson, R. N. (2014). Foodies and food events. *Scandinavian Journal of Hospitality and Tourism, 14*(3), 315-330.

Giulianotti, R., & Klauser, F. (2010). Security governance and sport mega-events: Toward an interdisciplinary research agenda. *Journal of Sport and Social Issues, 34*(1), 48–60.

Hanlon, C. & Cuskelly, G. (2002). Pulsating major sport event organizations: a framework for inducting managerial personnel. *Event Management, 7*, 231–43.

Heath, R. L. (1998). *Crisis Management for Managers and Executives: Business crises, the definitive handbook to reduction, readiness, response, and recovery*. Financial Times/Pitman Pub.

Higgins-Desbiolles, F. (2020a). The 'war over tourism': challenges to sustainable tourism in the tourism academy after COVID-19. *Journal of Sustainable Tourism*, doi.org/10.1080/09669582.2020.1803334

Higgins-Desbiolles, F. (2020b). Socialising tourism for social and ecological justice after COVID-19. *Tourism Geographies, 22*(3), 610-623.

Hoye, R., Cuskelly, G., Auld, C., Kappelides, P., & Misener, K. (2020). *Sport Volunteering*. Routledge.

Hsieh, Y., Apostolopoulos, Y., & Sönmez, S. (2013). World at work: Hotel cleaners. *Occupational and Environmental Medicine, 70*(5), 360–364.

Jago, L., Dwyer, L., Lipman, G., van Lill, D., & Vorster, S. (2010). Optimising the potential of mega-events: an overview. *International Journal of Event and Festival Management, 1*(3), 220-237.

Kim, E., & Cuskelly, G. (2017). A systematic quantitative review of volunteer management in events. *Event Management, 21*(1), 83–100.

Kim, E., Fredline, L., & Cuskelly, G. (2018). Heterogeneity of sport event volunteer motivations: A segmentation approach. *Tourism Management, 68*, 375-386.

Lee, S., & Goldblatt, J. (2001), *An exploratory study of the potential impacts from changes in the US economy in the event management industry,* unpublished thesis, George Washington University, Washington, DC.

Lee, S., & Goldblatt, J. (2012). The current and future impacts of the 2007-2009 economic recession on the festival and event industry. *International Journal of Event and Festival Management, 3*(2), 137-148.

Levinson, B. (2020). *New survey reveals impact of COVID-19 on events industry.* Spicenews. https://www.spicenews.com.au/industry-news/new-report-reveals-impact-of-covid-19-on-events-industry/ (Accessed 5 Nov 2020).

Liu, C. H. S. (2018). Examining social capital, organizational learning and knowledge transfer in cultural and creative industries of practice. *Tourism Management, 64,* 258–270.

Ludvigsen, J.A.L, & Hayton, J.W. (2020). Toward COVID-19 secure events: considerations for organizing the safe resumption of major sporting events. *Managing Sport and Leisure,* 1-11.

Maguire, K., & Hanrahan, J. (2017). Assessing the economic impact of event management in Ireland: A local authority planning perspective. *Event Management, 21*(3), 333-346.

Mair, J. (2009). The events industry: The employment context. In T. Baum, M. Deery, C. Hanlon, L. Lockstone, & K. Smith (Eds.), *People and Work in Events and Conventions: A research perspective.* Wallingford, UK: CABI.

McCabe, V. S. (2012). Developing and sustaining a quality workforce: lessons from the convention and exhibition industry. *Journal of Convention & Event Tourism, 13*(2), 121-134.

Michopoulou, E, Azara, I, & Russell, A. (2020). Investigating the triangular relationship between temporary event workforce, event employment businesses and event organisers. *International Journal of Contemporary Hospitality Management, 32*(3), 1247–1273.

Michopoulou, E. E., & Melpignano, C. (2019). Challenges in managing peripheral workers within diverse environments. *Event Management, 23*(4), 527-539.

Mills, B. M., & Rosentraub, M. S. (2013). Hosting mega-events: A guide to the evaluation of development effects in integrated metropolitan regions. *Tourism Management, 34,* 238-246.

Muskat, B., & Mair, J. (2020). Knowledge sharing and power in the event workforce. *Event Management, 24*(5), 597-609.

Muskat, B., & Mair, J. (2021). Managing the event workforce: Analysing the heterogeneity of job experiences. In V.V. Cuffy, F.E. Bakas & W.J.L. Coetzee (Eds.), *Events Tourism: Critical Insights and Contemporary Perspectives.* London: Routledge, (Chapter 3)

Nyaupane, G. P., Prayag, G., Godwyll, J., & White, D. (2020). Toward a resilient organization: analysis of employee skills and organization adaptive traits. *Journal of Sustainable Tourism,* 1-20.

Parnell, D., Widdop, P., Bond, A., & Wilson, R. (2020). COVID-19, networks and sport. *Managing Sport and Leisure,* 1–7.

Ritchie, B. W., & Jiang, Y. (2019). A review of research on tourism risk, crisis, and disaster management: Launching the annals of tourism research curated collection on tourism risk, crisis and disaster management. *Annals of Tourism Research, 79*, 102812.

Robinson, R. N. S., & Brenner, M. L. (2020). Wage theft in professional kitchens: Conned or complicit? *Hospitality & Society, 10*(4).

Robinson, R. N. S., Barron, P., & Solnet, D. (2008). Innovative approaches to event management education in career development: A study of student experiences. *Journal of Hospitality, Leisure, Sports and Tourism Education, 7*(1), 4.

Robinson, R.N., & Getz D. (2016). Food enthusiasts and tourism: Exploring food involvement dimensions. *Journal of Hospitality & Tourism Research, 40*(4), 432-455.

Robinson, R. N. S., Getz, D., & Dolnicar, S. (2018). Food tourism subsegments: A data-driven analysis. *International Journal of Tourism Research, 20*(3), 367-377.

Robinson, R. N. S., Martins, A., Solnet, D., & Baum, T. (2019). Sustaining precarity: critically examining tourism and employment. *Journal of Sustainable Tourism, 27*(7), 1008-1025.

Santos, J. R., Herrera, L., Yu, K. D., Pagsuyoin, S. A. , & Tan, R.R. (2014). State of the art in risk analysis of workforce criticality influencing disaster preparedness for interdependent systems. *Risk Analysis, 34*(6), 1056-1068.

Santos, J., Yip, C., Thekdi, S., & Pagsuyoin, S. (2020). Workforce/population, Economy, Infrastructure, Geography, Hierarchy, and Time (WEIGHT): Reflections on the plural dimensions of disaster resilience. *Risk Analysis, 40*(1), 43-67.

Sigala, M. (2020). Tourism and COVID-19: Impacts and implications for advancing and resetting industry and research. *Journal of Business Research, 117*, 312-321.

Solnet, D., Nickson, D., Robinson, R. N. S., Kralj, A., & Baum, T. (2014). Discourse about workforce development in tourism—An analysis of public policy, planning, and implementation in Australia and Scotland: Hot air or making a difference? *Tourism Analysis, 19*(5), 609-623.

Sönmez, S., Apostolopoulos, Y., Lemke, M. K., & Hsieh, Y.-C. (2020). Understanding the effects of COVID-19 on the health and safety of immigrant hospitality workers in the United States. *Tourism Management Perspectives, 35*.

Stadler, R., Fullagar, S., & Reid, S. (2014). The professionalization of festival organizations: A relational approach to knowledge management. *Event Management, 18*(1), 39–52.

Van der Wagen, L. (2007). *Human Resource Management for Events: Managing the event workforce*. Routledge.

Van der Wagen, L. & White, L. (2015), *Human Resource Management for the Event Industry*, 2nd ed., Oxford: Taylor and Francis.

WTTC. (2020). To recovery & beyond: The future of travel and tourism in the wake of COVID-19. https://wttc.org/Research/To-Recovery-Beyond (Accessed 12 January, 2021).

Practice Insight 3:

Interview with Vern Biaett (consultant, expert witness, retired Event Management Professor, and long-time event manager and volunteer)

Q1 – In your experience what have been the most important aspects of the current pandemic on the event sector?

First, I would say a deeper realization that there is a lack comprehensive leadership across the festival and events 'industry'. Trying to get event professionals on the same page is similar to herding cats. With a diversity of independent professional associations, a disconnect between working professionals and academics, and everything spread across public, non-profit, and corporate sectors, the festival and events industry failed to respond to the pandemic with a clear voice or direction. In past years Steven Wood Schmader, the CEO of the International Festivals and Events Association, has attempted to bring a number of professional associations together with only limited success. Event professionals could be more successful if they become less sectionalized and join together as a true professional industry.

Second, a realization that virtual events cannot replace important aspects of live events, on so many levels. Sponsors can buy print, electronic, and digital media from many sources including events, but they can only buy event media (the ability to have attendees actually reach out, touch, and interact in person with products and services) from live events. Virtual events may be able to partially stimulate attendees' senses of seeing and hearing, but only live events stimulate those plus smell, taste, and touch as well as the sensual modalities such as vibration, temperature, and balance. In-person events will always outshine virtual events in terms of increased bonding and bridging social capital.

Third, I never realized how many event 'experts' were on social media. It seems like everyone and their brother has been posting, blogging, even phishing about how events can survive the pandemic. Some is common sense, a little is creative, a lot is guesswork, and mostly it seems to be people promoting themselves or their businesses. Hopefully event professionals have been using this information to brainstorm their own solutions.

Q2 – What does this crisis require from various stakeholders? Who are the most important ones?

I have always believed that everyone is an event stakeholder. I teach students there are three kinds of stakeholders: 1) those that you want to be part of and they want to be part of your event; 2) those that you want to be part of but they do not want to be part of your event; 3) those that you do not want to but they want to be part of your event. I'll answer the second part first – they are all important. I feel like your question is more focused on my first group, however, so I'll address those.

The most important thing this group needs is a sense of ownership – event managers need to make this happen. When they have this sense of ownership they will have more understanding, more patience, a greater feel that what they have to contribute is important, a sense of pride, a feeling of belonging to something bigger than themselves, a sense of family. There are events that are planned and produced by single parents, but the best events have always been about family.

Q3 – What are the recovery and resilience strategies you would recommend for events?

There are many. For one, take time to review and reassess everything you do that has do with your finances. Look at your financial plan and budget – make sure you employ cost-revenue accounting to separate expenses from revenues, convert to a line item budget, prioritize expenses, re-exam cash flow and ROI, and do all those other business accounting things you have been avoiding in the past. Second, start brainstorming on some creative revenue generation ideas. The number one reason events fail is because of financial issues.

People have missed live events and the experiences and senses of happiness and community that come with them. Make sure you have a great product and great services to establish a WOW factor, but you have to know experience is more than that. How can you move attendees from being spectators to being more physical, collaborative, and creative? How will you infuse their senses? How will you rollercoaster their emotions? Give attendees a sense of flow, rapture, ecstasy or turbulence to create the experiences they want.

6 Redesigning Events in the Post COVID-19 Crisis: A Design Thinking Approach

Kom Campiranon

Introduction

The World Health Organization (WHO) declared COVID-19 a pandemic on 12 March 2020. Since then, COVID-19 has significantly influenced the global economic, political, and socio-cultural systems (Sigala, 2020). This pandemic is arguably one of the most substantial challenges facing businesses in the past 100 years (Hall et al., 2020). Although the tourism industry has been generally resilient in recovery from a variety of crises (e.g. terrorism, earthquakes, and outbreaks such as SARS), tourism is one of many industries in which COVID-19 has caused severe adverse effects (UNWTO, 2020b) and has given rise to profound and long-term changes (Sigala, 2020). Moreover, it is not yet clear if, or when, businesses will return to normal (Cankurtaran & Beverland, 2020).

As COVID-19 has continued to spread across the world, travel restrictions and border shutdowns have been enforced in many countries to curb its spread (Qiu et al., 2020). Flights have been canceled (Haywood, 2020), forcing millions of travelers to postpone their travel plans (Rwigema, 2020). People all over the world have experienced quarantine or isolation, whilst businesses have been closed in response to the outbreak of COVID-19 (Kabadayi et al., 2020) which has caused supply chain disruptions.

Whilst the events sector is considered as a vital part of the tourism industry (Mohanty et al., 2020; Rwigema, 2020), it has been disrupted the most (Gajjar & Parmar, 2020; Gössling et al., 2020) due to the sudden outbreak of COVID-19 (Congrex Switzerland, 2020; Margolis et al., 2020; Min Ho & Ming Sia, 2020; Mohanty et al., 2020; Ranasinghe et al., 2020) which lead to social distancing (Rwigema, 2020; Sigala, 2020), the avoidance of crowd gatherings (Hao et al., 2020), travel restrictions, border controls, and involuntary quarantine (Disimulacion, 2020).

Consequently, all kinds of events with large groups of participants have b een restricted, including events ranging from concerts, meetings, conferences, sports, to large family gatherings (e.g., weddings) (Gössling et al., 2020). Hundreds and thousands of events all over the world have been postponed or canceled (Congrex Switzerland, 2020), which has negatively affected stakeholders such as sponsors and suppliers (Min Ho & Ming Sia, 2020). Key events that have been affected by COVID-19 include the 2020 Summer Olympics and Paralympics, Facebook's Annual F8 Conference (Min Ho & Ming Sia, 2020), and major sports leagues across Europe, North America, and other regions. The total economic impact is not yet known but will be in the hundreds of billions of US dollars (Gössling et al., 2020).

When compared with other sectors of the tourism industry, the events sector will require a significantly longer period of time to recover as a number of events have already been postponed or cancelled and the marketing and travel budgets of companies are limited due to COVID-19 (Suau-Sanchez et al., 2020). In turn, this has resulted in significant losses to the events sector (Mohanty et al., 2020). Therefore, it is a challenge for the events sector to launch and manage events with minimal disruption (Disimulacion, 2020).

Regardless of such challenges, the implications of COVID-19 on the events sector have been largely understudied (Mohanty et al., 2020). Further studies on COVID-19 and the events sector are needed to accurately identify the key factors that contribute to the success of events in the future (Min Ho & Ming Sia, 2020). Moreover, the current situation requires study on how the events sector could be prepared to mitigate risks in the post-COVID-19 period (Mohanty et al., 2020).

Given the likelihood of a reoccurrence of the pandemic, design thinking is one of many problem-solving methods which can be used to cope with such challenges (Cankurtarana & Beverlandb, 2020; Thakur et al., 2020). Moreover, a number of authors (e.g. Higgins-Desbiolles, 2020; Sigala, 2020) have pointed out that COVID-19 tourism research, including events, should generate de-thinking, re-thinking and un-thinking of pre-assumptions and mindsets. Therefore, this chapter aims to discuss the role of design thinking during the COVID-19 pandemic to generate innovative solutions to address unique challenges in the events sector. By using design thinking as a framework, this chapter will discuss various solutions which address these challenges. Finally, recommendations for future studies will be provided.

Literature review

Crisis management in tourism and events

There is a growing number of crises that have affected the tourism industry, including the events sector, ranging from natural to human influenced incidents (Faulkner, 2001) including the '9/11' terrorist attacks on the USA in

2001, the tsunami in the Indian Ocean region in 2004, the swine flu crisis in 2009, and the Fukushima nuclear disaster in 2011 (Higgins-Desbiolles, 2020; Reddy et al., 2020) and COVID-19 in 2020 (Gössling et al., 2020; Hao et al., 2020; Ranasinghe et al., 2020; Sigala, 2020).

The tourism industry, especially international tourism demand, is vulnerable to crises due to many external factors, including political instability, economic conditions, the environment and the weather (Ritchie & Jiang, 2019). Tourism crises have affected the willingness of tourists to travel (Jin et al., 2019) as such crises create negative destination images and consequently reduce the number of tourist arrivals (Rittichainuwat et al., 2020). As a result, crises have impacts on both event organizers when selecting event destinations, as well as event participants when deciding whether to attend events.

To understand crisis management in the tourism and event contexts, it is crucial to examine multiple stages or crises (Lai & Wong, 2020). While opinion varies greatly in regard to the most suitable stages of crisis management, a number of authors have agreed that tourism crisis management involves the following stages: 1. The identification or discovery of threats, 2. Crisis management planning, 3. Crisis response, 4. Crisis recovery, and 5. Learning from the crisis (Campiranon & Scott, 2014). Another approach is to categorize crises into three stages: before, during and after a crisis (Sigala, 2020). The predisaster stage is the period of time that precedes the event, and research can determine the state of preparedness. Research in the post-disaster phase aims to examine the lessons learned and recommend crisis management responses for future incidents. However, in the during-crisis stage, the aim of research is different as it involves the development of a crisis management plan (Lai & Wong, 2020).

As there are no specific models or frameworks for event crisis management, this chapter has relied on literature and models from the general tourism field. Whilst a number of authors have proposed a crisis management framework in the tourism industry, Faulkner (2001)'s model remains one of the most cited crisis and disaster management frameworks. Faulkner's Tourism Disaster Management Framework discusses the following stages of disaster management (Table 6.1).

A number of authors (e.g. Muskat et al., 2014; Pacific Asia Travel Association, 2003; Ritchie, 2008) simplified the stages of tourism crisis management into four stages: reduction, readiness (pre disaster), response (disaster), and recovery. Following the review of 142 papers published between 1960 and 2018 on tourism risk, crisis and disaster management, Ritchie and Jiang (2019) identified the following three broad management stages of disasters and crises: 1. Preparedness and planning 2. Response and recovery 3. Resolution and reflection (Table 6.2).

Table 6.1: Tourism disaster management framework

Stage	Description
1. Pre-event	When actions can be taken to prevent or alleviate the effects of potential disasters.
2. Prodromal	When it is clear that a disaster is imminent.
3. Emergency	The effect of the disaster is felt, and action is needed to protect people and property.
4. Intermediate	Short-term needs of people have been addressed and the focus of activity is to restore services and the community to normal.
5. Recovery	Continuation of the previous phases; , issues that could not be attended to quickly are attended to in this phase.
6. Resolution	Normality is restored or there is a new improved solution.

Source: Faulkner (2001)

Table 6.2: The stages of disaster and crisis management

Phase	Explanation
1. Preparedness and planning	Crisis management planning.
2. Response and recovery	Recovery strategies from the perspective of government, industry/sector, and businesses.
3. Resolution and reflection	Crisis learning, organizational learning, and tourist destination resilience.

Source: Ritchie & Jiang (2019)

In regard to the research gaps in tourism crisis management, a number of authors have pointed out that more research should be conducted to understand the different aspects of an epidemic crisis (Lai & Wong, 2020). The COVID-19 outbreak, in particular, has rapidly changed business operations as well as people's travel behavior. Therefore, research on resilience related to COVID-19 is needed (Rittichainuwat et al., 2020). It should be pointed out, however, that the events sector has certain specific characteristics, particularly in regard to COVID-19. In turn, it has been argued in this chapter that tourism crisis management frameworks need to be adapted for the events sector to cope with COVID-19. Therefore, a new and specific event-focused model is needed, which will be discussed in this chapter.

Design thinking

One of the most widely-used problem-solving approaches is design thinking, which has been discussed extensively by a number of authors since 2000. Due to its fast-changing nature, there are several definitions of, and views about, design thinking. In general, design thinking is a method to solve complex problems (Sándorová et al., 2020) by creating innovative solutions with a user-centered approach. It can be implemented in a wide variety of fields, from product and service innovations to other related areas (Oeveren, 2020). By driving innovation (Moscardo, 2020) and creating customer value (Vogt et al., 2020), design thinking can generate solutions which are technologically feasible, economically viable, and desirable from a customer point-of-view.

Problems to be solved with design thinking are typically highly complex issues that cannot be solved using standard methods. Such problems range from global issues such as climate change and poverty to challenges that affect almost all businesses such as managing change, achieving sustainable growth, and maintaining a competitive edge (Stevens, 2020). To solve complex problems, as shown in Table 6.3, the design thinking process includes five stages: empathize, define, ideate, prototype, and test (Nakata & Hwang, 2020; Hasso Plattner Institute of Design, 2018). It is important to note that these stages are not always sequential, and designers can often run the stages in parallel, out of order or repeat them in an iterative fashion (Interaction Design Foundation, 2020).

Table 6.3: Design thinking stages

Stage	Explanation
1. Empathize	Acquire an understanding of the problem through customer research. In this stage, an organization needs to interview a range of customers to examine what they do, how they think, what they want, what motivates or discourages them, and where they experience frustration.
2. Define	Create an actionable problem statement. Arguably, one of the most challenging stages, as the definition of a problem, also known as a 'design challenge' or 'problem statement', requires organizations to analyze data acquired from the empathize stage.
3. Ideate	Set up brainstorming workshops to ideate solutions as brainstorming is one of the key methods used during the ideation stage.
4. Prototype	Research conducted during the empathy, define, and ideate stages cannot determine whether such ideas can be implemented successfully. Testing prototypes is a crucial customer-centric approach that is required no matter how thorough the research.
5. Test	Test the product using the best solutions identified in the prototype stage. In the test stage, it is recommended that an organization return to their customers for feedback. Does this solution meet customer needs? Has it improved how they feel, think, or perform their tasks?

Source: Various authors

The pandemic offers opportunities to organizations to use design thinking. To cope with COVID-19, organizations can use design thinking to change how customers access their products and services and also how to tackle organizational change and disruption (McCausland, 2020). Design thinking can accelerate the development and implementation of prototypes through a process of inspiration, ideation, and implementation. Moreover, design thinking can be utilized to develop human-centered solutions and to enhance the user experience (Thakur et al., 2020) using an unambiguous, collaborative, constructive, empathic, holistic, iterative, non-judgmental, and curiosity mindset (Sándorová et al., 2020).

Given that there are numerous rapid design thinking models, this paper has adopted Thakur et al.'s (2020) approach by focusing on three essential stages and their relevance in the events sector during the COVID-19 pandemic. The first stage, inspiration (empathize and define) draws inspiration from the problem or opportunity at hand. The second stage is ideation during which innovative ideas are generated. Finally, implementation (prototype and test) focuses on execution, such as putting innovations into practice.

Redesigning events with design thinking

During COVID-19, the events sector rushed to move their in-person events online (Russell, 2020a). In this pandemic scenario, event organizers are required to reconsider their options and to balance two priorities: on the one hand, to ensure the health and safety of staff, sponsors, and attendees; and on the other, to meet financial obligations, or to minimize the losses caused by disruption (Congrex Switzerland, 2020). In this section, we explore how these three stages of design thinking (inspiration, ideation, and implementation) can be used to address such challenges in the events sector (Figure 6.1).

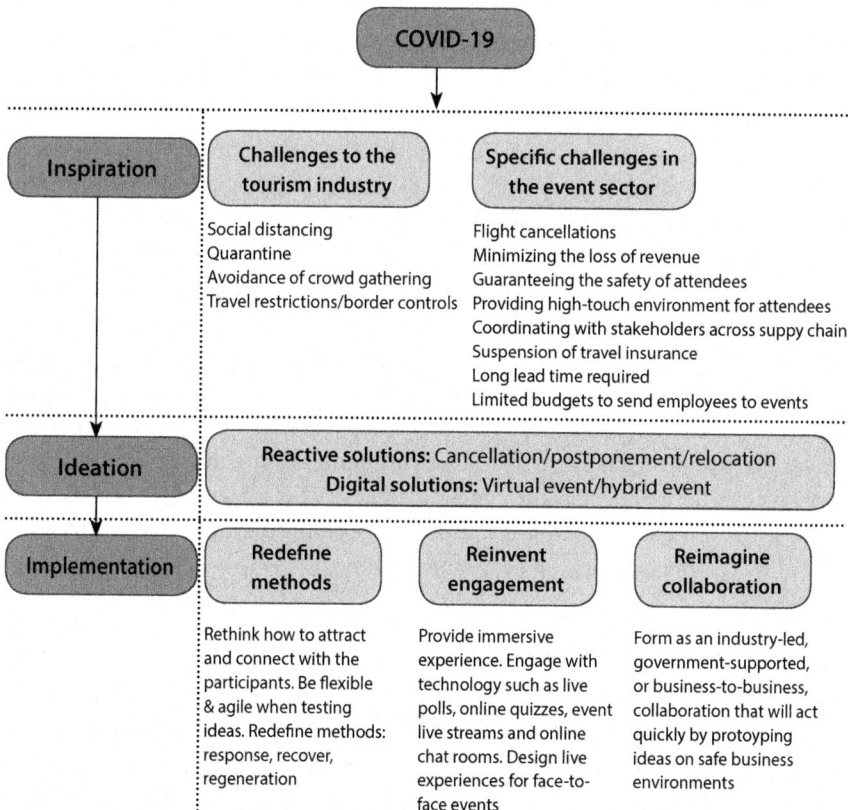

Figure 6.1: Design thinking approach to overcoming COVID-19 challenges in the events sector. Source: Adapted from Thakur et al. (2020)

Inspiration (Empathize and define)

The first stage in design thinking is to understand the challenges that an organization is trying to address before searching for solutions. Linke (2017) argued that most people do not put much effort into exploring the problem before finding a solution. Instead, they make mistakes by creating a solution based on their experience, and then try to empathize. This leads them to misunderstand the situation. By avoiding preconceived assumptions, empathy is crucial to a human-centered design process because it allows organizations to set aside their own assumptions and gain real insight into customer needs (Interaction Design Foundation, 2020) in order to avoid rushing into poor solutions (Cankurtarana & Beverlandb, 2020).

Finding patterns and making sense of the data collected during the empathize stage is a daunting challenge (Liedtka, 2018). By examining secondary data, including scholarly journals and events-related online sources, this chapter has defined the emerging patterns of the impact of COVID-19 on stakeholders in the events sector as follows: Challenges to the tourism industry; and Specific challenges in the event-sector.

Challenges to the tourism industry

Despite the ongoing reopening of many destinations since May 2020, the anticipated improvement in international tourism arrivals during the peak summer season in the Northern Hemisphere has not occurred. As the second-hardest hit of all global regions, Europe has experienced a 66% decline in tourist arrivals in the first half of 2020. The Americas (-55%), Africa and the Middle East (both -57%) also suffered. The Asia-Pacific region, the first tourism region that was affected by COVID-19, was the hardest hit, with a 72% fall in tourists for the six-month period (UNWTO, 2020a). Clearly, the tourism industry has been negatively affected by COVID-19. As discussed in the introduction, a number of authors (e.g., Haywood, 2020; Kabadayi et al., 2020; Qiu et al., 2020; Rwigema, 2020) have pointed out that COVID-19 has caused travel disruption such as social distancing, quarantine, avoidance of crowd gatherings, flight cancellations, and travel restrictions as well as border controls. In turn, business activities and supply chain disruptions have caused global wave effects across all economic sectors.

Specific challenges in the event sector

A number of COVID-19 challenges particularly affect the events sector. Event organizers are required to reconsider their options and to balance two priorities. On the one hand, they must follow the guidelines of public health officials and the directions of government; on the other hand, they have to sustain their event businesses after lockdown (Gajjar & Parmar, 2020) and minimize the losses caused by COVID-19 (Congrex Switzerland, 2020).

From a safety perspective, event organizers must sanitize the venue and provide hand sanitizers, on-call doctors, temperature measurement and other medical facilities, careful food preparation and storage while ensuring service staff safety. They must also strictly follow the guidelines provided by the government (Gajjar & Parmar, 2020). Although safety is the top priority for the event organizers, it should be pointed out, however, that the events sector, particularly business events or MICE (Meetings, Incentives, Conventions, and Exhibitions) is normally a high-touch environment (Disimulacion, 2020) which relies heavily on human relationships, connections and sharing knowledge and skills through networks. Participants who attend business events are naturally sociable and interactive (BBC, 2020b).

Another challenge is the decline in business-to-business (B2B) events, as lockdowns by governments around the world have resulted in an almost immediate loss of markets, as the rapid collapse in customer demand has a domino effect on the supply chain (Cankurtarana & Beverland, 2020) including the hospitality, travel, restaurant and other related sectors (David, 2020).

It should be pointed out that the decision-making process for business travel is complex and different from the leisure market. The events sector may be more vulnerable than the leisure market due to long lead times, the complex decision-making process and the status of participants (Rittichainuwat et al., 2020). Moreover, business travelers also have budgetary constraints as their employers may lack funds to send them to meetings, conventions, and conferences due to the economic downtown (Russell, 2020b). It may also mean that business travelers cannot travel due to the suspension of travel insurance (Rittichainuwat et al., 2020).

Ideation

The COVID-19 pandemic has deeply impacted events planned for 2020. For the meetings and conferences scheduled in the first half of 2020, event organizations were challenged with little time for planning and response (Margolis et al., 2020). Therefore, many event organizers rushed into solutions, focusing on leveraging capabilities to produce quick outcomes (Cankurtarana & Beverland, 2020) by deciding either to cancel, postpone, or relocate their events (Disimulacion, 2020), or by organizing virtual or hybrid events (Congrex Switzerland, 2020). Such ideation can be categorized into two types, which are reactive solutions and digital solutions (Table 6.4).

Online events such as virtual and hybrid events offer the organizers the possibility to hold the event in many different ways (David, 2020), and therefore virtual events and hybrid events represent a major strategy for the events sector to recover (Disimulacion, 2020; Min Ho & Ming Sia, 2020; Ranasinghe et al., 2020).

Table 6.4: Event organizer solutions

Solutions		Explanation
Reactive solutions	Cancellation	All efforts must be focused on communication and avoiding the negative effects of the cancellation, as well as delivering high standards of service to suppliers, sponsors, and those who had registered (Congrex Switzerland, 2020). People appreciate when organizations are transparent, and therefore a refund policy should be clearly stated and communicated (CVENT, 2020).
	Postpone-ment	Postponement is not an easy decision since hosting an event at a later time requires approval from venue managers, suppliers, and sponsors (Congrex Switzerland, 2020). Some participants may be unable to attend on the new date (CVENT, 2020).
	Relocation	Events take months to plan (Congrex Switzerland, 2020). If an event could not be canceled, some event organizers decided that the best solution would be to change its location, similarly to what the PGA Tour did when they moved a tournament from China to Indonesia during COVID-19 (David, 2020).
Digital solutions	Virtual events	This format is perhaps the best alternative to face-to-face meeting during COVID-19. By their very nature, virtual events welcome participants irrespective of travel restrictions (Congrex Switzerland, 2020).
	Hybrid events	Events that combine a live in-person event with a virtual component (Min Ho & Ming Sia, 2020) usually running simultaneously with overlapping content and interactive elements streamed over the Internet (PCMA, 2020). In this model, a number of speakers or participants may be present at a physical location while the audience at large attends the event remotely.

Source: Various authors

Virtual and hybrid events have a number of advantages. First, the platform enables event organizers to reach a larger audience through social media. These also empower participants to access events using mobile applications (Disimulacion, 2020). Second, the platform would allow event attendees to attend a wide array of event sessions and have networking opportunities that participants expect from attending a face-to-face event while situated safely at home (Min Ho & Ming Sia, 2020). Third, as budgets become tighter during COVID-19, incorporating technologies that allow for video conferencing and virtual meetings are increasingly seen by many organizers as a cost-effective option when hosting events (Ranasinghe et al., 2020). Fourth, the shift from face-to-face events to online platforms cause relatively minor disruption in terms of schedules and venue preparation (Disimulacion, 2020).

Whilst the demand for effective virtual/hybrid event platforms will increase significantly (Min Ho & Ming Sia, 2020), there are certain limitations to virtual events, particularly formats with live activities via web conference, or webinar. As BBC (2020a) explained, event organizers cannot simply shift what they do in a physical meeting and relocate it online as most participants will tune out. Margolis et al. (2020) added that such a virtual event is not well suited to remote access due to the lack of interaction between participants.

Clearly, managing events during COVID-19 is a challenging task for both reactive solutions (cancellation, postponement, relocation) and digital solutions (virtual, hybrid). The next section will discuss opportunities on how the events could be redesigned following the COVID-19 crisis.

Implementation (Prototype and Test)

During the COVID-19 pandemic, the implementation stage of design thinking focuses on prototyping with iterative feedback from stakeholders during testing (Thakur et al., 2020). This pandemic has provided opportunities to use new event delivery tools (Cankurtarana & Beverland, 2020). In particular, IDEO, a global design and innovation company, conducted research in April 2020 with over 700 business owners, community leaders, and entrepreneurs across more than 36 industries and 71 countries to examine how businesses can quickly adapt to support their COVID-19 response (IDEO, 2020). After examining the data, IDEO identified the following areas of opportunity for business adaptation that can be applied in the events sector: 1. Redefine methods, 2. Reinvent engagement, and 3. Reimagine collaboration (Russell, 2020a). These areas of opportunity encourage the events sector to first redefine their methods and then to thoughtfully consider engagement and collaboration.

Redefine methods

COVID-19 puts pressure on organizations, event organizers and event planners, who need to quickly shift their event into the digital sphere while offering outstanding value to all stakeholders (Congrex Switzerland, 2020). Moreover, event organizers need to show strong creative, innovation and resilience skills to put in place innovative solutions to rebuild a sustainable tourism industry (Rwigema, 2020). Arguably, face-to-face events cannot be simply replaced by digital platforms since virtual events need a different event design approach. Therefore, it is vital for the events sector to start developing innovative strategies that can deliver engagement and meet financial objectives through virtual delivery. Getting ready for a new landscape in the events sector also means rethinking how to connect with, and attract participants to, events by listening to their expectations and limitations and by learning from what other industry players are doing (Congrex Switzerland, 2020).

To redefine methods, it is crucial to test the prototype to determine its feasibility and success (Russell, 2020a). In order for organizations to redefine methods and to test new ideas, IDEO (2020) recommended key steps that can be employed in the events sector.

1   *Now (Response)*: How can events be adapted to new ways of working? Which existing protocols need to be changed in order to move quickly?

2   *Near (Recovery)*: Which new practices implemented during the pandemic will be carried forward? Which practices will be left behind as they are no longer meaningful or valuable?

3   *Far (Regeneration)*: How can an organizational culture characterized by adaptivity and flexibility be promoted in the future? How can today's event be adapted in preparation for a new post COVID-19 future?

By focusing on the three stages of crisis (response, recovery, regeneration), Russell (2020a) pointed out that event organizers need to carefully redefine their methods by improving the digital event experience and by providing greater value to their stakeholders, including sponsors. One example of a redefined event was the 2020 Peritoneal Dialysis Extended Congress. According to Margolis et al. (2020), this event was originally designed as a live two-day conference, including parallel sessions. The conference was originally scheduled for 27-28 March 2020 and was focused on healthcare professionals from neighboring countries (300 to 400 participants). In response to COVID-19 challenges, this event was redefined using the 'extended congress' concept as follows (Figure 6.2).

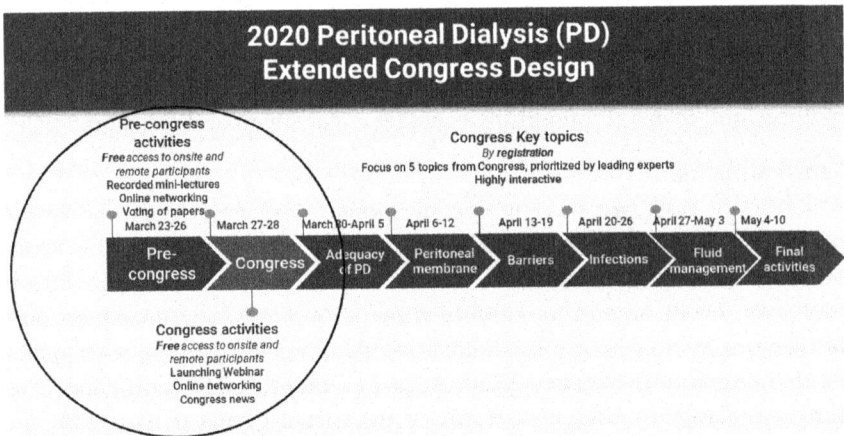

Figure 6.2: The 2020 Peritoneal Dialysis Extended Congress. Source: Margolis et al. (2020)

During the 'pre-congress' and 'congress' stage, the event provided both onsite and remote participants with full access to the virtual components of the congress. Remote participants who started the registration process but did not finish it had free access to this week as well. The following five weeks were focused on the main topics of the conference, with short lectures, reading materials, clinical simulations and case discussions in forums (Margolis et al., 2019). By offering free access during the pre-congress and congress, but requiring the payment of a registration fee during the following interactive five weeks, this event reached a much wider audience than a traditional on-site event.

Reinvent engagement

Despite advances in technology, virtual and hybrid events may not fully replace the experience of face-to-face interaction. Furthermore, virtual/hybrid events need to provide an immersive experience in order to enhance engagement for the participants (Disimulacion, 2020). Therefore, participant engagement is the most challenging aspect of a virtual event (Min Ho & Ming Sia, 2020) and event organizers may need to rely more on event technology such as live polls, online quizzes, event live streams and online chat rooms (Min Ho & Ming Sia, 2020).

For an example on how the engagement could be reinvented, the American Psychological Association (APA) quickly switched its in-person 2020 annual convention to an entirely virtual event due to COVID-19. With the objective of creating engagement, APA utilized the chat feature which enabled the speakers to participate in the chat. As a result, there was more engagement in the chats than at the face-to-face event (Russell, 2020c).

Another example is the seafood company Kvaroy Arctic, which planned to attend two of the world's leading trade shows. When both events were postponed, Kvaroy Arctic offered online tasting with fresh fish delivered to selected customers. These customers then watched an online video as the company prepared the fish as if they were at the trade show booth. The tasting experience was further enhanced by asking taste questions borrowed from a sommelier's wine test. Kvaroy Arctic then moved this and other content to social media, which led to a very high level of engagement (MPI, 2020).

Apart from virtual/hybrid events, there has been a limited number of face-to-face events post COVID-19. As Boley (2020) pointed out, the events that take place face-to-face need to have a very strong reason to happen, due to health and safety concerns. Such events are likely to be limited to domestic events using virtual or hybrid alternatives until there has been a high uptake of vaccinations globally. However, small, drive-to meetings such as internal meetings, workshops, and seminars, can be held locally with attendees from a close geographic area.

To engage with participants at face-to-face events, it is crucial that event organizers have the ability to design live experiences in post-COVID-19 physical environments with more stringent hygiene standards (Russell, 2020a). One of the examples to reinvent engagement in the events sector was Pfizer's global congresses. The company has led a group of over 20 business-event strategists through a months-long workshop in applying design-thinking processes to medical meetings (Palmer, 2018).

During the design thinking workshop, the teams of medical planners spent a few hours to brainstorm how materials, such as Styrofoam trays, sponges, pipe cleaners, paper cups and hair curlers, can be utilized to create prototypes that aim to address questions they formulated after talking to stakeholders. The main question was 'how can face-to-face interaction in the exhibit hall be improved?'. After crafting models of redesigned exhibit halls and a prototype of a redesigned meeting app, the event strategists tested the prototypes by inviting groups of users to critique the proposed solutions (Palmer, 2018).

Another example of a safe engagement during face-to-face events is the COVID Safe Event Solutions Framework (Figure 6.3), which visualizes how engagement could be enhanced on a safe user-journey (Fielddrive, 2020). The framework comprises both online and physical user-journeys starting with careful consideration of event planning and registration, through to onsite event access, check-in, show floor and session activities all the way through to exiting the event (Parry, 2020).

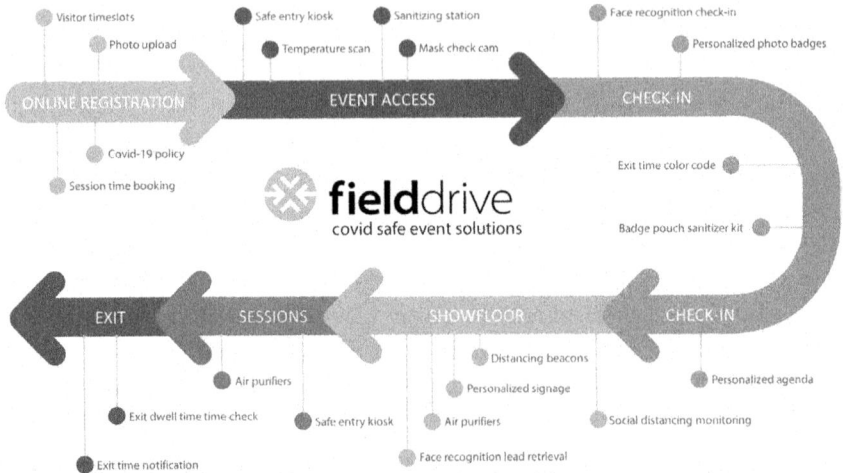

Figure 6.3: COVID safe event solution framework. Source: Fielddrive (2020)

Reimagine collaboration

Collaboration is one of the key success factors during COVID-19. On a policy level, policy makers in the tourism sector have used the COVID-19 outbreak to improve crisis management strategies and to strengthen international and domestic tourism coordination mechanisms. This yields a more sustainable and resilient tourism system to respond to any future shocks in a cohesive manner (Rwigema, 2020). To provide an example of reimagined collaboration, Singapore Tourism Board (2020) emphasized that the safe resumption of business events requires close partnership and coordination between public and private sector stakeholders. To do so, the Singapore Together Alliances for Action was formed as an industry-led, government-supported coalition that will act quickly by prototyping ideas on key strategic areas for Singapore.

On an organizational level, as organizations re-evaluate their value proposition and reimagine their offerings during COVID-19, many have turned to partners for support (Russell, 2020a). In the context of the events sector, there have been numerous examples of industry associations, convention and visitors bureaus (CVBs), and event venues collaborating with other entities to create protocols for a safe environment. Russell (2020a) stated that one example can be seen in the guide, *Essential Considerations for Safely Reopening Exhibitions and Events* which was developed in partnership with a number of key stakeholders in the events sector, including the International Association of Exhibitions and Events, the Experiential Designers and Producers Association, and the International Association of Venue Managers.

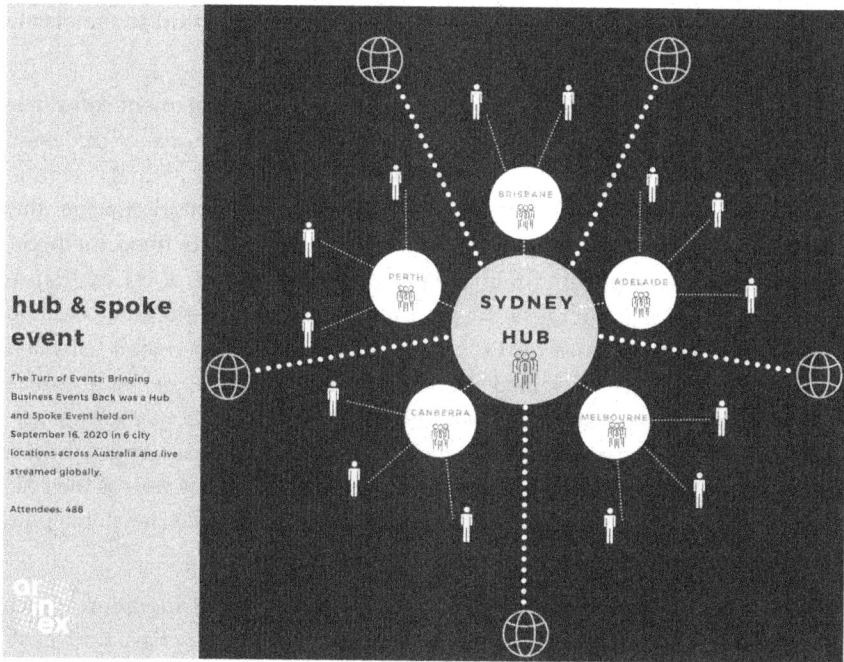

Figure 6.4: Hub & spoke events. Source: Arinex (2020)

In Australia, 'The Turn of Events, Bringing Business Events Back' in a wide 'hub and spoke' event format was held in September 2020 (Figure 6.4). This event brought together over 25 organizations to showcase business event readiness. Live and virtual events from six capital cities in Australia, including Sydney and Melbourne, launched the process to reignite the passion of 500 business event planners and associations in Australia and globally (Arinex, 2020). Business event professionals and clients were able to attend in their preferred city, either in person or virtually, with Melbourne Convention and Exhibition Centre offering only virtual attendance due to the safety restrictions (Colston, 2020).

Clearly, collaboration during COVID-19 has increased resilience and revealed unforeseen opportunities. With these partnerships lies the possibility to shift the governance of our societies and economies towards more sustainable and resilient approaches (IDEO, 2020).

Conclusion

The COVID-19 pandemic in 2020 created a number of challenges for the events sector, which were suddenly faced with a lack of markets and a loss of revenue. To cope with such challenges, this chapter attempts to conceptualize how events could be redesigned using design thinking during COVID-19. This chapter has made a number of contributions in regard to the events sector as follows.

First, design thinking can be utilized to develop and implement solutions. Drawing on the literature, this chapter has identified a three-stage design thinking process that involves inspiration (empathize and define), ideation and implementation (prototype and test). In the implementation stage, this chapter has discussed case studies which illustrate the redefined methods, reinvented engagement, and reimagined collaboration. One of the case studies is Pfizer's global congresses which adopted a design-thinking method for medical meetings. As a result, prototypes of redesigned exhibit halls and meeting apps have been created and tested. Other examples of events which have been redesigned due to COVID-19 include the COVID safe event solution framework focusing on both online and physical user-journeys, hub & spoke events with live and virtual events in multiple cities, as well as the 2020 Peritoneal Dialysis event using 'Extended Congress', which enabled both onsite and remote participants to engage at the events.

Second, event specific challenges need to be taken into consideration at each stage of crisis management: before (pre-crisis), during the crisis, and post-crisis. Unlike leisure tourism, the events sector requires a longer lead time in order to prepare. Nonetheless, crises such as COVID-19 are unpredictable in terms of severity and duration. Consequently, event organizers need to have an action plan and an appropriate event method for each crisis management stage. Whilst virtual events have mostly been adopted during the crisis, hybrid events could be more effective in the post-crisis stage in order to achieve a higher level of engagement among the participants.

Third, future research should be focused on how design thinking can be implemented in other types of crisis, such as natural disasters, political unrest, economic crisis, and so on. Whilst organizing events during political unrest does not have the same social distancing challenges as the COVID-19 pandemic, events are often required by local authorities to be suspended due to safety concern once unrest occurs. This would cause specific challenges for on-site participants, exhibitors, and event-related providers. Moreover, future studies could examine how event organizers could employ design thinking to re-design events during crises by employing the latest technologies such as Extended Reality (XR), which covers new and emerging technologies, including virtual, augmented, and mixed reality, to create immersive digital event experiences.

References

Arinex. (2020). The biggest face to face business event industry collaboration of 2020. https://arinex.com.au/the_biggest_face_to_face_business_event _industry_collaboration_2020/

BBC. (2020a). The future of business events during Covid-19. http://www. bbc.com/storyworks/capital/planning-your-next-business-event-in-japan/ the-future-of-business-events-during-covid-19

BBC. (2020b). How is Japan's business event industry adapting to Covid-19? http://www.bbc.com/storyworks/capital/planning-your-next-business-event-in-japan/ japans-business-event-industry-during-covid-19

Boley, M. (2020). Safe meetings and events: How COVID-19 could change the industry's future. https://www.cvent.com/en/blog/hospitality/ safe-meetings-events

Campiranon, K., & Scott, N. (2014). Critical success factors for crisis recovery management: A case study of Phuket hotels. *Journal of Travel & Tourism Marketing, 31*, 313–326.

Cankurtaran, P., & Beverland, M. (2020). Using design thinking to respond to crises: B2B lessons from the 2020 COVID-19 pandemic. *Industrial Marketing Management, 88*, 255-260.

Colston, P. (2020). Arinex brings Australia's business events sector back with biggest event of 2020. https://www.c-mw.net/arinex-brings-australias-business-events-sector-back-with-biggest-event-of-2020/

Congrex Switzerland. (2020). Disruption in the business events industry: Rising to the challenges of Covid-19. https://congrex.com/download/white-paper-10-disruption-in-the-business-events-industry-rising-to-the-challenges-of-covid-19/

CVENT. (2020). Event Postponement and Cancellation Guide. https://www.cvent. com/en/blog/events/event-postponement-and-cancellation-guide.

David, I. (2020). The impact of covid-19 on the events industry. https:// www.hartehanks.com/insights/our-insights/2020/04/27/the-impact-of -covid-19-on-the-events-industry.

Disimulacion, M. (2020). MICE tourism during Covid-19 and future directions for the new normal. *Asia Pacific International Events Management Journal, 2*(1), 11-17.

Faulkner, B. (2001). Towards a framework for tourism disaster management. *Tourism Management, 22*, 135–147.

Fielddrive. (2020). COVID safe event solutions. https://fielddrive.eu/covid-safe-events.

Gajjar, A., & Parmar, B. (2020). The impact of Covid 19 on event management industry in India. *Global Journal of Management and Business Research, 20*(2), 37-43.

Gössling, S., Scott, D., & Hall, C. M. (2020). Pandemics, tourism and global change: a rapid assessment of COVID-19. *Journal of Sustainable Tourism,* (ahead-of-print), 1-20.

Hall, C. M., Prayang, G., Fieger, P., & Dyason, D. (2020). Beyond panic buying: consumption displacement and COVID-19. *Journal of Service Management* (ahead-of-print). doi:ttps://doi.org/10.1108/JOSM-05-2020-0151.

Hao, F., Xiao, Q., & Chon, K. (2020). COVID-19 and China's hotel industry: impacts, a disaster management framework, and post-pandemic agenda. *International Journal of Hospitality Management, 90,* 1-11.

Hasso Plattner Institute of Design. (2018). Design thinking bootleg. https://dschool.stanford.edu/resources/design-thinking-bootleg.

Haywood, K. (2020). A post COVID-19 future – tourism re-imagined and re-enabled. *Tourism Geographies, 22*(3), 599-609.

Higgins-Desbiolles, F. (2020). Socialising tourism for social and ecological justice after COVID-19. *Tourism Geographies, 22*(3), 610-623.

IDEO. (2020). COVID-19 Business Pivot Challenge. https://www.openideo.com/content/covid-19-business-pivot-challenge-report-and-webinar.

Interaction Design Foundation. (2020). Design Thinking. https://www.interaction-design.org/literature/topics/design-thinking.

Jin, X., Qu, M., & Bao, J. (2019). Impact of crisis events on Chinese outbound tourist flow: A framework for post-events growth. *Tourism Management, 74,* 334-344.

Kabadayi, S., O'Connor, G., & Tuzovic, S. (2020). Viewpoint: The impact of coronavirus on service ecosystems as service mega-disruptions. *Journal of Services Marketing,* (ahead-of-print).

Lai, I. K. W., & Wong, J. W. C. (2020). Comparing crisis management practices in the hotel industry between initial and pandemic stages of COVID-19. *International Journal of Contemporary Hospitality Management, ahead-of-print*(ahead-of-print). doi:10.1108/IJCHM-04-2020-0325.

Liedtka, J. (2018). Why Design Thinking Works. *Harvard Business Review.*

Linke, R. (2017). Design thinking, explained. https://mitsloan.mit.edu/ideas-made-to-matter/design-thinking-explained.

Margolis, A., Balmer, J., Zimmerman, A., & López-Arredondo, A. (2020). The Extended Congress: Reimagining scientific meetings after the COVID-19 pandemic. https://www.mededpublish.org/manuscripts/3148.

McCausland, T. (2020). Design thinking revisited. *Research-Technology Management, 63*(4), 59-63.

Min Ho, J., & Ming Sia, J. (2020). Embracing an uncertain future: COVID-19 and MICE in Malaysia. *Local Development & Society,* 1-15. doi:10.1080/26883597.2020.1818533.

Mohanty, P., Himanshi, D., & Choudhury, R. (2020). Events tourism in the eye of the COVID-19 storm: Impacts and implications. In S. Arora & A. Sharma (Eds.), *Event Tourism in Asian Countries: Challenges and Prospects*: Apple Academic Press, https://ssrn.com/abstract=3682648 or http://dx.doi.org/10.2139/ssrn.3682648.

Moscardo, G. (2020). Stories and design in tourism. *Annals of Tourism Research, 83*(July).

MPI. (2020). Special report: novel coronavirus. https://www.mpi.org/docs/default-source/covid-19/coronavirus_report-3-30-20.pdf.

Muskat, B., Nakanishi, H., & Blackman, D. (2014). 2014. Integrating tourism into disaster recovery management. In: B. Ritchie & K. Campiranon (Eds.), *Tourism Crisis and Disaster Management in Asia-Pacific* (pp. 97-115). UK: CABI.

Nakata, C., & Hwang, J. (2020). Design thinking for innovation: Composition, consequence, and contingency. *Journal of Business Research, 118*, 117-128.

Oeveren, R. (2020). The difference between design thinking and service design. https://www.koosservicedesign.com/blog/difference-between-design-thinking-service-design/

Pacific Asia Travel Association. (2003). *Crisis: It Won't Happen to Us.* Bangkok: Pacific Asia Travel Association.

Palmer, B. (2018). Design Thinking: An Event Strategist's Toolkit. https://www.pcma.org/design-thinking-event-strategists-toolkit/.

Parry, A. (2020). COVID safe event solutions introduced by fielddrive. https://www.eventindustrynews.com/news/covid-safe-event-solutions-introduced-by-fielddrive#.

PCMA. (2020). Essential digital event terms. https://www.pcma.org/wp-content/uploads/2020/04/PCMA-DEI-Essential-Digital-Event-Terms.pdf.

Qiu, R., Park, J., Li, S., & Song, H. (2020). Social costs of tourism during the COVID-19 pandemic. *Annals of Tourism Research, 84*, 102994.

Ranasinghe, R., Damunupola, A., Wijesundara, S., Karunarathna, C., Nawarathna, D., Gamage, S., Ranaweera, A., & Idroos, A. (2020). Tourism after Corona: Impacts of Covid 19 pandemic and way forward for tourism, hotel and MICE industry in Sri Lanka. https://papers.ssrn.com/sol3/papers.cfm?abstract_id=3587170.

Reddy, M., Boyd, S., & Nica, M. (2020). Towards a post-conflict tourism recovery framework. *Annals of Tourism Research, 84*, 102940.

Ritchie, B. (2008). Tourism disaster planning and management: From response and recovery to reduction and readiness. *Current Issues in Tourism, 11*(4), 315-348.

Ritchie, B., & Jiang, Y. (2019). A review of research on tourism risk, crisis and disaster management: Launching the Annals of Tourism Research curated collection on tourism risk, crisis and disaster management. *Annals of Tourism Research, 79*(2019), 1-15.

Rittichainuwat, B., Laws, E., Maunchontham, R., Rattanaphinanchai, S., Muttamara, S., Mouton, K., Lin, Y., & Suksai, C. (2020). Resilience to crises of Thai MICE stakeholders: A longitudinal study of the destination image of Thailand as a MICE destination. *Tourism Management Perspectives, 35*.

Russell, M. (2020a). 5 ways to move forward, from the design-thinking community. https://www.pcma.org/5-ways-recovery-design-thinking -community/

Russell, M. (2020b). How events and host destinations will move forward. https://www.pcma.org/destinations-move-forward-post-covid-19/

Russell, M. (2020c). How the American Psychological Association 'crushed' its virtual event. https://www.pcma.org/ virtual-event-american-psychological-association-conference/

Rwigema, P. (2020). Impact of Covid-19 pandemic to meetings, incentives, conferences and exhibitions tourism in Rwanda. *The Strategic Journal of Business and Change Management, 7*(3), 395-409.

Sándorová, Z., Repáňová, T., Palenčíková, Z., & Beták, N. (2020). Design thinking - A revolutionary new approach in tourism education? *Journal of Hospitality, Leisure, Sport & Tourism Education, 26,* 100238.

Sigala, M. (2020). Tourism and COVID-19: Impacts and implications for advancing and resetting industry and research. *Journal of Business Research, 117,* 312-321.

Singapore Tourism Board. (2020). Safe and gradual resumption of MICE events. https://www.stb.gov.sg/content/stb/en/media-centre/media-releases/Safe-and-Gradual-Resumption-of-MICE-Events.html

Stevens, E. (2020). What is design thinking, and how do we apply it? https://www.invisionapp.com/inside-design/what-is-design-thinking/

Suau-Sanchez, P., Voltes-Dorta, A., & Cugueró-Escofet, N. (2020). An early assessment of the impact of COVID-19 on air transport: Just another crisis or the end of aviation as we know it? *Journal of Transport Geography, 86,* 1-8.

Thakur, A., Soklaridis, S., Crawford, A., Mulsant, B. & Sockalingam, S. (2020). Using rapid design thinking to overcome COVID-19 challenges in medical education. *Academic Medicine,* 1-6. doi:10.1097/ACM.0000000000003718

UNWTO. (2020a). International tourist numbers down 65% in first half of 2020, UNWTO reports. https://www.unwto.org/news/ international-tourist-numbers-down-65-in-first-half-of-2020-unwto-reports

UNWTO. (2020b). Supporting jobs and economies through travel & tourism. https://webunwto.s3.eu-west-1.amazonaws.com/s3fs-public/2020-04/ COVID19_Recommendations_English_1.pdf

Vogt, C., Andereck, K., & Pham, K. (2020). Designing for quality of life and sustainability. *Annals of Tourism Research, 83.*

Practice Insight 4:

Interview with Neil Alderson of Events Nova Scotia and Sport Tourism Canada

Q: What have been the pandemic's impacts on the event sector?

Early on in the pandemic the event sector did grind to a halt. It was one of the first industries impacted and will probably be one of the last to recover. This has had an immediate impact on the revenue (bottom line) of event organizations and organizers. The results have led to layoffs or downsizing for some organizations, however for those who have taken advantage of funding programs (most notably the Federal programs) it's provided a lifeline or at least helped to stop the bleeding for now. Most events rely on the revenue from tickets and activities to support their organizations, with little of this happening it means little revenue coming in. On the positive side expenses for the organizations are down as they are not paying out to put the events and activities on. Unfortunately, the lower expenses are not enough to be covered by the lower revenue.

The supply chain sector or those that supply events have been hit very hard. Most suppliers have good years when there are lots of events in the market and not so good years when there are fewer events. As you can imagine this will not be a good year for them. We worry about the impact on the supply chain. When events return will the supply chain be there to support events? Or will they be in any kind of shape to support the industry? That still remains a big question.

There's also been an impact on the non-profit sector. Many larger events in our region have a charity component to their tickets or offer the event audience as a way to fundraise for those non-profit organizations. Without the events happening those non-profits are struggling to find a new source of revenue or a way to fundraise. This could have some longer term impacts.

We also understand the social impacts the loss of events will have on the communities but also to individuals. Many people in rural Nova Scotia enjoy events as a provider of social connection and many volunteers like to be part of them. For some it's a great way to keep connected to the community and for others like musicians and artists it's mean less income this year and losing exposure. We've seen many musicians turn to an online model to try and keep a connection with their audience, but most have failed at translating that into income. People don't want to pay for online content, when they aren't use to paying for it.

Q: How is recovery being organized/planned?

Nationally, from a sport event perspective Sport Tourism Canada has developed and led a Sport Event COVID-19 Recovery Task Force that I've been a part of. The purpose is to develop an action plan for the responsible, safe and effective reopening of the $6.8 billion sport tourism industry. The work has been completed and a report will be released very soon. (Their report, entitled *Bouncing Back*, can be accessed from their website: https://www.sport-tourismcanada.com.)

From a provincial perspective we made an early decision in the pandemic to let organizations keep their funding for events for this year. We did not pull any funding back if their event was cancelled or impacted. We also opened up communication with event organizations and sector groups to collect information on the impacts and where the problem areas were. The positive out of this is a closer working relationship between levels of government, connection between government departments that may not work closely together (e.g. Events and Public Health) and closer connections to industry associations.

The Province of Nova Scotia, led by us, has an Event Advisory Group that meets on a regular basis to discuss the industry and challenges it may face. The group is made up of various representatives of regions across the province and a number of different industry sectors. We were equipped to deal with a number of situations and the pandemic has really activated this group. We have since developed a Provincial Event Recovery Task Force made up of some members of the Advisory Group as well as other missing industry representatives. This work is just starting but will focus on the challenges events are facing and how we can work together to find some common solutions. Not having the Advisory Group would have slowed this work down and perhaps not had the same close connections.

We are fortunate here in Atlantic Canada to have less restrictive public health measures due to the Atlantic Bubble. Our mass gathering sizes in Nova Scotia are large compared to many other parts of the county and this has allowed us to open up and host some events.

Q: Who are the key stakeholders in the process?

Internally or within government we are working with number of Departments including Public Health, Labour & Environment (oversee enforcement of public health measures), Alcohol & Gaming, Tourism, Sport & Rec. We meet on a regular basis to identify potential issues, but also find solutions to problems we all may be seeing or experiencing around events. This has proven to be very helpful and will continue past the pandemic. For example we've been able to produce event guidelines that meet the needs of public health order, but also provide guidance to the event sector so they can operate safely.

Externally, we are working with industry groups in the tourism sector, sport, culture, event organizations and other provincial groups related to events. Most of this work will be part of our Event Recovery Task Force to help identify who needs to be included and how we involve them in the recovery process. The goal will be to provide some best practices to the industry and also help to identify opportunities with events through the recovery and beyond. For example how can we build a provincial calendar of events so that the activity is coordinated for communities and the sector. It doesn't help the supply chain or the event industry to reschedule events all on the same weekend.

Here are a few final thoughts on the event industry moving forward.

1   *More focus on local events*. Some of the larger national and international events will have to adapt to thinking local. How can they use more local performers? How do they attract more locals and maximize revenue from them? Travel restrictions are not changing any time soon.

2   *Sharing financial risk*. The pandemic will impact the business model of events. The answer will not be turning to government for more support. There's no question attendees may have to pay more to attend events or sponsors may have to pay more.

3   *Custom COVID approach*. COVID-19 is here to stay for a while, so events will have to figure out a way to adapt their events to implement public health measures. There is no cookbook or instruction manual, so it's a lot of figuring out how to do things differently with a customized approach for each event.

4   *Doing less with more*. Everyone around events will have to figure out how to do more with less income. The cost of implementing public health measures will be expected by attendees, and if the attendees don't feel safe they won't attend.

5   *Increased collaboration*. This may be a positive result from the pandemic. We need to look at how we share best practices of what's working and not working. We have a saying on the East Coast that "A rising tide, raises all boats", the same is true here with events. When one event is successful we need to work together to learn from that success and apply it to other events.

7 The Future of Events will be Hybrid

Tim Brown

Introduction

In early 2020 a pandemic was declared following the rapid spread of COVID-19 across the globe. As a result, numerous governments worldwide implemented strict measures to limit the movements of their populations to prevent increases in COVID-19 infections (Ludvigsen & Hayton, 2020; Mohanty et al., 2020). These restrictions included regional and national 'lockdowns' which severely restricted personal activities, with all but essential workers urged to work from home, schools and universities closed and moved online, and only critical business (such as supermarkets and pharmacies) to remain open (Richter, 2020). Many industries were affected by the lockdowns, with the tourism, hospitality, and events industries most severely affected (Mohanty et al., 2020).

The Meetings Industry Association (mia) reported that in the UK the impact of COVID-19 on the events industry has resulted in £ billions lost in revenue through cancelled events and declines in enquiries, and that over 126,000 event jobs in the UK have been lost to date (mia, 2020), with fears this could increase to over 500,000 job losses without more government support (Fullard, 2020). This picture is mirrored in other countries, such as the USA, where it is outlined that 46% (8 million people) of those working in food, travel and events have lost their jobs (Dubay, 2020). Events are a global industry, worth $ trillions annually (Events Industry Council & Oxford Economics, 2018), and the shutdown of events presents an existential crisis to the industry which may take years to recover (EventMB, 2020b; mia, 2020; Mohanty et al., 2020).

There has, however, been some small green shoots that provide some optimism for the future recovery of events and the event industry. The business events sector in particular has turned to technology to provide a platform for creating and delivering events (specifically meetings and conferences), providing continuity of service, and experimenting and enhancing the consumer experience. Whilst not at the same level of capacity as live in-person events pre-pandemic, the 'pivot' to online is providing a lifeline for event professionals (EventMB, 2020b).

The purpose of this chapter will be to predominately explore the business events context in relation to the development and benefits of virtual and hybrid events, the impact of COVID-19 on the events industry, the pivot to online, designing virtual and hybrid event experiences, current trends of virtual and hybrid events, and postulate the future direction of events emerging from the COVID-19 pandemic crisis.

Virtual events

Technology has been an intrinsic and integral element within events for decades, and as the quality and capabilities of technology has enhanced so has the reliance on it to transform event experiences (Bowdin et al., 2011). The developments in web-based applications and platforms, and mobile applications, have further changed the event industry, enabling event professionals to create more meaningful event experiences, reach wider audiences, and increase returns on investment (Raj, Walter, & Rashid, 2017).

Despite the technological advancements over the last 20 years the growth of virtual events has been slower than predicted. This is due to several key factors. First, the atmosphere, ambience and emotive response of a live event are difficult to replicate online (Getz & Page, 2020). Second, whilst technology is embedded within our normal lives there is still a reluctance to use this in place of tried and tested event experiences. Third, a lack of confidence exists from some event organizers and consumers in using technology for events (Sox et al., 2017a), as well as the perceived costs associated with developing and delivering online events. Finally, the socialization and networking that live events offer are hard to artificially construct online (Nolan, 2018). The potential that virtual events can offer, therefore, has not been fully realized by the event industry, except for the business events sector (Davidson, 2019).

Virtual events are not a new genre but have existed for nearly 40 years since the development in the early 1980s of videoconferencing as a meetings platform (Sox et al., 2017b). It was not until the early 2000s, however, before virtual events began to build traction as a viable platform to conduct events, primarily meetings and conferences, due to breakthroughs in reducing the size and speed of the data being transmitted (Nolan, 2018), ease of use, and the reducing costs associated with using these platforms (Rogers, 2013). The financial crisis in 2008 had a major impact on the meetings and events sector with businesses reducing their capacity and budgets for delivering or attending events (Goldblatt & Lee, 2012). As a result, virtual events witnessed a significant growth to bridge the gap that had emerged during this recession and demonstrated their potential as a viable alternative to in-person events, and were expected to become a dominant aspect of the event industry (Briodagh, 2010; Shapiro, 2009). It was estimated that virtual events would grow to be worth $18.6 billion by 2015 and (Raj et al., 2017) and were predicted to grow exponentially (McLoughlin, 2014; Rogers, 2013; Sadd, 2014; Sox et al., 2017a). Sadd (2014) explored the technological possibilities for the future of events and argued that a blend of virtual and live elements would be the norm. The timeframe for this future was rather opaque, however, as the technology and prohibitive costs meant that for the foreseeable future the interconnectivity that in-person events provide could not be completely replaced or replicated online (Rogers, 2013; Sox et al., 2017b).

Virtual events also have their detractors with Getz and Page (2020, p. 51) commenting that all events are *"social in nature, and that is because people have a need to be together – to socialize, celebrate and do business"* and these elements cannot be replaced via technology. This is echoed by Sadd (2014, p. 216) who posits that despite the significant advances, technology *"cannot yet allow for total connectivity and immersion and that integral face-to-face reaction, co-creation and co-production are crucial elements to the event experience"*. There are real barriers, physical, technological, and sociological that are preventing the potential for virtual events to become fully integrated in the events industry. Whilst business events are seeing the benefits of virtual events, they have not fully replaced the demand for attending in person (Bladen et al., 2018).

Defining virtual and hybrid events

There are numerous definitions of what is meant by the term event but Dowson and Bassett (2018, p. 2) provide a succinct yet encompassing definition by outlining that an event is *"a planned gathering with a purpose"*. This definition can be attributed to any type of event, irrespective of size, scope, or scale, and can therefore align to both physical and virtual events. In contrast virtual events are defined as *"events represented on the internet"* (McLoughlin, 2014, p. 242), and are therefore an online gathering with a purpose. The focus of virtual events, therefore, is to create an effective online environment for people to engage with the event content and each other (Beech, Kaiser, & Kasper, 2014; Sa, Ferreira, & Serpa, 2019). The business events sector has been able to benefit from virtual events in particular given the relative ease that these events can be developed and delivered virtually (Beech et al., 2014; Davidson, 2019; Raj et al., 2017; Rogers, 2013; Sox et al., 2017a, 2017b), whereas other event typologies do not translate as readily to a virtual context, for example sporting events and fundraising events.

From a hybrid events context, Nolan (2018, p. 136) states that this can be defined as *"a live event that also includes elements of a virtual event or has an online component*". This is echoed by Sox et al. (2017b, p. 946) who comment that a hybrid event *"involves a mixture of physical events with elements of virtual events usually running simultaneously and with overlapping content and interactive elements"*. Fryatt, Garriga, Janssen, John, and Smith (2012) also outline that technology is integral to the development and delivery of a hybrid event that connects all participants digitally across multiple locations. The hybrid event should also be used to enhance the live event rather than to replace it, creating meaningful experiences for all participants (Fryatt et al., 2012). Hybrid events provide opportunities to engage with new audiences and previously untapped markets due to the virtual elements reducing physical barriers to attendance (Sa et al., 2019; Sox et al., 2017a). Hybrid events, therefore, lie at the intersection of where live in person events and virtual events overlap and this is portrayed in Figure 7.1, which is an adaptation of the hybrid models proposed by Fryatt et al. (2012) and Nolan (2018).

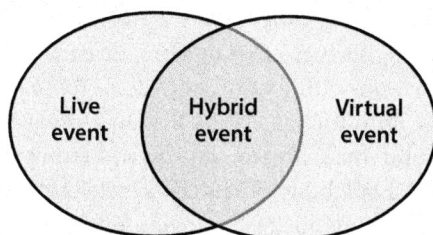

Figure 7.1: Hybrid event intersection

For hybrid events to succeed there is a requirement that the event experience is not impinged by either those attending in person or those online (Martin & Cazarre, 2016). The technology must be used to support and enhance the experience from both perspectives and add value (EventMB, 2020b). Designing the overall event experience and building in interactivity via appropriate technological platforms and applications is critical to the event audience, both virtual and in person (Antchak & Ramsbottom, 2020). Therefore, the intersection of live and virtual needs to be planned and mapped out fully to enable the intended event outcome, experience, and impact to be realized (Fryatt et al., 2012). Hybrid events also have a broader application for events and will benefit many event types, such as sporting events, fundraising events, festivals, and business events.

Development of hybrid events

Whilst virtual events have been a developing genre over the last 40 years, hybrid events are relatively new. According to Sox et al. (2017b), the first mention of hybrid in academic literature appeared in 2003 in context to teaching methods, where higher education establishments experimented with delivery methods mixing in-class and online sessions for synchronous learning. As of 2020, and due to the COVID-19 pandemic, hybrid teaching has now become a reality for most higher education establishments globally, who are opting to provide a flexible learning approach that incorporates face to face teaching with live streaming and interactions with students online (Boettcher & Conrad, 2016).

Whilst hybrid may be a relatively new term from an academic perspective, it can be argued that it has been a key characteristic of events for decades, although it would not have used the specific term of hybrid. It can be demonstrated that sporting and entertainment events operated as early pioneers for hybrid events and is sometimes referred to as 'event television' (Bowdin et al., 2011). An audience of spectators at a sporting fixture, festival or contest within a venue is engaged in watching and reacting to the event activity, which is simultaneously being broadcast live to viewers at home (Bowdin et al., 2011; Hill, 2011). Whilst this is a simplistic view it provides the broad scope of how a hybrid event can be defined. Early hybrid events predominately related to sporting events, with the 1927 BBC broadcast of the England versus Wales rugby union match being the very first live broadcast of its type in the world. This was quickly followed with live broadcasts of football and horse racing events but it was not until the late 1960s that live event broadcasts became more sophisticated and mainstream, due to technological enhancements, growing demand, and availability of television sets (Hill, 2011). In the last 10 years the advancements in mobile technologies now enable viewers to engage with these live events 'on the go', as well as interacting with the content via dedicated comments pages, polling and voting, use of hashtags and social media interactions (Antchak & Ramsbottom, 2020). Watching (streaming) live sporting events, festivals, conferences and lectures, ceremonies, religious services, and even personal events has become the norm, and we have the technological capabilities to consume this practically anywhere (Dowson & Bassett, 2018).

One of the key facets for events, including virtual and hybrid events, is the experience and connection that is made between the participant and the event (Quinn, 2013; Smit & Melissen, 2018). The audience's engagement and response at the live element of the event is therefore critical to this in its transmission. The action and enjoyment for the viewer at home is heightened by the atmosphere being conveyed, making them feel a part of the event (Smit & Melissen, 2018). Without this the broadcast or virtual experience can feel flat and lackluster. In late 2020 with sports and other events starting to return, albeit either behind closed doors or with very small audiences, a need to enhance the atmosphere and ambience of these events was required (Keh, 2020). Many sporting events, for example, added artificial soundtracks of fans' reactions to the broadcast to boost the atmosphere for audiences at home. In the UK, England's Football Premier League worked with Electronic Arts (a video games producer) to provide crowd noises to simulate the crowd dynamic and atmosphere (Keh, 2020). Whilst this works to an extent in generating an ambient atmosphere, excitement and tension, it can also create a disconnect with the images being viewed, due to empty stadiums being clearly visible, as well as issues with the syncing of 'fan' reaction to the live action (Keh, 2020). Sports governing bodies will continue experimenting with virtual and hybrid approaches to engage with fans until full capacity is enabled (Keh, 2020). These recent innovations in sport events will no doubt filter into the broader development of virtual and hybrid events in enriching the ambience and atmosphere to enhance the consumer experience.

COVID-19 and the pivot to online

Nolan (2018, p. 136) prophetically posited that *"the general consensus is that live events cannot be replaced by virtual ones and many of us would only choose to attend a virtual event if a live event were not available"*. In late 2019 and early 2020 a new disease, COVID-19, emerged that rapidly spread worldwide, resulting in unprecedented closures of numerous industries, including tourism, hospitality, sport, and events (Dams, 2020; Linthicum, 2020; Mohanty et al., 2020). The disease is a coronavirus and is aligned to a specific viral strain known as severe acute respiratory syndrome coronavirus 2 (SARS-CoV-2) which was termed COIVD-19 by the World Health Organization (WHO) in February 2020 following increases in global infection rates (WHO, 2020a). On the 11th March 2020 a pandemic was officially declared by the WHO (Ludvigsen & Hayton, 2020; WHO, 2020b), resulting in regional and national lockdowns in attempts to reduce the infection rates. As of December 2020, there have been over 70 million confirmed cases of COVID-19 and over 1.6 million deaths (WHO, 2020c).

One of the key reasons behind the sudden closure of events was due to the fact that *"historically, sporting, religious, music, and other MGs [mass gatherings at events] have been the source of infectious diseases that have spread globally"* (McCloskey et al., 2020, p. 1096). As COVID-19 was a novel coronavirus, which was spreading rapidly, the cancellation of events, such as weddings, sports events, trade shows, meetings, conferences, concerts and festivals, was inevitable, in order to combat the spread and in line with government guidelines (Mohanty et al., 2020). The cancellation of events also included numerous high-profile events, such as the Tokyo Olympic Games, UEFA (Union of European Football Associations) Euro 2020 football championship, the Cannes Film Festival, and Rugby Six Nations (Ludvigsen & Hayton, 2020; Mohanty et al., 2020). Whilst the closure of events was the only option, concerns were raised of the impact this would have on the industry and communities. McCloskey et al. (2020, p. 1098) posited that *"cancellations have social and economic impacts on public morale, on national economies, and on individual livelihoods"* and that cancelling events would have a significant impact on *"the future wellbeing of communities through economic recession or job losses"*.

Prior to the pandemic the global events industry was estimated to be worth $ trillions annually (Events Industry Council and Oxford Economics, 2018; Mohanty et al., 2020). According to the Events Industry Council and Oxford Economics (2018), business events represented more than $1.5 trillion to global gross domestic product, with over 1.5 billion participants attending events annually, and supported over 26 million jobs around the world. In the UK, for example, the Business Visits and Events Partnership (BVEP) estimated the event industry to be worth £70 billion annually, with business events being a crucial element, estimated to contribute over £31 billion, with over 95 million delegates attending approximately 1.48 million conferences and meetings each year (BVEP, 2020). The cancellation of events due to the pandemic has resulted in $ billions lost in revenue and millions of events related job losses globally (Dubay, 2020; Fullard, 2020; Mohanty et al., 2020).

COVID-19 has presented the most significant crisis management challenge to the entire events industry. Whilst crisis management plans and response mechanisms are common practice for event professionals (Bladen et al., 2018), COVID-19 was unprecedented in its scale and speed of disruption. Despite the significant negative impact across the event industry, many professionals identified opportunities for recovery via a pivot from in person events to online virtual events, particularly in the business events sector, as there was an unprecedented demand for events to continue (Amirkhanian, 2020; Dams, 2020). As a result, event professionals across the globe have focused on enhancing the techniques and caliber of virtual events and the supporting platforms, in order to enhance the consumer experience, and therefore evolve the commercial opportunities of virtual events (EventMB, 2020b). It is predicted that there will not be a return to 100% capacity at in-person events for the foreseeable future (Ludvigsen & Hayton, 2020; mia, 2020), even with the arrival of several vaccines, and therefore virtual events will maintain their importance until the crisis has passed (EventMB, 2020b).

With lockdowns resulting in businesses relocating to a 'work from home' mode, this has had an unexpected positive effect for virtual events, as people have become far more adept at working virtually and utilizing new technologies and platforms (Ritcher, 2020). Whilst a lack of confidence from event professionals and consumers in utilizing technology for events has created barriers previously for engaging new audiences with virtual events (Sox et al., 2017a), the COVID-19 crisis has resulted in an unique development in people's technological capabilities and confidence in order to stay connected and work (EventMB, 2020b; Ritcher, 2020). This has resulted in an exceptional growth in virtual events, such as meetings and conferences, as well as social events (Ritcher, 2020).

Koetsier (2020) notes that *"virtual events are up 1000% since Coronavirus"*, and the State of the Event Industry report also highlights a significant transition to virtual events, although this is not without its challenges (EventMB,

2020b). The global value of virtual events was estimated to be worth $18.6 billion in 2015 (Raj et al., 2017) which increased to $78 billion in 2019 and is now anticipated to grow to over $770 billion by 2030 (Grand View Research, 2020). This growth is due to the exceptional demand created by the COVID-19 crisis as well as the rapid innovations that have been developed for creating and delivering virtual events during the crisis (EventMB, 2020a). These innovations include enhancing the caliber of the virtual event platforms to enable these to link and integrate more easily to other applications (such as social media), developing guidance on better delivery styles for meetings and business events (such as using interview formats for presentations, and increased question and answer opportunities), and more interactivity for the audience (through live polling, chat functions, and voting) (EventMB, 2020a).

Whilst virtual events have been critical throughout 2020, the start of a limited return to in-person events now opens the opportunities for hybrid events, as they provide a link between the live event and wider online audience (Fryatt et al., 2012). This is due to two reasons. First, national regulations governing mass gatherings are still very restrictive in many countries to maintain control of the spread of COVID-19 (Ludvigsen & Hayton, 2020; McCloskey et al., 2020; Mohanty et al., 2020). In the UK for example, from December 2020 under government legislation, business events, as well as spectators to sporting events, can take place but these are capped depending on the local restrictions (Tier ratings) that the venue is located in. The guidelines state that there is a cap of 50% of the venue's capacity, which for Tier 1 (medium alert level) equals 4,000 people outdoors or 1,000 people indoors, for Tier 2 (high alert level) it equals 2,000 people outdoors or 1,000 people indoors, and for Tier 3 (very high alert level) no large events are permitted but meetings of up to 30 are allowed, and no multi-day events are currently permitted under any tier (Gov.uk, 2020a). For personal events, such as a wedding, only a maximum of 15 people can attend (Gov.uk, 2020b). Second, the planning time for most large scale events can take many months (Bladen et al., 2018), and with uncertainty remaining about the control of COVID-19, and reduced public confidence in attending events, event professionals are understandably being cautious about hosting wholly live in-person events (EventMB, 2020b). Hybrid events, therefore, offer a positive solution to this.

Benefits of virtual and hybrid events

As the technology has developed so have the range of benefits that virtual and hybrid events can provide. One of the most significant benefits is that they enable the event organizers to reach a wider audience who may not be able to attend otherwise, due to time constraints, travel logistics, and cost (Fryatt et al., 2012; Martin & Cazarre, 2016; Sox et al., 2017a; Rogers, 2013). Virtual events are becoming significantly cheaper to develop and deliver than conventional in-person events (Amirkhanian, 2020; Sadd, 2014) and are estimated to be approximately 90% cheaper (Rogers, 2013). Virtual events are also faster to develop and get to market, meaning that event organizers can quickly develop and market events that reflect the needs of consumers. The interactivity of virtual and hybrid events also aids in engaging the audience and enabling real time questions, polling, and content sharing to take place, thereby enriching the overall event experience (Sox et al., 2017a; Rogers, 2013).

Another significant benefit is the ability to archive and access content post-event (Martin & Cazarre, 2016). This means that attendees will be able to review elements of the event, such as a specific presentation or key note speech, as part of the attendee benefits, as well as creating an additional revenue stream for non-attendees who wish to access all or part of the content at a future point (Fryatt et al., 2012). The automated functions within the online platforms will also provide an invaluable tool for analyzing the data captured and even provide real-time analytics for events professionals to use (Dowson & Bassett, 2018; Fryatt et al., 2012). Finally, the sustainability agenda will benefit significantly from the move to virtual or hybrid events, as both formats will generate less travel as well as an overall reduction in waste and CO_2 (Linthicum, 2020; Sarabipour, 2020). Whilst there will be attendees in-person to hybrid events these will not be at the same volume as traditional wholly in-person events. This will reduce the need for venue space, catering, marketing collateral, amount of waste produced, and need for long distance travel (as most attendees will be local / regional) (Beech et al., 2014). Whilst hybrid events will be more costly than a virtual event, due to the need for a physical space and costs associated with hosting a live audience and technical set up, they are still more cost effective than wholly in-person events (Fryatt et al., 2012).

Despite the range of benefits for virtual and hybrid events there are several disadvantages which also need to be considered. First, whilst the carbon footprint is reduced due to reductions in travel, catering and other logistical requirements, there are still technical requirements that need to be factored in. For a virtual event this is essentially the energy production and resource consumption for powering the technology to deli ver the event (Holmes et al., 2015). For a hybrid event there will be additional logistical support and energy consumption required – although this does create an opportunity to develop hybrid events that are more environmentally sustainable, such as by utilizing renewable energy (Holmes et al., 2015). Accessibility can also be a barrier if consumers do not have access to appropriate technology or devices, or lack internet access, to access or engage with the event (Sarabipour, 2020). Similarly, if the platforms do not have subtitling, live descriptions, or good quality sound this could negatively impact attendees with disabilities (Leary, 2020). The technology can also now enable presentations and sessions to take place in multiple languages with the aid of captioning, translation systems, and transcripts, thereby creating a fully accessible global marketplace (Sarabipour, 2020). Engaging with disabled community groups will aid event professionals in ensuring online events, virtual or hybrid, are accessible and provide the appropriate support and mechanisms for everyone to participate (Leary, 2020).

For business events, particularly meetings and conferences, virtual events are, in principle, relatively easy and low cost to develop and deliver – they simply need a computer, webcam and microphone – which enable anyone to broadcast from anywhere and share material and ideas with ease (Shapiro, 2012). Hybrid events, in contrast, are more complex, as they require more technical know-how to provide a seamless and meaningful quality to the broadcast elements to enable both in-person and virtual attendees to be engaged (Davidson, 2019). A low-quality bandwidth for the event team and/ or delegates is a serious drawback (Martin & Cazarre, 2016; Sa et al., 2019). If the audience is unable to see, hear or interact with the content then this will result in a poor event experience. Therefore, ensuring venues (for hybrid events) have appropriate stable bandwidths is a critical requirement (Fryatt et al., 2012). Aligned to this is data consumption, which may affect some virtual attendees depending upon the platform or device they use to access the event.

From an experience perspective there can be a disconnect between in-person and virtual attendees, particularly at hybrid events, and therefore developing the overall experience for hybrid events is fundamentally important (Davidson, 2019; Sox et al., 2017a). A further disconnect can arise due to additional technological distractions which compete for attention by attendees, who may be multitasking or engaged in other social media activities (Ritcher, 2020; Sa et al., 2019; Sox et al., 2017a). Another issue linked to the experience is the quality of content and delivery. If done well this will result in an outstanding event and engaged audience. Therefore, investing in developing the content and delivery modes and methods is critical (Sa et al., 2019). Finally, the lack of networking opportunities at virtual events is seen as a major drawback, as many business events excel at enabling business to be conducted, deals struck, and connections made, including the serendipitous meetings that often take place in between formal sessions, which cannot be replicated online (Rogers, 2013).

Designing virtual and hybrid event experiences

Designing and creating meaningful event experiences are essential for all events, as this not only aids in bringing the event to life but also in marketing and selling this experience to consumers (Antchak & Ramsbottom, 2020; Getz & Page, 2020; Quinn, 2013; Smit & Melissen, 2018). Virtual and hybrid events must similarly give considerable attention to the event design to ensure that the experience is as rich and immersive as in-person events. This is of particular importance for hybrid events due to the differing needs of the in-person event and virtual aspects (Fryatt et al., 2012).

In facilitating the virtual or hybrid event experience it is critical to map the audience journey (Smit & Melissen, 2018). This will enable the event professional to visualize the event from the consumer's perspective and perceive how the event will be experienced (Berridge, 2007). This will highlight any potential difficulties that an attendee may encounter and develop solutions for these. The process is the same irrespective of the event being in-person or virtual. The complexity of hybrid events, however, means that the event professional does not only need to visualize both the in-person and online journeys but also how to link these two audiences and deliver equally meaningful experiences to both (EventMB, 2020a; Shapiro, 2009). To facilitate the design for a virtual or hybrid event there are three core considerations that need to be examined. These are the event objectives, the space, and the people.

Developing and defining the event objectives are a critical starting point for any event and are fundamental in shaping the concept, impact and experience being proposed (Bladen et al., 2018; Dowson & Bassett, 2018; Fryatt et al., 2012). The objectives will be contextualized to the type of event, the desired organizational outcomes, and consumer expectations. Therefore, the objectives for virtual and hybrid events are of significant import as this will affect the development and experience (Doyle, 2010). Working alongside key stakeholders, including consumers, will result in more meaningful objectives being developed, as this approach encapsulates co-creation, and more meaningful event experiences as a result (Smit & Melissen, 2018). The space refers to either the physical or virtual space within which the event occurs, or for hybrid events, the need for both (Fryatt et al., 2012). From an online perspective this space will be the platform that is best aligned to the event context, and with an ever-increasing diversity of specialist online event platforms to select from, it is important to remember that 'no one size fits all' (EventMB, 2020a). Therefore, utilizing a platform that enables the best integration with other applications (such as social media) and provides online interactivity and engagement is an important consideration (Doyle, 2010). For any virtual or hybrid event, the online platforms must be designed for interactions, such as polling, chat feeds, live streaming and break-out sessions, as well as enabling linking to other appropriate platforms, such as LinkedIn, Twitter, Facebook, websites and so on (EventMB, 2020a). For hybrid events the online elements should be available to all attendees to enable greater connectivity between those attending in-person and those attending virtually (Martin & Cazarre, 2016).

The final element, people, refers to the proposed audience and stakeholders of the event, who all need to be considered within the mapping of the event design and experience (Berridge, 2007; Smit & Melissen, 2018). For example, how can the event sponsors enhance their brand through both the online and in-person components (Sadd, 2014); for any speaker or presenter, how user-friendly is the technology to enable high quality delivery (Martin & Cazarre, 2016); how easy is it for virtual attendees to interact and enhance their own experience of the event (Doyle, 2010); and how well can staff navigate, manage and problem solve any online technical issues, or in-person needs (Fryatt et al., 2012). Event planners also need to consider the technological capabilities and confidence of their attendees, which is intrinsically linked to generational differences, with younger participants more readily engaged than more senior counterparts (Sox et al., 2017a). As participants can be global for a virtual or hybrid event, creating a seamless event is a priority as it will encourage inter-actions and enhance confidence for all stakeholders, resulting in a willingness to participate in future virtual or hybrid events (Shapiro, 2009).

The virtual and hybrid event experience is demonstrated in Figure 7.2. The three aspects of environment, interactions and immersion are all intrinsically linked to the overall event experience. The environment is both physical and virtual, and incorporates aspects such as music and audio, film, video and live stream, design, layout, and flow, which combined create the event aes-thetics (Fryatt et al., 2012). The quality of the environment design, therefore, will result in increased interactivity and immersion by participants, which is critical for virtual and hybrid events in particular, as *"active participation, interactivity, and engagement lead to audience satisfaction"* (Antchak & Ramsbot-tom, 2020, p. 38).

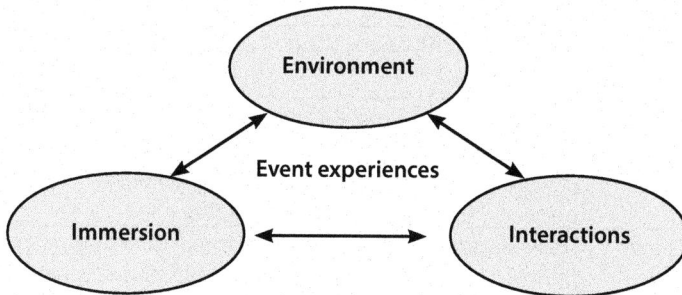

Figure 7.2: Event experiences, adapted from Antchak & Ramsbottom (2020).

In designing virtual events, the caliber of the content is fundamental to engaging with an audience in both the marketing and delivery of the event (Davidson, 2019; Linthicum, 2020). The content, therefore, must be relevant for the audience, and event planners must be cognizant that some concepts may not transfer well online and vice versa (Martin & Cazarre, 2016; Sox et al., 2017b). For hybrid events, providing exclusive content not available to those attending live, adds value to both attendee perspectives, as both provide unique experiences (Martin & Cazarre, 2016). Attracting engaging speakers or performers is therefore important and undertaking research into the appro-priateness of these in the context of the event concept and experience must be thoroughly examined. If a speaker, for example, cannot sustain the audience's attention, this will detract the interactivity and connection needed to sustain the event. Therefore, as Tripp (2020, p. 30) commented *"if content is King, delivery is Queen!"*, and attendees will willingly pay for high quality content. From a delivery perspective, managing the length of time for speakers has become important to maintain engagement; incorporating shorter, more succinct sessions; increasing live polling or interactivity with the audience (Fryatt et al., 2012); greater use of question and answer sessions as well as chat functions (Linthicum, 2020); and most significantly, the use of an emcee or interviewer to interact with speakers and keep the pace of the event moving (Cross, 2018). Whilst the caliber of speakers is important, the quality of the emcee is fundamental, as they will act as the glue that binds and strengthens the event (Cross, 2018).

Technical equipment	Virtual events	Hybrid events
Visual – lameras	One or two high definition video cameras (or a high-quality web camera).	At least two high definition video cameras.
Visual - lighting	Good quality natural light and positioning of speaker to this or small LED lighting.	LED lighting to full lighting rigs needed.
Audio – microphones	A separate source plug in microphone to provide clear sound quality.	Multiple microphones (such a lapel mics and boom mics) to provide clear sound quality.
Audio – speakers	Separate sound source (such as a sound bar).	Medium to large PA system.
Computer	Either a PC or laptop with high processing speeds. One to two monitors.	Multiple PCs or laptops with high processing speeds. At least two monitors needed per PC or laptop.
Broadband / bandwidth	Reliable broadband and speed.	Ensure venue has an appropriate bandwidth and speed.
Mixing desk	Small video mixing desk or video capture converter.	Medium to large video and sound mixing desk.
Software (if required).	Supporting software for broadcasting – such as OBS Studio.	Supporting software for broadcasting – such as OBS Studio.
Streaming	Platform being utilized – such as Zoom, Teams, YouTube or private platform.	Platform being utilized – such as Zoom, Teams, YouTube or private platform.
Interactivity tools	Polling, chat functions, video, and audio interactions, social media linking.	Polling, chat functions, video, and audio interactions, social media linking.

Table 7.1: Technological considerations for virtual and hybrid events

In line with the quality of the delivery is ensuring familiarity and proficiency with the technology being used, both the software and hardware (Cal, 2020; Matthews, 2016). Whilst a virtual event can be staged with just a laptop, the investment in higher specification equipment will enhance the production values immensely, particularly for hybrid events (Fryatt et al., 2012), resulting in increased event experiences (Davidson, 2019). The technological considerations for virtual events and hybrid events are outlined in Table 7.1. As well as the hardware and software, will be the requirement for appropriately cabling to connect to power and the technical equipment to the computer systems through which the events are being delivered. There will also be a requirement for specific event delivery roles, such as technical director, camera operators, audio and visual engineers, and event staff to manage the online interactivity (Fryatt et al., 2012). For hybrid events there would need to be a differentiation between staff managing the in-person elements and those specifically supporting the online engagement.

Current trends of virtual and hybrid events

There are several trends which need to be considered in the designing and development of virtual and hybrid events. One of the most critical to emerge in 2020 due to lockdown is the psychological concept known as Zoom Fatigue (Fosslien & West Duffy, 2020; Ritcher, 2020; Sander & Bauman, 2020). With the sudden pivot to online working, and virtual meetings replacing physical meetings, there was an increase in adverse effects to this mode of work which has been linked to Zoom Fatigue (Ritcher, 2020). As Sander and Bauman (2020) comment, the reason behind this is that *"meeting online increases our cognitive load, because several of its features take up a lot of conscious capacity"*. Sander and Bauman (2020) discuss that there are several reasons for Zoom Fatigue which include: having to concentrate harder to process and decipher nonverbal signals (such as body language, tone of voice, and facial expressions); heightened anxiety about personal surroundings; stress in using technology and technology failing; lacking appropriate breaks and mental rest; and reduced creativity. Added to this are issues around over stimulation via online and physical distractions, and a perceived need to constantly multitask (Fosslien & West Duffy, 2020). Zoom Fatigue is leading to decreased performance and increased stress and anxiety as a result. Therefore, from an events perspective it is important to create virtual and hybrid events that are immersive, engaging, interactive and enjoyable to reduce cognitive discomfort and enhance the experience (Sarabipour, 2020).

A trend that has emerged because of the lockdown and Zoom Fatigue scenario is the growth of audio only platforms, rather than visual interactions (Solaris, 2020a). This enables participants to listen and focus more easily and is in turn aiding engagement with the event or activity. This approach also has the benefit of not being reliant on bandwidth or high data usage, meaning it is more accessible to a wider audience (Solaris, 2020a). As it is audio only, there is less likelihood of sensory overload, due to Zoom Fatigue and other attributes (Fosslien & West Duffy, 2020), and therefore the simplicity and effectiveness of audio only platforms have merit.

Another recent trend for virtual and hybrid events is the use of ephemeral content (Owyang, 2020). According to Mialki (2019), ephemeral content is media, predominately images or videos, that are only accessible for a temporary period, from a few seconds to 24 hours, before it disappears. Incorporating ephemeral content into events will aid the event in several ways. If used appropriately, ephemeral content should result in higher engagement and can be incorporated to develop the story of the event as it happens, provide behind the scenes exclusives, create sponsorship and advertising opportunities, and grab the audience's attention (Owyang, 2020). Whilst ephemeral content may appear counterintuitive for events and marketing (as the content disappears) it possesses significant potential as it aids in developing brand awareness and builds relationships with the audience, driving conversions (Mialki, 2019). It is important if using this approach to ensure the content is authentic as this helps to build trust with the brand or event. They can also be designed to be fun as well as engaging, such as using memes that could link to the event context, and can be used in marketing pre-event, to respond to content during the event, and for post-event engagement.

Gamification has been utilized for several years to help enhance engagement at events, both physical and online (Antchak & Ramsbottom, 2020; Martin & Cazarre, 2016; Matthews, 2016). According to Davidson (2019, p. 434), gamification *"applies the elements of games that makes them engaging – such as interaction, competition and a sense of achievement – to non-game domain"*. Incorporating gamification into events, especially virtual and hybrid events, can result in increased motivation, engagement, interactivity, socialization, and satisfaction (Antchak & Ramsbottom, 2020; Martin & Cazarre, 2016). Event planners therefore need to consider the benefits that gamification can create without using it as a gimmick. As with all aspects of event design, introducing games, tasks or challenges needs to compliment the event concept and not detract from it (Beech et al., 2014). For virtual and hybrid events, gamification can be embedded within the event concept more easily than live events due to the technology and platforms already being employed. Setting simple challenges, such as creating a profile, linking to external sources, building a virtual event network, can be rewarded with badges or points which provide the participants with personal prestige and recognition from peers (Martin & Cazarre, 2016). The benefits of gamification for events are summarized by Martin and Cazarre (2016, p. 51) who state that *"gamification techniques exploit the natural tendency for people to socialize, collaborate, learn, compete and win status or position of prominence among their peers"*. Virtual and hybrid events, therefore, can benefit from gamification as it can create social and collaborative contexts from the outset of the event, leading to greater engagement, interactivity, and enjoyment.

Linked to gamification is the application of augmented reality (AR) and virtual reality (VR) which can also be incorporated into the event design to enhance engagement and the experience (Flavián, Ibanez-Sanchez, & Orus, 2018). AR is the layering of a virtual world onto a physical environment and is usually associated with a smartphone application (McLoughlin, 2014). Sadd (2014) argued that AR would become more prevalent in events, and whilst there have been some developments in incorporating AR into events this has not taken off to the extent predicted. One notable exception was the development and launch of the Pokémon Go mobile game in 2016 which has generated events all over the world for users to seek, hunt and train virtual Pokémon, with events taking place in parks, museums, and zoos, among other venues. Similarly, virtual reality has also yet to be fully embraced within events but has more potential than AR. Antchak and Ramsbottom (2020) note that VR is starting to be incorporated into events, enabling consumers to be fully immersed in a virtual experience and environment. It can be used in numerous event formats, from concerts and exhibitions, to sports events and product launches (Flavián et al., 2018).

A final trend concerns the potential use of 'hybrid event ambassadors' to act as a direct link between online users and the live experience (Flavián et al., 2018). For example, these ambassadors could receive direct instructions from virtual users to engage with specific exhibitors, interact with personnel, or collect and upload information (Martin & Cazarre, 2016). This could be enhanced using AR, such as Google Glasses, or video platforms such as twitch, that stream the live image to the virtual audience who can then engage and interact with the ambassador (Martin & Cazarre, 2016). This could also create high profile celebrity event ambassadors if the medium is well executed, which would help boast virtual event attendance as a result. The rapid rise in 'vlogging' and twitch 'celebrities' is testament to this, and as events offer unique opportunities and experiences, this will attract exuberant personalities to commentate and engage with their audience. The ITB Berlin and Berlin Travel Festival 2020 has switched to a hybrid event for the first time and will incorporate instagrammers and bloggers (among others) to help generate content and connections with the online audiences (Travelbiz Monitor, 2020). Event planners could capitalize on this within their event planning and design, as well as marketing opportunities.

The future of events will be hybrid

The impact of the COVID-19 crisis will be felt for years to come, with many industries being affected and transformed as a result (Mohanty et al., 2020). The events industry is no exception to this. Events, however, will return relatively quickly due to the human need for socialization and sharing of experiences (Getz & Page, 2020), whereas tourism and travel may be slower to recover (Mohanty et al., 2020). Whilst the pivot to virtual events has created a positive solution to the sudden void in events caused by the pandemic, it has not been able to provide opportunities for all event sectors, with meetings and conferences being the main beneficiaries so far. The learning and development of these virtual events, however, are providing a catalyst for the future of the entire events industry, with hybrid events being exemplified within the events industry as the future (Cal, 2020; EventMB, 2020c; Solaris, 2020b). As Copans (2020a) predicts *"the future of events will rely on virtual components that partner well with the live event. If done right, hybrid events will enable organizers to create a more dynamic experience and reach larger audiences as well as new sponsors"*.

As regional and national restrictions begin to ease, the transition back to completely live in-person events is still not possible on the size and scale previously, due to social distancing requirements, venue capacity, and concerns about infection rates persisting (Dams, 2020). The need for socialization is at the core of events and an intrinsic characteristic (Dams, 2020; Nolan, 2018) and virtual events cannot fully replace this (Getz & Page, 2020). Developing and delivering high quality hybrid events presents a crucial opportunity for event organizers to capture the ambience of the live elements and create meaningful and engaging event experiences for those attending in person, as well as those online (Dams, 2020; Fryatt et al., 2012). The mia (2020) have reported that more than 60% of UK venues are receiving enquiries for hybrid events, demonstrating the consumer demand that is starting to emerge. Similarly, research undertaken by EventMB (2020c) indicates that more than two-thirds or event professionals predict that hybrid events are the future direction for the recovery of the industry, with over 70% also outlining that digital strategies will continue to be critical for event delivery post-pandemic.

Hybrid events are not without their challenges, however, due to the technical capabilities and financial outlay required (Fryatt et al., 2012). Whilst consumers have an increased familiarity of virtual technology, tools, and applications, due to working and engaging remotely because of the pandemic (Ritcher, 2020), not all event professionals are fully versed in designing and delivering the technically challenging demands of a high quality hybrid event (Martin & Cazarre, 2016). With the exception of the business events sector, where more event professionals and venues will be proficient in the technical requirements of events (Cal, 2020), other event sectors may require retraining and upskilling of staff to ensure they are technically proficient for the future directions of the industry (McLoughlin, 2014).

Despite these challenges, however, there is a greater willingness by consumers to engage and participate in online events, as people feel more confident with the technology (Ritcher, 2020), which was previously seen as a barrier (Sox et al., 2017a). It is inevitable that social distancing will be the norm in many countries until 2022, reducing the capacity at live events, but rather than being a detractor it presents an ideal opportunity to transform events into a hybrid event experience (Cal, 2020). This will enable events to capitalize on larger global audiences, and if planned and managed correctly, should provide strong revenue streams (Martin & Cazarre, 2016). Hybrid events will continue to evolve in their design, delivery, and interactivity, enabling event organizers to enhance the consumer experience as a result (Cal, 2020). Hybrid events now represent the future direction for the recovery of the events industry, with all sectors able to benefit as a result.

Conclusion and further research

The COVID-19 pandemic has created a pivotal moment for the global events management industry, and related hospitality and tourism sectors (Mohanty et al., 2020). The immediacy of the impact created by event closures across the world resulted in job losses in unprecedented scales, which may take years to recover from. Events have been a vibrant industry for decades which play an important role within people's lives through the socialization and sense of belonging that they help to generate (Getz & Page, 2020). Whilst the transition to virtual events has aided the business events sector in particular, other parts of the events industry have struggled to pivot so easily. The impact of COVID-19, therefore, will have far reaching implications for the future of the industry. It can be hypothesized that there will be a significant evolution that takes place to ensure the safe return of events, which incorporates the use of technology (Sadd, 2014), enhanced professional skills and capabilities (Raj et al., 2017), and innovation in design and delivery (Dowson & Bassett, 2018). Social distancing will continue to be reviewed and analyzed as crowd density at events can result in the rapid spread of infections (Ludvigsen & Hayton, 2020; McCloskey et al., 2020), and increased safety protocols will no doubt continue to evolve in response to this. For example, the use of temperature monitors, rapid infection testing, enhanced track and trace systems, directional flow systems for consumers at events, and sanitizer stations, may all become a norm for events.

The supporting tourism and hospitality sectors which are integral to the events industry will also take time to recover, with international events being the most affected due to a reduction in air travel and capacity (Mohanty et al., 2020), and hence why hybrid events offer the perfect solution to this (Martin & Cazarre, 2016), as a global audience can still be engaged, as well as developing new markets (Sox et al., 2017a). The public may also be more cautious to return to events, as concerns about the transmission of COVID-19 will linger despite major vaccine programs being developed. The move to hybrid events will also increase sustainable practices (Beech et al., 2014) due to decreased travel and logistics, and through the integration of event applications which will create paperless events due to the fully online content (Holmes et al., 2015). Finally, the incorporation of event technology will enable events to engage directly with a wider audience who have, in general, become more technologically adept and more willing to engage in virtual activities (Ritcher, 2020), and the technological innovations will also result in increased accessibility and inclusivity at both virtual events and hybrid events (Layman, 2020; Sarabipour, 2020).

This chapter has explored the evolution and development of virtual events and posited that hybrid events will be a central component of events in the future. Whilst the event industry has been experimenting and providing best practice guidance and advice, there is still a gap in the academic perspective. McLoughlin (2014) commented that there is currently little exploration of virtual events, and particularly hybrid events, in the current academic literature, and this remains the case. Whilst more articles and chapters are being dedicated to technology, future trends, and virtual events, there is potential for developing this literature further and to explore hybrid events (Sox et al., 2017a). The sudden pivot to virtual events and expected focus and growth in hybrid events will most likely result in an increase in research, and this presents an opportunity for academia and industry to collaborate to examine the benefits and best practice approaches for this new event context. For the immediate future, however, this development will continue to be led by the event industry which continues to produce a significant output in content covering this topic. Whatever the future may hold, hybrid events will be a cornerstone of this new event landscape.

References

Amirkhanian, A. (2020). Virtual events take center stage: pivoting live events to virtual experiences. *Special Events Magazine*. https://link.gale.com/apps/doc/A625531281/ITOF?u=chesterc&sid=ITOF&xid=3945fc43

Antchak, V., & Ramsbottom, O. (2020). *The Fundamentals of Event Design*. London: Routledge.

Beech, J., Kaiser, S., & Kasper, R. (2014). *The Business of Events Management*. Harrow: Pearson.

Berridge, G. (2007). *Events Design and Experience*. Oxford: Elsevier.

Bladen, C., Kennell, J., Abson, E., & Wilde, N. (2018). *Events Management an Introduction*. (2nd ed.). London: Routledge.

Boettcher, J., & Conrad, R. (2016). *The Online Teaching Survival Guide: Simple and practical pedagogical tips*. San Francisco, CA: Jossey Bass.

Bowdin, G., Allen, J., O'Toole, W., Harris, R., & McDonnell, I. (2011). *Events Management*. (3rd ed.). London: Routledge.

Briodagh, K. (2010). Cisco takes its global sales meeting virtual. *Event Marketer*. Retrieved from: https://www.eventmarketer.com/article/cisco-takes-its-global-sales-meeting-virtual/.

BVEP. (2020). *The UK Events Report. Business Visits and Events Partnership*. https://www.businessvisitsandeventspartnership.com/component/phocadownload/category/4-bvep-research?download=396:the-uk-events-report .

Cal, O. (2020). *Hybrid events are the future: how venues can prepare*. Cvent. https://blog.cvent.com/uk/featured/hybrid-events-hotels-venues.

Copans, V. (2020a). *Hybrid events are the immediate future of the event industry*. Event Manager Blog. https://www.eventmanagerblog.com/post-coronavirus-hybrid-events.

Cross, B. (2018). *10 things to think about when preparing for a hybrid event*. Event Manager Blog. https://www.eventmanagerblog.com/tips-preparing-hybrid-event.

Dams, C. (2020). A peek into the events of the future: hybrid events. *Special Events Magazine*. https://link.gale.com/apps/doc/A630346858/ITOF?u=chesterc&sid=ITOF&xid=36fbf554.

Davidson, R. (2019). *Business Events*. (2nd ed.). London: Routledge.

Dowson, R., & Bassett, D. (2018). *Event Planning and Management*. (2nd ed.). London: Kogan Page.

Doyle, M. (2010). Developing a virtual/live hybrid event. *Meetings & Conventions*, 45(9), 36.

Dubay, C. (2020). *Analysis: Breaking down the unemployment crisis by industry*. U.S. Chamber of Commerce. https://www.uschamber.com/series/above-the-fold/analysis-breaking-down-the-unemployment-crisis-industry.

Events Industry Council and Oxford Economics. (2018). *Global economic significance of business events*. https://insights.eventscouncil.org/Portals/0/OE-EIC%20Global%20Meetings%20Significance%20%28FINAL%29%202018-11-09-2018.pdf.

EventMB. (2020a). *The hybrid event revolution – report*. Event Manager Blog. https://www.eventmanagerblog.com/hybrid-revolution-report.

EventMB. (2020b). *State of the event industry - report*. Event Manager Blog. https://www.eventmanagerblog.com/state-of-the-event-industry-report.

EventMB. (2020c). *Top 10 trends for 2021*. Event Manager Blog. https://www.eventmanagerblog.com/10-event-trends.

Flavián, C., Ibáñez-Sánchez, S., & Orús, C. (2019). The impact of virtual, augmented and mixed reality technologies on the customer experience. *Journal of Business Research, 100,* 547-560. DOI: https://doi.org/10.1016/j.jbusres.2018.10.050.

Fosslien, L., & West Duffy, M. (2020). How to combat Zoom Fatigue. *Harvard Business Review.* https://hbr.org/2020/04/how-to-combat-zoom-fatigue.

Fryatt, J., Garriga, R., Janssen, R., John, R., & Smith, S. (2012). *How-to guide: hybrid meetings.* Meeting Professionals International. https://www.mpi.org/docs/default-source/covid-19/hybridmeeting_howto.pdf.

Fullard, M. (2020). 525,000 jobs are at risk as business events industry campaigns for roadmap to recovery. *Exhibition News.* https://exhibitionnews.uk/525000-jobs-are-at-risk-as-business-events-industry-campaigns-for-roadmap-to-recovery/.

Getz, D., & Page, S. (2020). *Event Studies: Theory research and policy for planned events.* (4th ed.). Oxford: Routledge.

Goldblatt, J., & Lee, S. (2012). The current and future impacts of the 2007-2009 economic recession on the festival and event industry. *International Journal of Festival and Event Management, 3*(2), 137-148. DOI: https://doi.org/10.1108/17582951211229690.

Gov.uk. (2020a). *Closing certain businesses and venues in England* (3rd Dec). https://www.gov.uk/government/publications/further-businesses-and-premises-to-close/closing-certain-businesses-and-venues-in-england.

Gov.uk. (2020b). *COVID-19: Guidance for small marriages and civil partnerships* (4th December). https://www.gov.uk/government/publications/covid-19-guidance-for-small-marriages-and-civil-partnerships.

Grand View Research. (2020). *Virtual Events Market Size, Share & Trends Analysis Report By Event Type (Internal, External, Extended), By Service, By Establishment Size, By End Use, By Region, And Segment Forecasts, 2020 – 2027.* : https://www.grandviewresearch.com/industry-analysis/virtual-events-market.

Hill, J. (2011). *Sport in History: Aan introduction.* Basingstoke: Palgrave Macmillan.

Holmes, K., Hughes, M., Mair, J., & Carlsen, J. (2015). *Events and Sustainability.* London: Routledge.

Keh, A. (2020). We hope your cheers for this article are for real. *The New York Times,* June 16. https://www.nytimes.com/2020/06/16/sports/coronavirus-stadium-fans-crowd-noise.html.

Koetsier, J. (2020, May 27). *Virtual events up 1000% since COVID-19, with 52,000 on just one platform.* Forbes.com. https://www.forbes.com/sites/johnkoetsier/2020/05/27/virtual-events-up-1000-with-52000-on-just-one-platform.

Layman, M. (2020). *The ultimate guide to virtual events in 2020.* Cvent. https://blog.cvent.com/uk/feature/virtual-events-ultimate-guide/.

Leary, A. (2020). *How to make your virtual meetings and events accessible to the disability community.* Rooted in Rights. https://rootedinrights.org/how-to-make-your-virtual-meetings-and-events-accessible-to-the-disability-community/.

Linthicum, A. (2020). *Hybrid events: what you need to know*. Cvent. https://www.cvent.com/en/blog/events/hybrid-events-what-you-need-know.

Ludvigsen, J., & Hayton, J. (2020). Toward COVID-19 secure events: considerations for organizing the safe resumption of major sporting events. *Managing Sport and Leisure*. https://doi.org/10.1080/23750472.2020.1782252

Martin, V., & Cazarre, L. (2016). *Technology and Events: how to create engaging events*. Oxford: Goodfellow Publishers.

Matthews, D. (2016). *Special Event Production: The Process*. London: Routledge.

McCloskey, B., Zumla, A., Ippolito, G., Blumberg, L., Arbon, P., Cicero, A., Endericks, T., Lim, P., & Borodina, M. (2020). Mass gathering events and reducing further global spread of COVID-19: a political and public health dilemma. *The Lancet, 395*(10230), 1096-1099.

McLoughlin, A. (2014). The future of event design and experience. In Yeoman, I., Robertson, M., McMahon-Battie, U., Backer, E., & Smith, K. (eds). *The Future of Events & Festivals*, (pp 236-250). London: Routledge.

mia. (2020). *UK venue survey*. Meetings Industry Association. https://www.mia-uk.org/write/MediaUploads/Aug20_DCMS_Industry_Survey_Findings.pdf

Mialki, S. (2019). *5 reasons brands should consider ephemeral content & best practices when creating a strategy*. Instapage. https://instapage.com/blog/ephemeral-content.

Mohanty, P., Dhoundiyal, H., & Choudhury, R. (2020). Events tourism in the eye of the COVID-19 storm: impacts and implications. In S. Arora & A. Sharma (Eds.). *Event Tourism in Asian Countries: challenges and prospects,* (Chapter 6). Apple Academic Press. http://dx.doi.org/10.2139/ssrn.3682648.

Nolan, E. (2018). *Working with Venues for Events: a practical guide*. London: Routledge.

Owyang, J. (2020). What to watch in hybrid events. In EventMB. *The hybrid event revolution – report,* (pp 7-8). Event Manager Blog. https://www.eventmanagerblog.com/hybrid-revolution-report.

Quinn, B. (2013). *Key Concepts in Event Management*. London: Sage.

Raj, R., Walter, P., & Rashid, T. (2017). *Events Management: Principles and practice.* (3rd ed.). London: Sage.

Ritcher, A. (2020). Locked-down digital work. *International Journal of Information Management, 55*. DOI: https://doi.org/10.1016/j.ijinfomgt.2020.102185

Rogers, T. (2013). *Conferences and Conventions*. (3rd ed.). London: Routledge.

Sá, M., Ferreira, C., & Serpa, S. (2019). Virtual and face-to-face academic conferences: comparison and potentials. *Journal of Educational and Social Research, 9*(2), 35-47. DOI: 10.2478/jesr-2019-0011.

Sander, L., & Bauman, O. (2020). *Zoom fatigue is real — here's why video calls are so draining*. Ideas.Ted.Com. https://ideas.ted.com/zoom-fatigue-is-real-heres-why-video-calls-are-so-draining/.

Sadd, D. (2014). The future is virtual. In Yeoman, I., Robertson, M., McMahon-Battie, U., Backer, E., & Smith, K. (eds). *The Future of Events & Festivals*, (pp. 209-218). London: Routledge.

Sarabipour, S. (2020). Virtual conferences raise standards for accessibility and interactions. *eLife*, 9. DOI: https://doi.org/10.7554/eLife.62668.

Shapiro, M. (2009). Hybrid events: how meetings are blending virtual with face-to-face. *Meetings & Conventions*, 44(12), 30+. https://link.gale.com/apps/doc/A497735499/ITOF?u=chesterc&sid=ITOF&xid=ecda20c3.

Shapiro, M. (2012). Tech on the cheap: easy, low-cost ways to create hybrid events, meeting apps and more. *Meetings & Conventions*, 47(9), 31. https://link.gale.com/apps/doc/A306356901/ITOF?u=chesterc&sid=ITOF&xid=e3f154f1.

Smit, B., & Melissen, F. (2018). *Sustainable Customer Experience Design: Co-creating experiences in events, tourism and hospitality*. Abingdon: Routledge.

Solaris, J. (2020a). *The rise of audio in virtual events to combat Zoom burnout*. Event Manager Blog. https://www.eventmanagerblog.com/rise-of-audio-events.

Solaris, J. (2020b). *The future of events is definitely hybrid: what will they look like?* Event Manager Blog. https://www.eventmanagerblog.com/future-is-hybrid-events.

Sox, C., Kline, S., Crews, T., Strick, S., & Campbell, J. (2017a). Virtual and hybrid meetings: gaining generational insight from industry experts. *International Journal of Hospitality & Tourism Administration*, 18(2) 1-38. DOI: 10.1080/15256480.2016.1264904.

Sox, C., Kline, S., Crews, T., Strick, S., & Campbell, J. (2017b). Virtual and hybrid meetings: a mixed research synthesis of 2002-2012 Research. *Journal of Hospitality & Tourism Research*, 41(8) 945-984. DOI:10.1177/1096348015584437.

TravelBiz Monitor. (2020). ITB Berlin, Berlin Travel Festival to organize hybrid event 'We Love Travel' from Oct 16-18. *TravelBiz Monitor*. https://link.gale.com/apps/doc/A627976380/ITOF?u=chesterc&sid=ITOF&xid=d2a8dc24.

Tripp, J. (2020). Live experiences best practice. In EventMB. *The hybrid event revolution – report*, (pp 30). Event Manager Blog. https://www.eventmanagerblog.com/hybrid-revolution-report.

WHO. (2020a). *Naming the coronavirus disease (COVID-19) and the virus that causes it*. World Health Organization. https://www.who.int/emergencies/diseases/novel-coronavirus-2019/technical-guidance/naming-the-coronavirus-disease-(covid-2019)-and-the-virus-that-causes-it.

WHO. (2020b). *WHO Director-General's opening remarks at the media briefing on COVID-19 - 11 March 2020*. World Health Organization. https://www.who.int/dg/speeches/detail/who-director-general-s-opening-remarks-at-the-media-briefing-on-covid-19---11-march-2020.

WHO. (2020c). *WHO Coronavirus Disease (COVID-19) Dashboard*. World Health Organization. https://covid19.who.int/.

Practice Insight 5:

Interview with Dr. Amanda Cecil, CMP, 2012 PCMA[1] Foundation's Educator Honoree, 2012 MPI[2] "Member of the Year" RISE Award, Professor IUPUI[3],

Q1 - What have been the main impacts of the pandemic?

The impact on the meeting and convention segment has been financially devasting. With most meetings and conventions cancelled for 2020 and the 2021 outlook becoming increasing concerning, corporate, association and nonprofit meeting organizers are quickly shifting their strategy to virtual or hybrid events. Most meetings and expositions are held indoors with little space to social distance. Therefore, the logistical and liability impacts are significant, as well. This has forced convention and meeting planners to be become more creative in event design and quickly embrace different technologies to deliver content. Many associations and nonprofits that could not quickly shift were forced to close in 2020, as event registration, sponsorship and exhibitions were their main source of annual revenue.

When the MICE industry stalls – or in this case– comes to a complete stop, these impacts trickle down. Hotels, catering, audio visual, production, local restaurants and even specialty vendors – such as florists, entertainers, décor companies, destination management companies, are all significantly affected. Many small businesses are struggling to survive and even the large, international hotel chains will report bleak 2020 results. It is estimated to take 3-5 years to return to current levels of business travel and attendance at conventions and meetings. Until traveler confidence returns, many meeting planners will need to offer live, virtual and/or hybrid formats to attendees.

Q2 -What is being done to recover, including future plans?

The industry is coming together to create and implement a set of safety and sanitation standards. These comprehensive guidelines detail logistical changes (social distancing, maximum seating capacities), attendee behavioral adjustments (mask wearing, no contact) and increased cleaning requirements in public spaces.

In order for attendees to have confidence in returning to meetings and conventions, event organizations must demonstrate that risk management is

---

[1] PCMA: Professional Convention Management Association
[2] MPI: Meeting Professionals International
[3] IUPUI: Indiana University–Purdue University Indianapolis.

their top priority. The meetings industry must also partner with the travel and hospitality industries in the recovery, as one must feel safe throughout the travel journey to the meeting – in airports, taxi cabs, hotels, planes, food venues, etc. The partnership between these individual tourism and hospitality segments is critical for a successful recovery.

The recovery has begun and will take resilience and dedication by all event stakeholders to ensure the MICE industry returns, but returns safely.

Q3 - Who are the main stakeholders and what are their roles?

The MICE industry tends to have a variety of stakeholders for meetings and conventions, to include the meeting host/organizer, attendees, sponsors, the destination, convention centers, hotels, restaurants, production companies, ground transportation companies, airlines, marketing and communication specialists, and a variety of other suppliers. The roles of these individuals tended to focus on the meeting's logistical needs and communicating key messages to everyone that leads to a successful meeting outcome. As risk management has always been a part of the planning and execution process, it will become even more of a central focus, as the health and safety of those attending is the main priority in all decisions.

Notably, new segments of stakeholders are now increasingly involved in the day-to-day operations of MICE events. These could range from medical consultants, public health officials, technology/IT security vendors, government officials, insurance and risk mitigation partners, communication experts, and mobile application developers. These all become crucial in addressing and mitigating large gatherings of people in indoor facilities. Their role is vital and the meeting planner may now be taking direction from these professionals during the planning and onsite management of the convention.

8 Response and Recovery through Event Portfolio Management:

A Case Study from Des Moines, Iowa

Smita Singh and Eric D. Olson

Introduction

Des Moines, Iowa, hosts a variety of diverse events and festivals, reaping quite an event portfolio. A balanced portfolio of events is shaped by long term strategy: *"a full portfolio will consist of various types of events, for different target markets, held in different places, and at different times of the year, in pursuit of multiple goals"* (Getz, 2013, p. 23). Diversified and multiple events can bring more profits to the event organizers and the stakeholders by identifying overall risk-reward characteristics and minimizing the risk of not attracting the target audiences (Ziakas, 2014). Portfolio management of events also involves multiple stakeholders with distinct needs, priorities, and expectations (Reid, 2011). Thus, stakeholder theory is also considered a strategic tool within the events sector (Niekerk & Getz, 2019) which emphasizes the engagements between the events or the event portfolio and its stakeholders, hence putting the event at the core of the evaluation. This chapter utilizes the festival and event sector in Des Moines, Iowa as a case study to highlight the challenges of recovery and response to the COVID-19 pandemic and examines how Des Moines's portfolio management of festivals and events will position the city for a strong recovery in the festival and event sector. This chapter is organized as follows. First, we highlight key festivals and events in Des Moines. Next, we discuss how festivals and events in Des Moines have been responding to the impact of COVD-19. We then present four propositions, based on stakeholder interviews, how Des Moines can mitigate the effects of COVID-19 on its event portfolio.

City of Des Moines overview

Des Moines, with a population of 214,237, is the capital and most populous city in Iowa, according to 2019 estimates. It is the hub for the U.S. insurance industry and titled the third largest 'insurance capital' of the world (Des Moines Iowa, 2020). Major corporations, e.g., Principal Financial Group, Wellmark, and EMC Insurance, and more than 60 national and international offices, are headquartered in Des Moines. Employers and people alike are attracted to work and live in Des Moines due to its strong job market, low cost of living, strong schools, and high quality of life.

Festivals and events in Des Moines

Festivals and events are vital for the Des Moines community, as arts and culture are a way to generate business here. The success of these festivals and events is attributed to community engagement, economic assistance by local organizations, and voluntary participation of residents and local businesses. Des Moines has a history of hosting a wide variety of nationally acclaimed events and festivals. Locals and visitors alike attend the events annually to celebrate music, food, culture, agriculture, and the arts. For example, Des Moines has been hosting the Iowa State Fair, one of the largest state fairs in the country, for more than 150 years. In 2019, 1,170,375 people visited the Iowa State Fair, breaking the all-time attendance record by 40,115 (Carlson, 2019). The Des Moines Arts Festival is another annual event that attracts 200,000+ visitors (IFEA, 2017). In 2019, 177 professional artists participated from across the country in the live music and different community outreach programs (Kelley, 2019). Another popular event, the Downtown Farmers' Market, has been rated the second-best market in the United States (Des Moines Iowa, 2020) and attracts attendance of over 500,000 visitors over 26 weekends. In 2018, Des Moines hosted the Amateur Athletic Union Junior Olympic games, which attracted over 18,000 athletes and their families from across the country (AAU Junior Olympic Games, 2020). Other annual festivals and events include the 80/35 Music Festival, Bacon Fest, Wonder of Words, Capital City Pride, and Drake Relays, which are organized to attract visitors and support economic stability for the local economy. Research from Longwoods International states that annual visitor spending during the festivals accounts for approximately $838 million, including lodging, food and beverages, and retail segments, in 2016 (Catch Des Moines, 2018).

In 2017, the International Festivals and Events Association revealed that Des Moines was one of a few cities to earn the World Festival & Event City Award (Leimkuehler, 2017), to *"recognize and fly the flag of those cities and markets who have worked, through concerted efforts, to provide an environment conducive to successful festivals and events"* (IFEA, 2020, para. 1). Figure 8.1 highlights various events and festivals districts in the downtown Des Moines corridor. Table 8.1 states an overview of events in Des Moines.

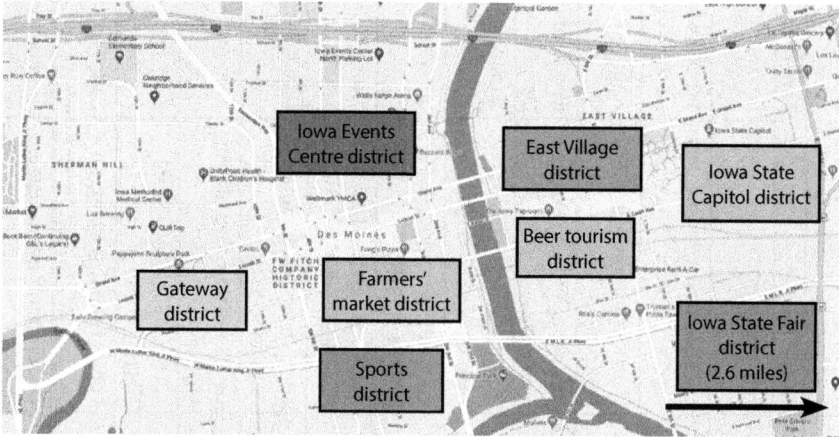

Figure 8.1: Map of festival and event districts in Des Moines. Retrieved from Google (n.d.). https://www.google.com/maps/@41.5877507,-93.623323,15.25z. Names of districts have been added by authors.

In early 2020, Des Moines metro area opened two new music venues, including an outdoor venue called The Lauridsen Amphitheater, and a smaller-scale venue called xBk Live, a space for smaller, live performances (Porter, 2020).

Impact of COVID-19 on the Des Moines event industry

On March 11, 2020, the novel coronavirus, COVID-19, was declared a pandemic by the World Health Organization (WHO, 2020). Two days later, on March 13, 2020, a national emergency was declared by the United States government. The state and the local authorities issued stay-at-home orders with social distancing guidelines prohibiting large social gatherings of more than 50 people (Schoening, 2020) to help slow the spread of the virus. As a result, large-scale events and festivals all across Iowa were either canceled or postponed. The cancelation of more than 100 events, meetings, and festivals resulted in an economic impact of more than $40 million loss during the summer season (Terrell, 2020).

People attend festivals and events to make emotional connections, as people tend to feel more connected if they share common experiences, which typically contribute toward their well-being. They also attend events for social interaction, which is critical in event attendance. A sense of belonging motivates people to attend events to spend time with their family and friends (Christine, 2020). For local businesses, getting involved with visitors and the local community provides opportunities to volunteer, facilitate businesses, and support

Table 8.1: Overview of Events in Des Moines

Event	District	Type of Event	Major Elements	Target Markets	Timeline
Iowa State Fair	Iowa State Fair	Fair	Agriculture contests, live music, food & beverage, midway carnival	Families, Iowans	Late Summer
Political Events	Iowa State Capitol	Political events	Fundraising, voter registration, rallies, & other types of political events	Local residents; Iowans; media; political coverage	1-2 Years Before Caucus/ Election
Capital City Pride	East Village District	Community festival	Parade, entertainment, expo	LGBT+ community and allies	June
Retail Events	East Village District	Holiday event	Live music events, ice skating, live ice sculpting	Residents and families Des Moines	Mid November - December
Beer-related events	Beer Tourism	Beer festival	Breweries, beer tasting, taprooms, entertainment, launch parties	Adults with a passion for beer and beer events	Summer
Downtown Farmers' Market	Farmers Market	Retail event	Sale of agricultural goods, foodstuff, plants, food and beverages	Local residents and families, Iowans, tourists	Summer-Fall
Iowa Cubs sport events; wedding expo	Sports District	Sport events; expo	Wedding, music, non-profit running events	Families from Des Moines; engaged couples	Spring, summer, fall
Business events, expos, live music, sports & others	Iowa Events Center District	Conventions, music, sports	Music performances, sports events, concerts, ice-skating, conferences	Locals from Des Moines; families Iowans	All year
Des Moines Arts Festival	Gateway District	Arts festival	Merchandise, art workshops and galleries, visual arts, music	Residents from Des Moines; families	Summer
Celebr Asian Heritage Festival	Gateway District	Cultural festival	Performances, cuisine	Local families from Des Moines	Early Summer
World Food and Music Festival	Gateway District	Cultural festival	Live music, performing arts, international cuisine	Locals from Des Moines	Early Fall
80/35 Music Festival	Gateway District	Music festival	Live music, interactive arts, food, and beverage	Generation Y and music lovers	Summer

economic development. However, as COVID-19 continued to spread within the United States, the consequences have been catastrophic for the events industry. On March 15, 2020, the Centers for Disease Control and Prevention suspended all large events and mass gathering for more than 50 people (Schoening, 2020); thus, events and festivals were either postponed or canceled, which resulted in economic and social costs.

Event cancelation or postponement has resulted in an estimated loss of $809 billion to the U.S. economy (Shapiro, 2020). On March 15, 2020, Des Moines declared a state of emergency in response to the community spread of novel coronavirus (City of Des Moines, 2020). Event managers and attendees deemed large events and gatherings as major financial and health risks. In July 2020, the Centers for Disease Control calculated 128,035 U.S. deaths and 783 Iowa casualties (Tefiowa, 2020). Event organizers faced many challenges to operate and conduct large events and to attract visitors to these events in the Des Moines area, with travel being a major concern, as visitors grew hesitant to travel due to social distancing guidelines and the number of travel restrictions and quarantine measures in and outside the country.

Additionally, event organizers never wanted to defame themselves for hosting large events and then spreading more infections in Des Moines. As a result, major events were either canceled or postponed. The famous 80/35 Music Festival was canceled for 2020 and postponed to 2021, followed by the Des Moines Arts Festival. The Director of the Des Moines Music Coalition (DMMC) stated that the pandemic has disrupted event ticket sales, volunteers, and community sponsorships (Maricle, 2020). The WHO DesMoines13 website featured the message about the cancelation of the 80/35 Music festival for its attendees and fans:

> The Des Moines Music Coalition (DMMC) Board of Directors has been closely monitoring all the developments to identify the best course of action for 80/35. It's with a sad song in our hearts to inform you, our friends, volunteers, artists and passionate music fans, that we have decided to cancel the 13th annual 80/35 festival originally scheduled for July 10 & 11. As a small, nonprofit organization that relies on ticket sales, volunteers, community grants, and corporate sponsorships, the COVID-19 global pandemic has profoundly disrupted our ability to responsibly prepare and produce the festival in a manner that ensures its future success. A future without 80/35 was something we couldn't risk. (Maricle, 2020, para. 3)

According to Catch Des Moines, the cancelation and delay of conventions and sporting events resulted in a revenue loss of more than $35 million for the Des Moines Community (Akin, 2020). Another annual event, the Capitol City Pride, was canceled due to COVID-19 and was planned virtually. The Iowa State Fair, one of the top events in the country, was canceled for the first time since World War II (Andrew & Henderson, 2020), which resulted in an estimated loss of $30 million in revenues (Linh, 2020).

The impact from COVID-19 has also been challenging for numerous independent music venues, including Vaudeville Mews, a music venue in Des Moines, which closed in October 2020, as highlighted by owner Amedeo Rossi in a recent interview in *The New York Times*: *"We couldn't pay our rent, and it was piling up, and we were constantly still getting drained by internet bill, insurance bill, utility bill,"* he said. *"Who wants to go into huge debt to float a business that we don't see any end in sight?"* (Casselman & Tankersely, 2020, para. 15). Wooly's is another independent music venue in the East Village neighborhood in Des Moines that has been impacted by COVID-19. Its co-owner Sam Summers stated in the *Des Moines Register* that he reopened the venue in June with a capacity from 680 to 200 and is currently focusing on scheduling performances for early spring 2021 (Porter, 2020, para. 38 & 41).

How Des Moines events have adapted

The COVID-19 pandemic has thus forced Des Moines to become creative in implementing and altering its festivals and events. The DSM Book Festival, a spring festival where attendees interact with authors, experimented with new financial models in the context of COVID-19. The festival offered a 'fee within a fee' concept and provided enhanced workshops and seating for limited VIP passes.

The Iowa Food & Music Festival, which celebrates the diverse cultures of Des Moines, is traditionally held in September in Downtown Des Moines and hosts a variety of food vendors, music festivals stages, and other programming. In 2020, the festival was repositioned as a *"community-wide celebration of food, music, heritage and culture"* (World Food Music Festival, 2020, para. 1). The Festival:

♦ Embraced a Community Cookout and encouraged Des Moines residents to decorate driveways and balconies by hosting a 'mini-World Food & Music Festival' by cooking global dishes;

♦ Created 'cultural kits' that included arts and culture activities for families that could be picked up at the Iowa State Historical Building;

♦ Repurposed international flags that are prominently displayed at the festival to the East Village neighborhood (Figure 8.2);

♦ Obtained festival sponsors including Bravo Greater Des Moines, Principal, Nationwide, MidAmerican Energy Company, Des Moines Area Regional Transit, and other prominent sponsors;

♦ Maintained a retail website where visitors could purchase festival-themed apparel, stickers & koozies, and other merchandise items.

Figure 8.2: Examples of World Food & Music Celebration modifications. Photos by authors.

Des Moines' Downtown Farmers' Market created a drive-through option, i.e., the Drive-Through Bite-Size Market, for its customers, in which participating vendors were featured online. Customers were able to pre-order goods by going online and picking them up from their vehicles at the Drive-Through Bite-Size Market on the assigned days. Staff monitored entry and exit points for vehicles driving to the market. A recent blog by Lydia Zerby on Des Moines Farmers' Market in *DSM Partnership* shared the experiences of the participating vendors and how the re-opening of the market had brought the community spirit and tranquility to the market. An owner of the American Pride Roasters who participated in the event commented, *"Last Saturday was our first Market back and it felt like we had finally come home! We saw our friends. We talked with old customers and met new ones. It was just so nice to feel normal again!"* (Zerby, 2020, para. 5).

Portfolio management

As previously noted, Des Moines employs a plethora of types of events and festivals across numerous locations in the city. *"They [events] mark important milestones and achievements, they are deployed to celebrate and engage communities, and they are inherent aspect of any public occasions"* (Pernecky & Luck, 2013, p. 1). According to Richards (2015), events reflect places of social interaction, which strengthen people by generating a sense of 'togetherness' via belonging to a specific subculture or society (Silvanto & Hellman, 2005) and influence the creation of a place identity. However, creating an event portfolio is a strategic approach to support the quality of life and to promote social, cultural, and economic development (Stone, 1989). An event portfolio is designed to put together various events, event stakeholders, community resources, and community goals by implementing collective strategies; it is defined by Ziakas

(2014) as *"the strategic patterning of disparate but interrelated events taking place during the course of the year in a host community that as a whole is intended to achieve multiple outcomes through the implementation of joint event strategies"* (p. 14). A portfolio must demonstrate a strategic link between events and a synergistic connection within the host city (Richards & Palmer, 2010; Ziakas, 2010). The purpose is to provide a workable comprehensive tool that can increase and improve tourism and create community spirit and planning.

Events and festivals in Des Moines provide a strategic framework for creating a place identity and can be associated with its competitive identity (Anholt, 2007, 2010). In 2017, Des Moines was honored with 'World Festival and Event City' by the International Festivals and Events Association (IFEA, 2017), as it has a history of hosting nationally acclaimed events and festivals e.g., Iowa State Fair, Des Moines Arts Festival and the Downtown Farmer's Market. These events are organized to promote local and regional development (Ziakas & Costa, 2011a). The Des Moines Arts Festival is celebrated every year to support the growing arts and culture within the state of Iowa; it not only attracts tourists from all over the United States but supports local businesses for economic stability. Another example is the Iowa State Fair, which is one of the largest and oldest agricultural and industrial expositions within Unites States. Large-scale public events and festivals act like a 'competitive identity magnet', which also transfers 'magnetism' to other objects.

Des Moines employs a symmetrization strategy for its event management portfolio (Ziakas, 2019). In this strategy, the city hosts a variety of small-scale and medium-scale events (i.e., cultural festivals in Des Moines) with an occasional large-scale event (i.e., Iowa State Fair). The variety of smaller and medium-size events include cultural festivals, agricultural events, sport events, and political events that aim to reach different target markets by balancing its portfolio reach. Examples of these target markets include Iowan families for the Iowa State Fair, Generation Y and music lovers for the 80/35 music festival; this portfolio also includes a few larger events, such as the Iowa State Fair with attendance typically over 1 million attendees a year. Des Moines has also aimed to diversify its portfolio through designation of event clusters of neighborhoods, such as the Gateway District, which hosts numerous cultural and music events as well as the East Village neighborhood, which hosts retail events and Capital City Pride. In order to enforce a successful event policy, cooperation from diverse stakeholders is required in this strategy; this includes public sector bodies, community groups, and volunteers (Ziakas, 2014; Ziakas & Costa, 2011b). Events and festivals in Des Moines have long been supported by the community and volunteers, along with financial support through stakeholders like Catch Des Moines, City of Des Moines, Bravo Greater Des Moines, and Greater Des Moines Partnership (Table 8.2).

These communities have remained active in providing funds to support the events that, thereafter, can help in creating and promoting Des Moines to build better career and business opportunities. The events become a source to unite these diverse and competitive stakeholders who share same goals and objectives (Anholt, 2007).

Methods

During Fall 2020, we conducted semi-structured interviews with event organizers, advocacy groups, and event entrepreneurs in Des Moines. The purpose of these semi-structure interviews was to examine the perceptions of the current state of events and festivals in Des Moines and how Des Moines would be able to recover from the impacts of COVID-19. Utilizing a snowball technique, we also asked our respondents to recommend other event stakeholders to meet with, and several of our respondents connected us to their personal network. Interviews were conducted via a virtual video platform, and ample notes regarding the conversations were kept in a research diary. The semi-structured interviews lasted between 35-45 minutes. Similar to Ziakas and Costa (2011a), these interviews were not recorded in order to avoid being obstructive. We asked questions pertaining to the current state of festivals and events in Des Moines, current relationships established with other organizations, and future challenges and constraints. Furthermore, secondary data was collected stemming from organization websites, marketing information, social media accounts, and local newspapers articles pertaining to festival and events in Des Moines. The results from our conversations and secondary data are reported next, by highlighting commentary regarding the future of Des Moines events, propositions to consider for recovery and response in Des Moines, and tactics event and festivals organizers should consider as it relates to portfolio management.

The future of Des Moines events

Effective portfolio management has the capacity to reach a wider audience (Chalip, 2004; Getz, 2008) and can serve a variety of purposes by making optimal use of available resources such that each event strengthens the benefits offered by other events (Ziakas & Costa, 2011a, 2011b). A strategic approach, which event portfolio management typically follows, is to integrate various stakeholders who come together to promote economic, social, and cultural development. Thus, stakeholders play vital roles in an event portfolio; in this case study, they are the visitors or attendees attending the events, the organizations providing financial support, and the local businesses and vendors participating in the events and festivals. Focal organizations, e.g., Catch Des Moines and Bravo, represent a collaboration to foster arts and culture and to market Des Moines as a destination and cultural identity. These organizations

Table 8.2: Overview of Major Festival & Event Des Moines Stakeholders

Organization Mission	Event Strategy and Goals	Funding of Events and Festivals	Ownership of Events and Festivals	COVID-19 Event Recovery & Response
City of Des Moines				
To promote economic and community development	To enhance quality of life; oversees collection of taxes and street closer fees	Minimal funding of events and festivals	No ownership of events and festivals	Current focus on COVID-19 response of city; safety and wellness of Des Moines citizens
Catch Des Moines				
To market the Des Moines region as a visitor destination to increase economic growth and enhance the visitor experience.	Events enhance economic success and the quality of life	Funding is obtained from local accommodation tax	No ownership of events and festivals	Marketing and communication of programs, events, reopening resources
Bravo Greater Des Moines				
To elevate and enrich a vibrant Greater Des Moines through arts, culture, and heritage	Strengthen the arts, culture, and heritage in central Iowa	Funded by hotel/motel tax revenues contributed local government partners	Financial and leadership support for arts, culture, & heritage of Des Moines. Hosts fundraising and awards events	Funding has decreased from hotel/motel tax
Greater Des Moines Partnership				
To drive economic growth through one voice, one mission and one region	Events can help promote businesses, career, and future of Des Moines area	Funds events through global collaboration with affiliate chambers of commerce, regional business members and investors	Numerous events including DSM Book Festival, Downtown Des Moines Farmers' Market, World Food & Music Festival, Holiday Promenade, and others	Created Rapid Response Hub with resources pertaining to small businesses, employment, government and public policy
Independent Events				
To support independent events and festivals.	Entrepreneurial; for-profit viewpoint	May receive funds from hotel tax	Variety of independent events	Recovery and response strategies

usually generate event funds through taxes from the hotel or service industry situated in the Des Moines region. However, in Des Moines, Bravo has been formed from the collaboration of local government to provide reliable funding and support to the arts, culture, and heritage community. The portfolio of their events can be characterized by beneficiaries receiving funds permanently. Effective event portfolio management of Des Moines will rely on collaboration and partnership among key stakeholders to combat the challenges of COVID-19. The key actors in this network in Des Moines are presented in Figure 8.3.

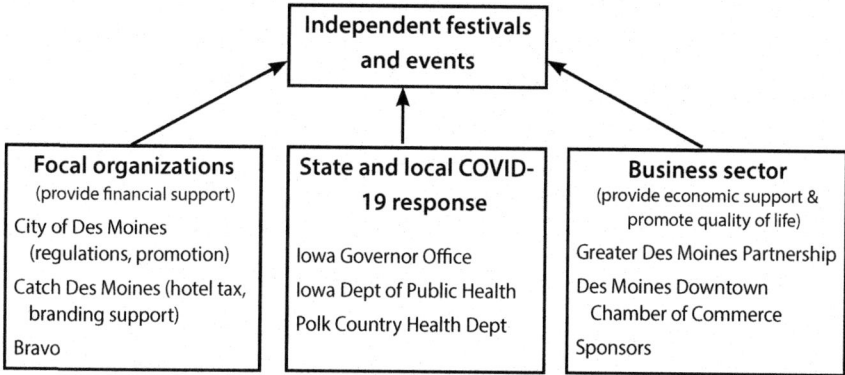

Figure 8.3: Network of Des Moines stakeholders

The recovery and response to COVID-19 for festivals and events in Des Moines are expected to be led by independent and entrepreneurial events and festivals. This will consist of major players (i.e., Iowa State Fair, Des Moines Arts Festival, Des Moines Farmers' Market, 80/35) as well as new event and festival concepts. The focal organizations (i.e., City of Des Moines, Catch Des Moines, Bravo) will continue to provide financial support through hotel and motel tax and also continue to promote increased quality of life. However, it is expected that the hotel and motel tax will be lower than expected over the next few years. State and local offices will continue to update COVID-19 mitigation strategies through rules and regulations that may have an impact on independent festivals and events.

As noted by Ziakas and Getz (2021), a portfolio development process has significant challenges, and the effective portfolio management strategy in Des Moines should recognize the constraints that sector faces. Integrating its event portfolio as it relates to its destination marketing tourism strategy could bring together missing relationships not previously linked. Additionally, Des Moines is a medium-size city that has obtained modest population growth in recent years compared its Midwest neighbors. In recent years, it has engaged in revitalization efforts downtown, attracting new residents and employers. Its citizens may not fully recognize the diversity and growth of its festival and event sector in relation to a city of its size. Des Moines was recognized as a

World Festival & Event City in 2017, and now stakeholders need to recognize the fruitful path of diversification of festivals and events in the near future. Several of our stakeholders also mentioned the financial constraints affecting their festivals and events due to COVID-19 cancelations. Traditionally higher levels of sponsorship of major festivals have been limited to a few major insurance companies. Thus, Des Moines will need to consider diversifying its sponsorship and revenue streams for the long-term survival of festivals. This portfolio management strategy could provide new sharing of resources, including human resources, such as leadership, volunteer efforts, and board of directors within the festival and event sector. Despite such challenges, Des Moines should be able to weather the impact of COVID-19 in recovery and response of festivals and events by these three propositions.

Proposition 1: Des Moines has a diverse event and festival portfolio

Des Moines currently takes a diverse and strategic approach to its portfolio of events and festivals, including a variety of events and festivals that occur in numerous event neighborhoods. Although a few events and festivals may be lost over the short-term due to economic challenges stemming from COVID-19, it is expected that Des Moines will emerge as a strong festival and event city. Many residents will have a new appreciation for face-to-face events, and events will continue to be linked with the quality of life in Des Moines.

It is also expected that the event and festival portfolio in Des Moines will experiment with new admission and entrance fees and policies as well as new and modified revenue streams. Events that are open to the public with no entrance fees will face pressure to charge an admission fee to recoup the increased costs of creating safety equipment as a response to COVID-19. Additionally, festivals and events in Des Moines will continue to explore innovative financial streams such as merchandising, event-in-an-event concepts, post-event opportunities, staggered attendee levels, and other types of creative financial streams.

Proposition 2: The event and festival portfolio of Des Moines will maximize the benefits of leveraging among key stakeholders.

According to Antchak, Ziakas, and Getz (2019), the *"major synergies made feasible through event portfolio management include:*

♦   *The leveraging of multiple events for social, cultural, economic, ecological, and built-in benefits;*

♦   *Efficiencies gained through resource and intelligence sharing, joint marketing, multiuse venues, and the pursuit of major goals through strategic planning;*

♦   *Greater public acceptance of events, venues and interventions through the demonstration of benefits and transparent accountability"* (p. 187).

Stakeholders in Des Moines will continue to assist festivals that will be impacted by COVID-19. How will they do this? For example, could a larger festival, such as the World & Event Festival, incorporate smaller festivals that face failure and economic challenges? Many festivals and events in Des Moines are cautious about overstepping their programming to include content and programming found at another festival. For example, the Des Moines Art Festival typically will not include a heavy presence on Latino programming since the Latino Festival already does this. Could festivals assist smaller, struggling festivals through financial, technological, and know-how support until they are independent? Could festivals in Des Moines assist others in suburban and rural areas? However, some stakeholders may not have the same level of commitment and remain open to collaboration, especially if competing against similar sponsors and event attendees. It has been stated that event planners outside Des Moines often face resistance from others inside the Des Moines event ecosystem, especially if they are not from the city. Such outside syndrome needs to be addressed among Des Moines stakeholders.

Proposition 3: Easy startup costs should cultivate a new area of entrepreneurship of festivals and events in Des Moines.

The Des Moines metro area has an educated workforce and a low cost of living; further, doing business in Des Moines is 16% below the national average (Des Moines Partnership, 2020). Additionally, Des Moines has a strong civic involvement, four seasons of recreation, and a long history of agriculture events, providing a vast opportunity for new events and festivals that may be introduced to the marketplace. In recent years, the city has a seen a strong start-up culture of new businesses and support to assist entrepreneurs; as it goes through this start-up culture, new festivals and events will emerge. Backed by entrepreneurship programs through local educational programs such as Iowa Pappajohn Entrepreneurial Centers located at five universities/colleges, Des Moines is poised for a new era of festival and event concepts. This proposition will complement Des Moines's symmetrization strategy of event management portfolio (Ziakas, 2019).

Tactics to overcome challenges

Despite the advantages of Des Moines' festival and event sector in recovery and response as it relates to portfolio management, we suggest the following four tactics to assist stakeholders in overcoming challenges related to COVID-19 recovery and response.

1. Umbrella organization to foster collaboration

Despite numerous stakeholders in Des Moines advocating for festivals and events, there appears to be a lack of a city-wide organization that can bring all stakeholders together to educate and advocate for the industry in Des Moines. At the state level, a nonprofit organization, i.e., Iowa Festivals and Events

Associations (http://iowafestivals.org/), was started in 2018 to *"specialize in the support, promotion, development and networking for professionals in Iowa's festival and event industry"* (Iowa Festivals & Events, 2020, para 3). The organization brought together over 110 event professionals and 500 festivals to host the Iowa Festivals & Events Conference in 2019.

An ad hoc group informally involved with producing events in the Gateway District, a downtown Des Moines district, which has received vast urban development in recent years, occasionally meets to discuss best practices in creating events in this district.

A larger organization in Des Moines, made up of industry leaders, government officials, event and festival suppliers, and educational programs could be utilized to share best practices, build partnerships, and advocate for the industry. Formal education, networking events, and informal training could also cultivate relationships in the industry. Additionally, to the best of our knowledge, a formal economic output report has not been completed on the economic and social impact of festivals and events in Des Moines, and such a group could lead these efforts. Such an umbrella organization could act as a catalyst for the sharing of resources among event and festival organizations to foster collaboration.

2. City of Des Moines' role in post-COVID-19

It is expected that the city of Des Moines will continue to implement new regulations and rules, as they relate to the number of people who may gather, capacity of streets, and other concerns to mitigate effects of COVID-19. Since Des Moines is involved in areas pertinent to event stakeholders, the city may also create a toolkit of best practices for operating events and festivals. The city should continue to be an advocate of bringing festivals and events to its downtown area. For example, in previous years, the Des Moines Arts Festival used to be held at Des Moines Arts Center (approximately four miles from downtown Des Moines). An informal advocacy group made up of industry and business leaders began a campaign to relocate the Arts Festival into the downtown area. Such efforts included the city of Des Moines, and the city is expected to continue such efforts in the future, adding to the vibrancy of downtown.

3. Partner with local education programs

Missing in this discussion of portfolio management and recover and response in Des Moines is the importance of educating future event and festival managers for Des Moines. Relationships and collaborations between event portfolio and educators should continue to be cultivated, as noted by the educational programs regarding event management that currently exist in central Iowa, as shown in Table 8.3.

Table 8.3: Event Management educational institutions in Iowa

Institution	Name of program/degrees	Connection to industry
Iowa State University, Ames	Bachelor of Science in Event Management; Master of Science in Event Management	The program provides expertise in a wide areas of event management; Event Management Executive Advisory Council provides support; THE MEETING ROOM provides a technology-based lab for student projects.
University of Iowa, Iowa City	Undergraduate certificate in event management	Combines experiential learning with academic coursework and provides practical and intellectual skills.
Des Moines Area Community College	Certification in Corporate Event Planning	An event planning certification providing expertise in implementing critical path methodologies, timelines, and project management best practices.
Grand View University, Des Moines	Sport management major	Provide opportunity to learn skills as it relates to the sports and recreation industry.

Such collaborations should provide educational opportunities for students, including internships, jobs, and other experiences, as well as content experts for industry panels and advisory boards, building the bridge between academia and industry. Additionally, faculty at these institutions should embrace to provide educational content in 'retooling' industry practitioners who may have been recently furloughed or those interested in getting into the event management field. Another constraint of portfolio management is that event portfolio development is typically not taught in event programs (Ziakas & Getz, 2021); thus, educational programs could partner with portfolio stakeholders in Des Moines to create curriculum that provides rich, industry examples of portfolio management.

4. Use event managers in city planning

Event managers have a variety of skills, attitudes, and knowledge from the event management planning process, that could aid city planners in recovery and response of mitigation effects stemming from COVID-19. Additionally, many festival and event spaces are used to facilitate public health initiatives. For example, the Polk County government opened a shelter at the Iowa State Fairgrounds in March 2020 for homeless who contracted COVID-19 (Cannon, 2020). In 2009, Polk County also used numerous event spaces to distribute the N1H1 flu vaccine at public vaccination events (Leys, 2020).

The relationship between event managers and local government officials is an intriguing one that needs to be utilized to facilitate mitigation programs of COVID-19. In other words, how can the festival and event industry in Des

Moines assist in the response efforts to COVID-19? Currently, the city's priorities are on the health and safety of the community. The festival and event industry professionals in Des Moines have the brand, the audience, the expertise and know-how, and the social inclusion elements to assist the city in meeting its objectives. Since event managers have transferrable skills of project management, marketing, and set-up/tear-down operations, these skillsets can be used to assist local government officials with testing sites, vaccine rollout programs, and other pandemic responses.

Conclusion

The purpose of this chapter is to highlight how Des Moines, Iowa, should use effective event portfolio management strategies through the collaboration of its key stakeholders (attendees, local businesses, and event organizers) for a strong recovery to adapt to the challenges presented by COVID-19. The case study mentions how Des Moines events have currently adapted by implementing creative strategies to boost the art, culture, and heritage of the Des Moines region. The chapter has offered suggestions to overcome the COVID-19 response and recovery by recommending forming an umbrella organization to brainstorm, share best practices, and build partnerships. It also encourages relationships and collaborations between event portfolio managers and educators to build a bridge between academia and the industry and advocates the use of event managers for efficient events planning in Des Moines. In summation, it is expected that Des Moines will emerge as a strong festival and event city due to its effective event portfolio management strategies and should be able to neutralize the impact of COVID-19 in recovery and response of festivals and events through the recommended suggestions.

References

AAU Junior Olympic Games. (2020). https://en.wikipedia.org/wiki/AAU_Junior_Olympic_Games.

Anholt, S. (2007). *Competitive Identity the New Brand Management for Nations, Cities and Regions*. Basingstoke: Palgrave MacMillan.

Anholt, S. (2010). A political perspective on place branding. (F. M. Go & R. Govers (Eds.). In *International Place Branding Yearbook 2010: Place branding in the new age of innovation* (pp. 12-20). Basingstoke: Palgrave Macmillan.

Akin, K. (2020). Silent spring: Coronavirus stifles Des Moines' post-winter celebrations. https://www.desmoinesregister.com/story/entertainment/2020/04/06/coronavirus-threatens-des-moines-summer-events-ragbrai-state-fair/5095265002/.

Andrew, S., & Henderson, J. (2020). The Iowa State Fair has been postponed for the first time since World War II. https://www.cnn.com/2020/06/11/politics/

iowa-state-fair-canceled-coronavirus-trnd/index.html

Antchak, V., Ziakas, V., & Getz, D. (2019). *Event Portfolio Management: Theory and methods for event management and tourism*. Oxford: Goodfellow.

Cannon, A. (2020). Polk County to open shelter at Iowa State Fairgrounds for homeless people who contract COVID-19. https://www.desmoinesregister.com/story/news/2020/03/24/coronavirus-iowa-polk-county-open-shelter-state-fairgrounds-homeless-people-who-contract-covid-19/2908415001/.

Carlson, B. (2019). Iowa State Fair marks record-breaking year in 2019. https://www.desmoinesregister.com/story/entertainment/dining/2019/09/13/2019-iowa-state-fair-record-breaking-year-attendance-sale-of-champions-grandstand-concerts-dart-food/2312571001/.

Casselman, B., & Tankersley. (2020). Iowa never locked down. Its economy is struggling anyway. *The New York Times*. https://www.nytimes.com/2020/10/22/business/economy/economy-coronavirus-lockdown-iowa.html.

Catch DesMoines. (2018). Des Moines draws record number of visitors to region. https://www.catchdesmoines.com/articles/post/des-moines-draws-record-number-of-visitors-to-region/.

Chalip, L. (2004). Beyond impact: A general model for sport event leverage. In B. W. Ritchie & A. Daryl (Eds.), *Sport Tourism: Interrelationships, impacts and issues* (pp. 226-252). Clevedon: Channel View.

Christine, W. (2020). Coronavirus event cancellations: Communication is key to retaining public trust. https://theconversation.com/coronavirus-event-cancellations-communication-is-key-to-retaining-public-trust-133594.

City of Des Moines. (2020). State of Emergency declared in Des Moines. https://www.dsm.city/news_detail_T2_R166.php.

Des Moines, Iowa. (2020). https://en.wikipedia.org/wiki/Des_Moines,_Iowa.

Des Moines Partnership. (2020). Key industries. https://www.dsmpartnership.com/growing-business-here/key-industries.

Getz, D. (2008). Event tourism: Definition, evolution, and research. *Tourism Management, 29(3)*, 403-428. doi:10.1016/j.tourman.2007.07.017.

Getz, D. (2013). *Event Tourism: Concepts, international case studies, and research*. Putnam Valley, NY: Cognizant Communication.

IFEA – International Festivals & Events Association. (2017). World festival & event city award. https://www.ifea.com/p/industryawards/worldfestivalandeventcityaward.

Iowa State Fair. (2020). About Iowa State Fair. https://www.iowastatefair.org/about/.

Iowa Festivals and Events. (2020). Iowa Festivals. http://iowafestivals.org/.

Kelley, M. (2019). Record attendance expected at the Des Moines Arts Festival. https://www.radioiowa.com/2019/06/24/record-attendance-expected-at-the-des-moines-arts-festival/.

Leimkuehler, M. (2017). Des Moines is one of the best festival cities in the world, says industry-leading group. https://www.

desmoinesregister.com/story/entertainment/music/2017/09/14/des-moines-best-festival-city-award/665299001/.

Leys, T. (2020). Here's how Polk County will distribute the coronavirus vaccine – when there is one. https://www.desmoinesregister.com/story/news/health/2020/09/22/polk-county-iowa-coronavirus-vaccine-covid-vs-flu/5831120002/.

Linh, T. (2020). Iowa State Fair estimates it will lose $30 million in revenue this year. Retrieved from https://iowacapitaldispatch.com/2020/06/12/iowa-state-fair-estimates-it-will-lose-30-million-in-revenue-this-year/.

Maricle, K. (2020). 80/35 Music Festival canceled for 2020 due to COVID-19. https://who13.com/news/80-35-music-festival-canceled-for-2020-due-to-covid-19/.

Niekerk, M. V., & Getz, D. (2019). *Event Stakeholders: Theory and methods for event management and tourism.* Oxford, UK: Goodfellow.

Pernecky, T., & Luck, M. (2013). *Events, Society and Sustainability: Critical and Contemporary Approaches.* Hoboken: Taylor and Francis.

Porter, S. A. (2020). 6 months into pandemic, Des Moines music venues hang on, holding out hope against a silent spring. *Des Moines Register.* https://www.desmoinesregister.com/story/entertainment/arts/arts-in-iowa/2020/09/11/covid-19-iowa-des-moines-6-months-pandemic-music-venues-survive-struggle/3435174001/.

Reid, S. (2011). Event stakeholder management: Developing sustainable rural event practices. *International Journal of Event and Festival Management, 2(1),* 20-36. doi:10.1108/17582951111116597.

Richards, G. W. (2015). Developing the eventful city: Time, space and urban identity. In M. A. Muhairi & S. Mushatat, Eds. *Planning for Event Cities* (pp. 37-46). Ajman, United Arab Emirates: Muncipality and Planning Department of Ajman.

Richards, G., & Palmer, R. (2010). *Eventful Cities: Cultural management and urban revitalisation.* Amsterdam: Butterworth-Heinemann.

Schoening, E. (2020). The Latest CDC Guidelines for Events. https://www.northstarmeetingsgroup.com/News/Coronavirus-CDC-Event-Meeting-Conference-Planning-Guidelines-Tips-Advice.

Shapiro, G. (2020). The events industry needs a future-forward mindset to survive coronavirus. https://www.northstarmeetingsgroup.com/News/Industry/Coronavirus-Events-Industry-Cancellation-Prevention-Hotels-Airlines-Convention-Centers.

Silvanto, S., & Hellman, T. (2005). *Helsinki—the festival city.* In L. Lankinen (Ed.) *Arts and Culture in Helsinki* (pp. 4-9). Helsinki: City of Helsinki.

Stone, C. (1989). *Regime Politics.* Lawrence: University of Kansas Press.

Tefiowa. (2020). The Economic Impact of COVID-19 on the Iowa Economy. https://www.tefiowa.org/covid/.

Terrell, L. (2020). $40 million lost by canceling metro events; Summer cancellations to make it worse. https://www.kcci.com/article/dollar40-million-lost-by-canceling-metro-events-summer-cancellations-to-make-it-worse/32648539.

World Health Organization. (2020). Coronavirus Disease (COVID-19) - events as they happen. https://www.who.int/emergencies/diseases/novel-coronavirus-2019/events-as-they-happen.

World Food & Music Festival. (2020). Enjoy the flavors of 2020. World Food & Music Celebration. https://www.dsmpartnership.com/worldfoodandmusicfestival/.

Zerby, L. (2020). Drive-Through Bite-Size Market in October 2020. https://www.dsmpartnership.com/desmoinesfarmersmarket/blog/one-more-month-to-shop-the-2020-drive-through-bite-size-market.

Ziakas, V. (2010). Understanding an event portfolio: The uncovering of interrelationships, synergies, and leveraging opportunities. *Journal of Policy Research in Tourism, Leisure and Events, 2(2)*, 144-164. doi:10.1080/19407963.2010.482274.

Ziakas, V. (2014). *Event Portfolio Planning and Management: A holistic approach.* London: Routledge, Taylor & Francis Group.

Ziakas, V. (2019). Issues, patterns and strategies in the development of event portfolios: Configuring models, design and policy. *Journal of Policy Research in Tourism, Leisure and Events, 11(1)*, 121-158.

Ziakas, V., & Costa, C. A. (2011a). The use of an event portfolio in regional community and tourism development: Creating synergy between sport and cultural events. *Journal of Sport & Tourism, 16(2)*, 149–175.

Ziakas, V., & Costa, C. A. (2011b). Event portfolio and multi-purpose development: Establishing the conceptual grounds. *Sport Management Review, 14(4)*, 409-423. doi:10.1016/j.smr.2010.09.003.

Ziakas, V., & Getz, D. (2021). Event portfolio management: An emerging transdisciplinary field of theory and praxis. *Tourism Management, 83*, 104233.

Practice Insight 6:

Case study of Transrockies Inc.

(The information provided in this case study is correct as of November 2020.)

This private event production and management company, based in Calgary, Canada, has been a leader in designing, producing and managing challenging events for runners and bicyclists. It has previously been profiled in the book *Event Tourism* (Getz, 2013), and that case study plus this current update have been written with the co-operation of TransRockies CEO, Aaron McConnell. Data from TransRockies events has been instrumental in several published papers on the Event Travel Career Trajectory (Getz & McConnell, 2011, 2014).

Quotes are from Aaron McConnell unless otherwise indicated.

Before the 2020 pandemic TransRockies (https://www.transrockies.com) owned and operated a portfolio of running, mountain-biking and cycling events in western Canada and the USA, under the brand TransRockies Race Series, as follows:

☐ Rundle's Revenge – Mountain Mule Trail Run, June (Canmore, Alberta).

☐ Under Armour Transrockies Run, August (Buena Vista - Leadville - Beaver Creek, Colorado).

☐ TranSelkirks Run, August (Revelstoke, British Columbia).

☐ Golden Ultra (3-day run), September (Golden, British Columbia). This event had been purchased from another organizer in early 2020 and TransRockies has yet to operate it.

☐ Moab Rocks (3-day mountain-biking), April (Moab, Utah).

☐ TransRockies Singletrack 6 (6-day mountain-biking), September (South Kootenay region, British Columbia).

☐ Golden 24 (mountain biking), June (Golden, British Columbia).

☐ Rundle's Revenge – Kick Ass Bike Race, June (Canmore, Alberta).

☐ ATB Financial Gran Fondo Highwood Pass (road cycling), July (Longview, Alberta).

These types of events for the most part attract already-accomplished athletes, with good incomes and the motivation to seek personal challenge and novel experiences. Profiles and motivations have been explored in detail in the Getz and McConnell articles (2011; 2014), and similar papers exploring involvement and event travel careers by Getz and Andersson (2020) and Andersson and Getz (2020).

In September 2019 TransRockies managed the first University of Calgary Chancellor's Ride, a multiple-distance road cycling event to raise money for scholarships. This was their only event managed under contract in that year, and they were expecting to provide this service again.

In their communications with sponsors, looking ahead to resumption of events, the company anticipated a 2021 season for the TransRockies Race Series with 3,650 participants and 10,950 participant days. Their customer base was described as "Affluent, Passionate, International; Average Age: 44; Median Household Income: Over $150,000; Target Markets: Alberta, British Columbia, Colorado, Utah, Western States".

Immediate Impact of Pandemic in 2020

Although 2016 had been a poor year in financial terms, the company was looking forward to a successful 2020. The demand for challenging running and cycling events was growing and pre-registration for TransRockies events was strong. However, by March of 2020 it was clear that their spring summer events could not be held, owing to the growing pandemic and more importantly to uncertainty regarding the emerging political environment in which every state in the USA and every province in Canada was imposing different regulations on events.

On April 29 registrants for the Under Armour TransRockies Run were sent this email:

"As we delved into the planning and logistics that we would need to undertake to keep everyone safe this summer, we realized the unprecedented challenges we would face including a complete reorganization of camps, aid stations and catering, a dedicated sanitation crew, and requiring physical distancing among our participants. We quickly realized that this would not be feasible. In addition, it appears that many restrictions on events and gatherings, as well as travel restrictions are likely to still be in place at the time of the event. With athletes and volunteers from over 15 countries and the current closure of the US/Canada border, we recognized that travel for many may not be possible."

By May 6 the TransRockies management team was still optimistic that some events could be held later in 2020. They specified these criteria through their mailing lists:

"In order to proceed with the final planning and preparation for our events we need to be sure with at least 2-3 months of lead time that:

1. The majority of our participants will be able to travel to attend the events

2. Our crew will be able to travel to operate the events

3. We will be allowed to operate our events by local, provincial/state and national authorities

4. Host communities are welcoming visitors

5. We can operate without risking the safety of our participants and crew with normal or modified operations"

Unfortunately none of the criteria could be met with certainty, and all 2020 events were postponed to 2021 – but with no guarantees they could be held. The impact on company revenues was severe, resulting in a very large financial loss – this despite efforts to cut costs and a refusal to refund prepaid registration fees. As CEO Aaron McConnell explained:

"Like most private event companies, huge costs are incurred before an event is held and it is simply not possible to make substantial refunds without having to declare bankruptcy. We want to get our customers back in 2021 for the same events, so their deposits will be moved forward. If you sell tickets only at the door to an event, that is another matter because cancellation means there is nothing to refund, yet staff, venues and suppliers have been paid so the financial loss is potentially the same. The losses then extend to partners and suppliers, all of whom face the same uncertainty as to when events will be able to resume."

Survival actions and key stakeholders

The obvious response of all businesses facing total loss of revenue is to either shut down completely or continue to operate with a new financial regime. TransRockies did let some staff go, but was able to keep others using government assistance packages. More importantly, investors were sought to keep essential operations going and plan for a future return to normal - or a new normal.

"We sought an investor group following the 2016 season when we experienced significant losses. The investor group came on board in 2017 and also became an informal advisory board – all of the investors are active endurance athletes. So far, we have not needed to raise more funds from the investors as a result of Covid-19 but we may need to if we are not able to operate in 2021. Having this access to capital may be a key to our survival in this crisis."

Maintaining contact with their customer base was a top priority, starting with facing the demands for refunds and ongoing event status reports. In events like those produced by TransRockies advance registration is always necessary, so fees must be paid and contact information obtained from customers. The company also did an online survey to determine future interests and employs its own website and social media to engage with existing and potential customers.

As to other key stakeholders:

"Volunteers and paid crew have stayed engaged through social media, primarily. We expect to see them return normally in 2021.

All sponsor payments and product contributions are being applied to the 2021 events. We have extended visibility to existing sponsors through ongoing participant communications and virtual challenges in 2020.

Regulators are typically following the lead of public health orders restricting events. Additional challenges have been experienced within Alberta Parks due to record visitation to parks during the COVID-19 pandemic. The record visitation has resulted in record demand for parking and search and rescue response. In British Columbia, public health orders are the same for indoor and outdoor events, with a limit of 50 attendees."

In August TransRockies produced a virtual run with registrants paying fees to participate. Some sponsors contributed prizes and gifts for participants, but they were not required to pay additional fees. The following is from a communication to participants:

"We are just 4 days away from the start of the 2020 TRR Virtual Race! You can choose to complete the 120 mile distance or the 60 mile distance over the course of 2 weeks. Each day, when you log your miles you will be able to track your progress on our virtual course map. Plus, each evening, we will be hosting a virtual ChillVille where you can connect with your fellow racers. We have over 400 folks participating from across the globe; don't miss out! Race registration ends this Sunday, August 2, 2020."

Planned recovery

All events in the race series have been rescheduled for 2021, and a new event has been added. Developed by the company during the summer shut-down period, the TransRockies Gravel Royale was announced in September and opened registration on Sept. 21. It was already over half full by November, thereby establishing a new revenue stream.

Uncertainty remains, both with regard to each individual event being able to occur as scheduled in 2021, and concerning the Canada-USA border. Restrictions on events have been tighter in Canada and it might be the case that USA events will get the green light sooner, and with fewer limits on the number of participants. The planned Moab Rocks event in Utah for April sold out well in advance and it is hoped that will re-start the entire series.

The TransRockies business model is to operate a portfolio of events, and this provides greater resilience. What is notable, indicated in the following quote, is that portfolio diversity relates to type of sport, location, target market, format and season.

"Having a portfolio of events is helpful to TransRockies because some events may be successful under different circumstances. Our events vary in the following aspects:

Sport/Discipline: Trail Running, Mountain Biking, Gravel Cycling
Location: Alberta, BC, Colorado, Utah
Reach: Local/Regional/Global Destination events
Duration: 2 days to 6 days
Format: Camp Based/Hotel Based/Local Audience

We may be able to operate again in the US before we can operate in Canada. Hotel based events may be easier to operate with Covid mitigations than camp based events."

As other practitioners and management gurus have said about resilience, optimism and perseverance are necessary for survival. Aaron McConnel believes that demand had been growing for challenging and endurance events and will bounce back following the pandemic.

"Our events have been steadily growing in the past few years. As we have re-opened registration for 2021 we have seen very strong response for some events. Two of our events were already sold out. On November 2 we re-opened Golden Ultra registration – with 225 runners rolled over from 2020, the event reached full capacity of 550 in just 4 hours. The cycling and running industries have boomed during the pandemic, with high demand for equipment that supports outdoor recreational activities. We expect some of this to transfer into interest in events."

During the pandemic there was evident in North America an increase in participation in running and cycling, with equipment sales soaring, as people realized they had to exercise while maintaining social distancing. It is uncertain, however, if this surge will result in higher demand for related sport events. Another possible trend to capitalize on is that of hybrid events. Aaron comment on the possible implications:

"Many races launched virtual events in 2020 as a replacement for traditional events. We also hosted a virtual TransRockies Run. While the experience is obviously much different from the in-person event, it allows more people to engage with the experience with lower costs and no travel requirements. We had more participants for the Virtual TRR than the in-person event and strong participant engagement. It is possible in the future that we will look to organize a virtual challenge alongside the in-person event to extend the reach and engagement of the event. It is possible that participation in a virtual challenge will eventually drive in-person participation."

Q: How do you build resilience for the company and for the events sector in general?

"After the 2016 event we found ourselves in a financial crisis which initiated a transformation of the company which has put us in a much better position to weather the pandemic. The primary changes involved better managing expenses, increasing prices to improve margins, and improving marketing methodology. Coming into the 2020 season we were seeing record revenue with a forecast for record profitability. Although we still service long-term debt, our cash position along with federal assistance allowed us to stabilize the company and redirect many of our resources into development activities.

Going forward, the importance of business fundamentals will increase. Higher margins will be required to recover from the losses of 2020 and create a better foundation to weather possible future shutdowns due to pandemics or other major events. The events industry has been shown to be particularly vulnerable to disruption during the pandemic. Event businesses without access to financial support may not survive, depending on how long the pandemic continues to impact operations. This may lead to consolidation within the industry as smaller operators look to sell struggling events."

By way of conclusion, this communication to stakeholders from TransRockies reflects both their optimism about the future and their commitment to proving their customer base with high-quality and safe experiences:

"For the past two decades, thousands of TransRockies event participants have created unforgettable memories crossing iconic finish lines in some of the most beautiful and wild places in North America. The community and connections made between the racers and the brands aligned with TransRockies events are equally special. Now the premiere event series in North America, TransRockies enters its third decade furthering its role as a pioneer in endurance races, and in 2021, will raise the bar once again. Our partners reach an engaged core audience of road and mountain cyclists and trail runners. Our event experiences are customizable for our sponsorship opportunities by region (U.S., Canada or global) and audience (road, mountain, gravel or trail running). TransRockies sponsors receive outstanding exposure, audience growth and engagement for their brands while also acquiring incredible visual brand assets and audience growth. Our suite of events and sponsorship opportunities will be thoughtfully expanded in the coming year, including a breathtaking gravel stage race based around the East Kootenay region of British Columbia.

TransRockies Race Series • Take place in iconic and rugged locations• Offer the highest standard of participant support• Celebrate the culture of endurance and trail sports• Represent authentic "difficult but doable" mountain challenges• Provide enriching social opportunities• Help our participants achieve their objectives of becoming a "finisher".

In the age of Covid – TransRockies will be a leader in participant and crew safety in all our operations."

References

Getz, D. (2013). *Event Tourism*. N.Y.: Cognizant.

Getz, D., & McConnell, A. (2011). Serious sport tourism and event travel careers. *Journal of Sport Management, 25*(4), 326-338.

Getz, D. & McConnell, A. (2014). Comparing trail runners and mountain bikers: Motivation, involvement, portfolios, and event-tourist careers. *Journal of Convention and Event Tourism, 15*(1), 69-100.

9 Swedish Sports Clubs and Events during the Covid-19 Pandemic: Impacts and Responses

John Armbrecht, Erik Lundberg, Robert Pettersson
and Malin Zillinger

Introduction

Sweden has 10 million inhabitants of which more than 30% are members of at least one sports club. Typically, sports clubs are organized under the Swedish Sports Confederation (*Riksidrottsförbundet*). On a national level, approximately 19,000 sports clubs exist, distributed over 72 specialist sports federations. Each club usually stages one or several sport events every year. For example, specialist sports federations organize all championships at national and international levels. From a sports club perspective, these events constitute important sources of income. From a societal perspective, clubs and events create considerable economic impacts, foster public health, and facilitate integration contributing with substantial social values (Brown et al., 2015; Pettersson & Wallstam, 2017; Wallstam, Ioannides, & Pettersson, 2020).

During the Covid-19 pandemic, most governments restricted individuals' possibilities for gatherings and movements. On March 12th the Swedish government responded to the pandemic by limiting the number of participants to events to no more than 500 people. Starting March 29th gatherings were limited to 50 people. During the end of year 2020 and the second virus wave, further actions were taken. The government limited the number of visitors and participants to eight people. These restrictions had considerable negative effects on many sport-related activities, events, and thus clubs.

While many clubs arguably suffer from event cancellations, little is known about the degree to which they are actually affected. What economic and non-economic (e.g., monetary, social and health-related) effects arise due to restrictions and subsequent event cancellations? This chapter describes and analyses consequences of cancelled events, organized by sports clubs in economic and non-economic terms. Previous research indicates that clubs are affected by factors such as size, type of sports, location or organizational form. A second objective of this chapter is therefore to describe how different clubs are affected, depending on a number of club characteristics.

The governmental restrictions that affected sports clubs as well as the event industry can be described in terms of a disruptive power. The theory of resilience concerns these powers which lead to changes. According to Lew et al. (2020), *"change is fundamental"* (p. 455) and positive since it implies development. Ideally, strategic changes incur through external powers such as the Covid-19 pandemic. In extension, this may result in innovations, which ultimately benefit the event industry. Such a development can create economic, social, hedonic values in the long-term, many of which also relate to sustainability (Lundberg et al., 2017). Recognizing the Covid-19 pandemic as a crisis and as a power affecting event organizers, this chapter describes important strategic reactions of Swedish sports clubs in response to the crisis. It ends with a description of the support that sports clubs need in order to meet existing challenges related to the pandemic. Adaptive capacities and vulnerabilities of the clubs are discussed, together with the question to what extent event managers can make use of these empirical results.

The chapter contributes to the field of event studies and crisis management by describing and analyzing a national case study that builds on extensive survey data. It provides a snapshot of the heavily affected event industry in Sweden during the pandemic.

Theoretical background: Crisis management and resilience

An external happening such as the Covid-19 pandemic urges the importance of crisis management and resilience. Both concepts lend useful perspectives to interpret the effects of the initial pandemic for Swedish sports clubs. The concepts also help us understand what factors are important when responding, and ultimately reviving the sport event sector in Sweden.

Managers, including event managers, need to deal with a new business environment. In a more globalized event economy, organizations are increasingly exposed to economic, political, social, and technological risks. When crises or disasters are linked to disruptive changes, they are difficult to foresee. Despite this, all organizations can work with crisis or disaster management in order to be prepared when the crisis arrives (Ritchie, 2004). Organizations that manage risks related to disruptive changes can reduce both negative economic and non-economic impacts. This capability of organizations to handle changes and recover is known as resilience (Hall, Timothy, & Duval, 2013; Lew, 2014; Shipway & Miles, 2020).

Resilience was originally used in system models within mathematical sciences and is today implemented to understand issues in a wide range of areas such as psychology, physics, engineering, and organizations. Within tourism and event studies, resilience has largely been used to explain reactions to changes caused by disasters and crises (cf. Lew, 2014). Examples of this are tourism actors' reactions to global climate change, previous pandemics, the tsunami in 2004, or earthquakes. The perspective supports our understanding of responses to slow and fast changes, respectively (e.g., climate change vs. natural disaster). It is also open to various adaptive behaviors for different individual actors and geographical scales. In a tourism context, actors' major concern to a shock like the pandemic is the critical loss of resources and primary tourist markets (Lew, 2014).

In recent research (Miles & Shipway, 2020; Shipway & Miles, 2020), disaster management and resilience have received increased attention. Shipway and Miles (2020) introduce an International Sports Events (ISEs) resilience continuum, which is an attempt to classify major sport events and how actors can work strategically with managing resilience, depending on their position on the continuum. In this context, resilience can be defined as the *"capability of a system to recover after undergoing significant disturbance"* (Shipway & Miles, 2020, p. 186). In the current study, this refers to the capability of sports clubs and federations to recover and organize sport events at a similar level as pre-Covid-19. The capability to recover varies between sports clubs and federations, depending on factors such as adaptive capacity, vulnerability, preparedness, responsiveness, learning processes (Biggs, Hall, & Stoeckl, 2012; Koronis & Ponis, 2018) and characteristics such as size or context (e.g., type of sport or geographical context). In the ISE resilience continuum, Shipway and Miles (2020) suggest that size and scale are imperative factors to develop greater resilience. While Shipway and Miles (2020) focus on large scale sport events, the model is underpinned by a bottom-up approach, which is beneficial for small-scale event organizations as well (as most actors in the current Swedish case). It focuses on the sport organization, the sport event, community aspects, the individual participants and event visitors in order to develop greater resilience. The context is therefore vital and we can assume that sports clubs, depending for instance on their level of resilience, need different types of support and resources (financial resources, support for innovation and change etc.) in order to recover.

In the current study, we analyze economic and non-economic impacts during the Covid-19 pandemic. Focus is on the initial crisis strategy of the sports clubs (i.e., impacts and measures), and on their perceived needs of external support. In this initial phase, focus is particularly on sports clubs' *responsiveness*, that is *"the ability of an organization to respond in a timely and constructive manner to a challenge critically influencing its resilience"* (Koronis & Ponis, 2018, p.37). Responsiveness assumes preparedness, but without a timely response it does not matter if your organization is prepared (Crandall et al., 2010). Moreover, both economic and non-economic support requested by sports clubs can be understood as assistance to adapt to a new environment (short-term and long-term) as well as a support for learning processes, that means both how to change and adapt to the new reality and how to learn from the crisis (Koronis & Ponis, 2018).

Methodology

The results are based on a data collection by the Swedish Sports Confederation. One of the authors of this chapter assisted in designing the survey. In April 2020, the Confederation sent the online survey to all 19,000 sports clubs in their organization, representing the majority of all sports clubs in Sweden. The aim was twofold: to measure the economic and non-economic impacts experienced by sports clubs due to cancelled events; and to develop a model for the state to compensate for forgone revenues and to cover costs. In the survey, the term 'events' refers to competitions, tournaments, cups and activities related to children's school holidays, or similar activities. The data covers events between March 12th, when the first national restrictions were put into place by the government, and June 30th (111 days).

The survey was directed to the sports club management level including chairmen, principals, or administrators. Respondents could answer to the survey between April 16th and 30th 2020. Altogether, 3,513 sports clubs participated in the survey, rendering a response rate of approximately 20%. The data describes both economic and non-economic consequences for clubs in three steps:

♦ First, lost revenues due to the pandemic; examples are a lower level of registration fees, ticket revenues, sponsor revenues, less sales during events, etc.

♦ Second, the costs for clubs due to event cancellation. These are sunk costs, meaning expenses that cannot be recovered in retrospect, e.g. . the expense for marketing an event that is cancelled.

♦ Third, non-economic consequences arising for event organizers, and their subsequent need of support.

The survey also contained a number of possible measures which clubs can undertake in order to respond to the restrictions of the pandemic, and with its economic consequences (see below).

Data analysis

The survey data was analyzed using a quantitative and a qualitative approach. The quantitative data was analysed using IBM SPSS Statistics 25. Descriptive statistics and regression analysis were used to estimate the size, proportions and reasons for lost revenues and sunk costs related to events. Outliers were removed before the statistical analyses.

To identify strategies pursued by the sports clubs, a binary cluster analysis was performed. A hierarchical complete linkage clustering for partitioning, and Sokal and Sneath 1 as the distance measure, were applied (cf. Griffin & Guttentag, 2020). The cluster variables consisted of nine measures taken by sports clubs to overcome the negative economic effects of the pandemic: short-time work allowance, reduced supply of sport activities, reduced daily operational costs, new fundraising activities, start/increase sales through members, increase training fees, increase membership fees, no refund of fees to events which have been cancelled. Sports clubs which took 'no measures' at the time of the survey, constitute a separate group and were not analyzed in the cluster analysis. The measures 'new loans' and 'close down the club' were not included in the cluster analysis wither, mainly for two reasons. First, these measures were taken by relatively few clubs (see Figure 9.1); and second, to close down the club prohibits all other measures.

In order to profile the clusters, items measuring size ('full-time employees', 'part-time employees', 'level of activity support from the Swedish Sports Confederation'); sunk costs from events; lost revenues from events; ownership of sport facilities; geographical location of sports club ('metropolitan area', 'large city area', or 'small city and countryside area'); and type of sport were used. T-tests and chi-square tests were applied to compare clusters. If differences among the clusters were statically significant, post-hoc tests were performed to further describe the differences between clusters (Bonferroni and adjusted standardized residuals, respectively, cf. Beasly & Schumaker, 1995; cf. Griffin & Guttentag, 2020).

The analysis of non-economic impacts is based on answers from open ended questions. It is based on specific questions on a) non-economic consequences for the clubs, and b) open answers about the need of support. To find the most frequent answers, an initial cluster analysis was done using the software NVivo. Further qualitative analysis was done by two researchers reading, sorting, and labelling the data in parallel. This procedure ensures a high inter-rater reliability (May, 2011). This procedure led to a number of mind maps, which consisted of word clouds that were, step by step, labelled and finally categorised. The question of non-economic impacts for the clubs resulted in five categories: i) loss of members; ii) decrease of activity levels; iii) physical and mental illness; iv) integration and v) joy and togetherness.

The question about needs for support resulted in four categories, which are i) interpretation of rules and regulations; ii) lobbying; iii) event innovation; and finally iv) marketing support.

Findings

This section starts with a description of the economic consequences of the Covid-19 pandemic for Swedish sports clubs. Cancelled events turn out to be the central aspect. On the one hand, event planning and organization have caused costs, which can no longer be recovered (i.e. sunk costs). On the other hand, clubs have lost considerable revenues due to event cancellations. Subsequently, lost revenues and sunk costs are analyzed in relation to sports club characteristics such as size, type of sport etc. to understand the effects for different types of clubs. The third part of the findings presents the strategic actions taken by clubs. The actions are described and analyzed both from an economic and non-economic perspective. This section ends with a description of support and recovery activities suggested by Swedish sports clubs.

Economic effects for sports clubs

Many sports clubs suffer economically from the Covid-19 pandemic. In Sweden, cancelled events accounted for 89.5% of the negative economic consequences. This amounts to roughly €100 million for the clubs included in this survey (which accounts for 20% of all Swedish sports clubs). The remaining negative lost revenues (10.5%) are associated with training activities.

The results suggest that events play a major role in generating revenues for many sports clubs during normal conditions. Another conclusion is that if we want to understand the negative economic effects of Covid-19 for sports clubs, then we need to understand the actions and decisions related to event cancellation and/or modification.

Lost revenues and types of sports

Lost revenues (as well as sunk costs) are distributed unequally among sports clubs. A considerable number (21%) indicate no decrease in revenues. The remaining clubs experienced decreased revenues. The pattern among those who lost revenues is clear; a few lost a lot while many lost some revenues. The fact that some sports are affected more than others (on an aggregated level) can partly be explained by the significance of particular sport in Sweden.

The uneven distribution of lost revenues is presented for the 15 largest sports (out of 68 represented in the survey) in Table 9.1. These sports account for 92.7% of all lost revenues. Football has by far the highest lost revenues (53.4% of all reported losses), but also the largest number of clubs. In relative terms, ice hockey clubs have the highest losses per club.

The lost revenues per club should be seen in the context of when the survey was carried out. The data concerns the period of April to June of 2020, which means that some sports have less events planned for this period than other sports. This explains the high ranking in this category for bandy (and ice hockey), having their playoffs during this period. Table 9.1 highlights sports that are highly dependent on staging events such as ice hockey, football, and handball. On contrary, equestrian sports seem to be less dependent on events (with more revenues from other sources like training and membership fees). Another interpretation of the distribution is that some sports are more pre-pared and responsive (i.e., more resilient) than others.

Table 9.1: *Revenue losses per sport (total and per club)*

Sports	Rank (total lost revenue)	Cumulative % of total	Clubs (n)	Rank (average lost revenue)
Football	1	53,40	815	2
Ice hockey	2	63,36	100	1
Athletics	3	69,36	217	8
Handball	4	73,44	77	3
Basketball	5	76,94	76	4
Equestrian sports	6	80,03	238	18
Floorball	7	82,38	98	9
Auto racing	8	84,20	62	7
Table tennis	9	85,92	108	15
Gymnastics	10	87,57	148	23
Bandy	11	89,11	37	5
Cycling	12	90,44	77	14
Golf	13	91,43	53	13
Sailing	14	92,14	31	10
Motorcycle & Snowmobile	15	92,71	30	12

Reasons for lost revenues and sunk costs

The decrease in event related revenues has several reasons. The largest share (33%) occurs due to a reduced number of participants and thus regis-tration fees. This loss highlights the importance of participatory events as a funding source for sports clubs. Ticket revenues from spectators and revenues from sponsors normally also constitute substantial sources of funding each accounting for approximately 20% of the lost revenues (see Table 9.2).

Considerable costs associated with the planning and organization arise prior to events. Some costs associated with e.g. equipment, planning and organization may not be completely sunk in the sense that the equipment may be used for future events. Services and labor as well as rent are, however, not storable products. Salaries already paid for the planning of an event, which could not be staged due to the pandemic, cannot be used in other ways. The latter accounts for almost 50%of the total sunk cost (Table 9.2).

Table 9.2: Decrease in revenues and sunk costs linked to events

Revenues and Costs	Decrease in revenues	Sunk costs
	%	%
Registration fees	33.4	
Ticket revenues	20.9	
Sponsor revenues	20.9	
Sales during events	11.3	
Other revenues	13.6	
Salary costs		46.5
Service costs		11.9
Rent costs		11.7
Equipment costs		10.3
Marketing costs		3.4
Other costs		16.2
Total	100	100

Note. Perceived costs between March 12th and June 30th, 2020

Sports club characteristics and lost revenues

Lost revenues vary not only according to type of sports, but also depending on club size. Three variables were used as proxies for club size. First, clubs were divided into four equal groups, according to how much they receive in (activity) support from the Swedish Sports Confederation. The support is a state grant, directed through the Confederation, to organize sport activities for youths (aged 7 to 25) (Swedish Sports Confederation, 2020). A large club with many members and activities for youths receives more state funding. State grants therefore represent a good proxy for club size. Two other proxies for club size are number of full-time and number of part-time employees.

Two multiple linear regression were calculated with the three proxies for club size as independent variables (activity support level coded as three dummy variables, number of part-time employees, and number of full-time employees) and revenue loss related to events as dependent variable in the first model and sunk costs related to events as dependent variable in the second model. The first model was significant ($F(5, 2267) = 303.109$, $p < .000$), with an R^2 of .401. Examining the independent variables (Table 9.3), number of full-time employees contributes most ($\beta = .498$), followed by part-time employees ($\beta = .192$). Having a large activity state support does also contribute to revenue losses ($\beta = .056$). While the number of employees and large activity state support are significant predictors of lost revenues, the remaining variables are non-significant.

The second model was also significant ($F(5, 2270) = 48.344$, $p < .000$), albeit with a much lower R^2 of .094. The level of activity state support does not contribute to sunk costs (statistically insignificant), but both number of full-time employees ($\beta = .200$) and part-time employees ($\beta = .172$) do (Table 9.3). These results show that club size had a more important role in terms of predicting revenue losses related to events, than sunk costs.

Table 9.3: The influence of club size on revenue losses and sunk costs

Club size	Revenue losses			Sunk costs		
	β	T	Sig.	β	T	Sig.
Full-time employees	0.498	26.71	0.000	0.200	8.52	0.000
Part-time employees	0.192	10.21	0.000	0.172	7.27	0.000
Activity state support, large	0.056	2.81	0.005	-0.037	-1.55	0.122
Activity state support, medium-large	-0.030	-1.67	0.096	-0.034	-1.51	0.131
Activity state support, small-medium	-0.002	-0.09	0.927	-0.007	-0.31	0.758

To conclude, the first model has a high R^2 explaining roughly 40% of the revenue losses from events. This means that it is essential that large sports clubs are active in regard to crisis management, their responsiveness when crisis hits, and their capabilities to recover and adapt (cf. Shipway & Miles, 2020).

Sports club strategies in response to crisis

When asked about the economic problems and how this crisis is managed, respondents could answer either 'no measures taken', or one or several of the measures in Figure 9.1.

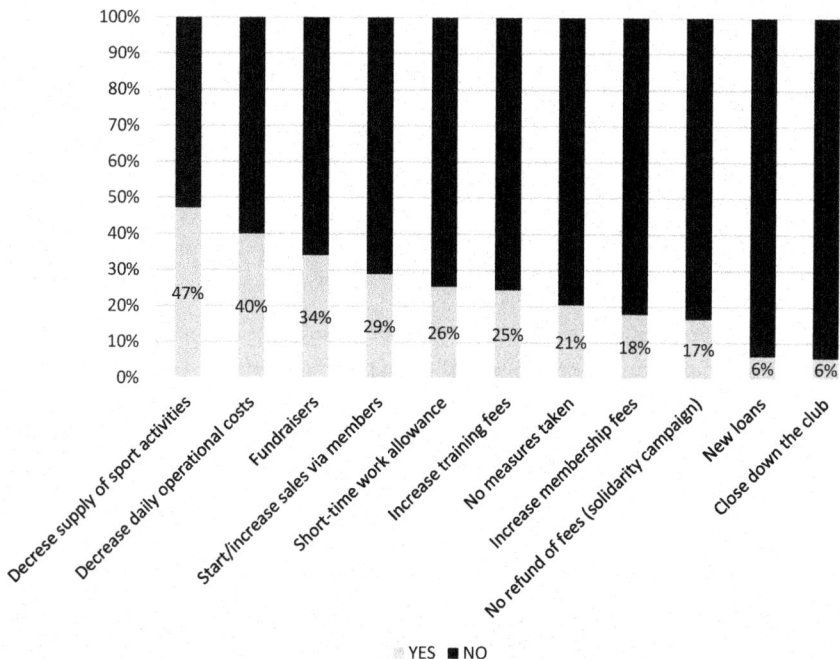

Figure 9.1: Sports club measures in response to Covid-19

On average, clubs plan to take 3.3 measures. In total 21% of the clubs took no measure, which means that 79% of the clubs took at least one measure. Thus, a majority of clubs show responsiveness to the crisis with timely measures (cf. Koronis & Ponis, 2018). More clubs seem to consider reductions in costs ('decrease supply of sport activities', 'decrease daily operational costs', 'short-time work allowance') before increased revenues ('fundraisers', 'start/increase sales via members', 'increase training fees', 'increase membership fees', 'no refund of fees'). This seems reasonable as the survey was conducted in an early stage of the pandemic when simple and fast measures to reduce costs were needed.

Clubs that took measures had considerably larger revenue losses (M = 297 862, SD = 1 075 181) and sunk costs (M = 91 233, SD = 1 046 718) than clubs that took no measures (M = 45 530, SD = 138 950 and M = 8914, SD = 49 831)[1]. They also had significantly more full-time (M = 1.95, SD = 4.41 versus M = 0.34, SD = 1.12) and part-time employees (M = 2.95, SD = 8.23 and M = 0.45, SD = 2.24) in their organizations[2]. Thus size, which is emphasized as an important factor by Shipway and Miles (2020), in terms of employees had an importance. However, geographical context of the club was not a factor. This shows that the urgency for clubs to respond with a variety of measures is directly linked to expected negative economic impacts.

As a second step, the cluster analysis tells us what combination of measures that were taken depending on the characteristics of the clubs. It shows the different strategies that clubs used and which clubs behaved similarly.

In the left column of Table 9.4, the measures that thematically belong together have been organized into three categories ('To decrease operational costs', 'To increase revenues', 'To increase fees/costs for members'). The remaining five columns to the right display five clusters of clubs which have taken different combinations of actions. In order to better understand the characteristics of the clusters and why they have chosen these strategies, five profiling variables were used (as described in the Methods section):

Multiple measures (a): This cluster of sports clubs launched multiple measures (more than any other cluster) to cope with the situation. This group has, more than other groups, focused on short-term allowance (78%), increase training fees (95%) and no refund of fees (51%). It is by far the smallest cluster (6.8%[3]), but contains the largest clubs. Ice hockey clubs are, to a larger degree, in this cluster.

---

1 The differences are statistically significant, t(3440) = -11.9, p < .001 and t(3444) = -4.1, p < .001.

2 The differences are statistically significant, $t(2817)$ = -15.4, p < .001 and $t(2414)$ = -11.7, p < .001.

3 The percentage refers to the share of all clubs that took any measures, i.e. the clubs that were included in the cluster analysis. This applies to all further references to the sizes of clusters.

Table 9.4: Results of cluster analysis, sports club strategies

Measures	Multiple measures (a)	Cost and revenue focus (b)	Cost focus (c)	Activity focus (d)	Members take the costs (e)
	(n = 185, 6.8%)	(n = 891, 32.7%)	(n = 609, 22.3%)	(n = 705, 25.9%)	(n = 335, 12.3%)
To decrease operational costs					
Short-time work allowance	**78%**	48%	32%	*14%*	*9%*
Decrease supply of sport activities	68%	46%	**70%**	**92%**	14%
Deacrease daily operational costs	**77%**	**66%**	**100%**	*2%*	*14%*
To increase revenues					
Fundraisers	39%	**93%**	*17%*	*12%*	33%
Start/increase sales via members	**79%**	**61%**	*16%*	22%	23%
To increase fees/costs for members					
Increase training fees	**95%**	34%	*7%*	*23%*	**53%**
Increase membership fees	37%	25%	*5%*	14%	**65%**
No refund of fees (solidary campaigns)	**51%**	27%	*16%*	*15%*	*15%*

Note. The percentages signify the share of sports clubs, in the cluster, that have taken the specific measure. The percentages in bold (**XX%**) are statistically significantly higher than the average for all sports clubs (i.e. their expected value). The percentages in italics (*XX%*) are statistically significantly lower than the average for all sports clubs (i.e. their expected value). Chi-square tests with post-hoc tests were performed.

Cost and revenue focus (b): These sports clubs, similar to the previous cluster, took multiple measures (more than average). The difference (compared to the previous cluster) is that they have not applied measures to increase fees and costs for their members to the same extent. Instead, they focus on cost cutting and revenue generation. In particular through fundraisers (93%), to decrease daily operational costs (66%), and to start/increase sales via members (61%). It is the largest cluster (32.7%) and contains large clubs. It contains more football and handball clubs, which were two of the most affected sports in terms of lost revenues linked to events (see above). Thus, the cost and revenue focus is based on their significantly higher losses (in comparison with cluster *d* and *e*).

Cost focus (c): This cluster has a focus on cutting costs. All clubs in this cluster focused on decreasing daily operational costs (100%) and many to decrease their supply of sport activities (70%). All percentages in the categories 'to increase revenues' and 'to increase fees/costs for members' are below the expected values (see Table 9.4). It consists of fairly large clubs (but smaller than in the preceding clusters). An outstanding feature of this cluster (linked to their cost focus) is that they are, more often than other clusters, operating and owning their own facilities. Thus, a strategy to respond to this fact is necessary.

Activity focus (d): The sports clubs in this cluster have mainly one focus: to decrease their supply of sport activities (92%). All other measures are below the expected outcomes (see Table 9.4). It is a fairly large cluster (25.9%) containing the smallest clubs (together with cluster *e*) and they take fewer measures than clubs in all other clusters. Seeing that they, to a smaller degree, own and operate their own facilities, the focus is on scaling down their activities to members in order to cope.

Members take the costs (e): In the last cluster, the focus is geared towards measures where the sports club members are targeted to endure the crisis. It is mainly to increase training fees (53%) and to increase membership fees (65%). This is a fairly small cluster (12.3%), containing smaller clubs. They take fewer measures than most clusters and have concentrated their strategy on making the paying members of the club increase their costs to support the club finances during this initial period of the pandemic. It is very similar to cluster *d* in many aspects, but have chosen a different strategy to cope.

To summarize, the strategies chosen are clearly related to the size of clubs, whether they own or operate their own facilities, and to some extent to lost revenues, sunk costs, and type of sports. The larger clubs have more urgent needs to react, to be responsive, with more employees, members and level of engagement in events, but it might also be a sign of higher levels of resilience (Koronis & Ponis, 2018; Shipway & Miles, 2020), which in turn might be linked to their level of professionalization. The first two cluster (*a* and *b*) could be said to have a more active or broad response, in terms of the variety of measures, while the other three are more limited (or specific), focusing on a smaller number of measures. Football, ice hockey and handball clubs are more prominent in the clusters with larger clubs, which reinforces the above argument since these clubs have relatively large costs and revenue losses linked to events.

Non-economic impacts on sports clubs

The above findings show that the demand for economic support varies, but that it is generally high among sports clubs organizing events. Economic support is the first support actors are asking for, and the support that was first provided by the Swedish government. But the situation for clubs is more complex than that, and results show a variety of impacts that the actors react to. The analysis has generated five areas that directly affect the clubs, and which lay the ground for subsequent needs of support. Overall, the results show that the impact of the pandemic on the sports clubs is far wider than merely economic, and that such impacts have wide-ranging influences on society. Such a situation calls for a varied responsiveness by the clubs in order to keep resilient in times when effects originate from spheres far beyond their control.

While the above economic impacts could be systematically measured, the non-economic consequences have been more difficult to identify and to classify, because they are wide-ranging and partly unexpected. The pandemic acts as a disturbance and its impacts on Swedish sports clubs are manifold. One possible road is to ask what values sports clubs and their connected events bring (cf. Lundberg et al., 2017). In non-pandemic times, several groups of people can benefit from events: internal participants within the clubs, volunteers and visitors. This can be seen in the answers that respondents give. By extension, we speak of benefits for a major part of society. This is interesting, because people may by default think of economic capital, based on clubs with huge revenues such as football or ice hockey (cf. Table 9.1). Results from this empirical study however show that social capital is of vital importance to virtually all sports clubs. Such social consequences appear both in the short and in the long run. In a first step, the everyday activities in the clubs are affected. In a second step though, there may be effects caused by cancelled events which the clubs arrange in regular intervals. The rest of this chapter presents how Swedish sports clubs deal with non-economic impacts caused by cancelled events.

Loss of members

One of the most frequent comments on negative consequences from the pandemic and cancelled events is the loss of members of the clubs. Events are a main motivator for people to exercise regularly. Consequently, when events are cancelled people drop out. They do so not only from the event itself, but also from everyday training. They may even end their memberships. In the short run, sports clubs are afraid of losing members. This feeling causes stress and instability, and consequently smaller training groups. In the long run, this can result in the closure of the club. Other consequences are a higher level of inactivity or, in the case of a swimming club, a decrease of swimming skills: *"We fear a loss of members as we now see a decline in the number of participants in our groups, which in the long run impairs swimming skills in the municipality."* A related category is the fear of losing leaders, referees, and coaches in the clubs. Such a loss can have many reasons, among them leaders' fear of working close to other human beings in pandemic times, not least on journeys to and from events. Another reason is the inability of clubs to keep staff and leaders when economic capital in the clubs goes missing. This causes stress not only for the leaders but also for the clubs: once lost, it takes time to find new staff. Besides being time-consuming, it is costly to improve leaders' skills after they have been recruited. All of these examples show that events are closely related to efficiency, excellence, and esteem values. The external development forces the clubs to react swiftly, and it may be difficult to find enough time for internal learning processes that are urgently needed when asked for adaptiveness.

Decrease of activity levels

When engagement is reduced, this has a direct influence on people's activity levels. In its first step, this is easily explained, because when numbers of exercise activities are reduced, the level of physical inactivity is simultaneously increased. In its indirect effect, bigger events are included in the line of argument. Such events, like the cross-country skiing event Vasaloppet, offer a great motivation to exercise for a long time in advance. In those cases, events can positively contribute to public health on a broad level. It also shows a close relationship between physical and social wellbeing because such exercise sessions are a reason for people to meet, to chitchat, and to aim for shared goals. Without doubt, such peer groups are important for people's mental health. This is true not only for participants, but for event organizers as well. Depending on the sport, both younger and older people are included, as the Stockholm orienteering club shows in this quote: *"Orienteering in general and our club in particular has a large proportion of active seniors, which means that both training activities and event participation are affected."* In this case, the club was particularly affected due to the high number of elderly individuals in the group. In times when elderly people constitute the risk group within pandemic effects, sports clubs have a difficult time in adapting actions.

Physical and mental illness

Among the most frequent comments are linked to physical and mental illness due to missed activities and cancelled events. The lack of physical exercise and a concomitant passive lifestyle are problematic far beyond a lower number of events, as is the scarcity of being in social contexts with peers, both on events, and while travelling to and from them. A parasport association writes that *"mental illness and weight gain are common dilemmas among our members. As we already have a vulnerable group with functional variations, we really suffer from cancelled events that would normally bring both physical and social training."* Apart from the above stated illnesses, answers often address stress, anxiety, and depression. People are pondering about their jobs, loss of income, and lack of social interaction, to name a few. As mentioned, worries about reduced participant numbers are frequent. All of these empirical results point to the fact that events are strong contributors to public health, both extensively and in a longer time-frame. The pandemic clearly has negative long-term impacts on the positive societal contributions of events. It is important though that this becomes visible, among others in a contribution like this book chapter.

Integration

Another issue that is affected by cancelled meetings and events is that of integration. Sports clubs and their related events act as major contributors to a heterogeneous society. This includes the incorporation by means of age, social and geographical background, gender and culture. Several respondents refer to integration that normally takes place via various events. Sports clubs, and not least football clubs, offer frequent opportunities for integration between children with different backgrounds. Coming together on a regular basis in a place where participants share a common goal is a great driver in this. This is obvious in the wake of the immigration wave in 2015 to Sweden. A Swedish bandy club puts it this way: *"We cannot arrange our big tournament where lots of children would have participated. Nor can we arrange our big annual meeting day where our members, their families and relatives, local residents, and our partners meet at our arena for a day in the spirit of integration and meetings between different cultures."* A similar argumentation goes for the amalgamation of different ages, when (grand)parents bring their kids to exercise sessions, elder people train younger ones, and else. This is true not only for the participants but also for spectators and volunteers. In this relation an orienteering club writes: *"We have many senior members for whom social integration during events mean a lot. Not only when they are participating but also, and not least, when they meet as volunteers during events. This has become like a second family for many people."*

Joy and togetherness

Finally, the possibly largest social effect of canceled events is the reduction of joy and togetherness. Results clearly show that most Swedish sports clubs focus neither on elites nor on performances. The driving forces of joy and togetherness could be said to be their core business. This extends to children and adolescents, parents, leaders, functionaries and spectators. One of the football clubs writes in its comment: *"Our team has collected money for several years to go to a big youth tournament in Gothenburg. Although we had no chance of winning, all of us have been looking forward to this trip that was now canceled due to the pandemic."* This category is apparently difficult to measure. Departing in parallel from a perspective of public health though, it is simultaneously apparent that the feeling of joy and togetherness is a major driver and consequence of events, on all levels of society. These are hedonistic values with no other means than feeling good and having a meaningful time. When analyzing events from a tourism perspective, such values may appear at first glance, but in relation to public health, such a result can be a major contribution to noticing social, sustainable, health-related, and economic values of events (cf. Lundberg et al., 2017).

Sports clubs´ need of support in times of a pandemic

The above (non-)economic effects have shown that impacts on the Swedish sports clubs are severe in many ways. Actors are trying to adapt to this disrupted situation. The support that is most often asked for is economic, but a development that builds on innovation, resilience, and a sustainable adaption of the event sector demands more from the actors than keeping things as they were with the help of economic contributions. This is especially true beyond the urgent phase of a collapse, in terms of resilience.

The pandemic has rapidly initiated governments to offer financial support to their suffering economies. This has enabled some of the affected sector to survive a bit longer, in times when expenses were high, but income was close to zero. Too much has changed, and too many factors need to be processed in new and different ways, instead of simply doing more or less of the same thing as pre-Covid-19. This is a rather painful part of resilience, and in every such process, there are actors that most of all want to return to what they once had, no matter what (Koronis & Ponis, 2018). Swedish event actors are no different to this. One club in floor ball states that: *"We hope to be back to normal soon so we can have our activities the way we are used to"*. Others are reasoning in terms of reorganization, trying to align with the new event landscape. It is for this adaption and innovation that they ask for external support beyond capital. The following text is a prolongation and subsequent result that is based on the above discussed consequences the pandemic has on Swedish event actors.

Interpretation of rules and regulations

It is clear that event organizations are doing their best to act according to the pandemic rules and regulations. This is not always easy. Swedish law regulates public gatherings, and its violation can lead to fines or even imprisonment. Breaking these regulations may lead to costly consequences and a possible shutdown of the whole business. However, temporary changes in these regulations may be difficult to interpret and understand. One of the most mentioned support needs beyond economic capital is the judicial assistance of understanding what regulations mean in relation to the own organization, and to implement such rules into day-to-day operations. One of the figure skating sports clubs for example, wonders how they should understand the upper limit for visitors: *"Today, there is a ban on gatherings with more than 50 participants, but there will be many questions of interpretation. Can you have several smaller groups in different rooms but in the same building or should the number of participants be added up?"* The indistinctness of the rules may be a result of their fast appearance, but the interpretation of laws is always associated with the inclusion of individual businesses.

Lobbying

The above question is closely related to another case in Swedish tourism, which is the theme park Astrid Lindgren's World. During summer 2020, the park arranged two parallel theater shows in the park, admitting 50 spectators in two different places. The authorities investigated the case and concluded that the theme park had acted against the rules. The park had to close down for the rest of the season. No wonder that event organizations ask for legal assistance. This may be related not only to economic values, but to peace of mind, and belief in the future, too. As with many other government aids, the pandemic aid has been experienced as both difficult to understand, and, to a certain degree, as unfair. While this may lie in the nature of things, a related need for support has been in the assistance in lobbying for the own organization. The aim of such consciousness raising is the improvement of conditions for events that are managed by one's own organization. One of the Swedish athletics sports clubs describes it in the following way: *"We wish that the Swedish Sports Confederation, in its communication with the government, can demand that the restrictions for events are changed. It is not as great a risk of infection in a running event as in a football match. Maybe one should also differentiate between indoor and outdoor events."* As the above examples show, rules and regulations are difficult to implement for individual organizations. In addition, rules have been changed during the pandemic. This is why organizations sometimes have had a hard time to implement and understand the logic behind the rules.

Event innovation

As time goes by, more and more sports clubs understand that there is no way back to how it used to be; and that a return to normality may take more time than initially expected. This is why a great number of the respondents are asking for assistance in the process of event innovation and renewal. This is an effect of actors' aims to learn more about how to adapt, and to open their eyes for the fact that changes may be inevitable (cf. Lew, 2014; Lew et al., 2020). Event actors realize that it is difficult to push changes forward by themselves. Instead, they look for cooperation, among others by supporting organizations on different geographical levels. Actors gain strength when they cooperate and learn together with others (Biggs et al., 2012; Crandall et al., 2010). Adaptive processes during such difficult times are both difficult and hard to advance, and event actors are asking for assistance that aims for conflict resolution, motivation, argumentation towards public authorities and other actors, and for seeking funding. Such requirements show that resilience in the sector is not limited to event-related questions only, but that factors such as idea generation, leadership, cooperation and administration are important when it comes to innovative development (cf. Biggs et al., 2012).

Marketing support

The last request for assistance that is mentioned here is the demand for help in the marketing processes. The sports clubs are in need of assistance when it comes to alternative events that are offered instead of ordinary events that stem from pre-covid times. They are also in need of support in starting up again when the crisis is over. Marketing is so important here because the events are central for the survival and prosperity of Swedish sports clubs. By means of events, clubs make money that can be spent on everyday activities and development as well as on health-related and social aspects within the clubs. This, again, shows the great importance of events not only for tourism and hospitality, but for a healthy society, as well. This goes hand in hand with the importance of value creation in event management (Lundberg et al., 2017). This argument is important also for the long-term contribution of events to sustainability, because it considers the social aspects of sustainability. It is notable that most respondents consider the need of marketing support to be the most important – not necessarily during the crisis, but afterwards. On the question of what kind of support is the most important, a judo sports club writes: "*Marketing when the crisis is over*".

Altogether, the results show that economic support maybe the most welcomed support. However, there is also a great need for non-monetary support in order to become a responsive and resilient event actor. The contribution of this book chapter lies in the joint discussion of these aspects.

Conclusion

This chapter shows that many sports clubs in Sweden have suffered in economic and non-economic terms during the Covid-19 pandemic. Cancelled events have been identified as the main driver of lost revenues. An important contribution from this study has been to pinpoint that clubs are heavily relying on their own sporting events. From a crisis management and resilience perspective, recognizing this relationship will help develop strategies supporting the economic resilience among clubs. An event portfolio approach including a diversification of events organized by a club is likely to reduce risks during similar crises.

During the lockdown of events, sports clubs took different strategies. They were adapting and innovating events, or simply waiting for the pandemic to be over so that things would get back to normal. Although the data in this study was collected early after the outbreak, it is remarkable that most respondents wait for better times. This is shown by the fact that most sports clubs ask for support in marketing events when the pandemic is over, rather than ask for support to rejuvenate the event supply. Maybe the early promise of state money to cover losses caused by the pandemic has reduced the incitements to adapt and innovate the events?

This is an entitled question, as results have shown that it takes time for the event business to become resilient actors. The data in this study was collected in the very beginning of the pandemic, and actors were mostly calling for economic assistance to keep things as they were. While there were calls for assistance in order to learn how to adapt, and to consider one's own vulnerability, this process became clearer as time went by. The level of preparedness for this pandemic was low. There is no one to blame for this, as one cannot be prepared for all the risks that may turn up during a lifetime. It is clear however that learning takes time. It is also clear that one actor cannot unfold all its adaptive capacity by itself. Learning works best in a group of actors, where individuals can help each other in appointing the problem, giving solutions, putting such solutions into place, communicating about it, and having a dialogue along the way with actors that can both support and benefit from such adaptive activities.

It is notable that several Swedish sports clubs experienced a strained relationship between the clubs on the one side, and members, practitioners, volunteers and staff on the other. Sports clubs risk closing down and members turning to other activities – less physical and less social. It is also likely that people will find their way to new sporting activities, and new sporting events, not least in open air. This might in turn lead to new travel patterns and changed environmental impacts. From a societal perspective, this study shows that events are important contributors to both public health and to sustainability in times when people can meet and plan for the participation or management of future events. In the pandemic year 2020, it becomes painfully aware that these possibilities are missing. This contribution is important to mention, as events are sometimes accused of their negative effects on, among other things, sustainability.

As the Covid-19 pandemic is still raging at the time of writing, it is difficult to recommend or advocate specific strategies to cope with negative economic impacts, because of the simple fact that we do not know to what extent these clubs will survive or recover to the same levels as before the pandemic. It is an empirical observation of what strategies clubs chose when the crisis hit. However, it gives us insights to what factors (size, lost revenues, sunk costs and type of sport) can be used to predict how clubs react in times of crisis and how different type of clubs manage crisis, and thus it contributes to the emerging literature on event resilience and crisis management for events (cf. Shipway & Miles, 2020). In particular, it contributes to the understanding of the responsiveness of sport event organizers, which e.g. Koronis and Ponis (2018) identify as a core feature to build resilient organizations.

Acknowledgement

The research in this chapter is part of the research programme Mistra Sport & Outdoors, funded by The Swedish Foundation for Strategic Environmental Research (Mistra), grant no. DIA 206/36. The authors would like to thank the Swedish Sport Confederation (*Riksidrottsförbundet*) for granting access to data based on their survey to *Swedish sport clubs in April 2020*.

References

Beasley, T. M., & Schumacker, R. E. (1995). Multiple regression approach to analyzing contingency tables: Post hoc and planned comparison procedures. *The Journal of Experimental Education, 64*(1), 79-93.

Biggs, D., Hall, C. M., & Stoeckl, N. (2012). The resilience of formal and informal tourism enterprises to disasters: Reef tourism in Phuket, Thailand. *Journal of Sustainable Tourism, 20*(5), 645–665.

Brown, S., Getz, D., Pettersson, R., & Wallstam, M. (2015). Event evaluation: Definitions, concepts and a state of the art review. *International Journal of Event and Festival Management, 6*(2), 135-157.

Crandall, W.R., Parnell, J.A., & Spillan, J.E. (2010). *Crisis Management in the New Strategy Landscape*, Sage Publications, Thousand Oaks, CA.

Griffin, T., & Guttentag, D. (2020). Identifying active resident hosts of VFR visitors. *International Journal of Tourism Research, 22*(5), 627-636.

Hall, C. M., Timothy, D. J., & Duval, D. T. (2013) *Safety and Security in Tourism: Relationships, management, and marketing.* Oxford: Routledge.

Koronis, E., & Ponis, S. (2018). Better than before: the resilient organization in crisis mode. *Journal of Business Strategy, 39*(1), 32-42.

Lew, A. A. (2014). Scale, change and resilience in community tourism planning. *Tourism Geographies 16*(1), 14-22.

Lew, A.A., Cheer, J.M., Haywood, M., Brouder, P., & Salazaar, N.B. (2020). Visions of travel after the global Covid-19 transformation of 2020. *Tourism Geographies 22*(3), 455-466.

Lundberg, E., Armbrecht, J., Andersson, T. D., & Getz, D. (2017). *The Value of Events.* Taylor & Francis.

May, T. (2011). *Social Research, Issues, Methods and Process.* Open University Press.

Miles, L., & Shipway, R. (2020). Exploring the COVID-19 pandemic as a catalyst for stimulating future research agendas for managing crises and disasters at international sport events. *Event Management, 24*(4), 537-552.

Pettersson, R., & Wallstam, M. (2017). Idrottsevenemangs samhällsnytta, in: Faskunger J. & Sjöblom, P. (Eds.) *Idrottens samhällsnytta - En vetenskaplig översikt av idrottsrörelsens mervärden för individ och samhälle.* Riksidrottsförbundet.

Ritchie, B. W. (2004). Chaos, crises and disasters: a strategic approach to crisis management in the tourism industry. *Tourism Management, 25*(6), 669-683.

Shipway, R., & Miles, L. (2020). Bouncing back and jumping forward: Scoping the resilience landscape of international sports events and implications for events and festivals. *Event Management, 24*(1), 185-196.

Swedish Sports Confederation (2020). LOK-stöd. Retrieved from https://www.rf.se/bidragochstod/lok-stod/

Wallstam, M., Ioannides, D., & Pettersson, R. (2020). Evaluating the social impacts of events: in search of unified indicators for effective policymaking. *Journal of Policy Research in Tourism, Leisure and Events, 12*(2), 122-141.

Practice Insight 7:

Case study of Musikfest (https://www.musikfest.org/)

Musikfest 2020, July 31-Aug. 9, Going from an In-person to Hybrid Event

The process of transforming Musikfest, typically the nation's largest free music festival, into a new format this year was one that took place over several months. The process involved two major steps – deciding if Musikfest should be offered in any format in 2020, and then how the event would and could be built and presented. The first step was to develop virtual programming and then, if state and city guidelines permitted, add in select in-person elements much closer to the event's start date. We also launched a major giving campaign, called the "One Million Festers" campaign (not a capital campaign,) for the first time in our history.

The 2020 festival ended up featuring 90 streaming concerts (Virtual Musikfest), six small-in person 'Outdoor Dining with a Show' experiences (250-person capacity per location) and an outdoor food vendor area featuring 10 of the festival's most popular vendors, where people could walk up and order food to go.

Major considerations/factors that went into planning Musikfest 2020:

1. Risk vs Reward – could we do the festival in an affordable, sustainable way by reducing expenses as much as possible and maximizing opportunity for revenue?

Process and Outcome: As an event where attendance is impacted greatly by weather, Musikfest revenues can and do vary greatly from year to year. Over the past decade, the surplus has ranged from a high of $1.5 million to a low of $75,000 in net revenues. As an organization, ArtsQuest focused on reducing expenses across the board after making the decision to move forward with the festival, with substantial savings realized due to eliminating physical festival setup, staging and lighting and performance fees for this year. Main stage performances, where possible, were moved to 2021, allowing the organization to keep a substantial amount of revenue in ticket sales (as new show dates for 2021 were announced, there were many patrons who had already requested refunds). For the first time in its history, ArtsQuest and its Foundation Board launched a major giving campaign during Musikfest, with a $500,000 matching gift campaign called 'One Million Festers.' (Every donation up to $500,000 in all is being matched dollar for dollar by the Foundation).

The development team focused on retaining as many existing sponsorships as possible, developing new benefits packages and opportunities for marketing and promoting partners' brands. In addition to the matching gift campaign, a partnership with video donation platform DUZY TV allowed people to make donations online while watching the Virtual Musikfest concerts. By reducing expenses and developing new digital and revenue opportunities such as a Virtual 5K, an incentivized giving campaign and transforming performances that were historically free to attend to a fee-based reservation system, ArtsQuest was able to present Musikfest 2020 in a format that was true to its mission and also generated approximately $200,000, coming in just above budget predictions for the reformatted event.

2: Could we offer an event that ensured, as best as possible, the safety of volunteers, vendors/artists, patrons and staff?

3: Could we be flexible in adapting to the constantly change rules and regulations pertaining to COVID-19 mitigation and safety efforts in the city and state?

Process and Outcome: The health and safety of patrons, performers, vendors, staff and volunteers was the top priority in establishing and offering any in-person programming. ArtsQuest established a number of best practices and procedures based on guidelines from the CDC, City of Bethlehem and the Commonwealth of PA. These include practicing safe social distancing; requiring staff, volunteers, vendors and patrons to wear facemasks in all indoor and outdoor areas except when eating and drinking; following event capacity guidelines established by the Commonwealth; and greatly expanding and enhancing cleaning and disinfecting procedures throughout the event. In addition, our two most dedicated groups, supporting members and volunteers, were surveyed to see if they would support in-person programming. All vendors were also required to adhere to all safety guidelines put in place for Musikfest.

Complete details on COVID-19 health and safety practices for ArtsQuest and our patrons can be found at www.steelstacks.org/wp-content/uploads/sites/3/2020/06/OutdoorEventsGuidelines.pdf.

ArtsQuest worked closely with City of Bethlehem and the city's Health Department to ensure all COVID-19 safety guidelines and regulations could be adhered to regarding its food court and its "Outdoor Dining and a Show" experiences at SteelStacks. Due to the constantly changing COVID-19 regulations in the state, the "Outdoor Dining with a Show" concerts were not announced until 10 days before the festival start date. Attendance was done via reserving a table of up to four people in same party in advance (all tables meet social distancing requirements), and reservations cost between $10 and $50 per table depending on the performer. Food purchases were an additional cost and did not come with the reservation. By offering a maximum of only 60 tables, we ensured we would not exceed the state's maximum attendance (250 people) for an outdoor gathering.

4. Could we develop a program/event that still fit the mission of our nonprofit organization – connecting people and supporting our city and community through music and the arts?

Process and Outcome: ArtsQuest's mission focuses on providing high-quality music, arts and festival experiences for the region while also supporting tourism and economic development in our city and region. Planning meetings determined a revamped festival would be possible, and Musikfest's virtual and in-person programming brought the community together at a time when it was needed most as many people had been sheltering at home for more than four months. A big focus was providing local vendors, many of whom had not operated all summer, with an opportunity to support their livelihood. To navigate the unusual circumstances, ArtsQuest developed a 73-27 revenue split with food vendors, a different revenue model than employed in previous years.

5. How could we develop new programming, both virtually and in-person, that was effective and impactful in the new normal?

Process and Outcome: This was a key area of focus for ArtsQuest. Early on we developed a virtual programming initiative called ArtsQuest@Home, providing online and digital programming for the community in music, arts, education, entertainment and more (including livestreamed SteelStacks at Noon concert series). Staff learned new skills and employed new digital technologies to developing streaming concerts, digital family programming and more, while in-person programs such as the Outdoor Dining with a Show were done on a small scale in early July to see if they could be offered successfully and safely during Musikfest. Virtual programming developed in spring and early summer helped pave the way to offer a Virtual Musikfest lineup of 40 performances. Using an existing partnership with a local cable company, Service Electric, another 40 shows were broadcast live from the cable company's garages and then streamed via Musikfest.org. Partnering with Martin Guitar provided for another 12 virtual shows by artists from across the country. Virtual Musikfest shows were seen by approximately 200,000 viewers in all 50 states and around the globe, helping to expand the Musikfest brand and festival awareness well beyond the region. Offering streaming concerts also allows us to re-purpose the performances via 'replays' that are promoted, providing additional content and additional opportunities to generate revenue.

10 A Chronicle of Event Postponement and Reorganization: Coming Back Stronger

Danai Varveri and Vassilios Ziakas

Introduction

Since the start of the COVID-19 pandemic, the global event industry has been deeply affected. In Greece, the scale of the coronavirus crisis brings back memories of the 2008 financial crisis; both are crises that reshaped society in lasting ways. The 2008 financial crisis showed that the event industry in Greece can survive adverse conditions. In the following years, although Greece has been under strict austerity measures and economic hardship, the Greek calendar continued to feature a range of cultural festivals and events, especially during the summer months of the peak tourism season. Music and dance festivals are a mainstay of the creative event industry in Greece, because they not only enhance local development and tourism but also contribute to artistic expression and the utilization of cultural capital.

The COVID-19 pandemic crisis has put at risk most events around the globe. According to chaos theory, the principle of 'butterfly effect' explains how small incidents may cause large effects to broader systems; in this manner alike the COVID-19 outbreak has plunged the global into a serious pandemic crisis. In the event industry, strict social distancing and restrictions to minimize the spread of coronavirus have set new norms in socializing and celebrating. Concerns about safety in gatherings have led to cancelling or reshaping events. The Greek government imposed consecutive lockdowns that paralyzed the already dismal social and business environment from a 10-year economic depression. Local or national lockdowns limit the range of managerial responses in event planning and make it more difficult for any level of crisis preparedness to be achieved. Thus, major uncertainties have arisen about the future and survival of events in Greece. How are event organizers responding to the crisis and adapting to the new conditions? What decision-making processes do they employ to deal with the consequences of the crisis? The purpose of this chapter is to throw light on the empirical decision-making of event managers to re-organize the National Ballet Competition of Greece as a virtual event. This experience is discussed alongside pertinent literature to highlight major issues and responses.

Organizational context and case study approach

A crisis can be understood as a major situation with harmful effects to both internal and external stakeholders. For events, a crisis may lead to their cancellation. Once an event is cancelled, there is always a risk that it will never take place; but also event-failure can be caused by financial deficiencies, lack of crisis management and detrimental external forces. Nevertheless, facing challenges can also bring opportunities, to which managers need to respond quickly in order to implement innovative policies for problem-solving and recovery (Advisory Board on Economic and Social Affairs, 2020). Swift responses to crises often mirror ad-hoc reactive decision-making by event organizers to particular issues. They might also represent creative ideas and innovative approaches that need to be recorded and examined. This chapter provides a case study that chronicles event organizers' decision-making in response to COVID-19 crisis.

To cancel vs. to postpone the National Ballet Competition

In Greece, Spring marks the beginning of the ballet competition season. In March of 2020, the COVID-19 outbreak led to a sudden national lockdown which lasted for three months. The organizers of the National Ballet Competition had to face the consequences of COVID-19 outbreak and manage effectively the crisis ridden event. The National Ballet Competition is a one-off, annual event, giving emphasis on celebrating 'the love for ballet', and promoting youth artistic development. It is a point of convergence for dancers, choreographers and ballet-school owners across Greece and Cyprus. This event is strongly related to art and culture and celebrates elements significant in the life of the ballet community, consolidating it. In addition, the National Ballet Competition has become a prestigious event by offering numerous scholarships and awards to young artists. More than 800 dancers perform their choreography, in front of a 12-member Judging Committee, in Solo, Duet or Group divisions.

The event is organized by the Hellenic Classical & Contemporary Dance Association, which is a non-profit organization established in 2015. The board of directors is composed of four members (i.e., President/Managing Director, Vice-President/Artistic Director, Secretary/Membership Coordinator, and Treasurer) and is elected every three years by stakeholders' vote at the annual meeting. According to Ingram (2015), the leadership of a social sector organization needs to fulfill its mission and advance the public good so that it can play a vital role in society. In order to accomplish that, the governing body meets at regular intervals to set policies for corporate management by adopting ethical and legal governance and overseeing the organization's activities. While the governance of the organization, strategy, oversight, and accountability are accomplished by the board of directors, the day-to-day operations are run by the management team, which is composed by four individuals. The management team is responsible for the implementation of the organizational mission and strategies. Two members from the board of directors have dual-capacity also in managing the team, which helps the mission of the organization and how it operates. These members have experience in overseeing business affairs, background in sport management and dance specialization, which all align with the organization's identity. The roles and responsibilities of the management team are described below:

♦ *Event Coordinator*: responsible for event planning and production within time limits, for choosing the venue, hiring guest dancers and coordinating volunteers. Part of the role is organizing transportation, accommodation, special equipment in the facilities and catering.

♦ *Communication Manager*: responsible for media and public relations and to ensure that the brand remains top of mind. Web and social media material, creation, editing and promotion, are part of this role's duties. This person also handles all complaints and press releases during crises.

♦ *Fundraising/Sponsor Manager*: responsible for overseeing communication with sponsors and developing a fundraising strategy aligning the organization's mission statement. This role looks for opportunities to reach and attract potential supporters, high-value donors, companies and governing bodies.

♦ *Virtual Event Technologist*: provides and manages the technical support to ensure a successful virtual event; responsible for monitoring each dance performance, chat, video stream, virtual meeting rooms and sponsors' exhibition booths, and addressing potential problems.

The first author of this chapter was a founding member and had a dual-capacity role as President and Managing Director, thus having first-hand access to the event and its management. In line with action research logics (Kemmis & Carr, 1986), the methodological approach in this chapter pursued a self-reflective enquiry of the event organizers' decision-making to deal with critical dilemmas and issues. This aimed to capture reflective practice where the practitioner is an insider action-researcher, actively involved in the cause for which the research is conducted (Coghlan, 2001). Self-reflection observations and interpretations were debated, contrasted and triangulated with the second author who acted as a detached observer. This enabled the production of a more balanced account of the event organizers' decision-making under crisis.

Due to the lockdown, the organizers had to make a difficult decision on how to proceed; would they cancel or postpone the event? The need for such a decision brought a great pressure due to the unpredictability and uncertainty of the COVID-19 pandemic. Methodical decision-making and flexible adaptation to changes were crucial for managing the event, which was facing such a severe crisis. Below we present the approach adopted by the organizers to manage the event under the crisis.

Making the decision and rescheduling

Developing a decision-making framework

The event organizers followed a decision-making framework in order to effectively design and apply an action plan, which would secure prompt responses and intelligence. The framework was developed by the organizers, based on practical experience, literature and instinct. This was in line with Matzler et al. (2007) who state that experienced managers often need to rely on 'gut instinct' to make complex decisions under pressure. Even though literature suggests different paths in crisis management (Coombs & Laufer, 2018; Mason, 2007; Seetharaman, 2020), the combination of theory with practical know-how and instinctiveness yielded a framework, which was suitably tailored to the artistic-participatory nature and identity of the event.

Crisis management is an administrative approach to deal with crisis conditions and to prepare and plan how to confront them (Berger et al., 2020). Scientific knowledge is foundational to develop a decision-making framework, though decisions within a pandemic context have to be made under overwhelming time pressure and amid high scientific uncertainty, with minimal robust evidence, and potential disagreements among experts and models (Berger et al., 2020). In agreement with the above, Al-Dabbagh (2020) states that modern crises, such as the COVID-19 pandemic, increase the need for skilled decision-makers and wise management in order to effectively face the severe economic, health, educational, and social consequences.

The following framework had to be made within a highly uncertain, complex and rapidly changing environment. In such a case, in which economy, education, sports and culture are at stake, ideas from modern decision theory were used. Modern decision theory has developed since the middle of the 20th century, through contributions from several academic disciplines. Based on Hansson (2005), the decision-making process is divided in sequential steps: 1. Identification of the problem; 2. Obtaining necessary information; 3. Production of possible solutions; 4. Evaluation of such solutions; 5. Selection of a strategy for performance. The organizers embedded elements of the decision theory in their framework. However, their framework had to reflect also their values and beliefs. In modern decision theory, the basic question of whether a decision is ethical or not, it is not provided in a thorough and operational manner.

The managers of the National Ballet Competition had a moral compass at the core of their decision-making. Their actions had to follow their vision statement that is 'empowering youth's artistic development' through offering scholarships and opportunities for recognition. Thus, ethics and educational values were indispensable elements in order to ensure that the opportunity to offer scholarships would not be lost. This fundamental value statement provided the keystone for instinctive decision-making and in line with literature the following framework was developed.

The decision-making framework included the following steps that are analyzed in the next section:

1   Identifying the reasons

2   Facing the option of canceling the competition

3   Identifying the alternatives

4   Ethical decision-making

5   Choosing among the alternatives

6   Rescheduling and redefining the strategic planning of the competition

7   Establishing a highly effective communication policy.

Step-by-step decision-making

1. Identifying the reasons

First, it was important to identify the reasons for canceling or postponing the event and also taking into account whether the event program would be updated by moving the date months later. It was fundamental for retaining the trust of attendees, dancers, choreographers and parents to communicate properly whether the postponement of the event would be due to an internal reason specific to the organization, or that it was due to a larger factor. External causes of crises are usually those that impact more than one sector and can range from environmental disasters to local dangers and global pandemics. Any company cannot have much influence and that is why they are also called exogenous causes (Dubrovski, 2016). External factors can be much more difficult to predict when it comes to rescheduling the event and COVID-19 pandemic is such a factor. The reason for not running the national competition in the originally scheduled date, Spring 2020, was that due to the sudden outbreak of COVID-19 and the new conditions created by the consequent preventive measures of the lockdown, its effective implementation was not feasible.

2. Facing the option of canceling the competition

The organizing team was always well prepared for problem-solving, but this unforeseen external force was beyond any crisis management plan they had. A debate started between the team members concerning the event cancellation or possible alternatives. As suggested by a member of the management team:

> *During this crazy time with events being canceled and postponed and the current restrictive language use such as 'government regulations', 'global pandemic' and 'center for disease control warnings', 'social distancing', we had a strong option to cancel the competition without a penalty.*

Considering that major events such as the Olympic Games were canceled for 2020, arguments leaned towards the decision to cancel, to avoid the spread of coronavirus. Before the final decision, alternatives had to be identified and evaluated. For example, after communicating with stakeholders and before any announcement, it was felt by the management team:

> *It helped us a lot to make the decision that we are keeping long-standing relationships with the dance teachers and usually they are very understanding and easy to work with. The communication client-by-client addressed that it will be very beneficial for both parties to postpone or reschedule the competition instead of canceling it.*

3. Identifying the alternatives

One possible alternative was to postpone the event until months later and changing the season in which the competition usually takes place. Nevertheless, announcing a new date was a challenge as the official guidelines for the pandemic were evolving rapidly. Based on Aligne and Mattioli (2011), crisis management functionalities are structured along three crucial steps: information gathering, situation understanding, and decision making. In the information-gathering step, the overall picture and the real-time situation awareness will be understood after providing trustworthy sources of information, like those offered by the World Health Organization and the national government, were gathered. Important questions were clearly stated: "*What are the updated guidelines and considerations for events and gatherings to prevent spread of coronavirus disease? Will the theaters operate after the lockdown and what are the precautions to be followed from staff and attendees in a theater?*"

Based on the answers of the officials, the organizers could not guarantee that the postponed competition would take place for sure at a new date due to the indefinite duration of the lockdown and the restrictions on theater operations. As stated by the management team:

> *Following the latest government guidance on COVID-19 left us feeling stressed, anxious, and powerless over the direction of the event. As we entered the second month of the pandemic, most theater companies have canceled their*

current contracts for spring and summer season and it was likely to face rolling theatre closures throughout autumn-winter 2020-2021.

Thus, the venue was also a big concern. Initially, the outdoor areas seemed to be a more possible option, rather than indoors, to host the event during the COVID-19 crisis. Nevertheless, this alternative was not considered, as it was taken into account that the national competition lasts more than twenty hours and the outdoor environment is not suitable neither for dancers nor for the judging committee. Therefore, the venue of the event should be indoors but theaters did not undertake new contracts due to the uncertainty about whether they would operate or not in the coming months. In addition, because of the dynamic nature of the competition, crowding by staggering arrivals and departures in the venue area as well as its overall complexity such as a crowd of dancers behind the scenes and similarly at the awards ceremony on stage, along with the increasing need for physical distancing and precautions to prevent the spread of coronavirus disease, a live event in 2020 could not stand as an option for this large-scale competition.

4. Ethical decision-making: Weighting the core values of the competition

Even if the existing alternatives, for realizing an in-person event, were weak and all evidence led towards the cancellation of the competition, the organizers wanted their decision to be in line with the event's ethical framework, their personal values and the 'common good approach'. This was in agreement with the 'ethical-decision processes' (Lozano, 2000), which maintain that business managers should not jump to solutions without first identifying the ethical issue(s) in the situation; also, by identifying the affected parties, they develop the perspective: *"Try to see things through the eyes of those individuals affected"* in order to formulate the appropriate decision or action based on the ethical organizational character and integrity (Lozano, 2000).

Organizing events is strongly connected to creating human experiences; they benefit people's psychology, social inclusion, increase awareness, connect communities and experts, drive dialogue and more. During a crisis, the organizers have to show their capacity to be visioners, big picture thinkers, optimists, dynamic and adaptive. From a psychological standpoint, the cancelation of the competition would promote a state of tension, anger and frustration between the participants, teachers and parents. If the national competition had been canceled for 2020, hundreds of young dancers would have been disappointed and disoriented from performance goals. As a member of the management team said:

Most of our participants are teenagers and it is even harder for a teenager to accept the dance school closure and the cancellation of the competition. Teens see this event as one of the biggest moments of their young lives. It's the culmination of a year's work and a social event. We wanted to lift them up, motivate them, remind them the value of determination and show them that we do respond to life-challenges with creativity.

At the same time, participating in the competition and winning a scholarship was indeed an important reason for ballet teachers and dance studio-owners to book private lessons, even online during the lockdown. As described by the management team:

When the pandemic hit Greece, dance studios across the country switched regular classes into virtual. Though many parents demanded refunds for tuition. To avoid this, dance teachers applied training for competition as a smart strategy to integrate dancers into their virtual classes and boost parents' motivation.

Keeping the competition period in progress and not cancelling this popular event, parents got a sense of satisfaction seeing their children active and expressing themselves creatively even in limited space at homes. Months of hard work, diligence, and commitment should not be placed in question 'all for nothing?' The organizers recognized that the competition worked as a 'strong motivation' for youths to 'stay active and creative during the COVID-19 crisis'. Also, it worked as a 'professional tool' for dance teachers and for the parents as an important part of children's 'educational development'. The organizers had to think outside the box and find potential alternatives to keep the competition running and meet everyone's expectations.

5. Choosing among the alternatives

The next alternative on the list was the use of modern technology to transition the competition into a virtual edition. Sending a dance video was never an option for the national competition, which was always based on live performances in front of judges and audience. The interaction between choreographers and dance school owners from Greece and Cyprus was also a key factor of the event's quality. A main objective was how to transition the event from in-person into virtual in an efficient and creative way. Organizers had to think outside the box, redefine the strategic plan and the context of the competition. Even in times of uncertainty and change, strategy remains a key to business success; because an effective strategy brings vision and execution together. The purpose of strategic planning was to set the new goals and to develop a plan to achieve them (Ranen, 2020). Although the venue was not to be a prestigious theater, by combining the right tools, streaming video services or all-in-one platforms, the virtual event could become bigger, unique, engaging and having a positive impact to attendees and stakeholders.

6. Redefining the strategic planning of the competition

The strategic plan included a six-month timetable from the postponed competition to the new virtual edition, both during 2020. The reconfiguration of strategic planning was aligned with value co-creation processes, viewing the event as a service ecosystem that comprises a range of stakeholders who interact and integrate resources in producing the event (Mervi et al., 2019; Woratschek et al., 2014). Co-creation is a form of collaborative innovation in which there is an open contribution to the event from all stakeholders. According to Akhilesh (2017), co-creation offers alternatives to deal with or overcome problem situations, but it cannot exist without the trust, respect, and mutuality that enable inclusive consumer involvement in the productive processes and overall success of organizations. Co-creative consumer behavior can be achieved when consumers are active and well aware that they too can contribute to value creation at certain points of exchange. This, in turn, may lead to open innovation and consequently collaborative consumption. Sharing power and co-creating with stakeholders helped the event grow fast, improved participants' insight and achieved alignment with the event's statements, such as 'Dance competition during COVID-19 crisis' and 'Stay safe – Keep dancing'. Four groups of stakeholders were identified and each is described below alongside how they contribute to the event's value.

Stakeholders' co-creation of value in the event

Co-creation of value aimed to promote and encourage active involvement in the event from experts, judges, participants and sponsors. Co-creation helped all stakeholders to be attuned in the importance of making this year's competition happen. As shown in Image 10.1, a partnership with international bodies associations and federations grounded the co-creation of the event with other organizers who all supported the concept 'Dance during COVID-19 crisis'.

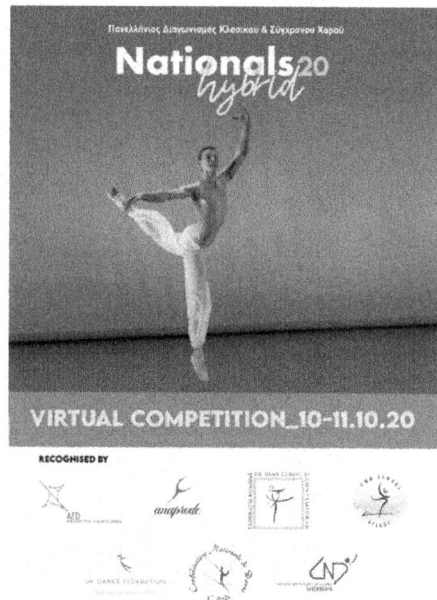

Image 10.1: Partnership for 'Dance during COVID-19 crisis'

Experts

The virtual edition of the competition brought an increasing need for expertise. Web designers and IT experts proposed ways to accomplish the production and provide a professional, unique and meaningful event. It also had to be fun and promote stakeholders' social interaction. A good slogan captured the essence, communicated the qualities and defined the purpose of the virtual event. It worked as a tool to advance the marketing strategies and helped to build in the participants' minds perceptions of trust, innovation, quality and commitment. IT experts secured an online platform for dancers to compete, gain valuable constructive feedback and receive recognition. As displayed in Image 10.2, the graphic designers realized the concept of connecting (net) Greece and Cyprus (countries' maps) using the slogan 'Dance Competition during COVID-19 crisis – Stay Connected' and with a talented dancer coming out of desktop window showing that all dance performances will reach the screen of the audience. Image 10.3 displays a range of promotional posts in social media.

Image 10.2: Concept design

Image 10.3: Promotional posts in social media

Judges

Choosing the right judges played a crucial role for the event's success. Judges were well-known dancers, choreographers and partner-organizers from other international competitions. Judges posted short videos on competition's social media to motivate participants. Phrases such as 'keep dancing and expressing yourself' and 'waiting to see all talented dancers from Greece and Cyprus' helped inspire the participation in the virtual competition. The feeling of 'coming together virtually', 'sharing the love for ballet' and the sense of 'belonging' brought excitement to participants and teachers. Image 10.4 shows the judges who were active and well-known dancers from the National Opera of Greece and offered to be dance models in promotional posters of the competition.

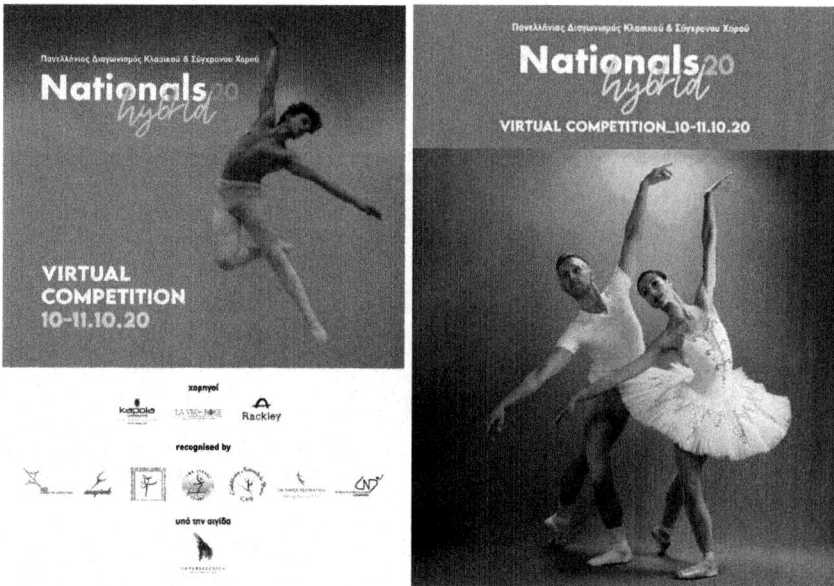

Image 10.4: Judges in promotional posters of the event

Participants

Dancers and teachers' efforts were focused on shooting the dance videos, which was the actual content of the competition. Teachers were free to decide the place and background where they would shoot the dance performance. Photos from the shooting period were posted from dancers sharing quotes and tagging on the competition's page. Image 10.5 shows examples of teachers and dance studio-owners who were posting photos in social media during the time of video shooting, thereby helping the promotion of the event.

Image 10.5: Teachers and dance studio owners photos in social media

Sponsors

The virtual event offered various possibilities to maximize the engagement between sponsors and attendees. A promotional campaign around the sponsor's mission was created and specific times for an elevator pitch were scheduled through social media. Sponsors' interaction and exposure was increased by using online tools such as 'virtual booths', interviews via web-stream and sharing their story through social media. For example, Image 10.6 shows a dancewear company, which was a sponsor of the event and helped promote the competition.

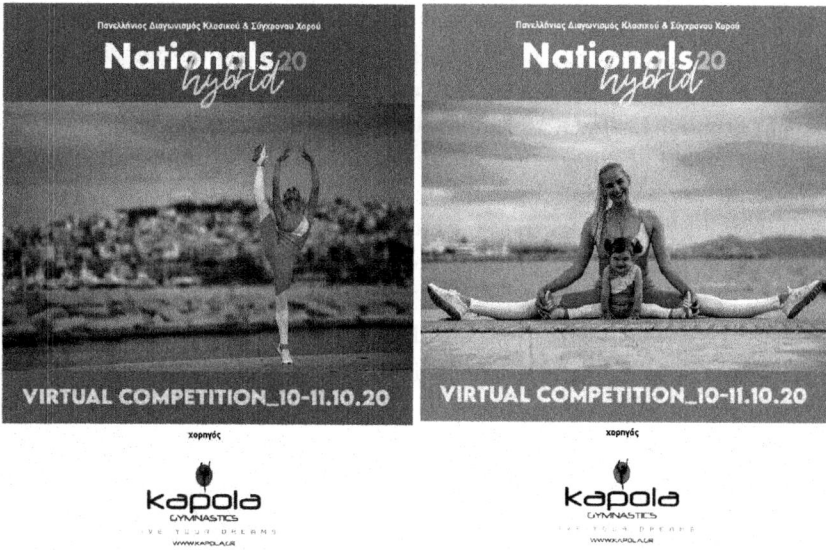

Image 10.6: Promotional poster by a dancewear company sponsor of the event

7. *Establishing a highly effective communication policy*

Announcing the postponement of the National Ballet Competition created a huge demand for information. Communication was important to keep stakeholders and attendees well-informed and engaged. According to public relations principles (Gilpin & Murphy, 2006), three key lessons appear in crisis communication: be *quick*, be *consistent* and be *open*. Public relations techniques also suggest 'getting the word out', letting stakeholders know. The objective is to fill the information vacuum with accurate information. The organizers had a quick response, which showed that everything was under control; and consistency that insured all team members were speaking 'with one voice' and delivering consistent messages. Openness and full transparency, being as communicative as possible and updating dancers, teachers and parents frequently, was the key behavior to instill trust (Gilpin & Murphy, 2006).

What are the dance video requirements?

When is the final date to send the video submission?

How to send the dance video?

What information is important to write in every video?

When will be the program announced?

How can people see the competition?

What are the awards?

Image 10.7: Questions on the F.A.Q webpage

The website of the event provided at least one way for people to get in touch with the organizers, and a question form and a F.A.Q page was created (Image 10.7). A person was always available to answer questions in a timely manner and worked as a consultant to help participants navigate the competition changes and suggested alternatives. Multiple announcement emails and mobile app notifications with the rescheduled date and time were sent out. When the stakeholders and the attendees saw that they could rely on the organization, new registrations and partnerships were secured.

The outcome: Enjoying the competition and getting satisfaction

With over 1000 registrations from dancers across Greece and Cyprus, the virtual event was run successfully in October 2020, one month before the second lockdown (coronavirus second wave). More than 30 scholarships were given to talented young dancers, whose elite performances captured judges and the audience. Stakeholders' feedback was received through an event app. With this mobile app, participants gave feedback instantly and even engaged by voting 'audience best performance'. A chat function enabled the interaction of dance schools with each other during the event – which was really fun. Reviews scored high (1) service quality and relationship satisfaction, (2) trust and affective commitment, (3) communication, and (4) willingness to participate again. In post-competition announcements, the organizers expressed their deep feelings with a thank you: *"You gave us the best moments of 2020".*

Conclusion

Crises challenge the hosting of events and bring the need for reorganization and identification of innovative solutions to ensure survival or future prosperity. During the COVID-19 crisis, creative minds in the event industry have turned their focus on finding ways to keep events running, reshaping them into virtual productions, while keeping participants, staff and contributors safe. As this case of the National Ballet Competition in Greece demonstrates, when facing hard and swift decision-making in rescheduling an event, the following key lessons are put forth:

1   Reacting to a crisis requires multi-dimensional thinking and methodical problem-solving for adaptation.

2   Choosing the right tools and experts is crucial.

3   Scaling up the event is possible when the strategic plan is redefined and an effective communication policy is applied.

4   Maximizing stakeholder engagement through investing in collaborative co-creation processes.

As the overwhelmingly positive responses from stakeholders on re-organizing this event showed, there was a general disposition and support to host it.

No doubt, there is still a need for events, even in times of hardship, to realize social, psychological and other functions. The survival of events in the context of Greece is noteworthy as this country has been under long-lasting multiple crises since 2008. Worse still, the lack of a proactive regulatory framework, government support and specific education for event management exacerbates the tough conditions under which events operate. Event organizers have to rely on their own abilities, resourcefulness and adaptability in order to stay in business. Subsequently, events are based on the empirical foresight and hindsight of their organizers. Despite the difficulties, this might create new event strategies and tools in dealing with crises. This case provides an example of adaptive thinking and planning processes, on how event organizers have responded to the crisis through methodical decision-making to re-organize the competition as a virtual event. While in general, responses of event organizers have been tentative and investigative, this also makes up a virgin ground upon which a more sophisticated event management outlook and specific event-focused crisis recovery techniques can be instituted and nurtured in the near future.

In this chapter, we examined a particular participatory type of event. Participatory ballet events are arguably harder to manage and re-organize as virtual due to the human bond between the dancers and the audience. Such an experience cannot be replaced and ballet events are seriously threatened from crises and necessary cancellations. Ballet is related to the arts, sport, culture and entertainment; such a combination is achieved in a theatrical atmosphere which is even harder to transfer in a virtual reality. Similar characteristics and exigencies span across artistic, sporting, cultural and entertainment events, so this case provides an example with which organizers of the above events can easily relate. Quite evidently, with the lasting global impact of the pandemic, ballet-event organizers have to take a deep dive into crisis management, and develop their expertise in leadership and communication practices to efficiently navigate these events on a safe path. As shown, this can be done through synthesizing creatively empirical insight and theory.

References

Advisory Board on Economic and Social Affairs (2020). *Recovering better: Economic and social challenges and opportunities.* New York: United Nations, Department of Economic and Social Affairs.

Akhilesh, K. B. (2017). *Co-creation and Learning: Concepts and cases.* New York: Springer.

Al-Dabbagh, Z. S. (2020). The role of decision-maker in crisis management: A qualitative study using Grounded Theory (COVID-19 pandemic crisis as a model). *Journal of Public Affairs, 20*(4), e2186.

Aligne, F., & Mattioli, J. (2011). The role of context for crisis management cycle. In F. Burstein, P. Brézillon, & A. Zaslavsky (Eds.), *Supporting Real-time Decision-making*. Boston: Springer.

Berger, L., Berger, N., Bosetti, V., Gilboa, I., Hansen, L. P., Jarvis, C., Marinacci, M., & Smith, R. (2020). Uncertainty and decision-making during a crisis: How to make policy decisions in the COVID-19 context? University of Chicago, Becker Friedman Institute for Economics Working Paper No. 2020-95, http://dx.doi.org/10.2139/ssrn.3647188.

Coghlan, D. (2001). Insider action research projects: Implications for practising managers. *Management Learning, 32*(1), 49-60.

Coombs, W.T., & Laufer, D. (2018). Global crisis management – Current research and future directions. *Journal of International Management, 24*(3), 199-203.

Dubrovski, D. (2016). Handling corporate crises based on the correct analysis of its causes. *Journal of Financial Risk Management, 5*(4), 264-280.

Gilpin, D., & Murphy, P. (2006). Reframing crisis management through complexity. In C. H. Botan & V. Hazleton (Eds.), *Public Relations Theory II* (pp. 375-392). Abingdon: Routledge.

Hansson, S. O. (2005). *Decision Theory: A brief introduction*. Stockholm: Royal Institute of Technology.

Ingram, R. T. (2015). *Ten Basic Responsibilities of Nonprofit Boards* (3rd ed.). Washington: BoardSource.

Kemmis , S., & Carr, W. (1986). *Becoming Critical: Education, knowledge and action research*. Abingdon: Routledge.

Lozano, J. M. (2000). *Ethics and Organizations: Understanding business ethics as a learning process*. Boston: Springer.

Mason, R. B. (2007). The external environment's effect on management and strategy: A complexity theory approach. *Management Decision, 45*(1), 10-28.

Matzler, B. M., Bailom, F., & Mooradian, T.A. (2007). Intuitive decision making. *MIT Sloan Management Review*. https://sloanreview.mit.edu/article/intuitive-decision-making/.

Mervi, L., Suomi, K., & Lepistö, T. (2019). Unraveling mechanisms of value co-creation in festivals. *Event Management, 23*(1), 41-60.

Ranen, M. (2020). Redefining strategy in disruptive times. *Chief Executive* (27 April). chiefexecutive.net/scenario-planning-redefining-strategy-in-disruptive-times/.

Seetharaman, P. (2020). Business models shifts: Impact of COVID-19. *International Journal of Information Management, 54*, 102173.

Woratschek, H., Horbel, C., & Popp, B. (2014). The sport value framework – A new fundamental logic for analyses in sport management. *European Sport Management Quarterly, 14*(1), 6-24.

11 Agility in the Events Sector: A Case Study of a Business Event in Finland

Valentina Gorchakova and Ekaterina Berdysheva

Introduction

The events industry was estimated at $1,100 billion in 2018 and was expected to grow to reach $2,330 billion by 2026 (Allied Market Research, n.d.). Year 2020, however, turned out to be perhaps the most transformative year in the industry in the last decades. Numerous events, from smaller family occasions, like weddings, to major events of the likes of the Wimbledon tennis tournament, the UEFA EURO 2020, Glastonbury Festival and the Cannes Film festival, had to be cancelled due to the Covid-19 pandemic. The combined economic impact is not yet known but will be a loss in the hundreds of billions of US dollars (Gössling, Scott, & Hall, 2021). This shows the vulnerability of the events industry to major crises.

Despite the negative impacts of crises on events, there is a paucity of research that explores organizational responses under unusual, unprecedented or critical circumstances in the events sector. This chapter applies the concept of agility in event organization within volatile, uncertain, complex, and ambiguous, so-called VUCA, environment (Bennett & Lemoine, 2014) that dominated year 2020 due to the unfolding pandemic. The agile approach is often seen as a stream of new ideas leading to elegantly simple solutions. It requires a high energy level of the team involved due to the tight constraints and deadlines. The authors introduce a case study of a business festival organized in Turku (Finland) and discuss the decision-making process, stakeholder involvement, introduction of a new modus operandi, and the new event format that was chosen.

2020: A crisis or a VUCA situation?

It is generally accepted, and has been discussed in previous chapters in this volume, that crisis is an unexpected and unpredictable event, characterized by lack of control and need for action; it can cause significant negative results, including instability of organizational processes and, potentially, threaten an organization's viability and survival (e.g., Pauchant & Mitroff, 1992; Pearson & Mitroff, 1993; Seeger, Sellnow, & Ulmur, 1998; Selbst (1978) in Faulkner 2001; Williams & Treadaway, 1992). Related terms – disaster, incident, problem, event – also feature in the literature, and some authors would argue that what differentiates 'crisis' is the extent to which management structures cope, or do not cope, with a situation and the level of control over the changes (Faulkner, 2001).

Crisis management can be conceived of as an art more than a science, because it relies on human beings, their actions, an array of emotions and skill set (Vanvactor, 2015). The way organizations, their managers and leaders respond to crises, disasters and incidents are, therefore, critical (Saleh, 2016; Useem, Cook, & Sutton, 2005). It has been suggested that creative thinking can be helpful, particularly in two ways (Pearson & Sommer, 2011):

♦ *Novelty*, a decision that is unconventional or unique as compared to previous decisions, and

♦ *Value*, a decision that is acceptable and effective.

If either is missing, then creativity cannot be deemed useful. Thinking creatively, in unconventional ways can be valuable when the purpose is clear and shared within an organization or a team, and there is the desire to achieve that purpose.

It has been argued that three conditions contribute to higher levels of creative thought (Paul & Elder, 2012, p. 14):

♦ A minimal level of innate intellectual capacity;

♦ An environment that stimulates the development of that capacity;

♦ A positive response and inner motivation on the part of the person.

Leaders of event organizations can foster creative thinking by creating a favorable environment within the team; one that would unlock the potential of each team member and use their inner motivation to discover a range of opportunities and possible actions.

Scholars have suggested various stages for a crisis lifecycle: from pre-crisis through to 'emergency' to recovery. Contrary to some natural disasters and previous epidemics, such as the severe acute respiratory syndrome (SARS) outbreak in 2003 and the Middle East Respiratory Syndrome (MERS) outbreak in 2015, Covid-19 has proved to have a significantly longer-term effect on the events industry, affecting, in one way or another, all scheduled business, cultural and sporting events. Due to the geographical spread and time span of this pandemic, it may be reasonable to suggest that starting from February 2020 the events sector operated within a VUCA environment. This is especially valid considering that many events were eventually organized in a virtual format, which testifies to the ability of the sector to adjust to the external environment and proceed with the core business – events.

The VUCA abbreviation stands for volatile, uncertain, complex, and ambiguous environment. It comes into the business world from a military one where *"confusion is part of the game"* (Johansen & Euchner, 2013, p. 10). Key characteristics of such environment have been summarized by Bennett and Lemoine (2014):

- ◆ *Volatility*: The change is unstable and unpredictable, and may be of unknown duration, but it is not necessarily hard to understand; knowledge about it is often available.

- ◆ *Uncertainty*: The situation's basic cause and effect are known. Change is possible but not a given; the scope of its effects is unknown.

- ◆ *Complexity*: The situation has many interconnected parts and variables. Some information is available or can be predicted, but the volume or nature of it can be overwhelming to process.

- ◆ *Ambiguity*: A lack of knowledge; causal relationships are completely unclear. No precedents exist.

Throughout year 2020, event organizers had to deal with numerous questions pertinent to all four components:

Volatility – the events sector faced an unstable situation. Although the information about the Covid-19 virus was available to some extent, it was still unclear how long the pandemic would last for and how the situation would be unfolding in each country. Changes could happen quickly and affect various regions, cities or countries. It was clear that the change was likely; however, its magnitude across locations could vary.

Uncertainty – there was a lack of knowledge about the impact of the pandemic on the motivation of event attendees, their behaviors and attitudes towards events in general, as well as about the wider regulations that might be introduced by the Government at any stage. Will there be any changes in guidance or regulations by the scheduled event's date? If a new format was introduced, would the usual audience attend? Would that new format be able to maintain the event's identity, interest and commitment from stakeholders?

Complexity – the complexity of organizing an event during the pandemic. This includes the changes in the ways an event organization used to work previously during preparation and delivery. Several levels of complexity could be identified; for instance, for the team dynamics if the event team members were used to working in an office environment and having regular conversations and discussions; for the logistics of an event; complexity associated with exploring various software and their applicability and viability for the existing event; complexity with implementing a new format or introducing media that previously had not been used, e.g. online or virtual software. All those parts were interconnected, and event organizations had to review and restructure their processes to respond to that complexity.

Ambiguity – the situation was new to the events sector. In the absence of a historical precedent of the same scale, it was challenging for the organizers to establish possible outcomes of causes or actions. How would event participants and attendees feel about attending an event if the decision would be to organize it on-site during the pandemic? Would the change in the original dates help in attracting the audience? And, overall, what would happen next? Experimentation with various options is required, but the price of a failed experiment can be detrimental for the event's future.

It is evident that under the circumstances such as above, the onus to steer organizations both strategically and on a day-to-day operational level falls on leadership and management.

Agility

Even in non-VUCA times, organizations, arguably, need strong visionary leadership and effective management (Morden, 1997). A style that could embrace both was termed 'visionary management'. *"The vision speaks the language of the people, the company's employees. It is a means for the company to communicate to its own people, its clients and other parties about its prospects, interests, trust in the future and its way of doing business"* (Malaska & Holstius, 1999, p. 356). A vision can serve to work on specific management tasks, empower and engage people, and leads to the commitment. Competent management is also critical as decisions need to be timely and effective. Leading and working under time and/or resource constraints is one of the differentiating features of agility.

In VUCA times, the agility of organizational leaders, their ability to lead into the uncertain, unexpected, complex and unknown, becomes critical. As a concept, agility comes from flexible manufacturing systems and automation, further expanding to the wider business context, more as an organizational orientation (Aitken, Christopher, & Towill, 2002). Organization agility is a so-called dynamic capability that represents the capacity to sense opportunities and threats, and solve problems, when changing circumstances require it (Winby & Worley, 2014). Agility has been conceived of in various ways, but, in essence, in business operations, it is often associated with the speed in responding to changes (Gong & Janssen, 2012). Van Oosterhout et al. (2006, p. 53) define business agility as:

> the ability to sense highly uncertain external and internal changes, and respond to them reactively or proactively, based on innovation of the internal operational processes, involving the customer in exploration and exploitation activities, while leveraging the capabilities of partners in the business network.

An agile organization has a sense of shared purpose, an identity and intent (Winby & Worley, 2014). The shared purpose is the one that extends beyond monetary profit and is shared by the key stakeholders of the organization; the identity encompasses the organization's culture and brand; while the intent is the market position and the company's unique selling proposition (USP). These three components are essential when leadership decisions on innovation are made.

Hugos (2009) suggests a three-steps process for agility and innovation in business: Define (2-3 weeks); Design (1-3 months); Build (2-6 months). During the first step, Define, business goal and performance requirements are being defined, conceptual design suggested, and initial plan and budget developed. The second step, Design, involves the introduction of a new business process design, a system prototype and actual plan and budget. The final step, Build, is characterized by launching a working system with supporting technical documentation and manual. The pre-determined deadlines and timeframe for completing each step underscores the urgency to both the decision-making process and actions.

The model, albeit suggested in a context that is different to events, can be applicable, with variations, to the agile organization of events: Define – Design – Deliver. During the first step, Define, an event's goal, vision, resources, and target audience are defined; conceptual design of the event suggested; action plan and budget developed. The second step, Design, involves the development of an event's program, format, venue/platform, and actual plan and budget. The final step, Deliver, is characterized by working on the delivery of the event, including the technical aspects, specific program elements, working with event participants and attendees, partners and other stakeholders.

Agility embraces a wide range of processes and activities, including marketing, design, organization, management, and people (Aitken et al., 2002). Beyond processes, agility can also be seen as an integrated set of behaviors (Hallanbeck, 2016) and it starts with a frame of mind (Hugos, 2009). Agility is grounded in one's own experiences but requires versatility and adaptability under novel and complex circumstances; the ability to see new and challenging situations as opportunities of growth and new learning. Curiosity and willingness to experiment characterize this approach and prompt to explore a range of available options and their applicability and practicality. Thinking and acting differently can lead to a range of innovations – from adoption of new technologies to new business models or formats (Doz & Kosonen, 2008).

New technology and virtual events

The technological advancement of the last decades made a significant impact on the MICE sector across the world, in particular in the areas of information and communication (Locke, 2010). Despite the fact that technologies had been emerging and continuously implemented in events of various formats over the past decade, the pandemic caused by Covid-19 forced most events to embrace new ways of management and organization. Event organizers had to explore and employ technologies, including the ones that provide an opportunity for an event to take place in a virtual space. As a result, the use of the online or virtual platforms, such as 6Connex, Google meet, Hangout, Zoom, WebX, experienced significant growth. Virtual meeting software market is estimated to more than triple from $12.1 billion in 2019 to $41.58 billion in 2027 (Fortune Business Insights, n.d.).

Online and virtual events have received some attention in the events literature. The words, online and virtual, have been often used somewhat interchangeably (e.g., Getz & Page, 2016; Seraphin, 2021); however, they denote different formats. Online is associated with the use of the Internet, i.e. available, done, bought, used, as well as *"using a computer to communicate with other computers, or of or about a computer that is connected to another computer"* (Cambridge Dictionary, 2021a). The term 'virtual' has got several meanings to it, including, as per Cambridge Dictionary (2021b):

◆ created by computer technology and appearing to exist but not existing in the physical world;

◆ done using computer technology over the internet, and not involving people physically going somewhere.

The focus of 'virtual' becomes more on the technology and a non-physical word, or reality. Virtual world has been defined as *"an imaginary space often manifested through a medium"* (Sherman & Craig, 2019, p. 8). According to the authors, the key elements in experiencing virtual reality are the following: the virtual world, immersion, interactivity, and the people on the creating and receiving side of the medium (Sherman & Craig, 2019). Therefore, watching a lecture via a YouTube stream, for instance, or attending a conference via Zoom, or a team meeting on Microsoft Teams can all be considered online ways of participation, and the format for the said events is online, too. A virtual event calls for additional software and attributes, and a different experience for the attendees.

Case study: Overview of SHIFT festival

SHIFT Business festival is an annual two-day networking event that combines speaker line-up, workshops, round-table discussions, and expo-like business visibility opportunities. It was founded in 2015 in Turku, Western Finland, by a group of like-minded people interested in promoting innovative ways of doing business. It is a non-profit organization, and the stakeholder support is carried out by the Board of both SHIFT Association and SHIFT Events Ltd. Participants of the Board have various backgrounds, such as multi-entrepreneurs, digital business pioneers, and event industry experts. The festival has been supported by the City of Turku, Turku Science Park, Turku Technology Properties, and University of Turku, among other partners over the years.

The program topics have been changing from one year to another, and event organizers endeavored to cover both global mega-trends and the specifics of regional business environment. In the first year the festival was organized, 2016, the key themes were health, education and energy industries. Subsequently, in 2017, the topics were human-machine and human-human collaboration. The 2018 festival focused on the ethical tech and artificial intelligence (AI), as well as maritime industry and mobility. In 2019, the event's main topics were circular economy, AI, and maritime industry.

The themes for each year had been chosen based on the relevance and currency of these mega-trends for both local and international businesses. For example, the maritime industry featured repeatedly for 2 years in a row, 2018 and 2019, because Turku is a port city and a part of maritime cluster in Southwestern Finland and is, therefore, critical for the economy and overall vitality of the Turku region.

A distinct feature of SHIFT has been its unusual venues. For the first two years the festival was held in the medieval Turku castle – a historical monument with more than 700 years of history. In 2018 the festival was moved to a former prison building that nowadays hosts a hotel and commercial property. The event's 2019 venue was an old shipyard in Ruissalo, once the biggest boatyard in the Nordic countries.

The number of participants has been rising gradually. Over 1000 people attended the event in its first year, 2016. In 2017 the festival attracted over 2500 visitors and in year 2019, SHIFT hosted over 3000 visitors from more than 40 countries. The attendees represented such sectors as business and finance, technology, industry, academia, and public and third sectors. The attendees' job roles varied from university students to C-level executives and company founders.

Organizing an event during the pandemic: Key decisions

With the pandemic unfolding in 2020, all large business events in Finland and worldwide were faced with a choice of whether to find a safe way to organize the event, postpone till 2021 or to cancel the event altogether. The SHIFT Business Festival team was determined to find an option that would not just allow the event to happen, but also provide the value and experience for attendees compatible with the high standard that it had become known for. In this effort, the event team demonstrated their commitment to the shared purpose, although pursuing it required high energy level of all members of the team and creative thinking while facing a lot of ambiguity, complexity, and uncertainty.

At the Define and Design stages, the questions about the dates, event concept, and topic of the festival were on the agenda. Traditionally, the festival was held in August. As the restrictions were changing throughout spring and summer, it was decided to, first, move the festival from August to October, in the hope that by the end of the year the restrictions could be eased. Second, the organizers came to the decision to switch to a hybrid event format, so SHIFT would combine features of online and on-site events. That way it could be possible to create some real-life experience for a limited number of participants and, at the same time, provide an opportunity for others to join online.

Even before the pandemic started, it had been decided to introduce a broader topic for the event – Intelligent business, i.e., doing business both sustainably, profitably and with the help of new technologies. The rationale was that the festival had been growing in both the number of attendees and their profile characteristics, and that introducing one overarching theme would allow for a wider variety of keynote speakers and topics, thus, offering greater value to attendees.

Another important event design decision was to change the format from a two-day event to a two-month's series of events that would start with a kick-off in August on the original dates of the festival, continuing with bi-weekly expert webinars delivered by the festival's partners, and culminating in the main event in October. Maintaining the original dates was deemed important to retain the regular audience of the festival and maintain their interest. This way, attendees could still get a sense that the event was organized in August, as it normally would. The follow-up webinars were aimed at teasing out the contents of the main festival and giving people more time to familiarize themselves with the new format – online instead of on-site, and the new, broader theme of the festival, as compared to more specific topics in the previous years. That helped prospective attendees to experience the unique value of the festival, get more insights into the Intelligent business area and to decide if they wanted to attend the main event. The capacity to sense opportunities and pursue innovative solutions in programming demonstrates an agile approach to event management of the festival.

While many other business events in 2020 were getting canceled, the SHIFT team decided to respond proactively to changes and do the opposite. The solution to change the format of the festival and make it happen in 2020 in a new format, despite the ambiguity of the situation, was a unanimous opinion of the event team and its management and was supported by key stakeholders. The idea of a virtual event had not been considered before the pandemic in 2020, so that was a truly novel format forged as a response to the changes in the event industry and the external environment.

The inspiration for the event's format came from looking at the essence and identity of SHIFT Business Festival, in particular, to create an environment for people from different industries and roles to come together and meet each other. This diverse and co-creative atmosphere facilitates both learning and networking across geographical and industry borders. In this sense, the festival's ambition differs from sector-specific events where the players generally already know each other.

A creative solution was required in order to maintain the traditional SHIFT atmosphere and to allow for people to 'randomly run into each other', as they would do on-site. A webinar format was considered not good enough for the main event due to it being a passive form of participation and not allowing for serendipitous meetings. Different options and media were evaluated by the event team. As a result, a 3D virtual platform as an event 'venue' was found to meet the key criteria for the uniqueness of the environment and the overall event experience. The previous years' events set the expectations bar very high, as the festival had been a combination of outdoor and indoor experiences and was held in unusual locations. In a 3D format, attendees would get to join the virtual part of the event as an avatar and would be able to move in the 3D world between locations, interact with other attendees through voice as well as through the chat. In addition, in order to make the networking for participants more convenient, a possibility of introducing a business-to-business 'matchmaking' tool was also explored.

Different 3D platforms and digital networking software options were carefully considered in terms of functionality, price and user experience. VirBELA 3D platform and Talque Event Matchmaking tool were chosen. Other options were considered but found less suitable for this particular event for various reasons, for example, their inability to get the functionality ready in time for the event or the technological requirements that were too high and would require hiring a technical partner and, thus, raise the costs. The price of these relatively novel technologies in combination with a smooth user interface and engaging features were major factors in the decision-making process.

Characteristically for the VUCA times, just three weeks before the main hybrid event, the restrictions for live events in Finland were tightened in a way that made it impossible to organize the on-site part of the festival. That was something the festival management team were prepared for as it was one of the scenarios developed earlier. In the first months of the pandemic, an assessment was made about how long the pandemic could last for and different scenarios were created and action plans for different scenarios and contingencies drawn, allowing for the possibility to adapt those plans in response to change. Three weeks before the event the festival was moved to a fully on-line mode. The event team demonstrated great flexibility with the process and the attendees were kept informed of the changing circumstances. Those who got onsite tickets joined the fully virtual event in 2020 and got complimentary pass to the 2021 festival.

During the final, Deliver, stage of managing the event, the focus was on its execution. In particular, the new and more sophisticated technical aspects, work with the speakers and attendees, as well as with the event's partners. The main event took place on 27-28 October 2020 on the virtual platform VirBELA (see Image 11.1). International speakers delivered their keynotes in live format remotely as avatars on VirBELA, whereas many Finnish speakers joined through a live broadcast from a studio in Turku and remotely. Twenty companies presented their services in the VirBELA expo hall through customized virtual booths of four different sizes.

Image 11.1: SHIFT 2020 Fair Artificial Intelligence session.

The format was new for the event organizers, and the production team had to tackle several unexpected technological challenges before the end of October and in the run-up to the event. For instance, less than a month before the event it became clear that the live stream was not possible to be brought directly into the platform, i.e., the professional camera stream was not compatible with the browsers in the platform, only streaming through personal webcams from speakers' laptops was available. That posed a significant technological challenge, but it was successfully resolved by the production team through using a video mixer on a separate computer that 'tricked' the VirBELA platform into believing this was the webcam.

Getting all the speakers to submit their materials on time and in formats compatible with the software was another important task, and the production team had to work with the speakers individually to achieve it. Local presenters speaking live from a studio in Finland had their own technological set-up that had to be handled differently. It required significant efforts from the team to predict, mitigate and resolve all the technological concerns as they were emerging.

The festival and networking events were attended by over 1000 visitors from more than 10 different countries in two days, with more than 300 business meetings having taken place. The game-like, virtual reality format proved to be very engaging, and attendees stayed at the event platform for a longer time as compared to such formats as webinars, and, consequently, were able to meet more people and interact with each other more. Participants commented on the uniqueness of the experience, as they were able to do things that would not have been possible in an on-site format or in real-life meetings, due to the restrictions being in place at the time. For example, shaking hands and speaking in groups, or the entertaining side of the virtual environment – the opportunity to easily move between different event locations, the ability to virtually dance with the avatar at a beach after-party to streamed live music, or to virtually do a boat trip with other attendees.

No other event in Finland nor the Nordic countries had done this specific format of the event before SHIFT. For example, the biggest Finnish start-up festival Slush was cancelled altogether in 2020, and so was another major event, Nordic Business Forum. The fact that the number of attendees was less than in 2019 highlights the fact that the new virtual format may have been found by some of the usual festival audience unfamiliar compared to the on-site event. This can also be a reflection of the tightened marketing budgets of some of the businesses as a response to the external volatility and uncertainty due to the pandemic. However, the attendance exceeding 1000 participants can be seen as a success under the VUCA circumstances and the associated challenges that the event team was facing. It was important for the organizers to keep the event running and relevant, maintain the value and spirit of the festival, as well as to keep the core audience engaged with the event.

Discussion and conclusion

In 2020, event managers and leaders were working under highly uncertain, volatile, unpredictable, complex, and ambiguous circumstances. This type of environment necessitates agility across a spectrum of areas, from event design to team management. Agility allows new products, services or operations to be created and is rooted in the processes and overall management of an event.

The model of a 3Ds process in agile event management, Define – Design – Deliver, is characterized by specific – and shorter – deadlines, an urgency associated with the decision-making, and the need to act under challenging environment. The case of a business festival demonstrates its applicability and indicates the focus of the event team on certain areas of event organization and execution at each stage.

The chapter explored the concepts of agility and the VUCA environment in the context of crisis management and recovery for events. The case of the SHIFT annual business festival organized in Turku, Finland, from 2016, evidences how the team used agility in the decision-making process and throughout the organization of the event as the situation in the events industry remained unstable and, overall, challenging. Thus, the event team demonstrated creative thinking and willingness to explore alternative formats, with the management providing support and motivation in the period of change. Without prior experience of working remotely or using virtual software, the festival had to adopt new systems and build on the expertise of team members and key stakeholders, and look for new partnerships outside of the existing network. Importantly, the event design and the program were developed in a way that would maintain continuity with the previous iterations, i.e., the decision to formally launch the event on the usual dates. The addition of workshops and webinars in the run-up to the main event was aimed at preparing the audience for the new version of the event, as well as developing their understanding of the key theme of the festival in 2020. The virtual platform had been prepared in advance for the off-line part of the event, although the decision not to proceed with any on-site activities was made three weeks before the start of the main event. The virtual platform and the b2b networking application were used to support the key element of the original event's identity, i.e., to provide attendees from all sectors, regions, and countries with an opportunity to meet and interact with each other in a serendipitous manner.

Aitken et al. (2002) suggest a framework of levels of activities and core characteristics in agile manufacturing. The activity levels are: marketing, production, design, organization, management, and people. Based on the analysis of the SHIFT event management, it can be proposed that all but one activity levels of the agile event management, i.e., programming instead of production, remain the same. Several of the agile characteristics, however, will vary from the manufacturing context (Table 11.1).

Table 11.1: Core characteristics of agile event management

Activity level	Agile characteristics
Marketing	Audience focused, individualized combinations of products and services.
Programming	Deliver an enriching experience via a program that caters to the interests of target audience segments and stakeholders.
Design	An event design that takes into account event vision, stakeholders' interests, business processes, attendees needs and wants.
Organization	Ability to synthesize new event management systems and capabilities from expertise of event team and key stakeholders regardless of their internal or external location.
Management	Emphasis of leadership, support, motivation, and trust.
People	Knowledgeable, skilled and innovative event team.

Source: Adapted from Aitken et al. (2002).

The novelty in the application of business concepts, such as agility, and wider terms pertinent to the environment, such as a VUCA world, can prompt academics in the event studies to develop that line of enquiry further. Future research could investigate specific areas for agile event management, such as new technologies implementation, event operations, event leadership, as well as to apply the suggested core characteristics of agile event management to specific events to better understand the manifestation of those characteristics in practice. Scholars could consider the attributes of a VUCA environment and suggest a more comprehensive framework that could be used for the events industry.

With the proliferation of tools, applications and other technological advancements in events organization, both academics and practitioners will benefit from a typology for the events that are organized using digital software, online tools and/or virtual reality elements. This will have practical implications for the planning and marketing of events, as well as for the purpose of setting out realistic expectations for the attendees.

References

Aitken J., Christopher M., & Towill D. (2002). Understanding, implementing and exploiting agility and leanness. *International Journal of Logistics: Research & Applications, 5*(1), 59-74.

Allied Market Research. (n.d.). Events industry market. https://www. alliedmarketresearch.com/events-industry-market (Accessed 5/02/2021).

Bennett, N., & Lemoine, J. (2014). What a difference a word makes: Understanding threats to performance in a VUCA world. *Business Horizons, 57*(3), 311-317.

Cambridge Dictionary (2021a). https://dictionary.cambridge.org/dictionary/english/online.

Cambridge Dictionary (2021b). https://dictionary.cambridge.org/dictionary/english/virtual.

Doz, Y. L., & Kosonen, M. (2008). *Fast Strategy: How strategic agility will help you stay ahead of the game*. Harlow: Pearson Education.

Faulkner, B. (2001). Towards a framework for tourism disaster management. *Tourism Management, 22*(2), 135-147.

Fortune Business Insights. (n.d.). Virtual meeting software (3D virtual event) market size. https://www.fortunebusinessinsights.com/virtual-meeting-software-3d-virtual-event-market-104064 (Accessed 5/02/2021).

Getz, D., & Page, S. J. (2016). *Event Studies: Theory, research and policy for planned events* (3 ed.). London: Routledge.

Gong, Y., & Janssen, M. (2012). From policy implementation to business process management: Principles for creating flexibility and agility. *Government Information Quarterly, 29*(Suppl. 1), S61–S71.

Gössling, S., Scott, D., & Hall, C. M. (2021). Pandemics, tourism and global change: A rapid assessment of COVID-19. *Journal of Sustainable Tourism, 29*(1), 1–20.

Hallenbeck, G. (2016). *Learning Agility: Unlock the lessons of experience*. Center for Creative Leadership.

Hugos, M. H. (2009). *Business Agility: Sustainable prosperity in a relentlessly competitive world*. Wiley.

Johansen, B., & Euchner, J. (2013). Navigating the VUCA World. *Research-Technology Management, 56*(1), 10-15.

Locke, M. (2010). A framework for conducting a situational analysis of the meetings, incentives, conventions, and exhibitions sector. *Journal of Convention & Event Tourism, 11*(3), 209-233.

Malaska, P., & Holstius, K. (1999). Visionary management. *Foresight, 1*(4), 353-361.

Morden, T. (1997). Leadership as vision. *Management Decision, 35*(9), 668-676.

Pauchant, T. I., & Mitroff, I. (1992). *Transforming the Crisis Prone Organization*. San Francisco, CA: Jossey-Bass Publishers.

Paul, R., & Elder, L. (2012). *The Nature and Functions of Critical and Creative Thinking* (3 ed.). Tomales, CA: The Foundation for Critical Thinking.

Pearson, C. M., & Mitroff, I. I. (1993). From crisis prone to crisis prepared: A framework for crisis management. *Academy of Management Executive, 7*(1), 48-59.

Pearson, C. M., & Sommer, S. A. (2011). Infusing creativity into crisis management: An essential approach today. *Organizational Dynamics, 40*(1), 27-33.

Saleh, Y. D. (2016). *Crisis Management: The art of success & failure: 30 case studies in business & politics*. Minneapolis, MN: Mill City Press.

Seeger, M., Sellnow, T., & Ulmer, R. (1998). Communication, organization, and crisis. *Annals of the International Communication Association, 21*(1), 231-276.

Seraphin, H. (2021). COVID-19: An opportunity to review existing grounded theories in event studies. *Journal of Convention and & Event Tourism, 22*(1), 3-35.

Sherman, W. R., & Craig, A. B. (2019). *Understanding Virtual Reality: Interface, application, and design* (2 ed.). Elsevier.

Useem, M., Cook, J. R., & Sutton, L. (2005). Developing leaders for decision making under stress: Wildland firefighters in the South Canyon fire and its aftermath. *Academy of Management Learning and Education, 4*(4), 461-485.

Van Oosterhout, M., Waarts, E., van Heck, E., & van Hillegersberg, J. (2006). Business agility: need, readiness and alignment with IT-strategies. In K. C. Desouza (Ed.), *Agile Information Systems: Conceptualization, construction and management* (pp. 52-69). Oxford: Butterworth Heinemann.

Vanvactor, J. D. (2015). *Crisis Management: A leadership perspective*. Nova Science Publishers.

Williams, D.E., & Treadaway, G. (1992). Exxon and the Valdez accident: A failure in crisis communication. *Communication Studies, 43*, 56-64.

Winby, S., & Worley, C. G. (2014). Management processes for agility, speed, and innovation. *Organizational Dynamics, 43*(3), 225–234.

12 Crisis Management and Recovery for Events: Issues and Directions

Vassilios Ziakas, Vladimir Antchak and Donald Getz

Introduction

The landscape of the event sector is dramatically changing as a result of the COVID-19 pandemic crisis. The crisis has accelerated structural change and aggravated the instability of what has traditionally been a highly volatile, disruptive and erratic sector. Crises are becoming the new normal. The probability of the advent of further crises should be considered and carefully evaluated by the event industry and the entire visitor economy sector. It is critical for event organizers and host communities to learn how to cooperate and manage their events under conditions of constant or episodic crises and turbulence. A holistic mindset in crisis management needs to be developed to create tools and strategies for enabling the effective adaptability, recovery, and resilience of events.

In this concluding chapter, we outline the pillars of a holistic crisis management perspective that makes use of complex adaptive systems, event portfolio and resilience theories. We encapsulate major issues in the crisis management of events and put forward an integrative framework that brings together crucial elements and processes. Finally, we discuss key trends and transformations of the sector, and in this context, suggest directions for future research.

Stages in crisis management

As indicated by both case studies and industry insights in the volume, the crisis caused by the COVID-19 pandemic has considerably increased the risks for event organizations concerning, for instance, their adherence to stricter safety and health regulations, dealing with financial losses and finding alternative revenue sources, managing effectively the workforce, communicating with stakeholders, as well as creatively readjusting event programming and delivery formats.

The evidence presented in the chapters reveals interesting aspects of the pandemic-related reactions that likely can be applied in many other situations including new crises. It is possible to highlight at least six stages of crisis management, including: awareness; acknowledgement or denial; anger and bargaining; leadership and decision-making; reaction and planning; and, finally, innovation, creativity and resilience. The stages might be overlapping and selectively applicable, depending on circumstances.

Awareness. At the beginning of the COVID-19 pandemic in 2020 there were many signs of an emerging global crisis, but the need for timely information, advice and decisive action from authorities was not met in most countries. This resulted in a period of confusion, mixed opinions and late responses within the visitor economy sector. Ineffective leadership and a lack of decision-making raise the question of responsibility in any given crisis situation, and how vital information is best shared.

Acknowledgment or denial. Many practitioners in the affected sectors were not at first willing to accept that a crisis loomed or that they had to change their business operations to adapt to new realities. Others acknowledged that the pandemic was going to have a profound impact and started to plan adequate response. What explains these differences – was it a matter of politics, culture or misinformation?

Anger and bargaining. Within a new and uncertain environment, organizations often engage in negotiation and bargaining. Faced with imposed restrictions, new costs and uncertainty, many organizations and businesses had little choice but to push back or react irrationally, which can be expected in a time of crisis. In events, anger and bargaining were related to the fact that many jurisdictions provided financial support, but not to every organization and not necessarily enough to meet needs. As well, some events were permitted, but with no audience or limited numbers; other events have occurred within so called 'bubbles' (another term to enter the vernacular in 2020) generating concerns about equity or the wisdom of allowing any events. As evidence demonstrates, a crisis response is not always rational; politics are inevitably part of the process, and equity is not always assured.

Leadership and decision-making. Many countries, cities and organizations that should have been able to respond to the pandemic in a timely manner, both to minimize impacts and prepare effective recovery, did not. In many cases this can be attributed to a lack of leadership, or to inefficiently dispersed leadership and decision making. There will always be a need for decisive leadership in a crisis, and who or what provides it is a matter of perceived legitimacy, the use of power, and a sense of urgency. A prerequisite is that leaders, and those stakeholders with power to affect change, must accept that a crisis exists, and that action has to be taken. The role of industry and professional associations is important here, as collective planning (see the IFEA and Cotter interviews) can be quicker and more effective. A number of contributors to this book have emphasized the need for 'hope' and particularly optimism. Undoubtedly, it is a big part of resilience and may be found in key leaders or within networks.

Reaction and planning. Determining the best response to a crisis is not always easy. Incidents can be handled through contingency plans and rehearsed responses, but there were no 'best practices' available to cope with the pandemic. Consideration of risks versus rewards had to be made when it came to decisions about postponements, cancellations, or modified formats. Virtual events and hybrid events had to be carefully planned and the outcomes evaluated before decisions could be made concerning the future. Uncertainty about the length and overall impacts of the pandemic has increased risks. New costs had to be considered, as well as the likelihood of reduced financial support from governments and corporations.

Innovation, creativity and resilience. Creative thinking and innovation have been evident in the event sector. The ability to think outside the box and adapt to new realities has been shown to be a vital leadership and management skill. It can also be a matter of fostering collective capacity among stakeholders and networks. This capacity can be facilitated within event portfolios. Specific areas of innovation that have been identified within the events sector include the design and presentation of new types of virtual and hybrid events, the use of technology, and new systems for increased health and safety management, communications strategies and media tactics to maintain relationships with audiences and other key stakeholders, and in generating revenue. Many events will have to 'go back to basics' when it comes to future operations, especially in terms of reduced costs and selective programming, and a greater emphasis on the generation of value for their community, sponsors and funders. When we consider the new paradigm of strategic planning, being the emphasis on systems and networks for creating value, it is certain that the pandemic has accelerated the process by which events collaborate and cities or destinations place their emphasis on managed portfolios of events for value creation and resiliency.

Issues and processes: A rounded crisis management framework for events

It is a central thesis of this book that event-related scholarship needs to look more tenaciously and systematically at the processes of crisis management and recovery for events. A range of theoretical perspectives have been presented in the foregoing chapters that provide a solid platform for developing sustainable plans of action within the event sector. These include chaos and complexity theories, portfolio management, design thinking, stakeholder management and resilience planning. Taking the COVID-19 pandemic crisis as a case in point, the impacts on the event sector have been identified through international case studies alongside the main responses by event organizers and stakeholders. This evidence demonstrates not only the devastating effects of the pandemic on the event sector but, more importantly, the sector's unavoidable restructuring both in terms of demand and supply. From this standpoint, a crisis might also engender opportunities that need to be identified and appropriately leveraged. For example, the emergence of hybrid events provides ample room for co-creation and innovation. Further, the capacity of events to address serious public concerns and heal people from pain and loss warrants their place as a means for community post-disaster recovery. In the same vein, crisis management can be seen as a process of identification of, and capitalization on, opportunities through the highly protean adaptation of events to new conditions, roles and functions.

Clearly, a more systematic and methodical approach is needed, incorporating research evidence; and event management scholarship has a significant role to play here. Thus, the hitherto dearth of study on crisis management needs to be addressed soon, especially as the event sector has reached maturity and faces several disruptions; therefore, specialized evidence-based knowledge is required to prepare and deal with the repercussions of different crises and take advantage of opportunities. We are in need of new integrative, adaptive and transformational models for crisis management, recovery and resilience of events, which should be able to link the diachronic gap between academics and practitioners.

Along these lines, Figure 12.1 presents an integrative, rounded framework that links focal components and processes in crisis management for events. The schematic representation of the framework is cyclical to capture the non-linear way that its interconnected parts function, with no definite start or end, but in constant interaction and co-construction as in adaptive systems. For the purpose of explaining the framework, an imaginable initial point is the extent to which event organizers are ready and prepared to effectively deal with a crisis. *Readiness and preparedness* means identifying threats and opportunities and developing a mindset of organizational flexibility that puts in place processes for *Adaptation*. Building adaptive capacity of events is a key requirement; however, the underlying challenge is how to achieve this across the diverse range of events. Apparently, there is no uniform solution. Adaptive strategies should be tailored to the contexts, scale and type of each event.

Event design is imperative here as it can be employed to reconfigure the nature, program and delivery mode of an event according to new conditions and requirements. Hybrid solutions can be applied, as well as new genres of events introduced to diversify the offer and target wider audience.

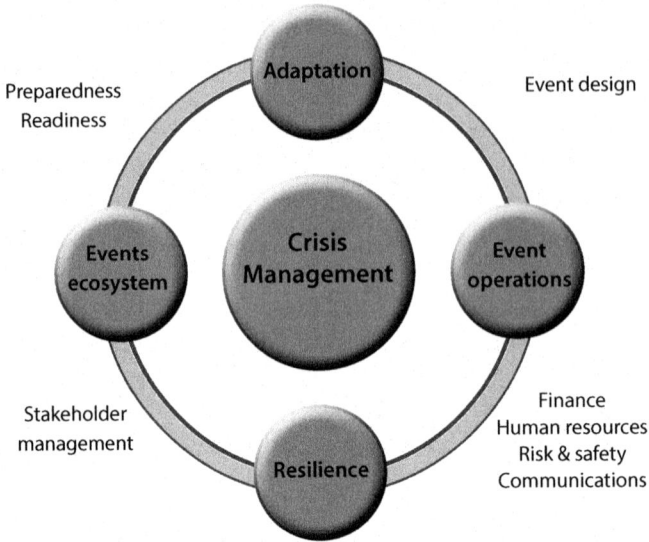

Figure 12.1: Crisis management and recovery for events

Similarly, *Event operations* have to be readjusted. This element of the framework may include *Financial management* (e.g., managing financial losses and re-financing event operations after events are canceled or postponed); *Human resources management* (e.g., re-engaging laid-off staff and volunteers after a long absence); *Risk and safety* (e.g., adhering to ne w stricter health regulations); and *Communications* (e.g., promoting a redesigned event or rectifying image/reputation). Moving forward from the pandemic, many event organizations will have to re-evaluate their business models and governance, especially if the trend to virtual and hybrid events results in structural changes to the sector.

Effective implementation of adapted operations may lead to the *Resilience* of events making them stronger to cope with adverse conditions. Leadership within and between levels of government has to be provided for the events sector, possibly requiring new arrangements among the many departments and agencies that regulate, support and otherwise deal with events and event venues. This requires prudent *Stakeholder management* to maintain stakeholder relations (e.g., sponsors, suppliers, community, politicians, etc.), especially when events are cancelled, re-scheduled or modified.

Without doubt the pandemic refocused attention on some stakeholders and brought new ones to the fore. Inter-dependencies have been stressed, with the inevitable conclusion that events and organizations cannot go it alone in a crisis, and especially when long-term resilience and sustainability are planned. For example, host communities have been identified as a big loser in the pandemic, owing to reduced economic and financial inputs, cancelled volunteer opportunities, and loss of celebration and entertainment. Event audiences is a broad stakeholder group that has to be given more nuanced attention, in part related to the move towards hybrid and virtual events, but also because of the necessity for maintaining engagement during a hiatus and informing segments of the implications of any crisis.

All the above-mentioned processes can be greatly facilitated within the *Ecosystem* of an event portfolio, which is able to assist individual events. Portfolio management can support individual events through stakeholder network synergies, operational efficiencies, combined effects and knowledge exchange amongst different events to cope with the crisis. This, in turn, may prompt a sense of readiness and organizational flexibility infused across the array of events and enhance practically their preparedness by sharing information, know-how, resources and methods for adaptation as well as implementing joint strategies and problem-solving actions. Effective portfolio management requires the coordinated planning and delivery of events, including adaptation strategies, redesign, operations and stakeholder management. As an event portfolio is a permanent but flexible structure in a host community, it can eventually ensure the continuity of the events ecosystem and enhance the resilience of events.

Given the wide scope of the events sector, event portfolio management and policy by appropriate levels of government has to bring together representatives of culture and arts, sports, corporations, tourism and hospitality, and many others who have a legitimate claim to be heard. As noted above, professional and industry associations might be able to fill this need. In particular, note that a major lesson communicated by many practitioners and experts has been the necessity for collaborative action, forging new partnerships, and strengthening support networks.

Based on this framework, we can understand more comprehensively and methodically emergent issues and archetypal processes in crisis management for events. As discussed in the chapters of this volume, the event sector is highly sensitive to exogenous shocks and environmental turbulence while response time is very limited. This makes it important for risk management to not only optimize levels of preparedness but also enable swift response to contingencies. Processes for sound, flexible and rapid decision-making are essential in order to readjust strategy and operations. The perspective of portfolio management creates a common ground for building adaptability and resilience of individual events within a portfolio. These considerations bring to the fore the considerable complexity of crisis management for events and the need to explore in depth the processes that can facilitate effective responses and recovery.

Lessons from industry insights

The professional practice interviews conducted for this book and selected case studies (i.e., TransRockies Inc. and Musikfest) provide numerous details of the impacts and responses to the 2020 pandemic. More importantly, the practitioners interviewed offer advice for future planning and the foundations of resilience for individual events and the event sector. If the terms 'event ecosystem', 'collaboration', 'resilience' and 'event portfolio management' were not relevant previously, they certainly are now.

The two case studies pertain to quite different types of events and organizations. TransRockies Inc. is a private event production and management company that suffered immediate and potentially devastating financial losses with cancellation and indefinite postponement of their events. As a consequence, existing and new investors – drawing from an established stakeholder network – became essential for survival and future planning. Like many other organizations the company innovated with virtual and new events, stressed continual communication with their customer base and other stakeholders, and sought new revenue sources. Portfolio management is central to their planning, consisting of events in different sports, locations and countries (Canada and USA). Of utmost concern for this company, and many other events, is the uncertainty surrounding the pandemic and when imposed regulations will permit a re-launch.

Musikfest is a community-based festival, and one of the largest of its kind. In deciding how to respond to the pandemic they evaluated risks versus rewards and then went with both hybrid and virtual events, including innovative programming and fund raising. Emphasis was placed on maintaining relationships with sponsors and vendors and finding new ways to create value for them. Adaptation to new health and safety regulations will be a key to future resilience.

Online interviews were conducted with a number of professionals with extensive and diverse experience in the events sector. Rebecca Cotter documented the direct impacts and discussed efforts by municipalities in Ontario, Canada to sustain events, adapt and provide leadership during the pandemic. The importance of a coordinated local response was highlighted, including the many governmental agencies and departments. Vern Biaett observed that a lack of a clear voice and leadership for the entire events industry was a major impediment in responding to the pandemic crisis. He emphasized the importance of professional associations and argued for greater integration of the various sectors of the events industry.

Neil Alderson spoke of the harsh negative impacts of the pandemic on sports, communities and the entire supply chain, and the work of the Province of Nova Scotia in attempting to hold together and recover the events sector. The importance of support from senior levels of government was stressed, as was the necessity for wide collaborative efforts to ensure future resilience. Amanda Cecil related to the meetings and conventions sector, pointing to huge disruptions and financial losses through the pertinent supply chains. The shift to virtual and hybrid events had been especially significant in 2020, and many new stakeholders and partnerships have been forged out of necessity. Resilience in this sector will require a much greater emphasis on risk management and adapting to stringent health and safety regulations.

Steve Wood Schmader discussed IFEA (International Festivals and Events Association) and their work through a number of task forces to development strategies for recovery and resilience. An important conclusion of their collaborative work was that no best practices existed for responding to what has been a worst case scenario and that a considerable amount of creativity and innovation is being displayed by event organization to adapt to new realities. A back to basics approach will likely be needed to ensure resiliency in the entire events sector. Another interesting highlight of this interview was Mr. Schmader's observation of the emotional, attitudinal and reactive stages by events and organizations during 2020.

Trends and transformations

As indicated by the chapters in this volume, the pandemic of 2020 has triggered and accelerated long-lasting structural changes to the economy and society. It is thus important to determine how the event sector as a whole might be impacted in the next years to come. This entails identification of key trends and structural transformations. Such an analysis pertains to the machinations of the capitalist supra-system under which the leisure, event and tourism industries converge in the production of their service bundles. It is possible to distinguish four categories and the underlying trends within each: (1) the weakened economy, including a decline in globalization; (2) the nature of work; (3) leisure and tourism; as well as (4) social and cultural change.

First and foremost, a global economic downturn threatens the event sector. Many countries have suffered huge losses in tax revenue, while making enormous expenditures to combat immediate losses in employment; innumerable businesses have been damaged or have failed. It is expected that, at least, in the immediate future, government spending at all levels on discretionary policy fields is probably going to decline, and this will include support for events and venues. Many events will likely fail and terminate. At the same time, a parallel decline in corporate sponsorship, and in producing or funding corporate events, is also expected as a result of a generalized economic recession. The overall result could be a structurally smaller and more vulnerable event sector, with on-going negative impact on hospitality and tourism, as well as on the entire supply chain.

The nature of work has already significantly changed. Employees are now being advised or asked to work from home, and many companies and government agencies are expected to make this a permanent feature of their operations. With more employment home-based there will be less physical commuting, with benefits to the environment, and more personal isolation that leads to a greater need for social gatherings. If health-related restrictions on the size and nature of planned events remain in place, and it is possible they will have to endure for years to come, then the ways in which events alleviate social isolation and foster healthy pursuits will have to adapt.

Going virtual does not replace meeting in person or exercising in participatory events. Another work-related consequence of the pandemic, one that is exacerbating an established trend, is the inequitable distribution of winners and losers. Those segments being economically disadvantaged include youth, women, minority cultural/ethnic groups, the aged needing care, the already poor, and immigrants. Subsequently, the need for planned events to foster social and cultural integration and promote community and self-development will increase even while financial support is likely to decrease.

The leisure and tourism industry is also expected to significantly change, including both new consumer behavior patterns and supply models. Analysts predict a slow return to normal in the leisure and tourism industry, largely owing to a combination of diminished disposable incomes and a fear of infection, which may cause structural changes to demand and supply. The home isolation of many families has led to an increase in home entertainment, gaming and over-consumption of food and alcohol; it remains to be seen if these consumer trends soon end. For example, even though the cruise market received extremely negative publicity during the early stages of the pandemic, cruise providers anticipate demand to rebound, which seems to be a questionable, if not unrealistic, expectation. More generally, it is doubtful if international tourism, including event-related travel, will ever be the same again. Another important market is sport events which had a rise in participation the past two decades. Some of these can exist even with strict health measures in place, while others are by nature prone to mass infections. For example, running events tend to bunch people together in very large numbers, while bicycle events can more easily accommodate social distancing. Contact sports of all types are in a difficult position, both to protect athletes from infection and to allow for spectators. The same problems arise in indoor theater and concerts, parties and private functions. Limits on crowd size and interaction might become permanent, or perhaps demand will diminish in response to fears of infection. The nature of certain events and the degree to which they can be adapted to new regulations will determine their continuation or termination and this, in turn, will restructure the event sector.

Finally, the implications of social and cultural change for the event sector are the most complex to analyze. It is certainly more difficult to monitor and predict the kinds of profound social and cultural changes that relate to fundamental values and attitudes towards leisure, travel, planned events and gatherings of all kinds. Will society become more fearful and intolerant? Or will, the acts of kindness and sacrifice demonstrated during the worst days of the pandemic, endure and a more caring society arise? How will changing socio-cultural values and behaviors affect supply and demand for events? One thing can be predicted with some degree of confidence is that many cities will re-launch hallmark events or create new, media-oriented events to announce they have survived, to encourage socializing and travel, and to convey a healthy image. This is grounded in the primordial value of events to bring people together to celebrate ideals and identities and/or create and sustain communities.

Future research

Based on the insights provided by the contributors to this volume, we suggest several directions for future research to understand the processes and pathways of crisis management and recovery in events.

First, it is necessary to employ a systemic perspective for examining the interactions of different theoretical components that to date remain unconnected in the literature. Drawing on principles of chaos and complexity theories, diverse processes that determine the adaptive capacity and self-organizing of events resulting in new forms of management and delivery need to be explored and fully appreciated. Similarly, we need to learn more about the conditions at the host destination that can enable collaboration and joint problem-solving for dealing with a crisis.

Second, portfolio management provides a holistic perspective and synergistic structure at destination-level and we need to better understand how its principles can be applied to the context of crisis management. Also, pathways and strategies for creative and innovative transformation of events as a response to crises should be identified and elaborated.

Third, future research should focus on crisis-proof solutions for Human Resource management, staff engagement, wellbeing and individual resilience during the course of any potential crisis or disaster. The post-COVID event industry will demand sustainable solutions to any emerging employment issues; hence the experience and insights from the industry should be accumulated and holistically analyzed to provide new relevant frameworks and models of workforce management.

Similarly, it is essential to explore the effect of design thinking and co-creation on the event resilience and development of the industry immunity to any potential crisis in the future. What are the ways of adapting the principles of design thinking to risk and crisis management at the level of small-, medium- and large-scale events? What are the requirements for developing a supportive network of diverse actors involved in co-creation of solutions for the event industry?

Furthermore, more research is needed to understand the perspectives of the emerging genres of events, including hybrid solutions, the use of augmented and virtual reality, increase in ephemeral content and gamification. What are the consequences of 'going virtual'? How would virtual and online events affect the sustainability of the industry?

Another area for research is how event risk management processes can be optimized in the new conditions of increasing volatility and uncertainty. It seems that the risk appetite and tolerance of event organizations will need to become even more agile requiring them to develop capacity to accept and deal with a range of new risks as these are augmented by intersecting crises (e.g., pandemic and global economic recession) and adapt their risk management plans according to changing circumstances. To an extent, this is shaped by organizers' perceptions of risk, which are often primarily based on intuition and praxis. How can academic research guide event managers to develop comprehensive, evidence-based and tailored risk management approaches?

In bringing together the range of interrelated issues and aspects covered in this volume, a comprehensive research framework for event crisis management and recovery is suggested in Figure 12.2.

This puts at the center the need to view event crisis management as a chaordic route entailing adaptive responses and self-organizing, while envisaging stronger linkages with the host destination context/stakeholders and portfolio management approaches that can positively contribute to the transformation of events in the new conditions. The volume builds firm foundations towards this direction. More specifically, drawing directly from the chapters, cases and interviews in the volume, a number of research questions emerge in the suggested research framework:

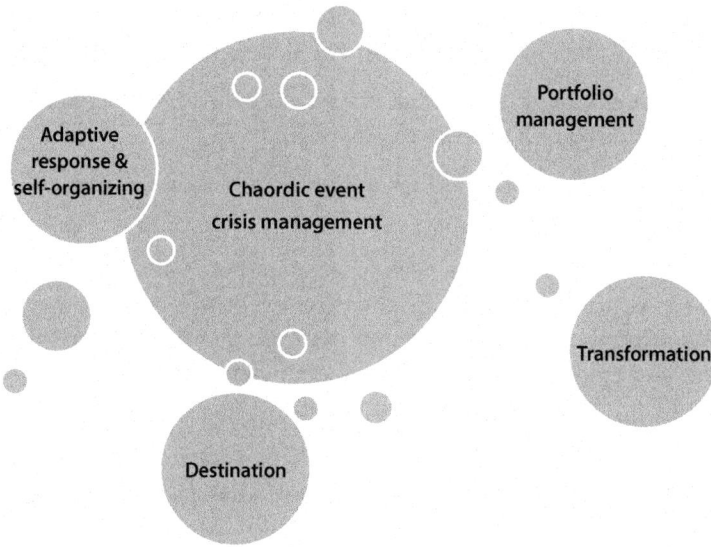

Figure 12.2: Towards chaordic event crisis management: Connecting the fragments

♦ In the post-pandemic period, will the events sector and ecosystem be the same, or have structural changes occurred? What are they?

♦ Will hybrid and virtual events threaten the status quo, or will the sector return to its emphasis on live events? What are the implications of hybrid and virtual events for work/careers, revenue generation, audiences' experiences and satisfaction, and stakeholder support?

♦ How many events will have failed, and are there now gaps to be filled through innovation?

♦ Which types of events will be prioritized by cities and destinations in the recovery stage (with implications for public, private and non-profit sectors)?

♦ What are the implications of the pandemic crisis for education, training and careers in the events sector? How can students and practitioners be prepared for crisis management and worst-case scenarios?

♦ What new forms of collaboration and stakeholder networking have emerged? Do these fit into the concept of event portfolio management, or enlarge it?

♦ Has the well-being of workers, volunteers, owners and other stakeholders suffered during the pandemic? What are the implications for the future of education, training, work and careers?

- Will events return to basics and adopt new, more conservative business models? Can new revenue streams be developed?

- How should crisis and risk management evolve? Will agile event management become a necessary component?

- Has the pandemic focused or re-directed attention on value co-creation, and in what ways?

- New collaborations have been forged and new stakeholders brought to the fore. What are the implications for event and portfolio governance? What forms of collaboration and portfolio management are most effective and efficient in terms of sustainability and resilience?

- Stages of crisis response, recovery and resilience building have now been hypothesized and they need to be verified or amended through empirical research in many settings; what explains differences in decision-making, for example?

- Research and theory development are required with regard to chaos theory and chaordic systems applied to events and event populations. What are the optimal pathways and events ecosystem configurations that lead to effective crisis management and recovery?

- How does the Maturity model of the event sector relate to sustainability and resilience?

In conclusion, by re-thinking hitherto event management practice we can develop and refine comprehensive perspectives, adaptive strategies and pertinent tools that will enable events' resilience and sustainability within an increasingly uncertain world. The pandemic crisis only triggered the need for a change in mindset how we view, treat, design and manage events. Change will configure a new landscape for the event sector that we have to consider with more perspicacity, forward-thinking mentality and evidence-based practice than previous decades the opportunities upon which we can capitalize to reshape events in line with new conditions. Event-focused scholarship has a key part here providing the specific theory, models and instruments capable of capturing comprehensively the unique contexts and complex processes involved in crisis management and recovery of events.

Index

Terms in italics are mentioned too numerously to list all page numbers.

acceptance 43, 178,
accountability 5, 32, 86, 88, 178, 219
action (see also: decision making; interaction; planning; reaction; strategy; tactics) 82, 84, 189
activity (see also: interactivity)
   decline/decrease 206
   focus 204
   level 245
adapt(ation)(adaptability) (see also: innovation; resilience; system; flexibility) 22, 25, 32, 172, 252, 259
agile/agility 233-247
Alderson, Neil 139-141
alternatives 221-225
ambiguity 235-6
anger 43, 90, 249
appeasement 85, 89-90
appropriate strategies 77, 84, 94
Armbrecht, J. 193-212
audience(s) 87-92
   development 91-2
   lost 83
Australia 36, 38, 107-110, 133
Australasia 101
autonomy 21
awareness 45, 53, 55, 59, 61-2, 67-71, 249

balance (see also: leverage; portfolio) 25
ballet competition 218-232
bargaining 43, 249
basic principles 9
benefits (see also: leveraging) 149-150, 178
best practices 32, 41-2, 44, 54, 67-9, 97, 141, 160, 180-182, 214, 250, 255

Bethlehem, PA (see: Musikfest)
Biaett, V. 118-119
business events (see also: hybrid; virtual) 170, 233-247
business sector 177

Canada 96-9, 139-141, 186-192
cancel(lation) (see also: postponement)
case study (see: Cluster Arts; Des Moines; Musikfest; National Ballet Competition; SHIFT Festival; Sky City; TransRockies)
Cecil, A. 165-6
challenges 125-7, 179
chaordic 8-10, 258-260
chaos (theory) 3, 6-10, 217, 251, 257, 260
city planning 181
classifying stakeholders 77
cluster analysis (see: Sweden)
Cluster Arts 107-112
co-creation 144, 152, 224-5, 230, 251, 258, 260
collaboration (see also: network; strategy) 22-3, 85, 125, 132, 141, 179-80, 259-60
commitment (see also: stakeholders) 17, 85, 87, 89
committee (see also: IFEA) 97
communications (see also: marketing; technology) 45, 56, 90-1, 96-8, 105-6, 113, 128, 166, 176, 187-192, 219, 221-2, 229-30, 252
community (see also: Alderson; Des Moines; IFEA; Musikfest; Sky City; stakeholder) 17, 96-99
   resilience 19-25

competence (see also: leadership) 3, 32
competition (see also: defense;
 National Ballet Competition) 5-6
complex systems 8-10, 31, 36-8,
complexity (see also: VUCA) 235-6
control (see also: risk management) 2,
 14, 43, 62, 125
conventions (see also: business events;
 Cecil; Des Moines; Sky City) 46, 127,
 131, 133
cost (see: impacts; Musikfest; Sweden;
 TransRockies)
Cotter 96-9, 250, 254
counter terrorism 57-62, 70
Covid (see also: post-Covid)
creativity (see also: co-creation; design;
 innovation)
crime (see also: cyber; terrorism) 58-9
customer (see also: stakeholder;
 TransRockies) 17-8, 83, 104-5, 124
cyber crime and security 62-70

dangerous stakeholders 78, 81-2
data analysis 197
data theft and malware 65-9
decision making 15-6, 22, 32, 49, 55-6,
 70, 127, 218-23, 234, 240, 244, 249-50,
 254, 260
decision support models 56
defense (see also: risk management) 90
demanding stakeholders 79, 83
denial 43, 249
depression 43
Des Moines 167-55
design /redesign 17-8, 105, 120-138
design thinking 123
develop(ment)
 of hybrid events 145
digital (see: cyber; virtual)
directions (and issues; research) 248-60
directors (board of) 82, 86, 89, 109, 171,
 178, 218-9
disaster (see also: crisis; risk)
 causes 4-6
disaster management framework
 122-3
diversified portfolio 20-1, 174, 178, 190
domestic terrorism 57-8

economy /economic
 conditions 5
 impact 34
effects for sport clubs 198-204
ecosystem
 continuity 25
 digital 63-9
events 2, 94, 179, 224, 252-4, 259-60
education(al) (see also: IFEA;
 workforce) 92, 97, 102, 145-6, 180-1,
 215, 220-1, 224, 231, 239, 259
efficiency(ies) 21, 23-4, 178, 205, 253,
 260
emergency (see also: crisis; disaster) 1,
 11, 19, 86, 97-8, 123, 169, 171, 234
response 4, 62, 77, 113
employment /employee 44, 62, 67, 76,
 81, 83, 87, 93, 100-117, 197, 200-1,
 204, 236, 255-8
engage(ment) 107-9, 111, 125, 129,
 131-4, 144-7, 150-9, 168, 173, 177, 189,
 191-2, 204-6, 228-30, 236, 243, 253,
 258
environment (see also: ecosystem;
 experience)
ethics 89-90, 94, 219, 221, 223, 239
event
 managers 119, 171, 181-2, 194, 218,
 244
 management (see also: agile; crisis;
 decision; portfolio; risk; strategy)
 26, 35-6, 181, 260
events sector maturity model 31-3
evil done 60
exhibit(ions) (see also: business events;
 MICE) 13-5, 127, 132-5, 157, 165, 219
experience
 designing virtual/hybrid 151-5
experts 225
external
 causes 4
 funders 86
fail(ure)
failure to act in time or appropriately 6
festival
 IFEA 41
 in Des Moines 168

Musikfest 213
SHIFT 239
financial
  losses 44
  management 252
  resources 17
  sharing risk 141
  support 176-7
Finland 233
flexibility 17, 25, 32, 36
focal organization (see also:
  governance) 177
formal /informal 32
framework 112, 123, 132, 220, 251-2
future 47, 69, 85, 87, 142, 158, 165, 175
  research 113, 257

globalism 33-4
goal 176
governance 22
governing bodies 88
Greece 217-232
hallmark events 14-7, 21, 80, 89, 257
health
  crisis 35-6
hub and spoke events 133-4
human error 4
  malfeasance 4
  resources (see also: education;
    workforce) 17, 252, 258
hybrid (see also: Musikfest;
  TransRockies) 125-34, 142-164, 259

ideation 124-5, 127
IFEA 41-8, 54, 93, 174
immersion (see also: experience) 153
impact
  cybercrime impacts 64
  economic 34
  immediate 12, 187
  long-term 12
  Nova Scotia/events sector 139-141
  on employment/workforce 100-117
  on Swedish sport clubs 193-212
  on municipal events 96
implementation
  in design thinking 125
  prototype and test 129

incident versus crisis 3
informal versus formal 32
innovation
  and creativity 250
  and sport clubs 209
  of products/programs 112
inspiration 125
integration 32, 206-7
interactions /interactivity 153, 154
interdependence (see also:
  stakeholder) 22, 25
internal causes (see also: stakeholder)
  5-6
investors 86, 189
issues 49, 112, 248, 251

joy and togetherness 207
judges 227

key
  decisions 240
  stakeholders 48, 56, 140, 178, 189

leader(ship) 92-3, 97, 118, 249-50
learn(ing)
  and resilience 25
legitimate / legitimacy 61, 78-80, 85-8
lessons 254
leverage 24, 112, 178
lobbying 85-6, 208-9
lost
  revenues 198-201
  audiences 83
Lundberg, E. 193-212

making sense 50, 126
manage(ment) (see also: event
  manager)
  agile 245
  chaordic 259
  club, sports (see: Sweden)
  crisis 8, 121, 194, 248, 251
  disaster 123
  event management education 181
  maturity 32
  portfolio 25, 167, 173
  resilience 194
  risk 44, 49

stakeholder 76
    weak or incompetent 6
    workforce 102
mapping, stakeholder 85-86
market, farmers (see: Des Moines)
market(ing)
    agile 245
    supplementarities 24
    support 209
    target (see also: TransRockies) 170
matrix
    blended stakeholder management
        84-6
    for risk assessment 52
maturity model 31-8, 260
McConnell, A. (see: TransRockies)
mega events 14-6, 36-39
member(ship)
    loss 205
messaging 48, 82, 91, 105-6, 113, 166
methods 175
    redefine 129
methodology 181, 196
    for decision support 56
MICE (see also: business events) 127,
    165-6, 238
mission 56, 176, 214-5
mitigation 66-7, 112
models
    decision support 56
    maturity 31-8, 260
    salience 78
monitoring 85
Musikfest 213-6, 254

National Ballet Competition 218-232
natural causes 4
network(ing) (see also: collaboration;
    portfolio; stakeholder)
    DesMoines stakeholders 177
    synergies 23
New Zealand 41, 105-7, 110
non-economic impacts on sport clubs
    204-8
Nova Scotia, Canada 139-141, 255

online
    media reports (see also: Cluster
        Arts) 40
    pivot to 147
Ontario (see: Cottler)
OODA Loop 56
operation(al)
    in crisis management and recovery
        model 252
    messaging and operational support
        48
    operational efficiencies 23
opportunity(ies)
    in resilience within portfolios model
        25
organizational culture conflict 5
organizer/organization (see also: case
    studies; decision support; IFEA;
    reorganisation; self organization)
    and agile event management 245
    and risk mitigation 66-8
    community event organisers 99
    event organizer solutions 128
    focal organizations 177
    organizational context and case
        study approach 218
    organizational mission 176
    organizing an event during
        pandemic 240
    umbrella organisation 179
owner(ship) 176
    as stakeholder 82, 86

pandemic (see also: case studies and
    interviews)
    crisis and event sector 11
    impacts and responses 12
    organizing an event during 240
    Swedish sports clubs 193
participant/participation (see also: case
    studies and interviews)
    participants in ballet competition 227
partner(ship) (see also: stakeholder)
    Greater Des Moines Partnership
        176-9
    with local education programs 180
perception of risk 50

physical
  physical and mental illness 206
plan/planned/planner/planning (see also:
  case studies and interviews; design;
  maturity; portfolio; risk; strategy
  city planning 181
  crisis recovery and resilience
    planning 15
population of events 20
portfolio (see also: Des Moines)
  and resilience 20-26
  portfolio management 259
  in Des Moines 173
post Covid
  in Des Moines 180
  redesign 120
postpone(ment)
  and event organizer solutions 128
  and reorganization 217-232
power 78-9 4
PPRR 19
preparedness (see also: PPRR) 123, 252
process
  and outcome (see: Musikfest)
  issues and processes 251
propositions (see: Des Moines)
prototype and test 124, 129

ranking risks 53-5
reaction and planning 250
readiness and preparedness 251-3
reasons
  for lost revenues and sunk costs 199
  in decision making 221
recover(y) (see also: case studies and
  interviews; DesMoines)
  and disaster management 123
  and sports clubs (see: Sweden)
  and stakeholders 85
  and workforce 112
  crisis management, recovery and
    resilience 15, 252
  event recovery model 17
redesigning events 17, 120-138
redundancy 21
reimagine(ing) 25, 132
reinvent(ing) 125, 131
reorganization 217-232

reschedule(ing) 220
research
  future 113, 159, 257
resilience / resilient (see also: case
  studies and interviews; risk)
  and crisis management 194
  and stakeholders 92
  community resilience 19
  event crisis recovery and resilience
    planning 15
  crisis management and recovery
    model 252
  organizational resilience defined
    18-9
  portfolio and population resilience
    20-5
resolution (see also: solutions) 100
risk
  and cyber crime 62-70
  and terrorism 58-62
  assessment matrix 52
  management 34, 44, 49
  perception 50
  ranking 53-5
  roles of stakeholders 92

safety (see also: health; risk)
  COVID Safe Event Solutions
    Framework 132-5
security and safety management plan
  62
salience 78-94
Schmader, S. 41-48, 118
security (see also: cybercrime; risk;
  safety)
  cyber security practices 68-70
  Event Security and Safety
    Management Plan 62
self organizing 9, 259
SHIFT Festival 239
Sky City 105-7
social
  and cultural conditions 5
  distancing 125
  media 82, 88, 226-8
solutions 125, 128, 132
sponsor(ship) 17, 86, 228-9

sport (see: Alderson; Des Moines;
    TransRockies)
    governing bodies 88
sports clubs 193-212
stability / instability 30-40
stages 85, 122-30, 248-50, 260
stakeholder (see also: case studies and
    interviews; Des Moines)
    and co-creation of value 225
    management 17, 76-95, 252
standards 32-8
strategy /strategic (see also: case studies
    and interviews; Des Moines)
    counter-terrorism 60-2
    sports clubs 201
    stakeholder 77-94
    strategic planning 224
    workforce 112
strength 22
structural change 12
support(ive) 17, 25, 48, 177, 207
    decision 56
    financial 201
    marketing 209
    stakeholders 85-8
survive / survival (see also: resilience;
    strategy)
    and key stakeholders 189
Sweden 193-212
synergy / synergistic (see also:
    portfolio) 23-25
system (see also: ecosystem)
    system-wide chaos 6
    systems perspective 8-10, 20

tactics 179
target
    attributes 61
    markets 170
technical
    equipment 154
    feasibility 17
technology /technological 125, 238 (see
    also: virtual)

technologist 219
terrorism (see also: risk) 4, 57-71
test
    and prototype 124-9
    statistical 197-203
theoretical background; perspectives
    1, 194
theory 251
    chaos 8-10, 217
    complexity 8-10
    criminological 59
    decision making 55, 220-1
    risk perception 36, 50
    stakeholder 76-94
    systems 26
threat(en) (see also: dangerous)
    cyber criminal 63-9
    stakeholder 85
    terrorism threat landscape 57
time(s)
    available 17-8
timeline 12, 170
timely response 6
tourist(m) 34, 121, 123, 125-6
TransRockies 186-192
trends and transformations 255-9

umbrella organization 179
uncertain(ty) (see also: VUCA)
    decision making under 55
urgency 77-89

value(s)
    co-creation 225
venue 17, 87-8
virtual (also see: hybrid) 125, 128, 143
volatility 235, 243
VUCA 234-7
vulnerable (see also: terrorism;
    resilience; risk)
    stakeholders 83

weak or incompetent management 6
workforce 100-117

Printed by Printforce, United Kingdom